CHAPTER 1

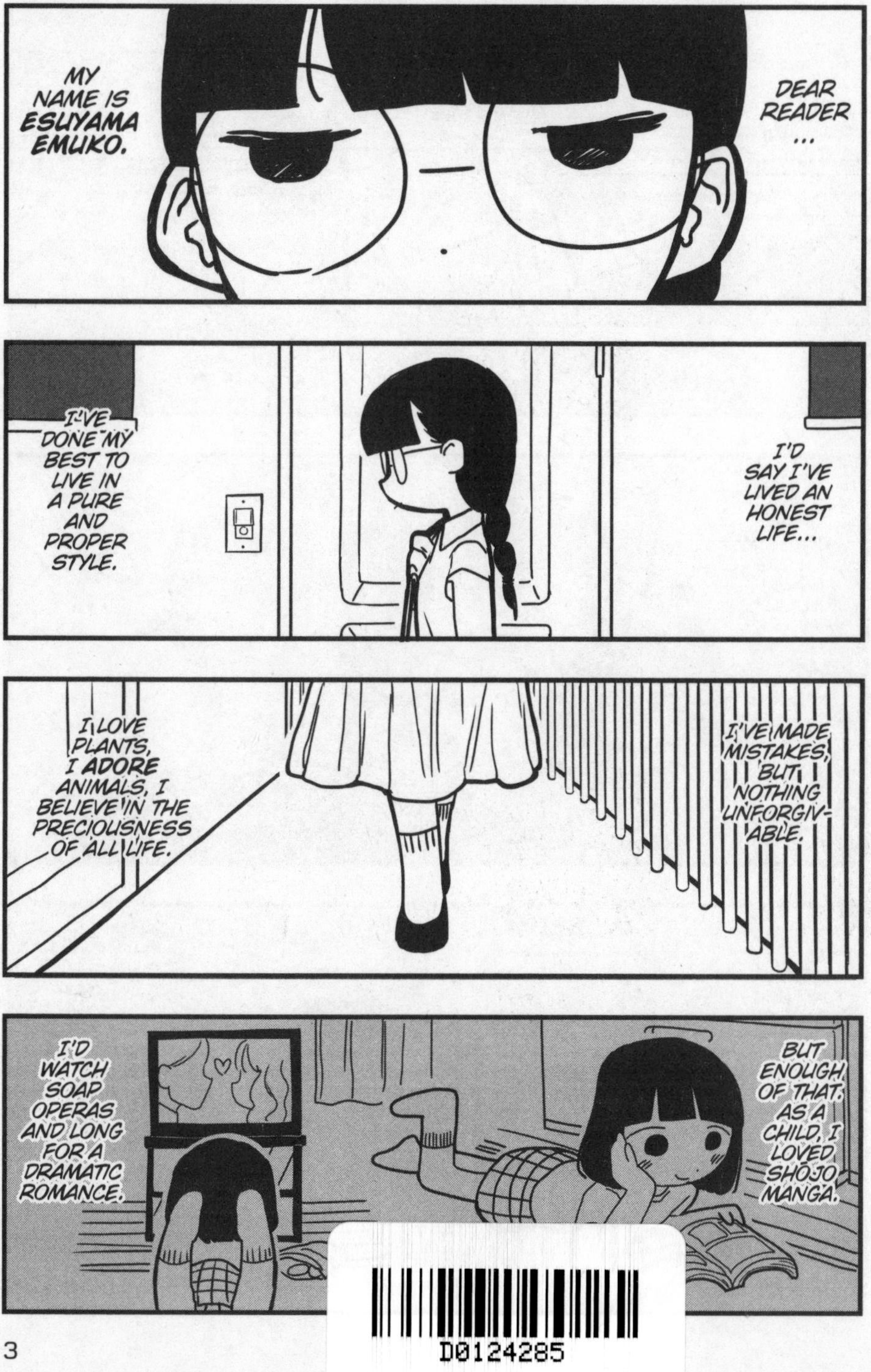
DEAR READER ...
MY NAME IS ESUYAMA EMUKO.
I'D SAY I'VE LIVED AN HONEST LIFE...
I'VE DONE MY BEST TO LIVE IN A PURE AND PROPER STYLE.
I'VE MADE MISTAKES, BUT NOTHING UNFORGIV-ABLE.
I LOVE PLANTS, I ADORE ANIMALS, I BELIEVE IN THE PRECIOUSNESS OF ALL LIFE.
BUT ENOUGH OF THAT. AS A CHILD, I LOVED SHOJO MANGA.
I'D WATCH SOAP OPERAS AND LONG FOR A DRAMATIC ROMANCE.

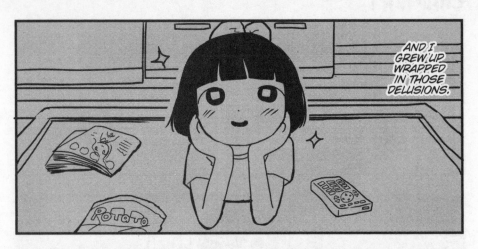

AND I GREW UP WRAPPED IN THOSE DELUSIONS.
POTATO
AS LONG AS I ACTED LIKE A LADY...
MY PERFECT PRINCE ON A WHITE HORSE WOULD APPEAR TO WHISK ME AWAY.
BUT MY PRINCE NEVER SHOWED.
HER~~?
NO WAY!
I DECIDED TO GO OUT AND FIND HIM MYSELF, BUT ALL MY EFFORT LED TO NOTHING BUT HEART-BREAK... UNTIL I GOT SICK OF TRYING.
Sorry.
-END-

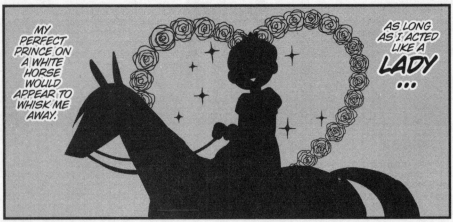

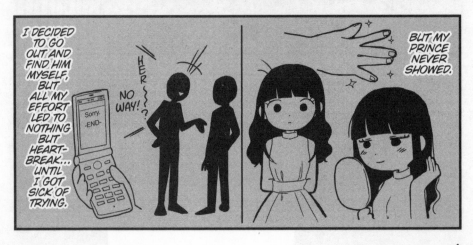

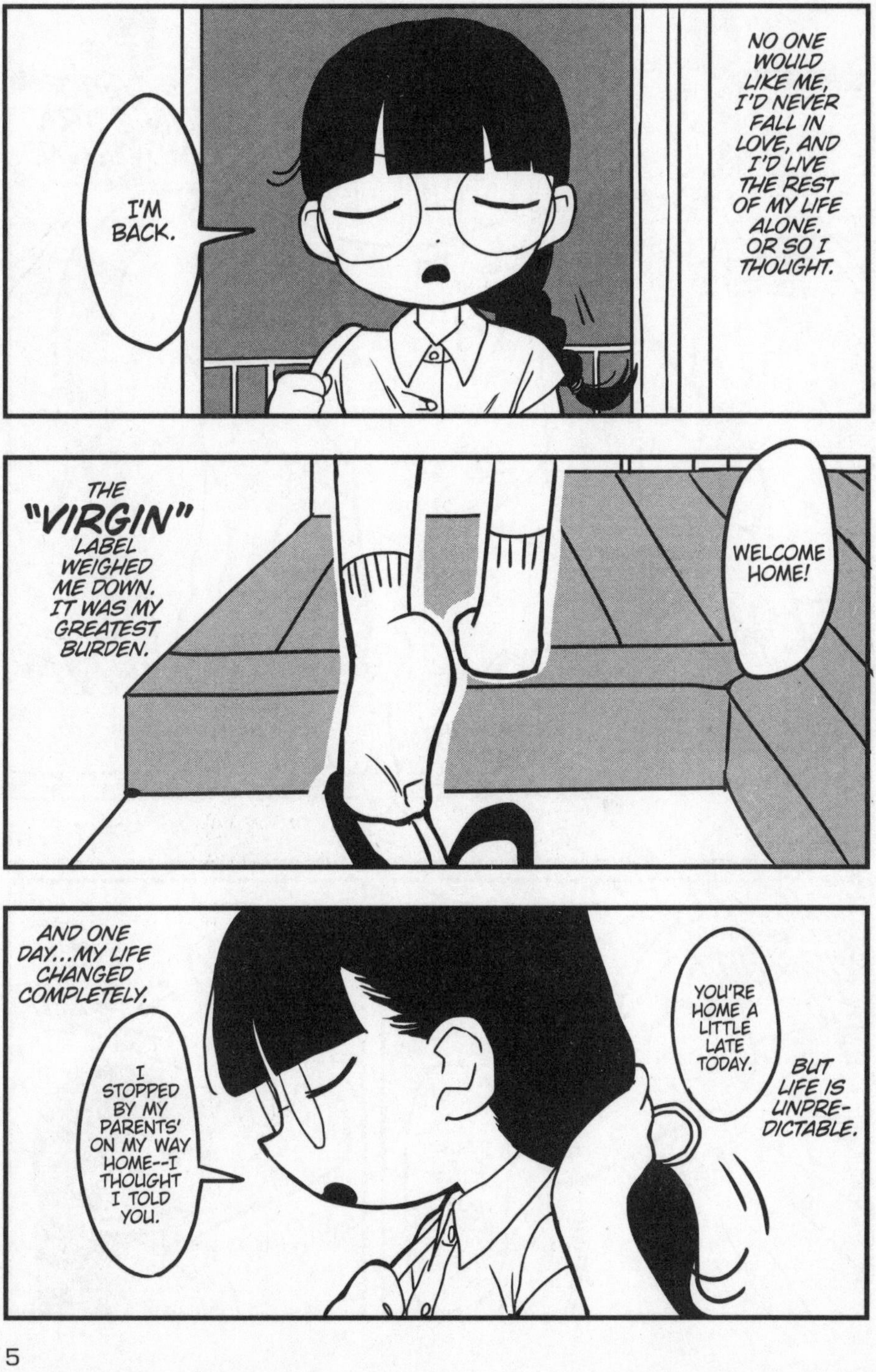
NO ONE WOULD LIKE ME, I'D NEVER FALL IN LOVE, AND I'D LIVE THE REST OF MY LIFE ALONE. OR SO I THOUGHT.
I'M BACK.
WELCOME HOME!
THE "VIRGIN" LABEL WEIGHED ME DOWN. IT WAS MY GREATEST BURDEN.
YOU'RE HOME A LITTLE LATE TODAY.
BUT LIFE IS UNPRE-DICTABLE.
AND ONE DAY...MY LIFE CHANGED COMPLETELY.
I STOPPED BY MY PARENTS' ON MY WAY HOME--I THOUGHT I TOLD YOU.

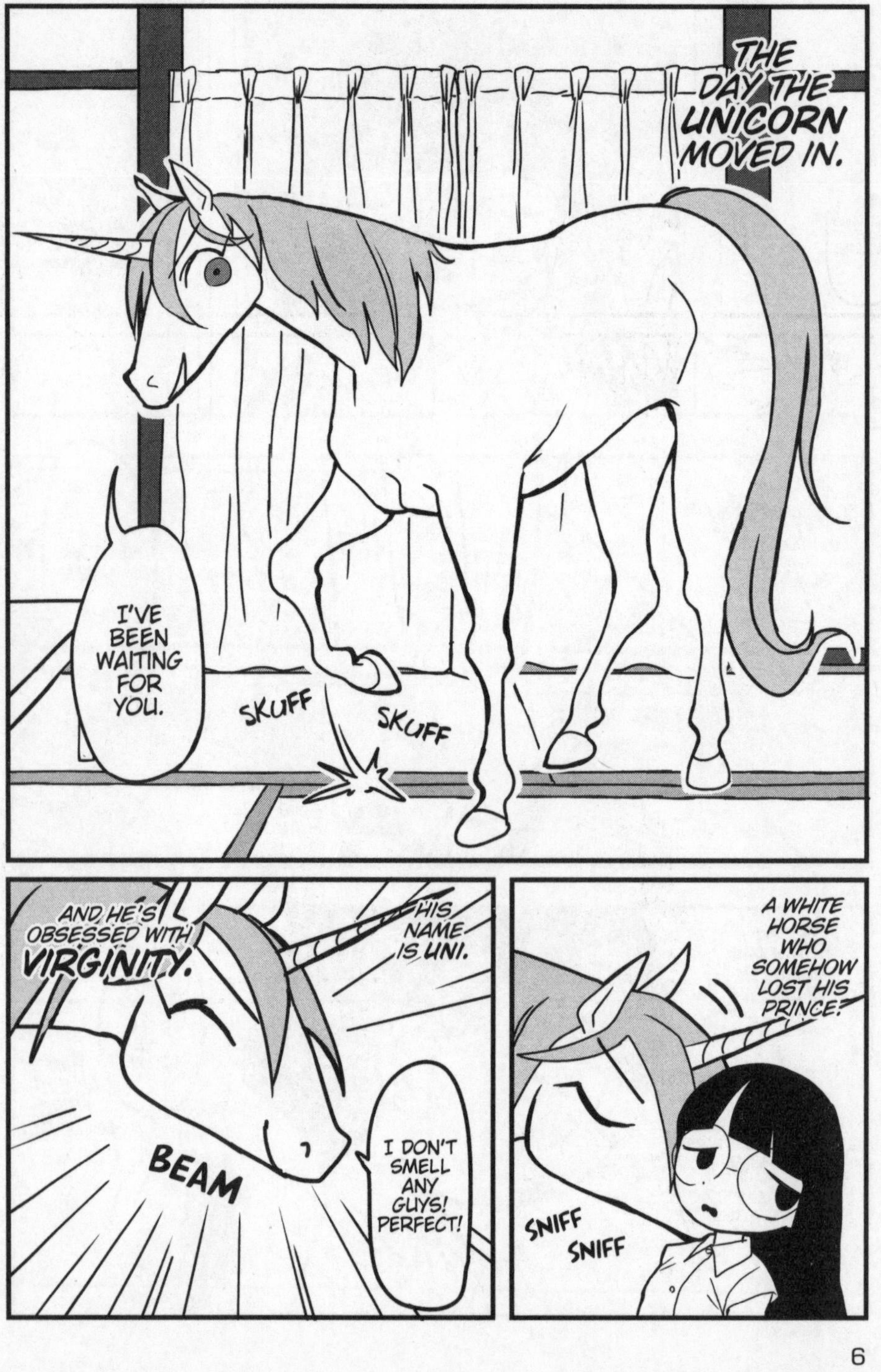
THE DAY THE UNICORN MOVED IN.
I'VE BEEN WAITING FOR YOU.
SKUFF
SKUFF
A WHITE HORSE WHO SOMEHOW LOST HIS PRINCE?
SNIFF
SNIFF
HIS NAME IS UNI.
AND HE'S OBSESSED WITH VIRGINITY.
BEAM
I DON'T SMELL ANY GUYS! PERFECT!

LIFE PLAN

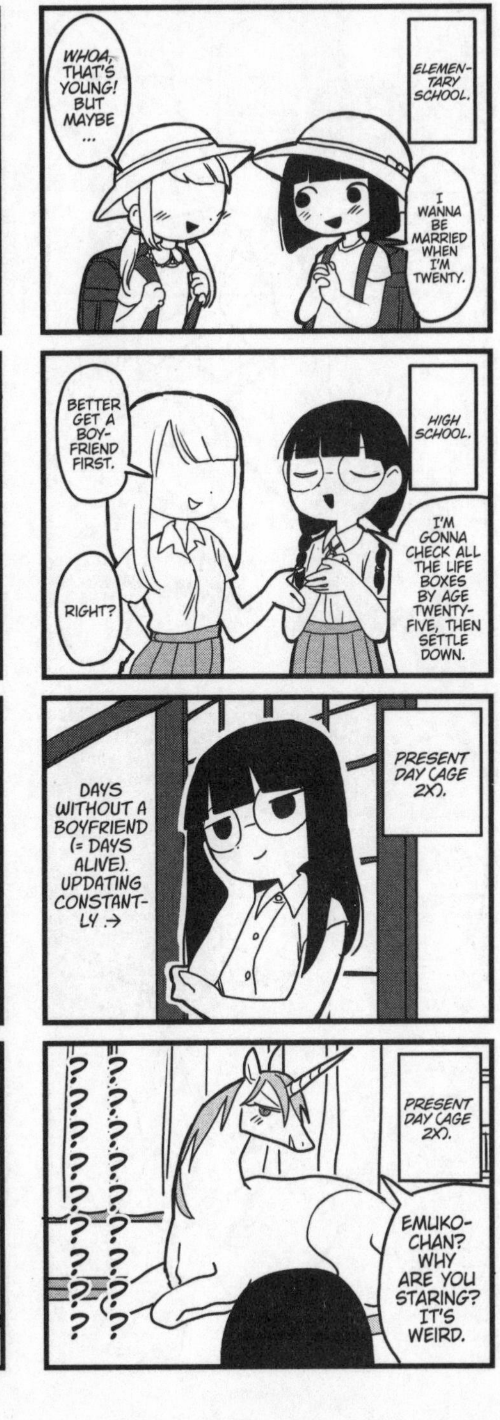
ELEMENTARY SCHOOL.
I WANNA BE MARRIED WHEN I'M TWENTY.
WHOA, THAT'S YOUNG! BUT MAYBE ...
HIGH SCHOOL.
I'M GONNA CHECK ALL THE LIFE BOXES BY AGE TWENTY-FIVE, THEN SETTLE DOWN.
BETTER GET A BOYFRIEND FIRST.
RIGHT?
PRESENT DAY (AGE 2X).
DAYS WITHOUT A BOYFRIEND (= DAYS ALIVE). UPDATING CONSTANTLY →
PRESENT DAY (AGE 2X).
EMUKO-CHAN? WHY ARE YOU STARING? IT'S WEIRD.
??????????
??????????

NICE GUYS

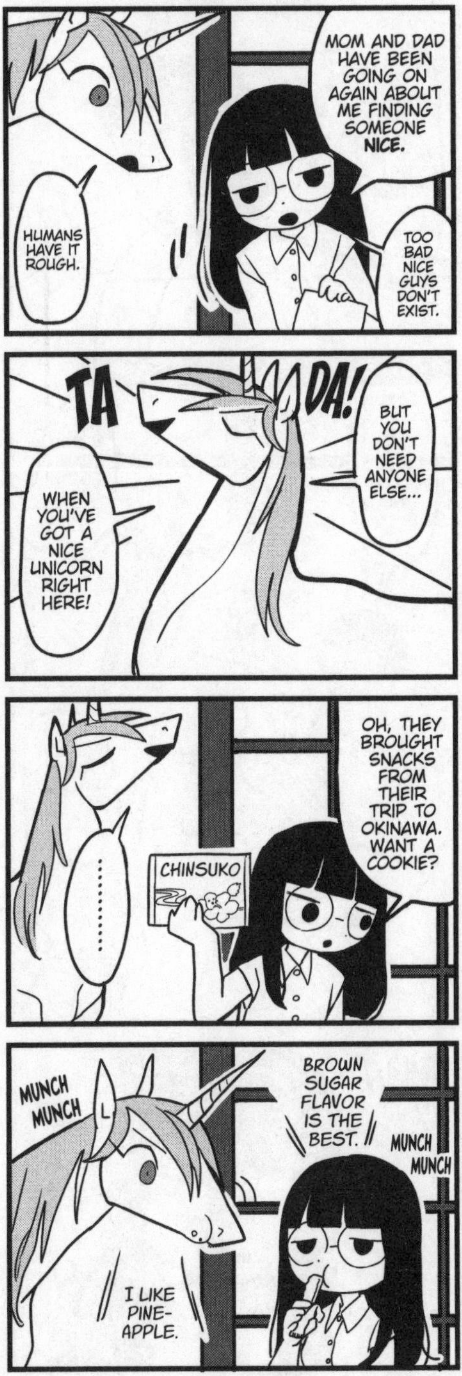
MOM AND DAD HAVE BEEN GOING ON AGAIN ABOUT ME FINDING SOMEONE **NICE.**
TOO BAD NICE GUYS DON'T EXIST.
HUMANS HAVE IT ROUGH.
BUT YOU DON'T NEED ANYONE ELSE...
TA DA!
WHEN YOU'VE GOT A NICE UNICORN RIGHT HERE!
OH, THEY BROUGHT SNACKS FROM THEIR TRIP TO OKINAWA. WANT A COOKIE?
CHINSUKO
......
MUNCH MUNCH
BROWN SUGAR FLAVOR IS THE BEST.
MUNCH MUNCH
I LIKE PINEAPPLE.

A DREADFUL CURSE

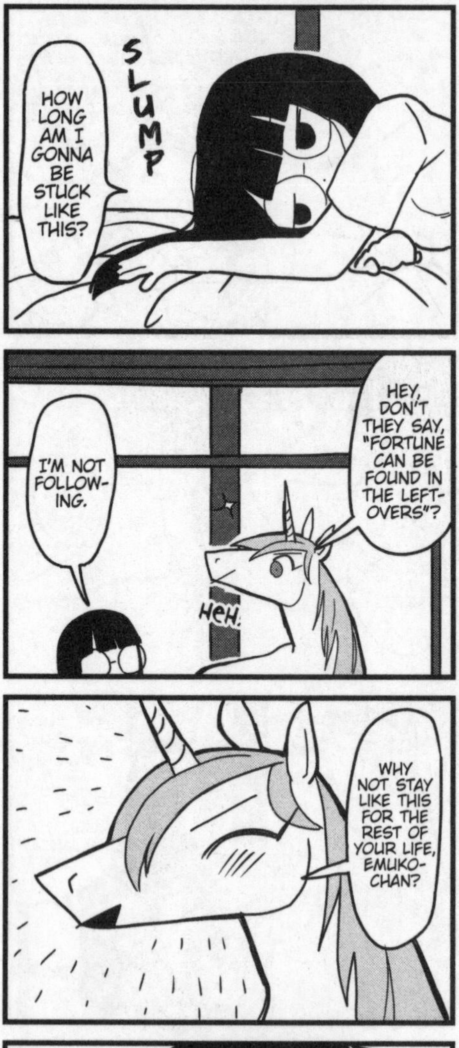
SLUMP
HOW LONG AM I GONNA BE STUCK LIKE THIS?
HEY, DON'T THEY SAY, "FORTUNE CAN BE FOUND IN THE LEFTOVERS"?
I'M NOT FOLLOWING.
HEH!
WHY NOT STAY LIKE THIS FOR THE REST OF YOUR LIFE, EMUKO-CHAN?
"THE REST OF YOUR LIFE" ...!!
GAAH!
"THE REST OF YOUR LIFE" ...!!

THE POMPOUS TYPE

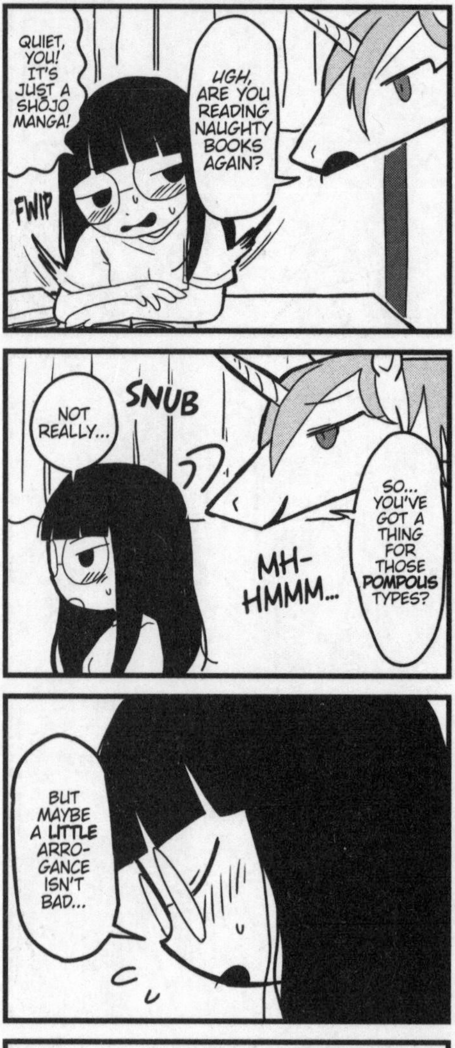
UGH, ARE YOU READING NAUGHTY BOOKS AGAIN?
QUIET, YOU! IT'S JUST A SHŌJO MANGA!
FWIP
SO... YOU'VE GOT A THING FOR THOSE POMPOUS TYPES?
SNUB
NOT REALLY...
MH-HMMM...
BUT MAYBE A LITTLE ARROGANCE ISN'T BAD...
WELL THEN, MY DEAR... YOU CAN ENTRUST YOUR VIRGINITY TO ME.
YEAH, WAY TOO MUCH. MINUS FIVE POINTS.

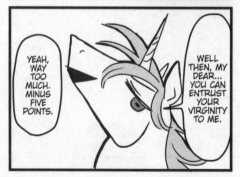

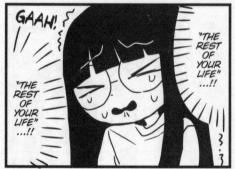

WHISPER TO ME

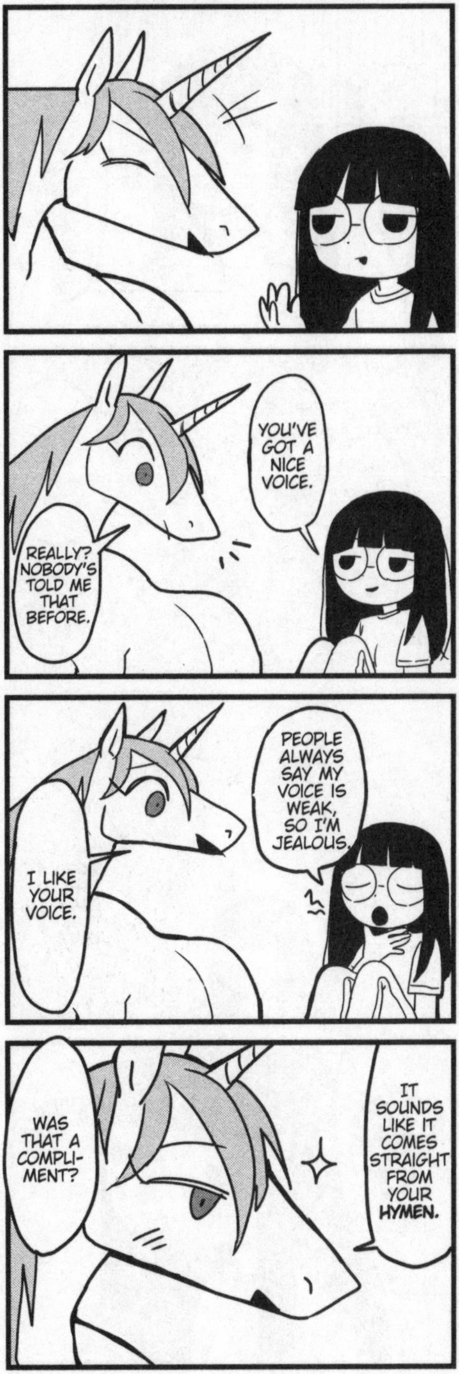
YOU'VE GOT A NICE VOICE.
REALLY? NOBODY'S TOLD ME THAT BEFORE.
PEOPLE ALWAYS SAY MY VOICE IS WEAK, SO I'M JEALOUS.
I LIKE YOUR VOICE.
IT SOUNDS LIKE IT COMES STRAIGHT FROM YOUR **HYMEN.**
WAS THAT A COMPLIMENT?

IF YOU CLOSE YOUR EYES

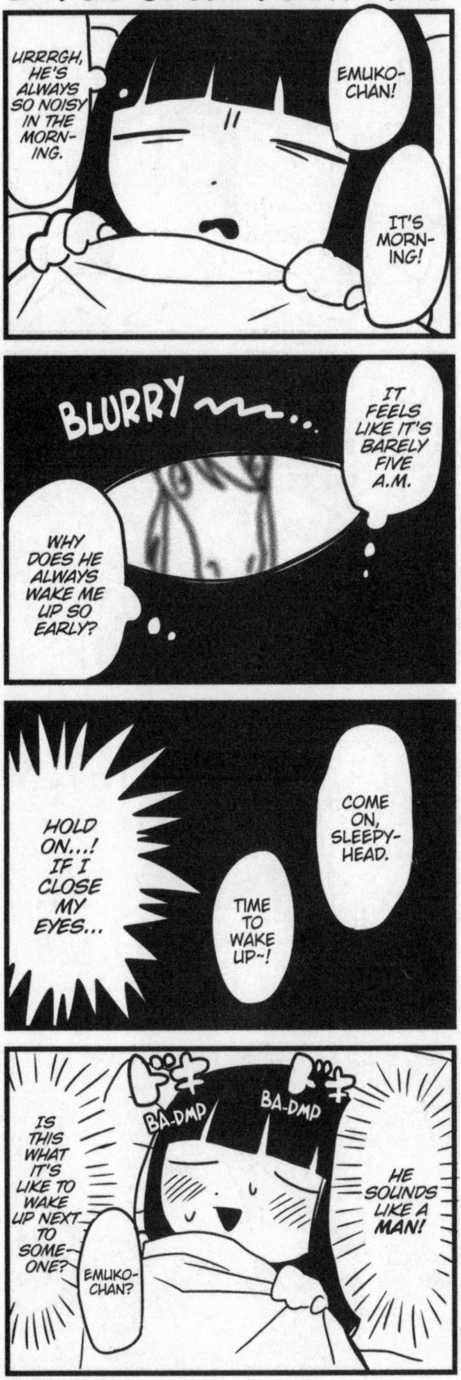
EMUKO-CHAN!
IT'S MORNING!
URRRGH, HE'S ALWAYS SO NOISY IN THE MORNING.
IT FEELS LIKE IT'S BARELY FIVE A.M.
BLURRY ~~~...
WHY DOES HE ALWAYS WAKE ME UP SO EARLY?
COME ON, SLEEPY-HEAD.
TIME TO WAKE UP~!
HOLD ON...! IF I CLOSE MY EYES...
ドキ
BA-DMP
ドキ
BA-DMP
HE SOUNDS LIKE A **MAN!**
IS THIS WHAT IT'S LIKE TO WAKE UP NEXT TO SOME-ONE?
EMUKO-CHAN?

FETISH

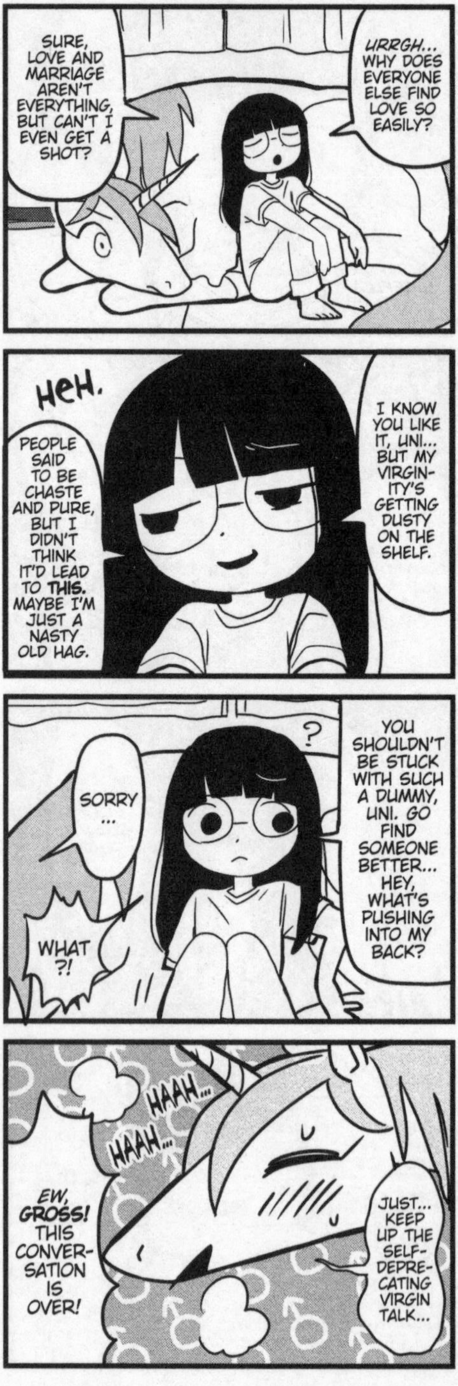
URRGH... WHY DOES EVERYONE ELSE FIND LOVE SO EASILY?
SURE, LOVE AND MARRIAGE AREN'T EVERYTHING, BUT CAN'T I EVEN GET A SHOT?
I KNOW YOU LIKE IT, UNI... BUT MY VIRGINITY'S GETTING DUSTY ON THE SHELF.
HEH.
PEOPLE SAID TO BE CHASTE AND PURE, BUT I DIDN'T THINK IT'D LEAD TO THIS. MAYBE I'M JUST A NASTY OLD HAG.
YOU SHOULDN'T BE STUCK WITH SUCH A DUMMY, UNI. GO FIND SOMEONE BETTER... HEY, WHAT'S PUSHING INTO MY BACK?
?
SORRY...
WHAT?!
HAAH...
HAAH...
JUST... KEEP UP THE SELF-DEPRECATING VIRGIN TALK...
EW, GROSS! THIS CONVERSATION IS OVER!

A BIT TOO FORGIVING

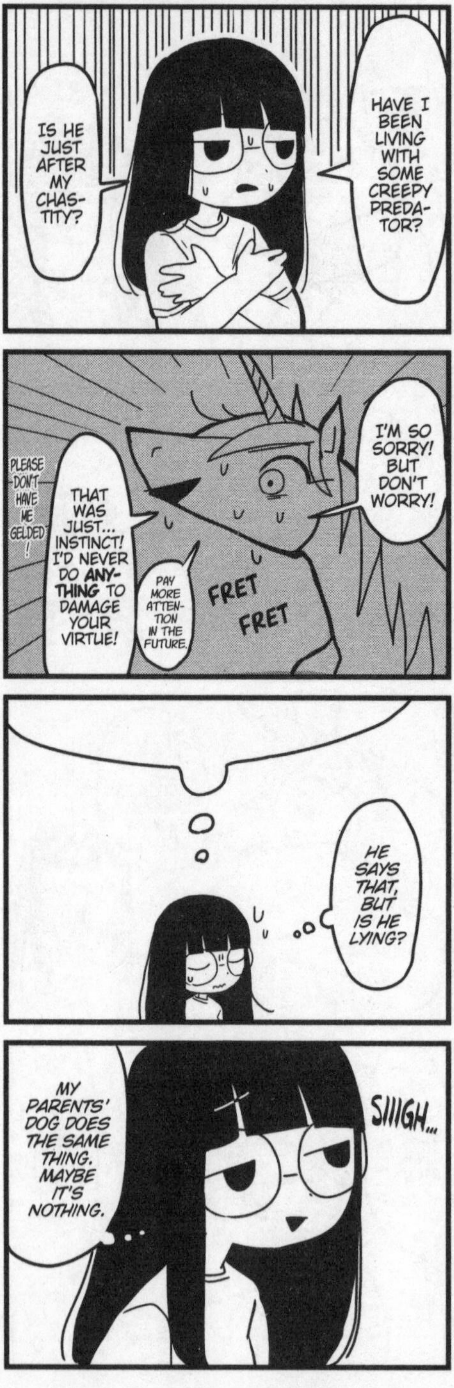
HAVE I BEEN LIVING WITH SOME CREEPY PREDATOR?
IS HE JUST AFTER MY CHASTITY?
I'M SO SORRY! BUT DON'T WORRY!
FRET FRET
THAT WAS JUST... INSTINCT! I'D NEVER DO ANYTHING TO DAMAGE YOUR VIRTUE!
PAY MORE ATTENTION IN THE FUTURE.
PLEASE DON'T HAVE ME GELDED!
HE SAYS THAT, BUT IS HE LYING?
SIIIGH...
MY PARENTS' DOG DOES THE SAME THING. MAYBE IT'S NOTHING.

SWEET OBLIVION

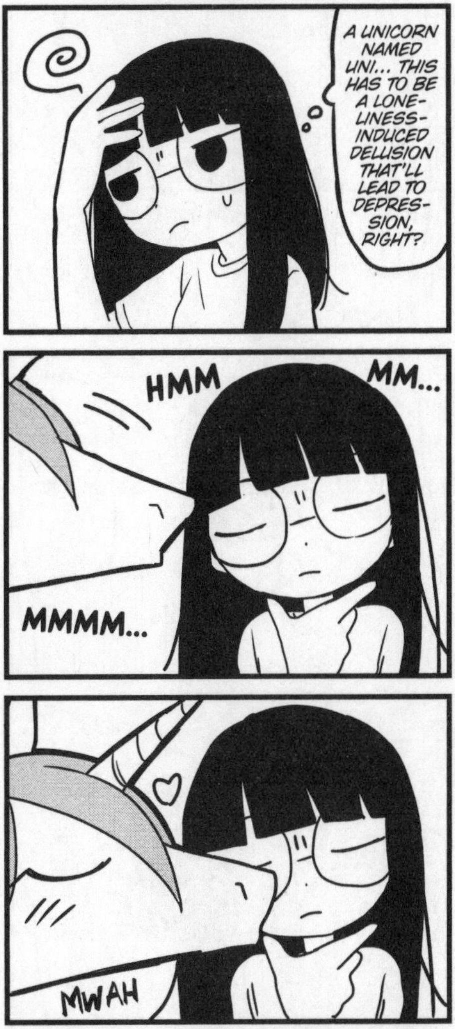
A UNICORN NAMED UNI... THIS HAS TO BE A LONE-LINESS-INDUCED DELUSION THAT'LL LEAD TO DEPRES-SION, RIGHT?
MM...
HMM
MMMM...
MWAH
HRRRGH...
YOU'D THINK I'D HAVE A MORE **NORMAL** DELUSION.

STUDY

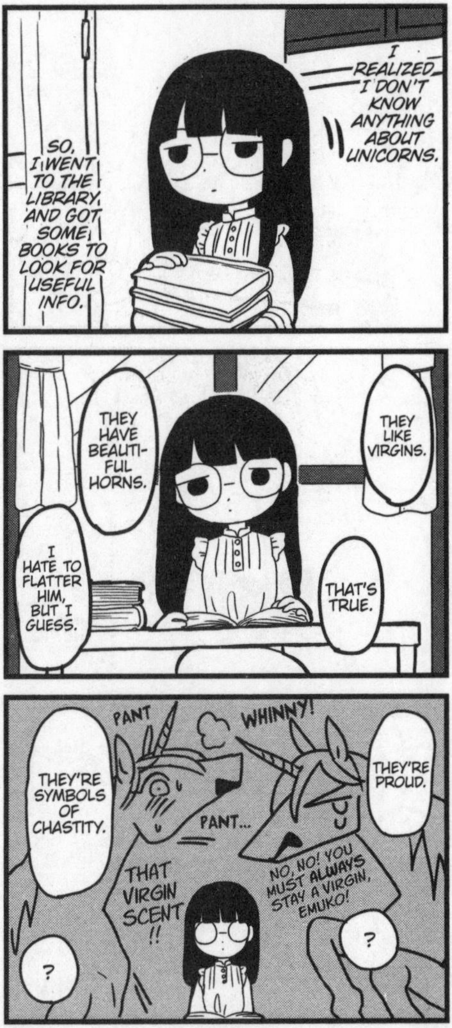
I REALIZED I DON'T KNOW ANYTHING ABOUT UNICORNS.
SO, I WENT TO THE LIBRARY AND GOT SOME BOOKS TO LOOK FOR USEFUL INFO.
THEY LIKE VIRGINS.
THEY HAVE BEAUTI-FUL HORNS.
THAT'S TRUE.
I HATE TO FLATTER HIM, BUT I GUESS.
THEY'RE PROUD.
WHINNY!
PANT
THEY'RE SYMBOLS OF CHASTITY.
PANT...
NO, NO! YOU MUST **ALWAYS** STAY A VIRGIN, EMUKO!
THAT VIRGIN SCENT !!
?
?
...
I GUESS THERE ARE ALL TYPES OF UNI-CORNS.

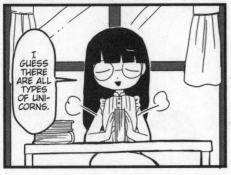

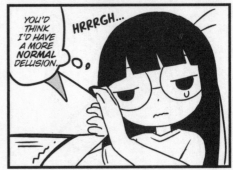

A UNICORN'S WEAKNESS

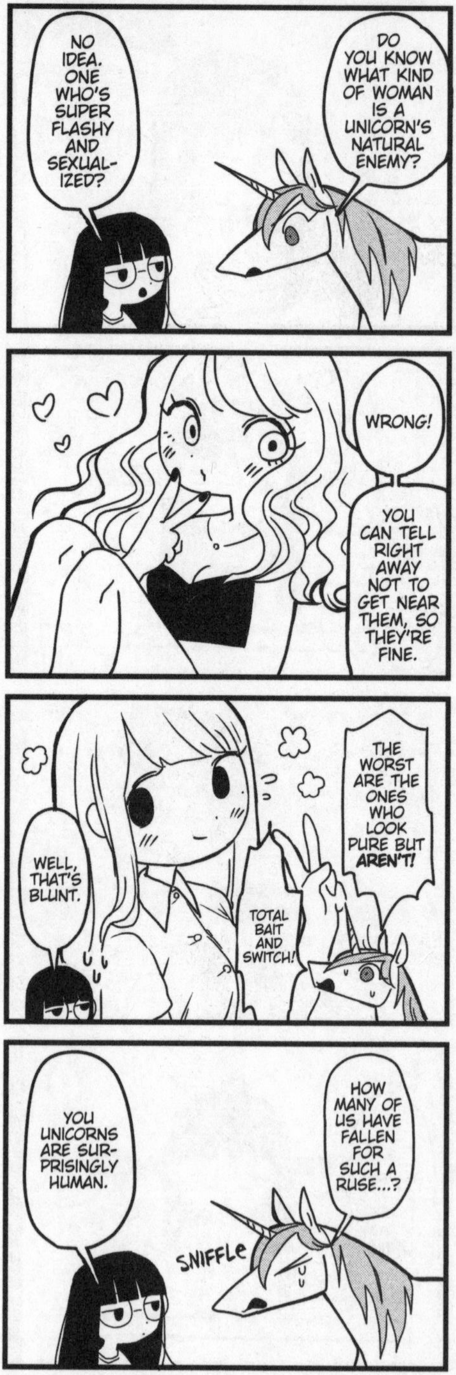
DO YOU KNOW WHAT KIND OF WOMAN IS A UNICORN'S NATURAL ENEMY?
NO IDEA. ONE WHO'S SUPER FLASHY AND SEXUALIZED?
WRONG!
YOU CAN TELL RIGHT AWAY NOT TO GET NEAR THEM, SO THEY'RE FINE.
THE WORST ARE THE ONES WHO LOOK PURE BUT **AREN'T!**
TOTAL BAIT AND SWITCH!
WELL, THAT'S BLUNT.
HOW MANY OF US HAVE FALLEN FOR SUCH A RUSE...?
SNIFFLE
YOU UNICORNS ARE SURPRISINGLY HUMAN.

RAINY DAYS

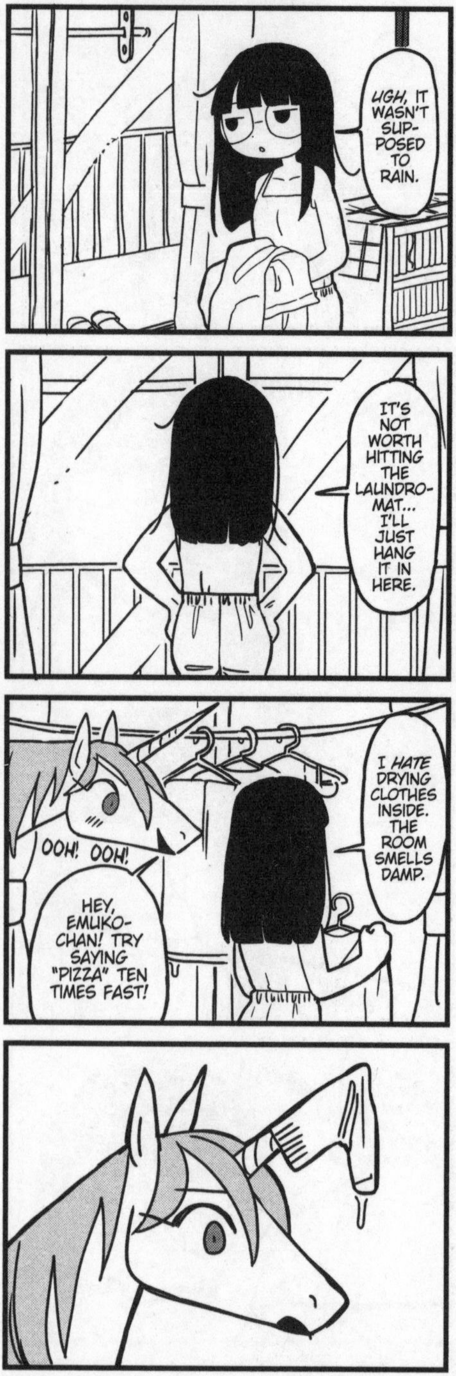
UGH, IT WASN'T SUPPOSED TO RAIN.
IT'S NOT WORTH HITTING THE LAUNDROMAT... I'LL JUST HANG IT IN HERE.
I *HATE* DRYING CLOTHES INSIDE. THE ROOM SMELLS DAMP.
OOH! OOH!
HEY, EMUKO-CHAN! TRY SAYING "PIZZA" TEN TIMES FAST!

OBLIVIOUS

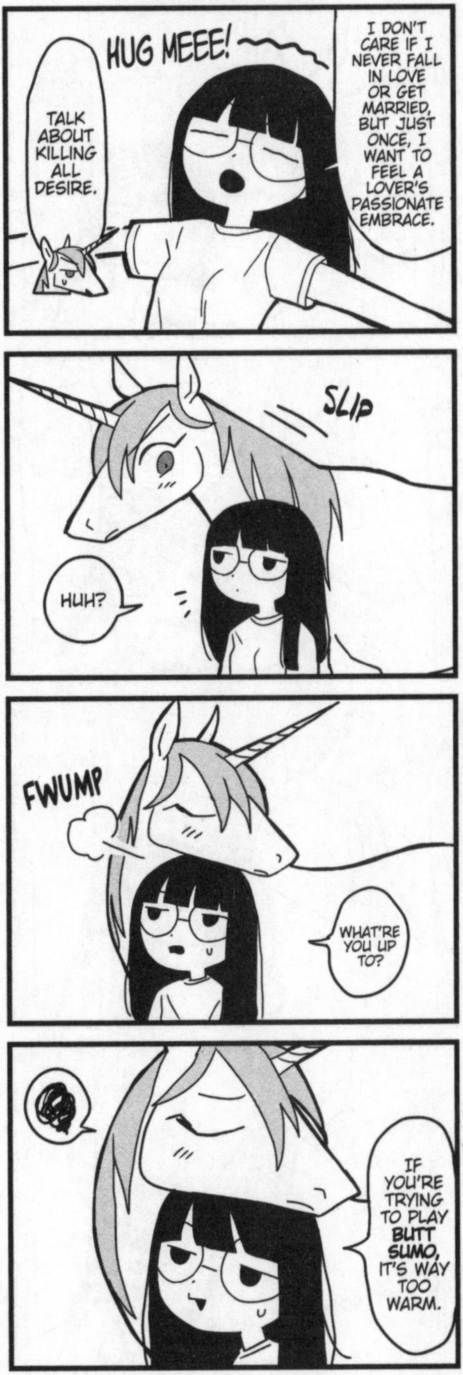
I DON'T CARE IF I NEVER FALL IN LOVE OR GET MARRIED, BUT JUST ONCE, I WANT TO FEEL A LOVER'S PASSIONATE EMBRACE.
HUG MEEE!
TALK ABOUT KILLING ALL DESIRE.
SLIP
HUH?
FWUMP
WHAT'RE YOU UP TO?
IF YOU'RE TRYING TO PLAY **BUTT SUMO,** IT'S WAY TOO WARM.

PERPLEXING

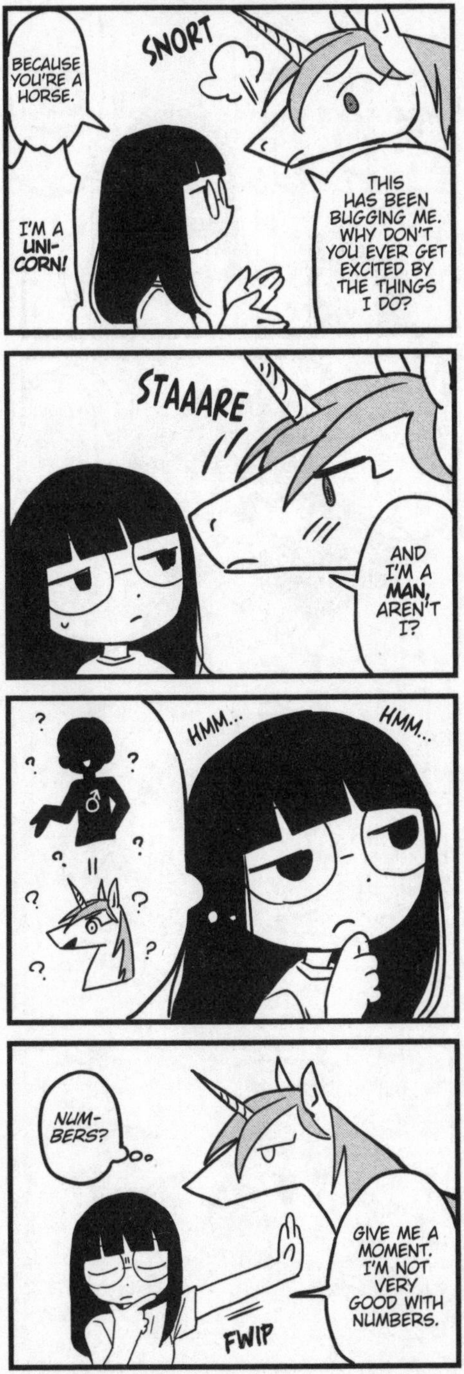
SNORT
THIS HAS BEEN BUGGING ME. WHY DON'T YOU EVER GET EXCITED BY THE THINGS I DO?
BECAUSE YOU'RE A HORSE.
I'M A **UNI-CORN!**
STAAARE
AND I'M A **MAN,** AREN'T I?
HMM...
HMM...
GIVE ME A MOMENT. I'M NOT VERY GOOD WITH NUMBERS.
FWIP
NUM-BERS?

MIXER

A FRIEND INVITED ME TO A MIXER.
A WHAT ?!
WATCH THE HOUSE WHILE I'M OUT.
NOOOOOO!
KA-CHK
TWO HOURS LATER ...
I'M HOME.
WEL-COME BACK.

JUST HOW UNICORNS ARE

YOU'LL NEVER LEAVE ME, RIGHT, UNI?
WELL, NOT AS LONG AS YOU'RE A VIRGIN.
SQUEEZE

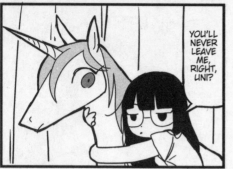

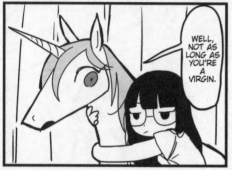

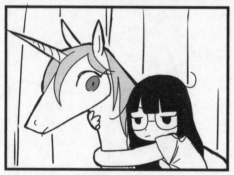

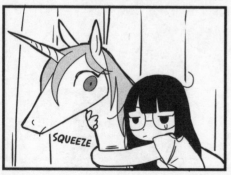

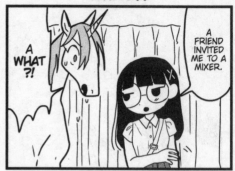

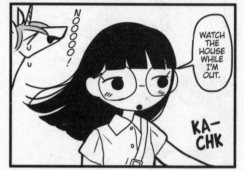

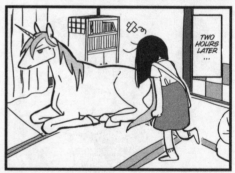

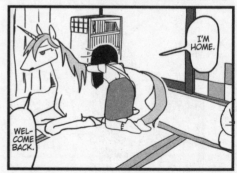

CHAPTER 2

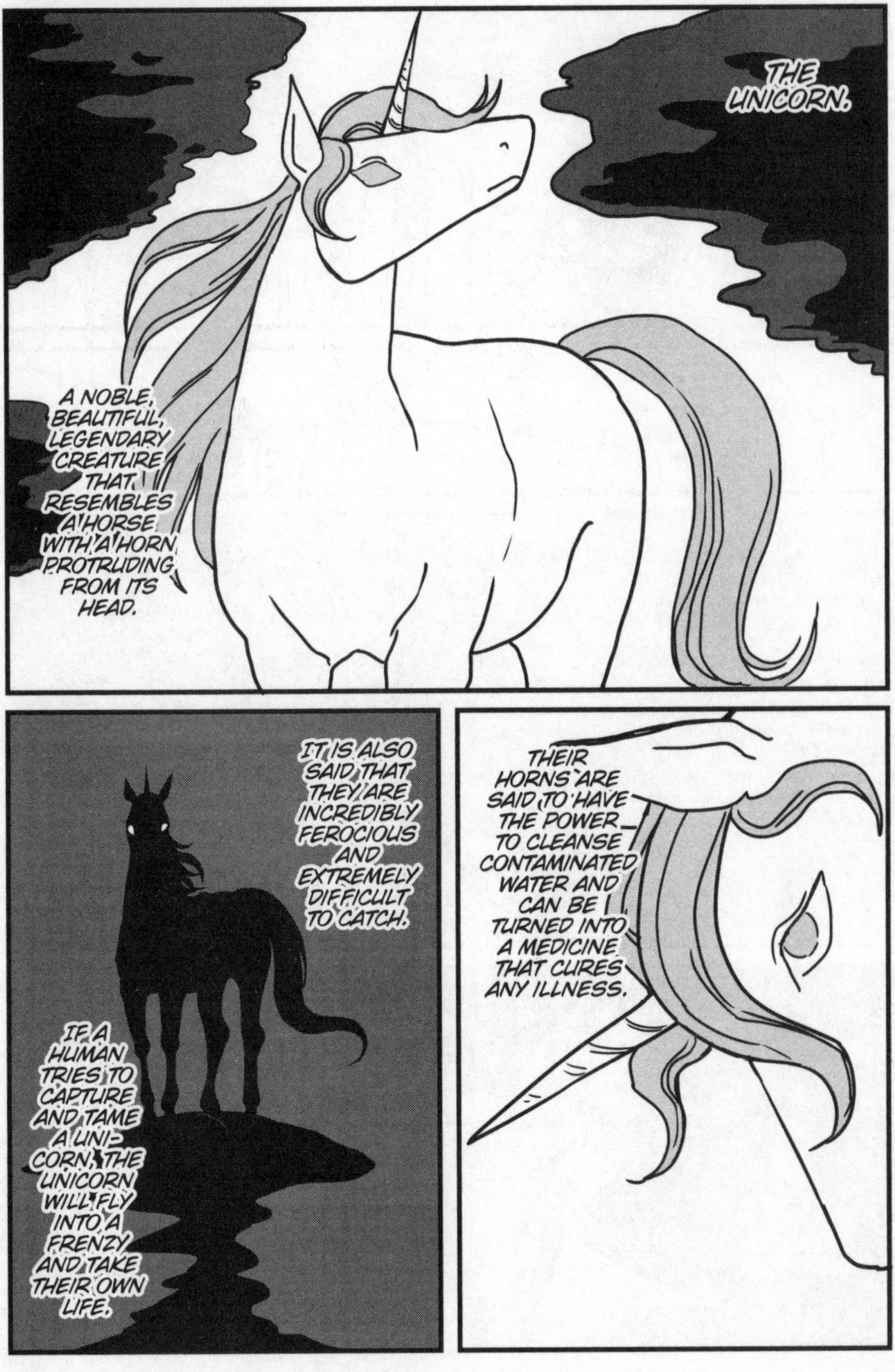
THE UNICORN.
A NOBLE, BEAUTIFUL, LEGENDARY CREATURE THAT RESEMBLES A HORSE WITH A HORN PROTRUDING FROM ITS HEAD.
THEIR HORNS ARE SAID TO HAVE THE POWER TO CLEANSE CONTAMINATED WATER AND CAN BE TURNED INTO A MEDICINE THAT CURES ANY ILLNESS.
IT IS ALSO SAID THAT THEY ARE INCREDIBLY FEROCIOUS AND EXTREMELY DIFFICULT TO CATCH.
IF A HUMAN TRIES TO CAPTURE AND TAME A UNI-CORN, THE UNICORN WILL FLY INTO A FRENZY AND TAKE THEIR OWN LIFE.

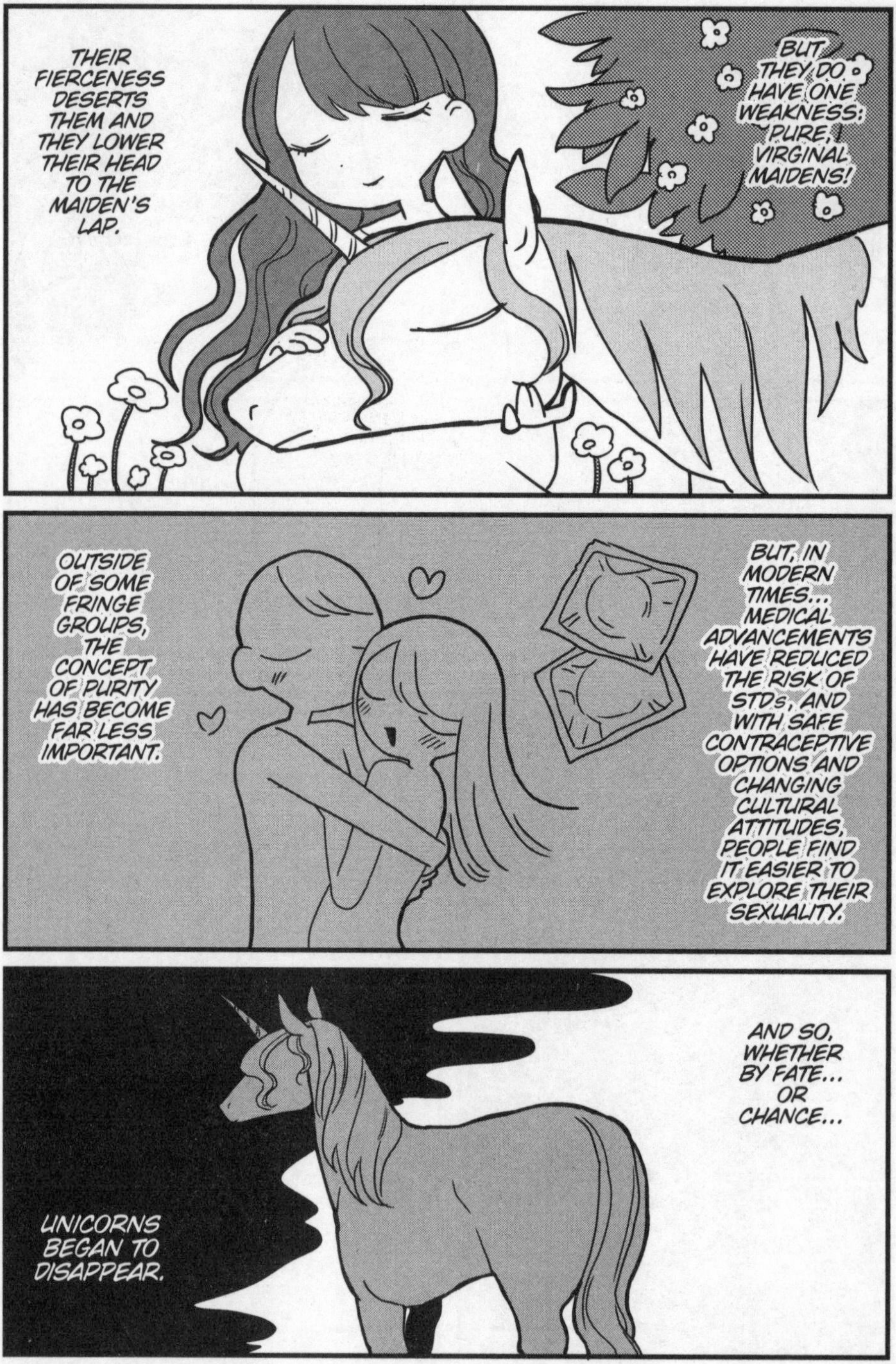
BUT THEY DO HAVE ONE WEAKNESS: PURE, VIRGINAL MAIDENS!
THEIR FIERCENESS DESERTS THEM AND THEY LOWER THEIR HEAD TO THE MAIDEN'S LAP.
BUT, IN MODERN TIMES... MEDICAL ADVANCEMENTS HAVE REDUCED THE RISK OF STDs, AND WITH SAFE CONTRACEPTIVE OPTIONS AND CHANGING CULTURAL ATTITUDES, PEOPLE FIND IT EASIER TO EXPLORE THEIR SEXUALITY.
OUTSIDE OF SOME FRINGE GROUPS, THE CONCEPT OF PURITY HAS BECOME FAR LESS IMPORTANT.
AND SO, WHETHER BY FATE... OR CHANCE...
UNICORNS BEGAN TO DISAPPEAR.

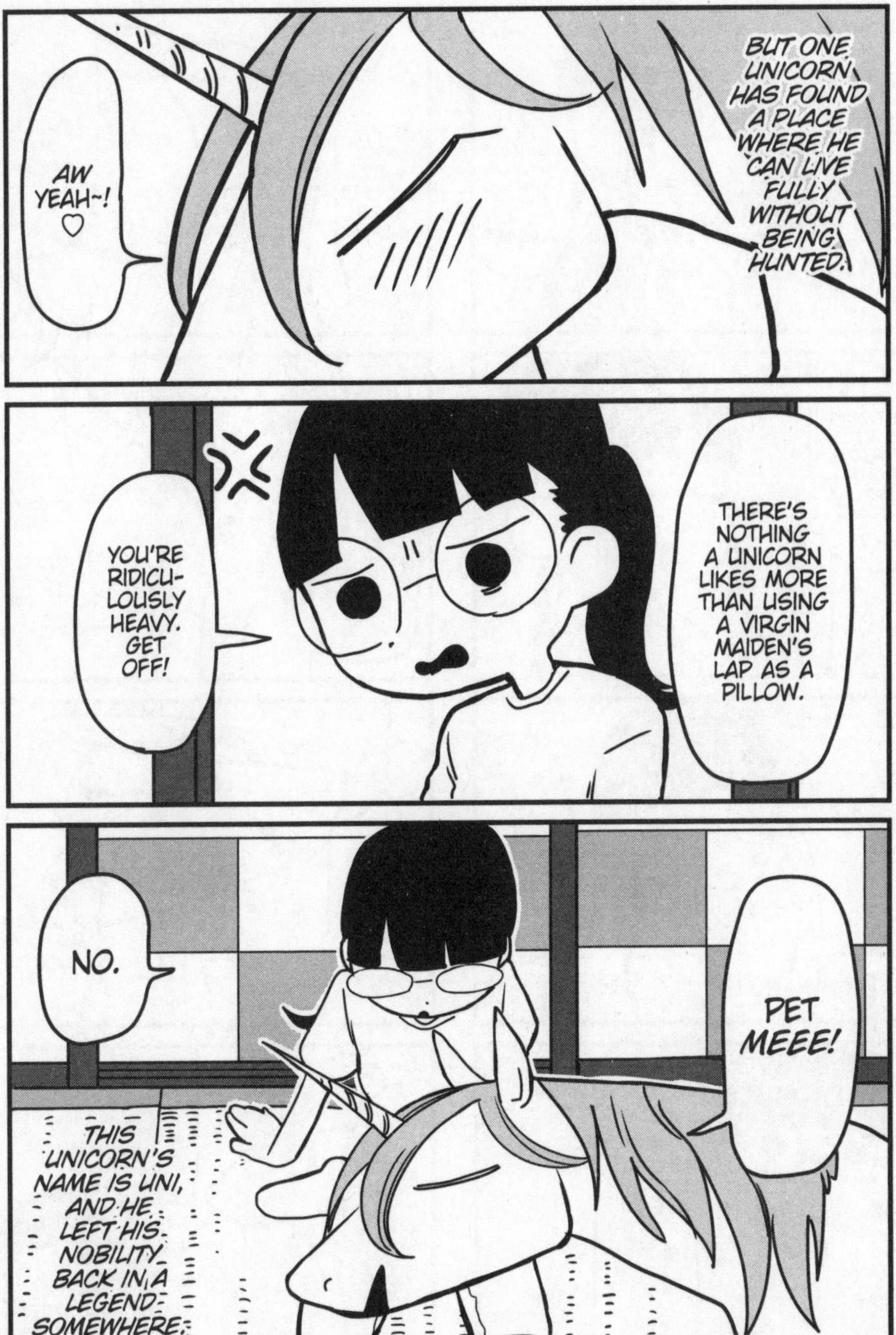
BUT ONE UNICORN HAS FOUND A PLACE WHERE HE CAN LIVE FULLY WITHOUT BEING HUNTED.
AW YEAH~! ♡
THERE'S NOTHING A UNICORN LIKES MORE THAN USING A VIRGIN MAIDEN'S LAP AS A PILLOW.
YOU'RE RIDICU-LOUSLY HEAVY. GET OFF!
PET MEEE!
NO.
THIS UNICORN'S NAME IS UNI, AND HE LEFT HIS NOBILITY BACK IN A LEGEND SOMEWHERE.

DAILY ROUTINE

TIME TO CHECK MY LOOK!
TAIL?! CHECK! HAIR LOOKING SILKY SOFT!
HORN? CHECK! SHARP AND MANLY! READY TO BE TOUCHED!
AND FINALLY...
MY FACE! PERFECT! NO COMPLAINTS!
AS ALWAYS, I AM CUTE AND SEXY!
DON'T YOU GET **BORED** DOING ALL THAT?
NOT AT ALL! THE MORE I LOOK AT MYSELF, THE MORE I'M IN LOVE.

GROOMING

YOU SHOULD TRY PRAISING YOURSELF, EMUKO-CHAN. MAKES YOU FEEL **PUMPED!**
NOPE, TOO EMBARRASSING.
ALL I NEED IS A QUICK GROOM, A CHECK, AND I'M DONE!
NO POINT IN WASTING PRECIOUS TIME.
GLEAM
YEAH, WELL, YOUR SKIRT'S CAUGHT IN YOUR UNDERWEAR.
YANK

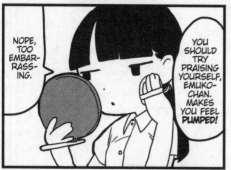

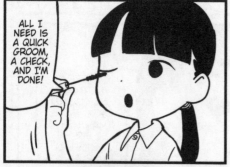

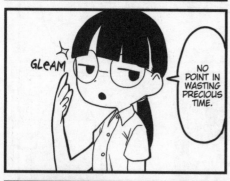

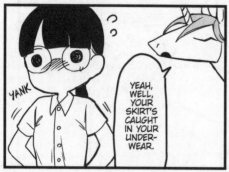

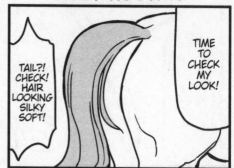

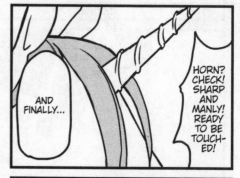

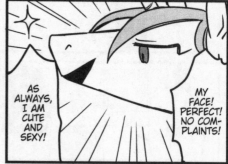

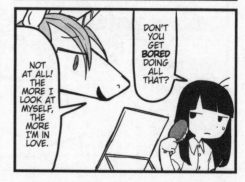

SELF-DESTRUCTION

SERI-OUSLY, EMUKO-CHAN...
I'M WORRIED ABOUT HOW **DEFENSE-LESS** YOU ARE SOME-TIMES.
REALLY ...?
I'VE NEVER THOUGHT OF MYSELF THAT WAY.
IT'S TRUE. ANYONE COULD SLIP THROUGH.
WELL, NO NEED TO WORRY. NO ONE'S EVER GOING TO SEDUCE ME, SO WHO CARES?
IT'S LIKE AN ETERNAL BYE WEEK! I CAN'T LOSE!
AH... ARRRGH ...
SLUMP
EMUKO-CHAN ?!

VIRGIN FILTER

HMPH! JOKES ASIDE, I REALLY **AM** WORRIED!
YOU WEAR YOUR UNDER-CLOTHES AROUND THE HOUSE...
YOU SLEEP HALF NAKED...
AND YOU EVEN LICK THE TOPS OF YOUR YOGURT CUPS!!
SLURP
TALK ABOUT GETTING THE WRONG IDEA... THAT'S ALL JUST **LAZINESS.**

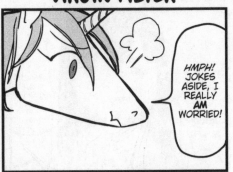

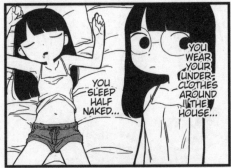

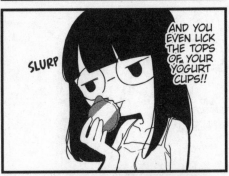

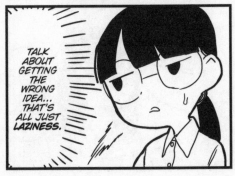

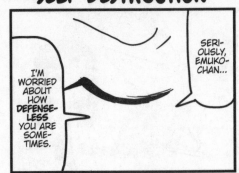

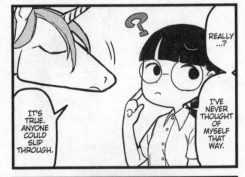

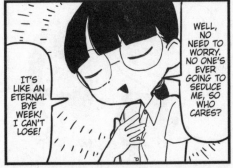

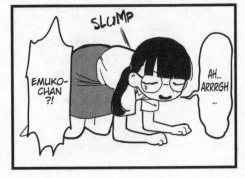

MOVIE NIGHT

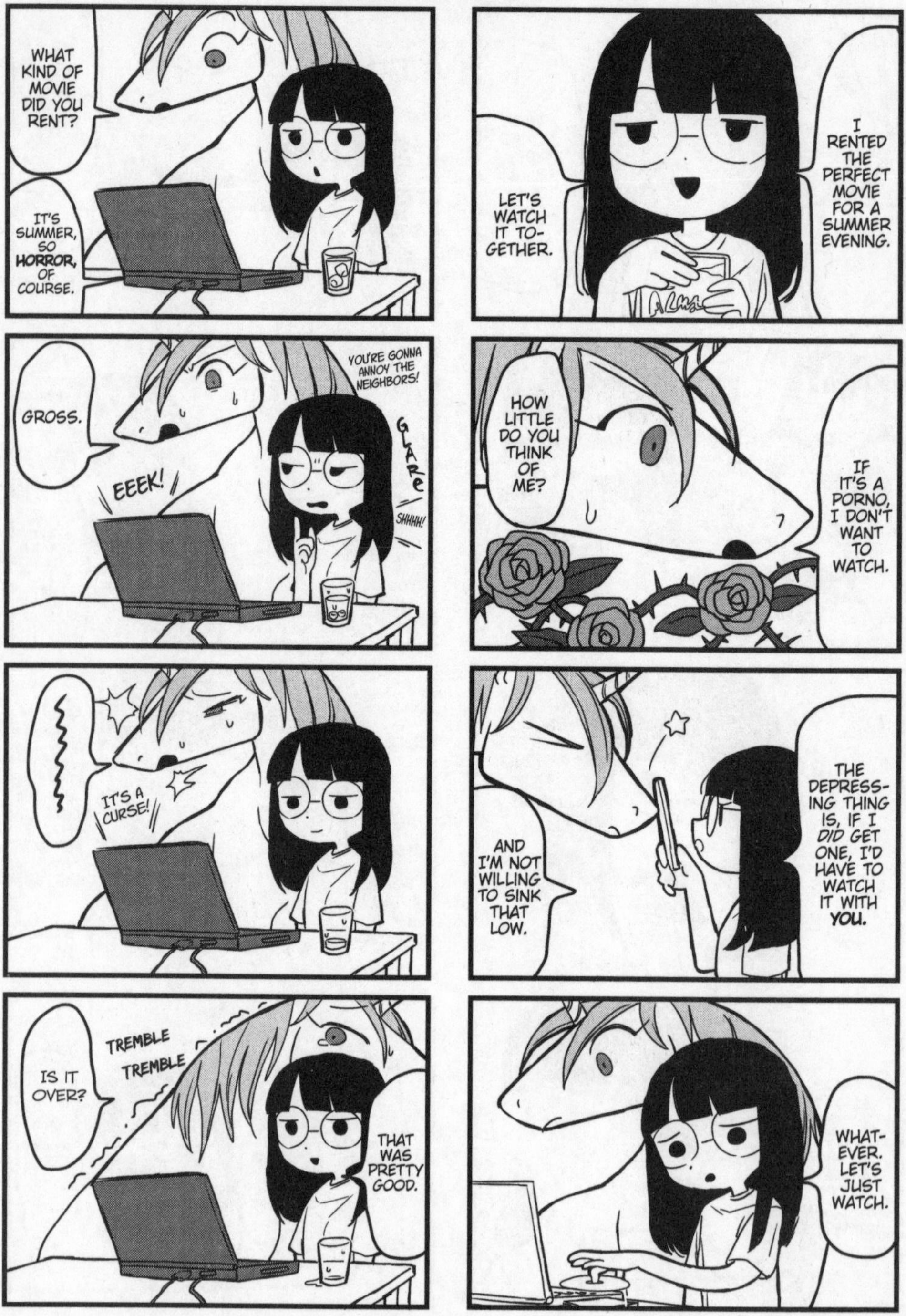
I RENTED THE PERFECT MOVIE FOR A SUMMER EVENING.
LET'S WATCH IT TO-GETHER.
IF IT'S A PORNO, I DON'T WANT TO WATCH.
HOW LITTLE DO YOU THINK OF ME?
THE DEPRESS-ING THING IS, IF I *DID* GET ONE, I'D HAVE TO WATCH IT WITH **YOU.**
AND I'M NOT WILLING TO SINK THAT LOW.
WHAT-EVER. LET'S JUST WATCH.
WHAT KIND OF MOVIE DID YOU RENT?
IT'S SUMMER, SO **HORROR,** OF COURSE.
YOU'RE GONNA ANNOY THE NEIGHBORS!
GLARE
GROSS.
SHHHH!
EEEK!
IT'S A CURSE!
TREMBLE
TREMBLE
IS IT OVER?
THAT WAS PRETTY GOOD.

WITH MY OWN EYES

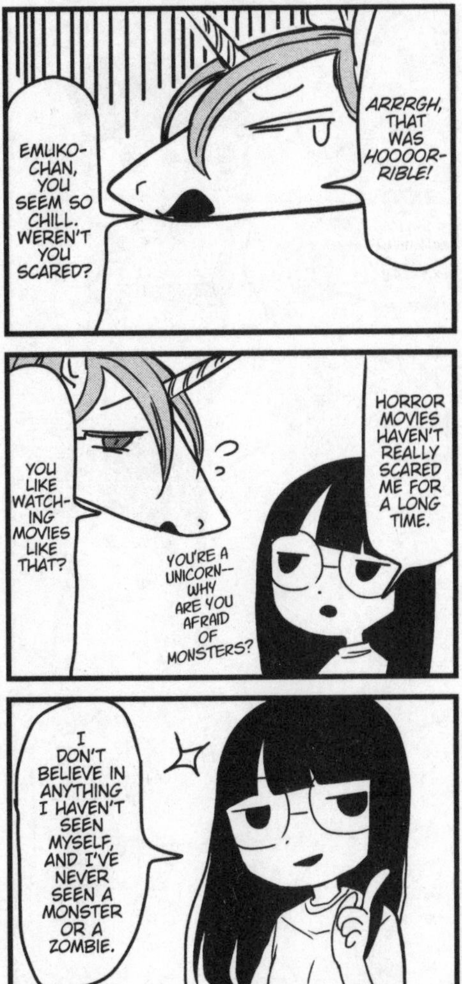
ARRRGH, THAT WAS HOOOORRIBLE!
EMUKO-CHAN, YOU SEEM SO CHILL. WEREN'T YOU SCARED?
HORROR MOVIES HAVEN'T REALLY SCARED ME FOR A LONG TIME.
YOU LIKE WATCHING MOVIES LIKE THAT?
YOU'RE A UNICORN--WHY ARE YOU AFRAID OF MONSTERS?
I DON'T BELIEVE IN ANYTHING I HAVEN'T SEEN MYSELF, AND I'VE NEVER SEEN A MONSTER OR A ZOMBIE.
BUT WAIT--WOULDN'T THAT MAKE **SEX** JUST ANOTHER URBAN LEGEND ...?
WHAT ?!

TRUE HORROR

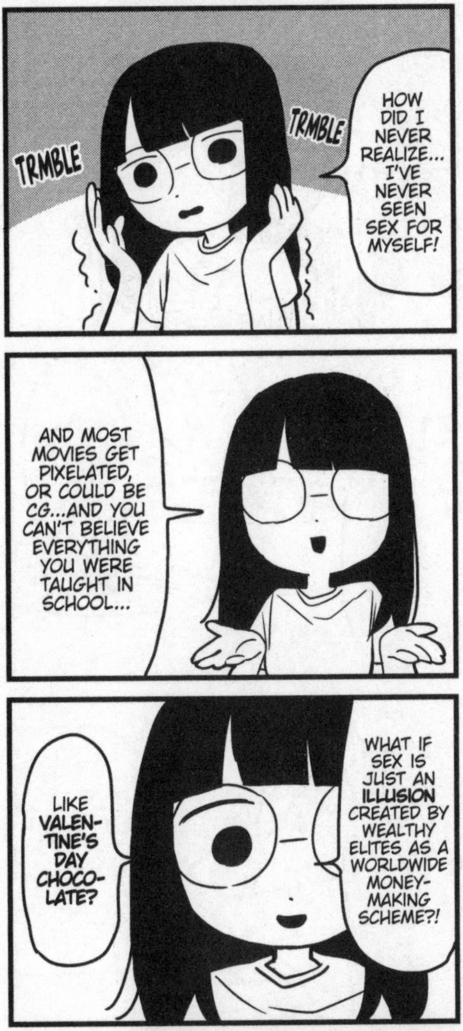
HOW DID I NEVER REALIZE... I'VE NEVER SEEN SEX FOR MYSELF!
TRMBLE
TRMBLE
AND MOST MOVIES GET PIXELATED, OR COULD BE CG...AND YOU CAN'T BELIEVE EVERYTHING YOU WERE TAUGHT IN SCHOOL...
WHAT IF SEX IS JUST AN **ILLUSION** CREATED BY WEALTHY ELITES AS A WORLDWIDE MONEY-MAKING SCHEME?!
LIKE **VALENTINE'S DAY CHOCOLATE?**
THAT *CAN'T* BE TRUE, RIGHT ...?
SHOULD I SAY SOMETHING, OR WILL SHE BE ALL RIGHT?

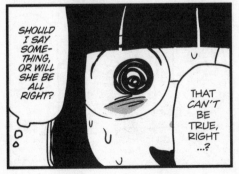

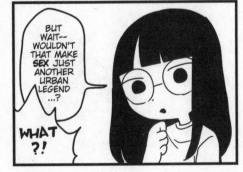

SUMMER TREATS

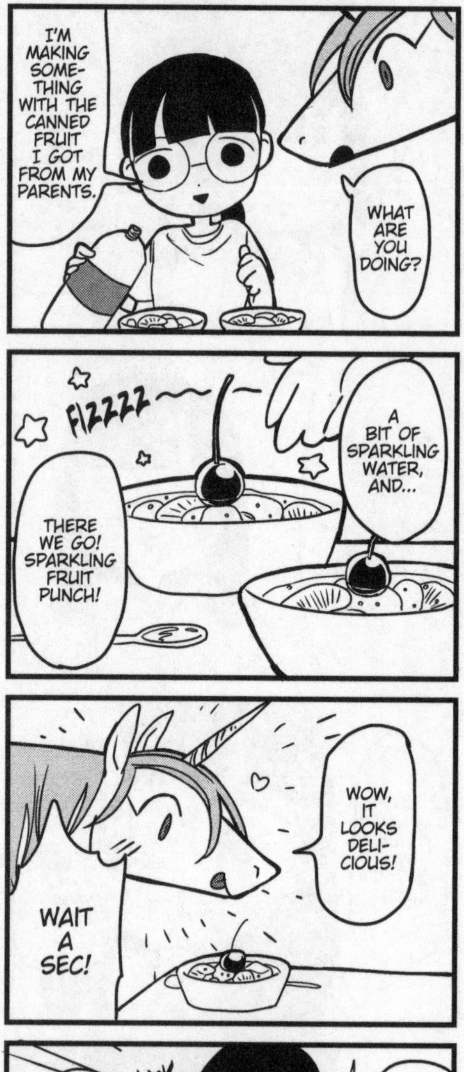
WHAT ARE YOU DOING?
I'M MAKING SOMETHING WITH THE CANNED FRUIT I GOT FROM MY PARENTS.
A BIT OF SPARKLING WATER, AND...
FIZZZZ~~
THERE WE GO! SPARKLING FRUIT PUNCH!
WOW, IT LOOKS DELICIOUS!
WAIT A SEC!
I NEED A PICTURE FOR THE INTERNET!
GET OUT OF THE SHOT.
CLICK
THAT'S UNUSUALLY MODERN OF YOU...
CLICK

TECHNIQUE

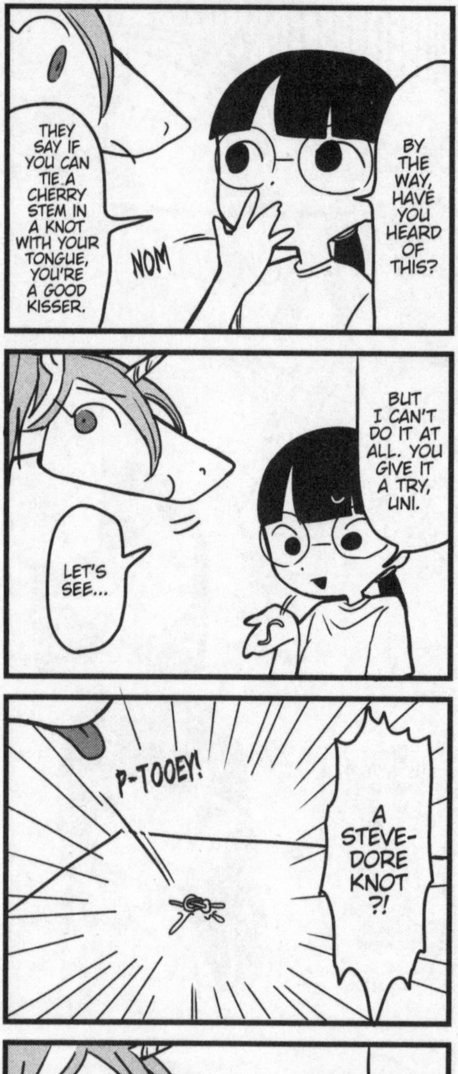
BY THE WAY, HAVE YOU HEARD OF THIS?
NOM
THEY SAY IF YOU CAN TIE A CHERRY STEM IN A KNOT WITH YOUR TONGUE, YOU'RE A GOOD KISSER.
BUT I CAN'T DO IT AT ALL. YOU GIVE IT A TRY, UNI.
LET'S SEE...
A STEVEDORE KNOT?!
P-TOOEY!
I'VE NEVER SEEN THIS BEFORE.
GROSS...
THIS IS, LIKE, SEXUAL HARASSMENT LEVEL.
WELL, **THAT'S** UNCALLED FOR.

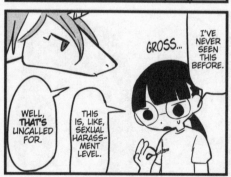

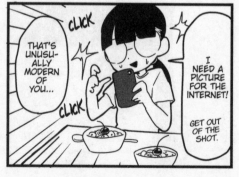

WISH FULFILLMENT

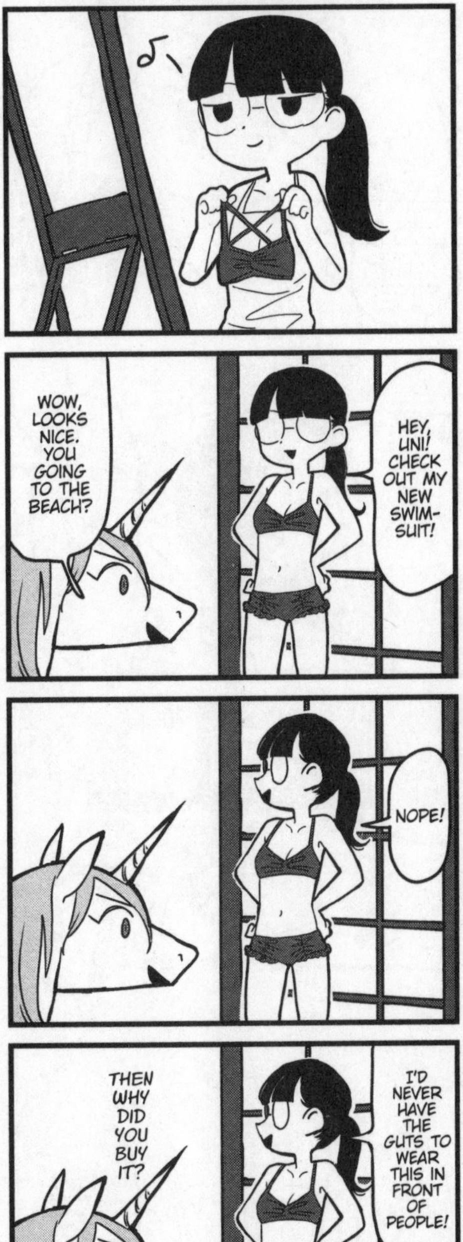
HEY, UNI! CHECK OUT MY NEW SWIM-SUIT!
WOW, LOOKS NICE. YOU GOING TO THE BEACH?
NOPE!
I'D NEVER HAVE THE GUTS TO WEAR THIS IN FRONT OF PEOPLE!
THEN WHY DID YOU BUY IT?

A MAIDEN'S SUPPLE SKIN

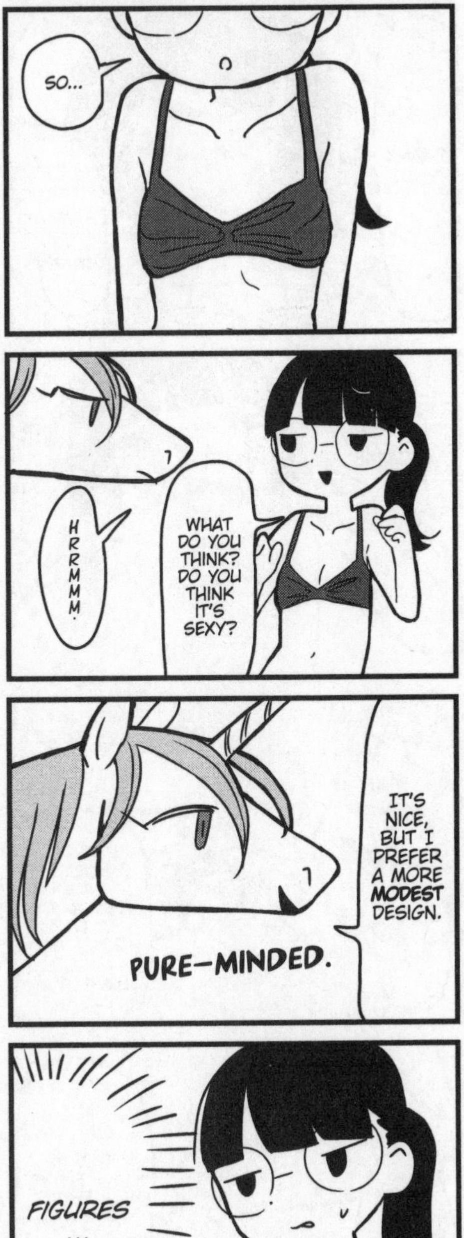
SO...
WHAT DO YOU THINK? DO YOU THINK IT'S SEXY?
HRRMMM.
IT'S NICE, BUT I PREFER A MORE MODEST DESIGN.
PURE-MINDED.
FIGURES ...

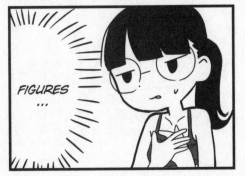

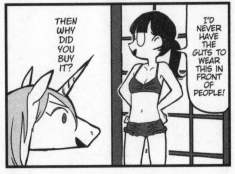

SUMMER COLD

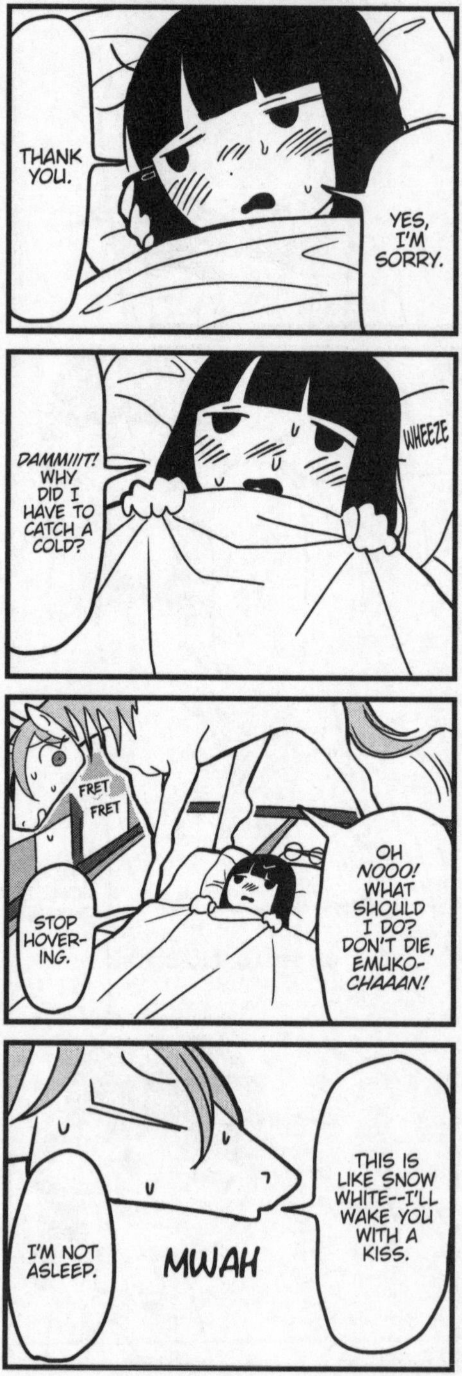
YES, I'M SORRY.
THANK YOU.
WHEEZE
DAMMIIIT! WHY DID I HAVE TO CATCH A COLD?
FRET
FRET
OH NOOO! WHAT SHOULD I DO? DON'T DIE, EMUKO-CHAAAN!
STOP HOVER-ING.
THIS IS LIKE SNOW WHITE--I'LL WAKE YOU WITH A KISS.
MWAH
I'M NOT ASLEEP.

SECRET SCHEMES

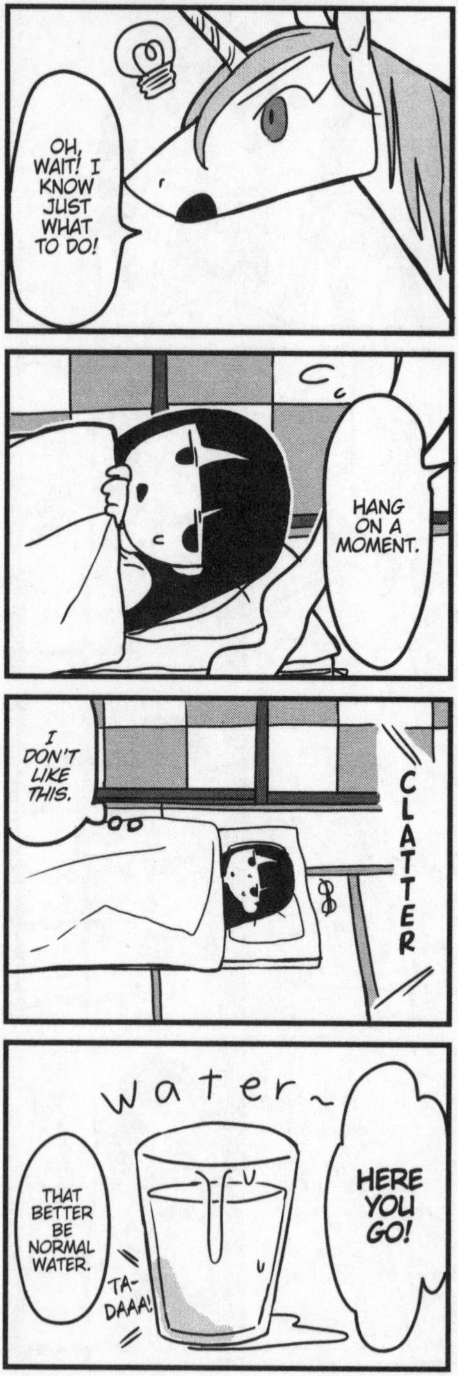
OH, WAIT! I KNOW JUST WHAT TO DO!
HANG ON A MOMENT.
CLATTER
I DON'T LIKE THIS.
HERE YOU GO!
water~
TA-DAAA!
THAT BETTER BE NORMAL WATER.

SECRET WONDER DRUG

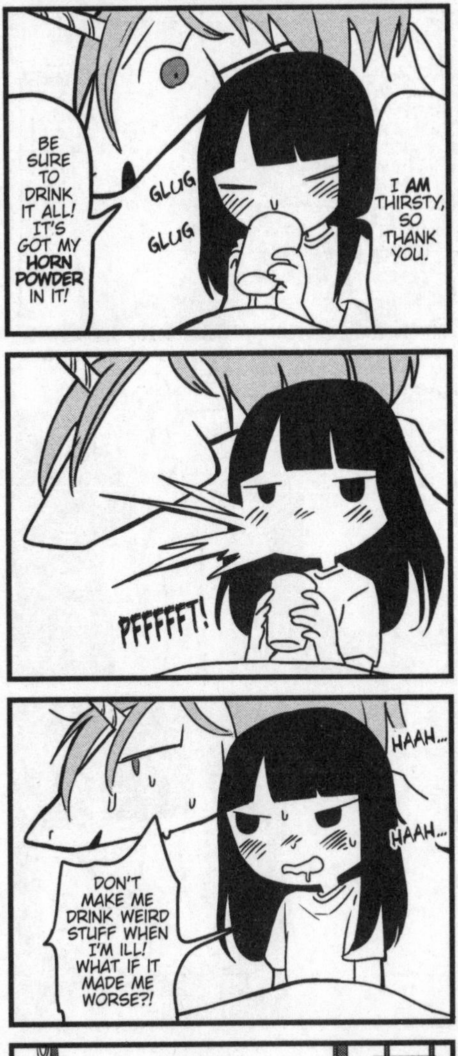

I AM THIRSTY, SO THANK YOU.
GLUG
GLUG
BE SURE TO DRINK IT ALL! IT'S GOT MY HORN POWDER IN IT!
PFFFFFT!
HAAH...
HAAH...
DON'T MAKE ME DRINK WEIRD STUFF WHEN I'M ILL! WHAT IF IT MADE ME WORSE?!
A FEW HOURS LATER ...
IT WORKED.

SOFT TOUCH

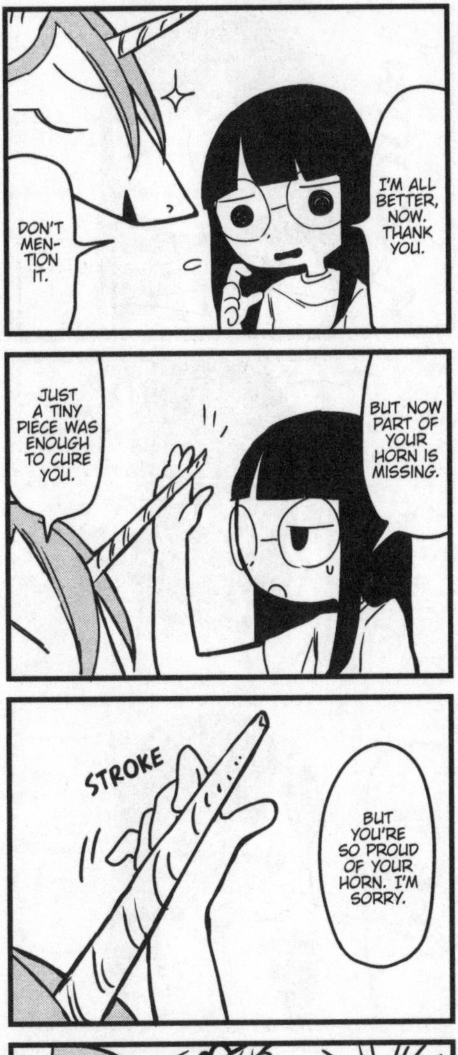

I'M ALL BETTER, NOW. THANK YOU.
DON'T MENTION IT.
BUT NOW PART OF YOUR HORN IS MISSING.
JUST A TINY PIECE WAS ENOUGH TO CURE YOU.
BUT YOU'RE SO PROUD OF YOUR HORN. I'M SORRY.
STROKE
PLAY IT COOL! C'MON UNI, KEEP IT TOGETHER!

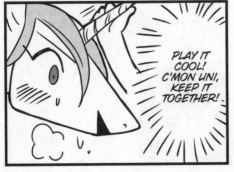

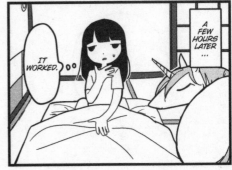

DISTANT FESTIVAL

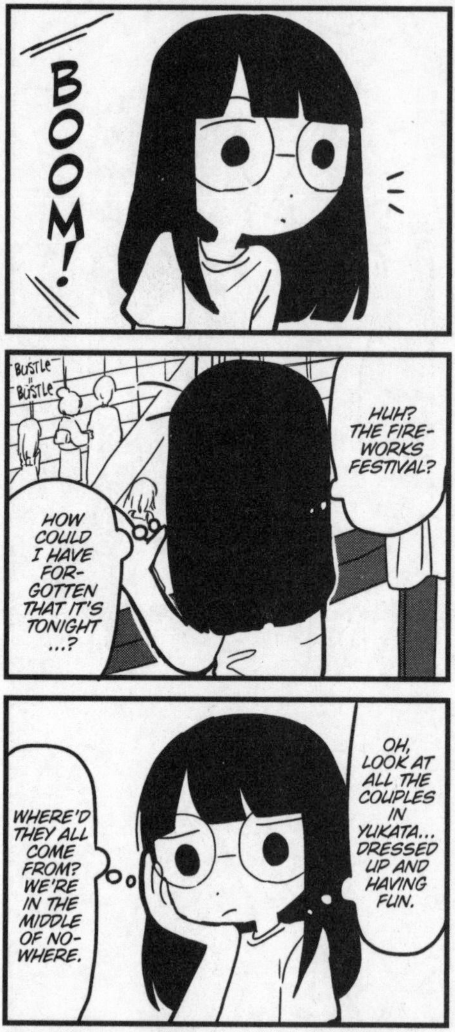
BOOM!
BUSTLE BUSTLE
HUH? THE FIRE-WORKS FESTIVAL?
HOW COULD I HAVE FOR-GOTTEN THAT IT'S TONIGHT ...?
OH, LOOK AT ALL THE COUPLES IN YUKATA... DRESSED UP AND HAVING FUN.
WHERE'D THEY ALL COME FROM? WE'RE IN THE MIDDLE OF NO-WHERE.
WHAT'S GOING ON? THERE'S AN OVER-WHELMING STENCH OF IMPURITY.
THIS GUY...
URK!

MY NEIGHBOR UNICORN

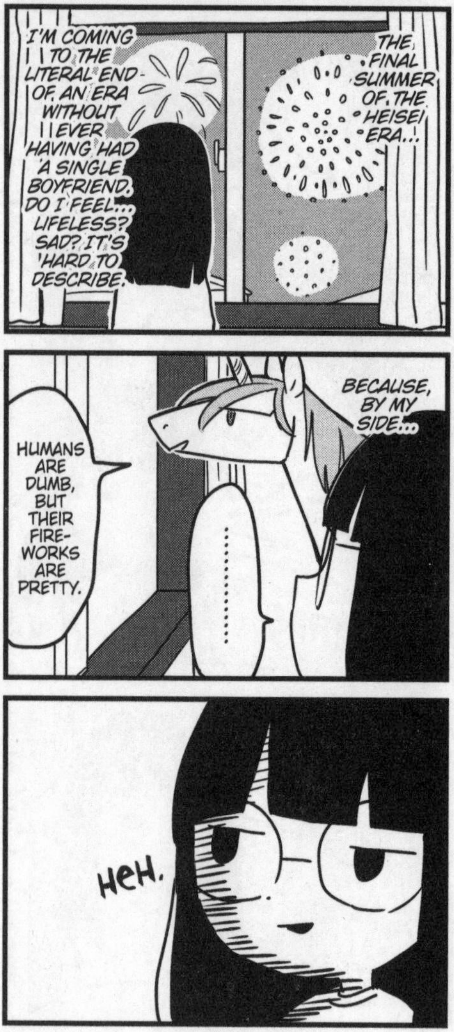
THE FINAL SUMMER OF THE HEISEI ERA...
I'M COMING TO THE LITERAL END OF AN ERA WITHOUT EVER HAVING HAD A SINGLE BOYFRIEND. DO I FEEL... LIFELESS? SAD? IT'S HARD TO DESCRIBE.
BECAUSE, BY MY SIDE...
HUMANS ARE DUMB, BUT THEIR FIRE-WORKS ARE PRETTY.
HEH.
WELL, MAYBE IT'S NOT SO BAD.

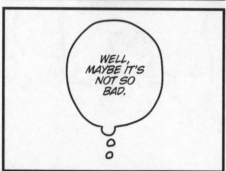

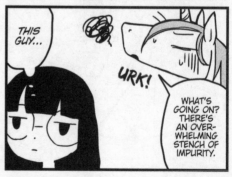

CHAPTER 3

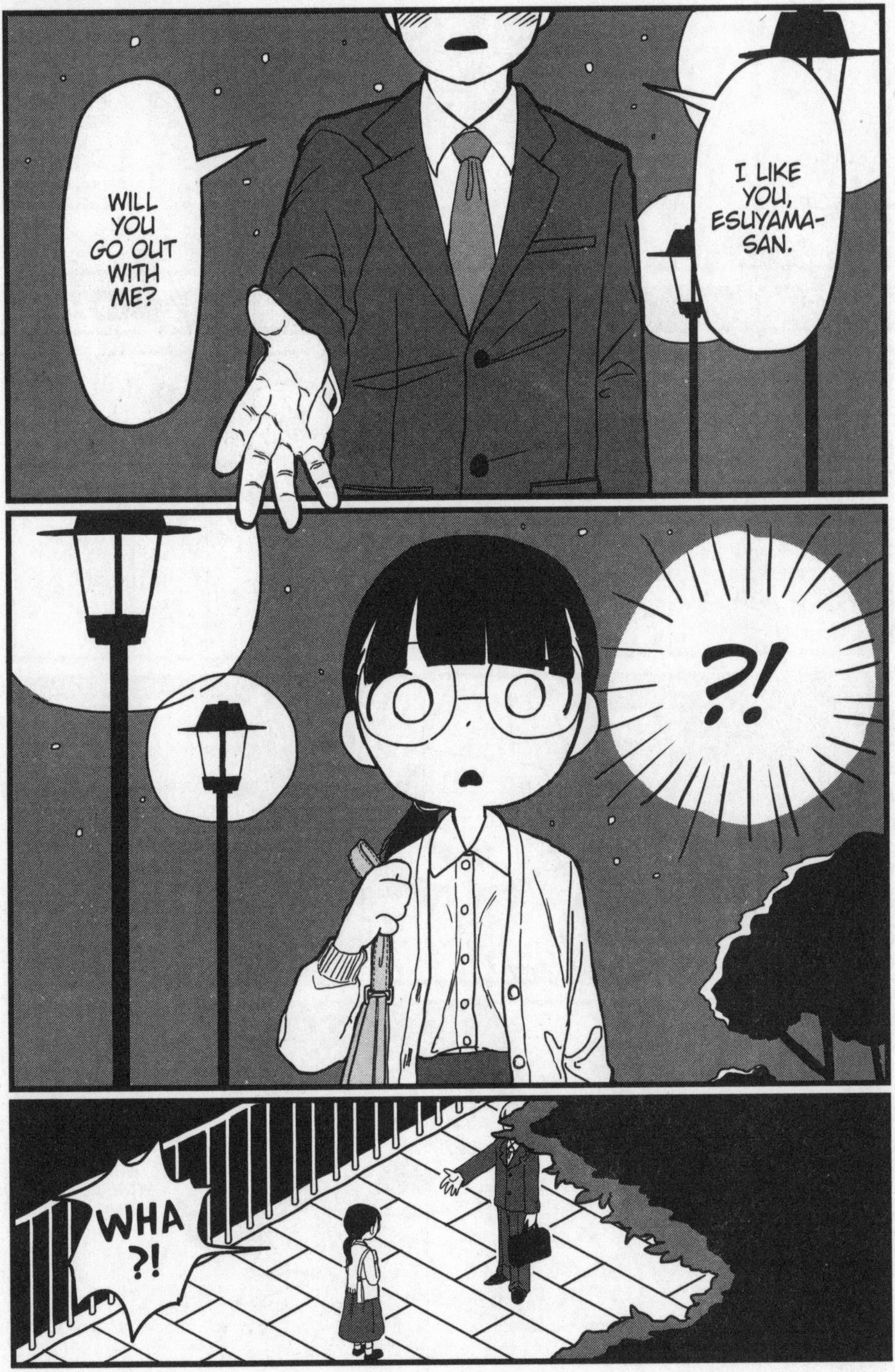

I LIKE YOU, ESUYAMA-SAN.
WILL YOU GO OUT WITH ME?
?!
WHA ?!

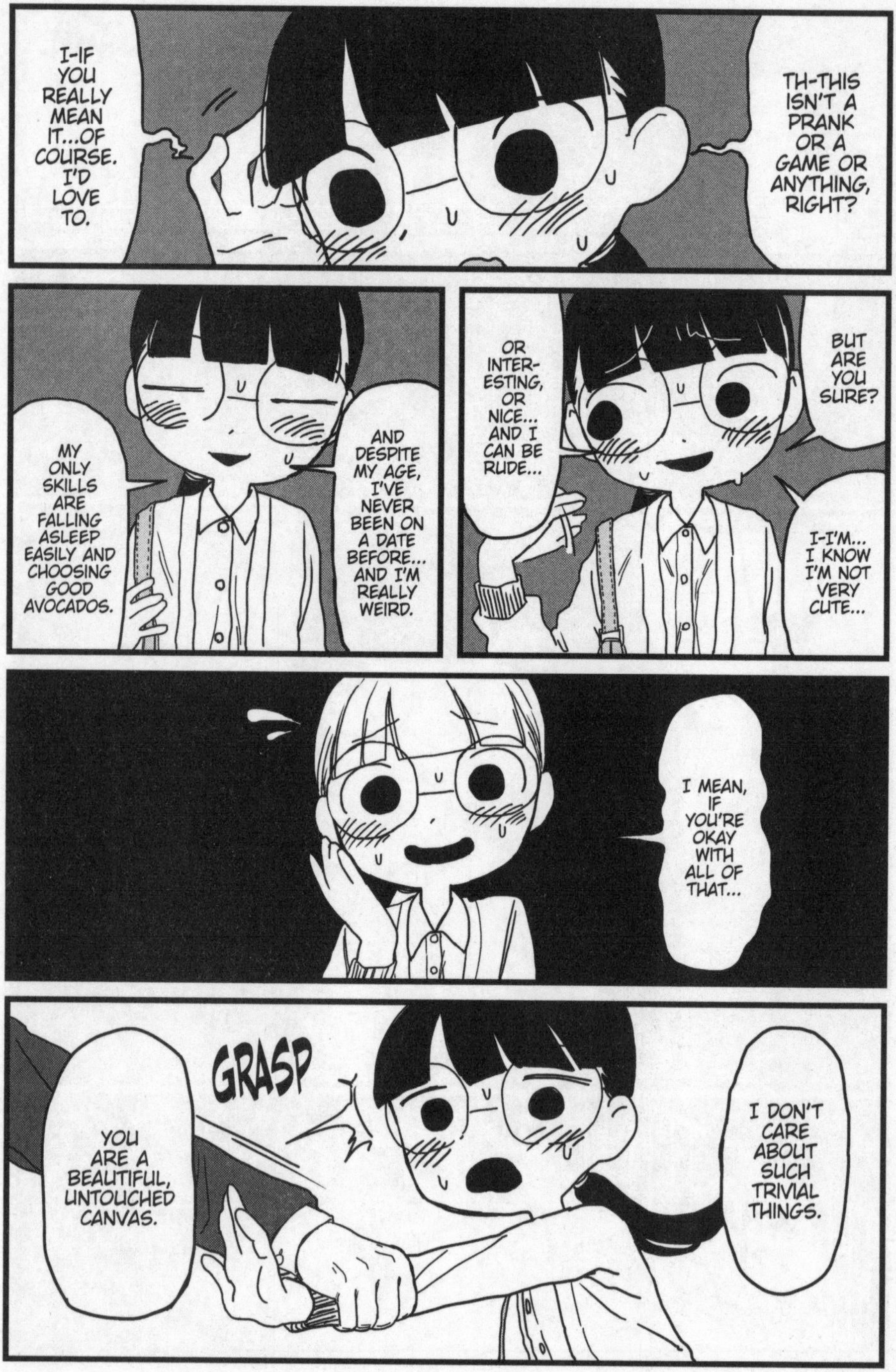
TH-THIS ISN'T A PRANK OR A GAME OR ANYTHING, RIGHT?
I-IF YOU REALLY MEAN IT...OF COURSE. I'D LOVE TO.
BUT ARE YOU SURE?
I-I'M... I KNOW I'M NOT VERY CUTE...
OR INTERESTING, OR NICE... AND I CAN BE RUDE...
AND DESPITE MY AGE, I'VE NEVER BEEN ON A DATE BEFORE... AND I'M REALLY WEIRD.
MY ONLY SKILLS ARE FALLING ASLEEP EASILY AND CHOOSING GOOD AVOCADOS.
I MEAN, IF YOU'RE OKAY WITH ALL OF THAT...
I DON'T CARE ABOUT SUCH TRIVIAL THINGS.
GRASP
YOU ARE A BEAUTIFUL, UNTOUCHED CANVAS.

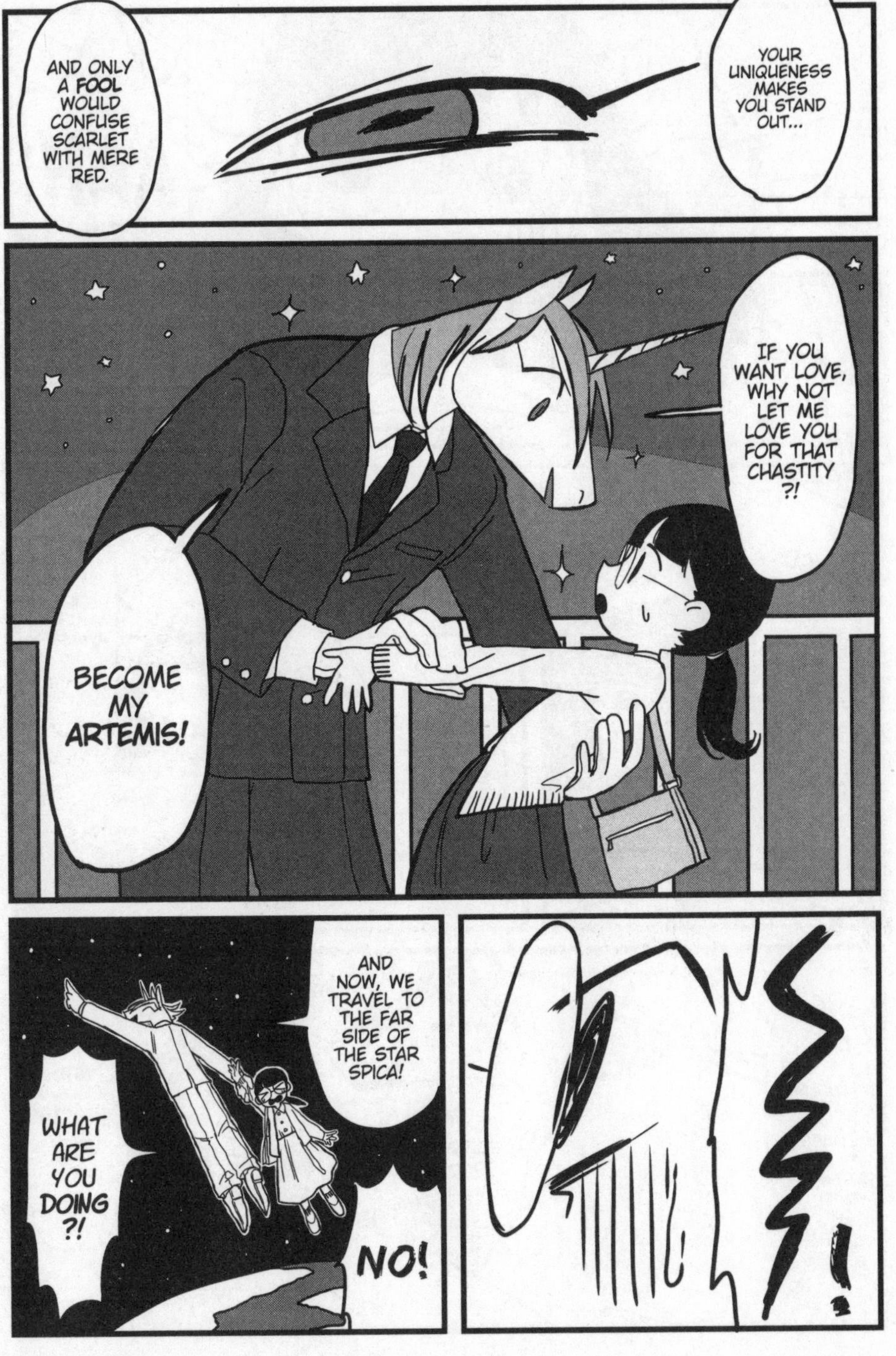
YOUR UNIQUENESS MAKES YOU STAND OUT...
AND ONLY A **FOOL** WOULD CONFUSE SCARLET WITH MERE RED.
IF YOU WANT LOVE, WHY NOT LET ME LOVE YOU FOR THAT CHASTITY ?!
BECOME MY **ARTEMIS!**
AND NOW, WE TRAVEL TO THE FAR SIDE OF THE STAR SPICA!
WHAT ARE YOU **DOING** ?!
NO!

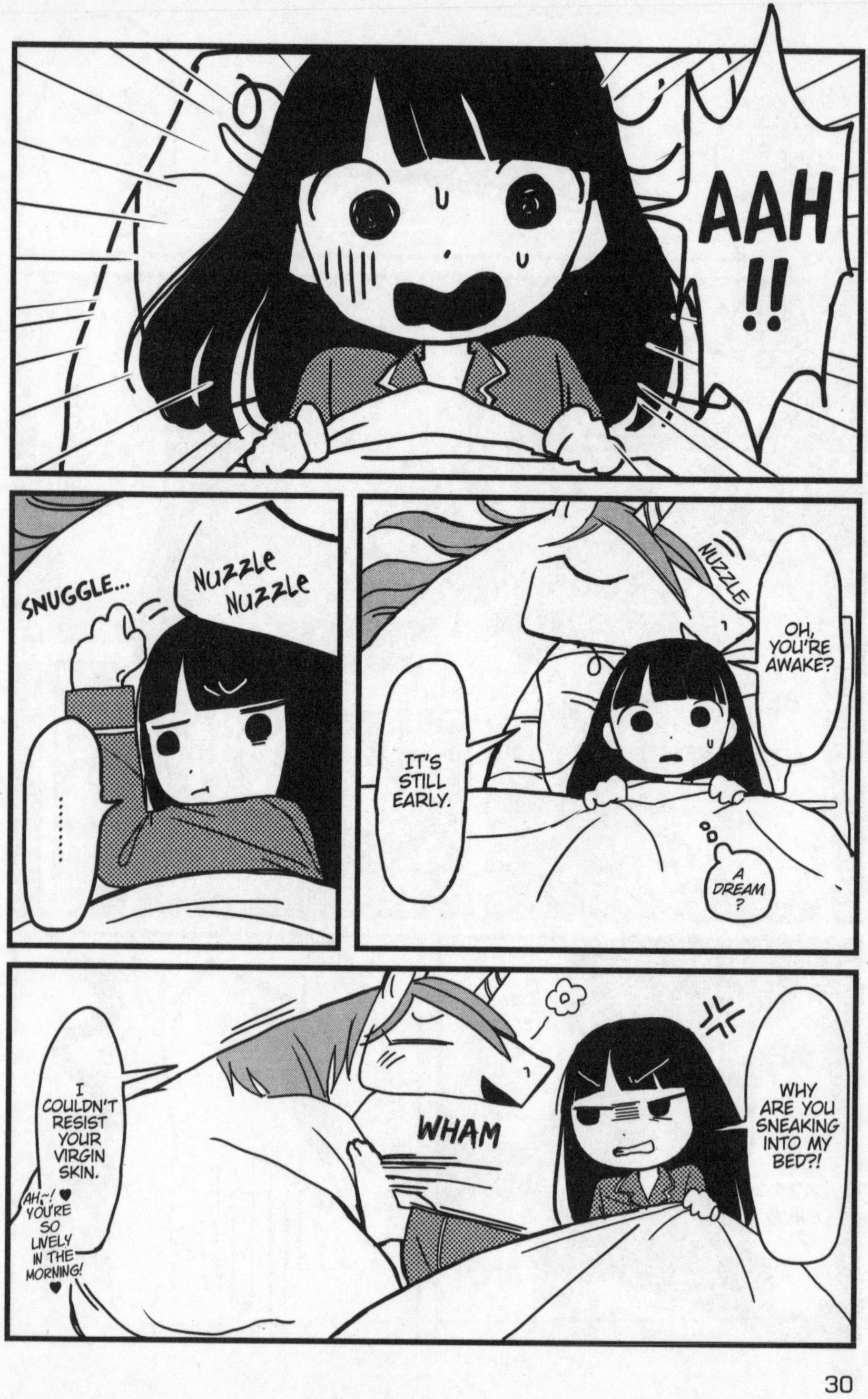
AAH!!
NUZZLE
OH, YOU'RE AWAKE?
IT'S STILL EARLY.
A DREAM?
Nuzzle Nuzzle
SNUGGLE...
......
WHY ARE YOU SNEAKING INTO MY BED?!
WHAM
I COULDN'T RESIST YOUR VIRGIN SKIN.
AH~! ♥ YOU'RE SO LIVELY IN THE MORNING! ♥

SWERVE

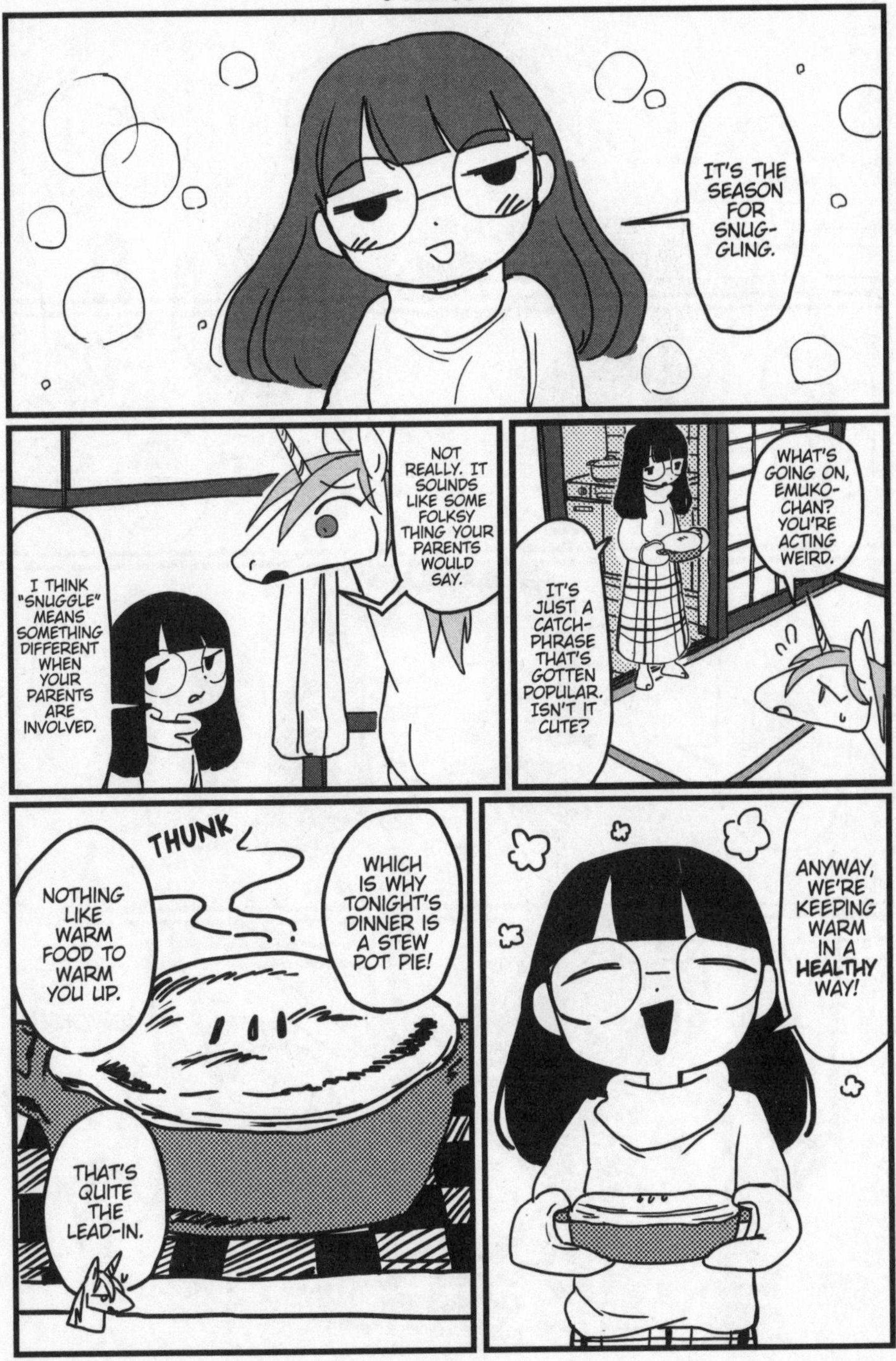
IT'S THE SEASON FOR SNUG-GLING.
WHAT'S GOING ON, EMUKO-CHAN? YOU'RE ACTING WEIRD.
IT'S JUST A CATCH-PHRASE THAT'S GOTTEN POPULAR. ISN'T IT CUTE?
NOT REALLY. IT SOUNDS LIKE SOME FOLKSY THING YOUR PARENTS WOULD SAY.
I THINK "SNUGGLE" MEANS SOMETHING DIFFERENT WHEN YOUR PARENTS ARE INVOLVED.
ANYWAY, WE'RE KEEPING WARM IN A **HEALTHY** WAY!
WHICH IS WHY TONIGHT'S DINNER IS A STEW POT PIE!
THUNK
NOTHING LIKE WARM FOOD TO WARM YOU UP.
THAT'S QUITE THE LEAD-IN.

APPROVAL

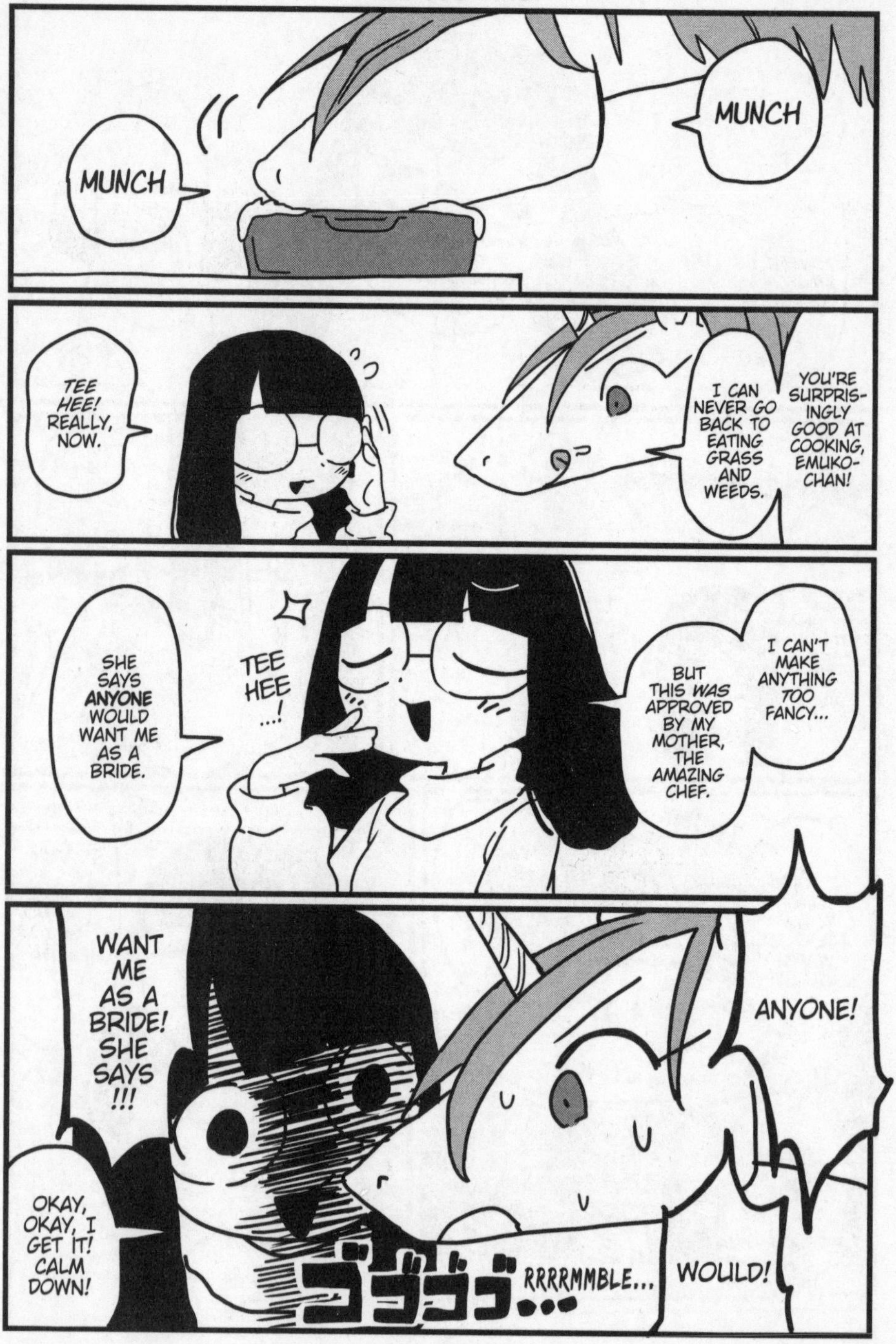
MUNCH
MUNCH
YOU'RE SURPRISINGLY GOOD AT COOKING, EMUKO-CHAN!
I CAN NEVER GO BACK TO EATING GRASS AND WEEDS.
TEE HEE! REALLY, NOW.
I CAN'T MAKE ANYTHING TOO FANCY...
BUT THIS WAS APPROVED BY MY MOTHER, THE AMAZING CHEF.
TEE HEE ...!
SHE SAYS ANYONE WOULD WANT ME AS A BRIDE.
ANYONE!
WOULD!
WANT ME AS A BRIDE! SHE SAYS!!!
ゴゴゴゴ...
RRRRMMBLE...
OKAY, OKAY, I GET IT! CALM DOWN!

DAILY GRIND

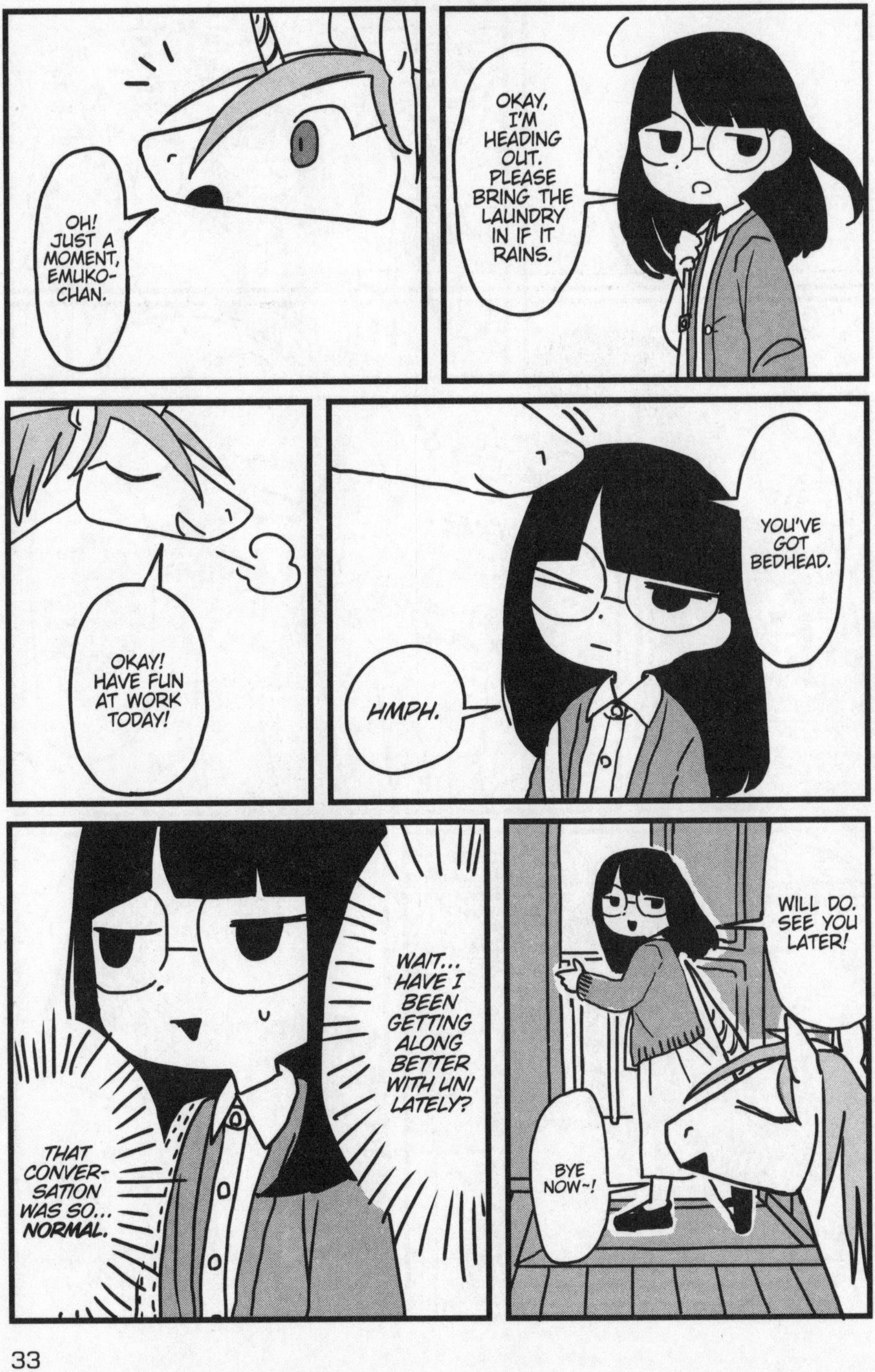
OKAY, I'M HEADING OUT. PLEASE BRING THE LAUNDRY IN IF IT RAINS.
OH! JUST A MOMENT, EMUKO-CHAN.
YOU'VE GOT BEDHEAD.
HMPH.
OKAY! HAVE FUN AT WORK TODAY!
WILL DO. SEE YOU LATER!
BYE NOW~!
WAIT... HAVE I BEEN GETTING ALONG BETTER WITH UNI LATELY?
THAT CONVER-SATION WAS SO... NORMAL.

FATE

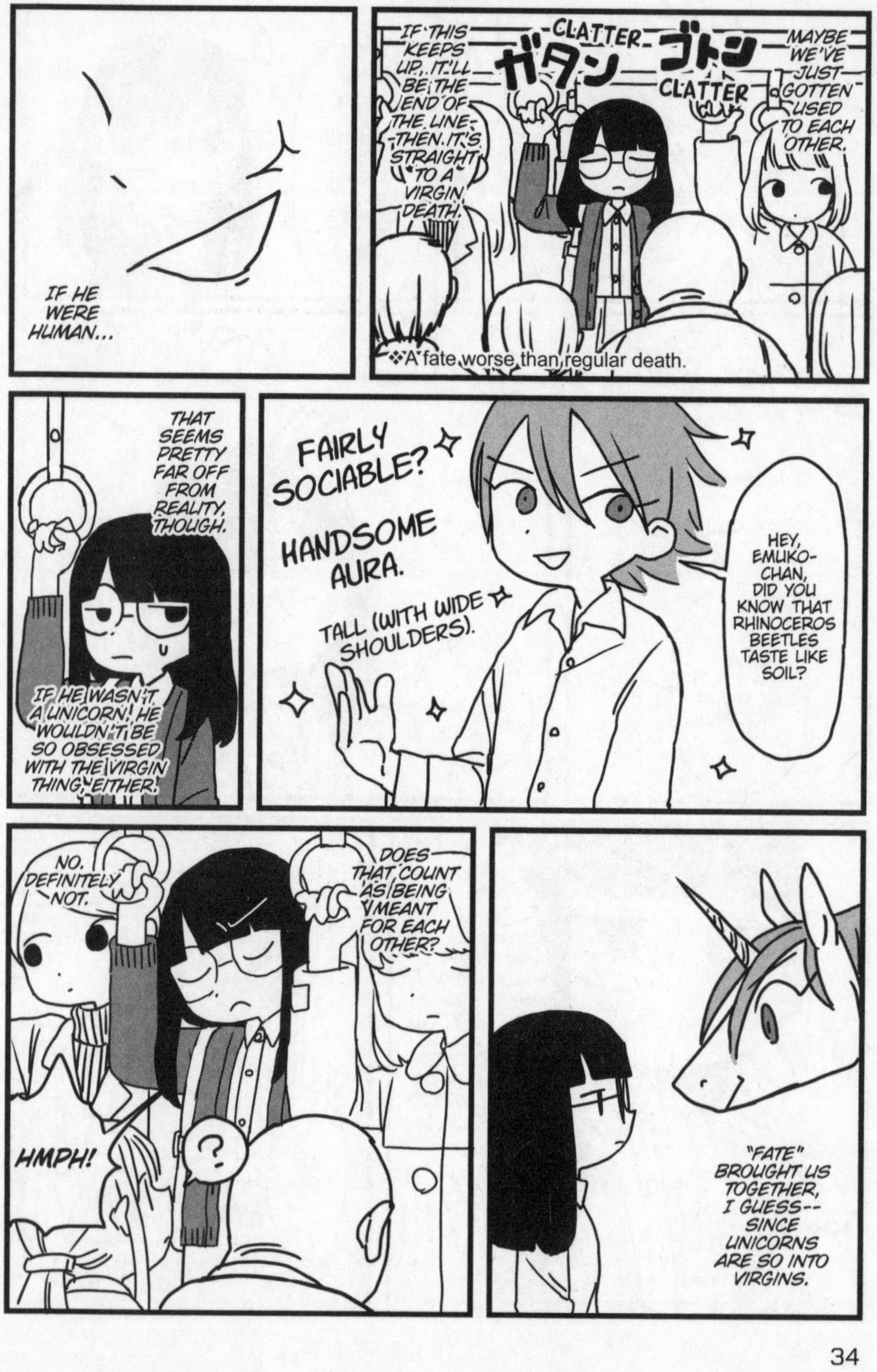
MAYBE WE'VE JUST GOTTEN USED TO EACH OTHER.
CLATTER
ゴトン
CLATTER
ガタン
IF THIS KEEPS UP, IT'LL BE THE END OF THE LINE. THEN IT'S STRAIGHT TO A VIRGIN DEATH.
❖A fate worse than regular death.
IF HE WERE HUMAN...
HEY, EMUKO-CHAN, DID YOU KNOW THAT RHINOCEROS BEETLES TASTE LIKE SOIL?
FAIRLY SOCIABLE?
HANDSOME AURA.
TALL (WITH WIDE SHOULDERS).
THAT SEEMS PRETTY FAR OFF FROM REALITY, THOUGH.
IF HE WASN'T A UNICORN, HE WOULDN'T BE SO OBSESSED WITH THE VIRGIN THING, EITHER.
"FATE" BROUGHT US TOGETHER, I GUESS-- SINCE UNICORNS ARE SO INTO VIRGINS.
DOES THAT COUNT AS BEING MEANT FOR EACH OTHER?
NO. DEFINITELY NOT.
?
HMPH!

REMINISCING

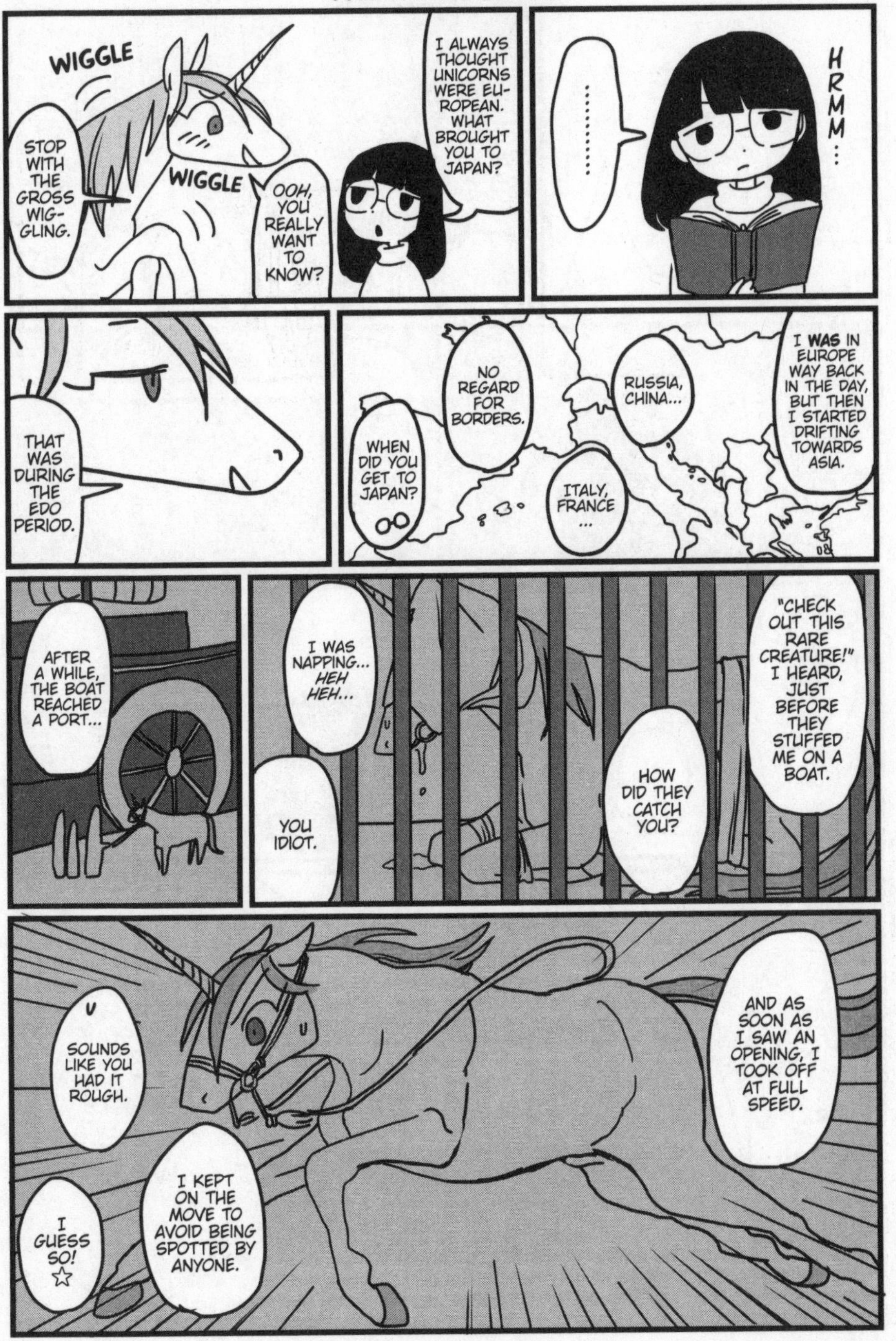
HRMM...
......
I ALWAYS THOUGHT UNICORNS WERE EUROPEAN. WHAT BROUGHT YOU TO JAPAN?
WIGGLE
OOH, YOU REALLY WANT TO KNOW?
WIGGLE
STOP WITH THE GROSS WIGGLING.
I **WAS** IN EUROPE WAY BACK IN THE DAY, BUT THEN I STARTED DRIFTING TOWARDS ASIA.
RUSSIA, CHINA...
NO REGARD FOR BORDERS.
ITALY, FRANCE ...
WHEN DID YOU GET TO JAPAN?
THAT WAS DURING THE EDO PERIOD.
"CHECK OUT THIS RARE CREATURE!" I HEARD, JUST BEFORE THEY STUFFED ME ON A BOAT.
HOW DID THEY CATCH YOU?
I WAS NAPPING... *HEH HEH...*
YOU IDIOT.
AFTER A WHILE, THE BOAT REACHED A PORT...
AND AS SOON AS I SAW AN OPENING, I TOOK OFF AT FULL SPEED.
SOUNDS LIKE YOU HAD IT ROUGH.
I KEPT ON THE MOVE TO AVOID BEING SPOTTED BY ANYONE.
I GUESS SO! ☆

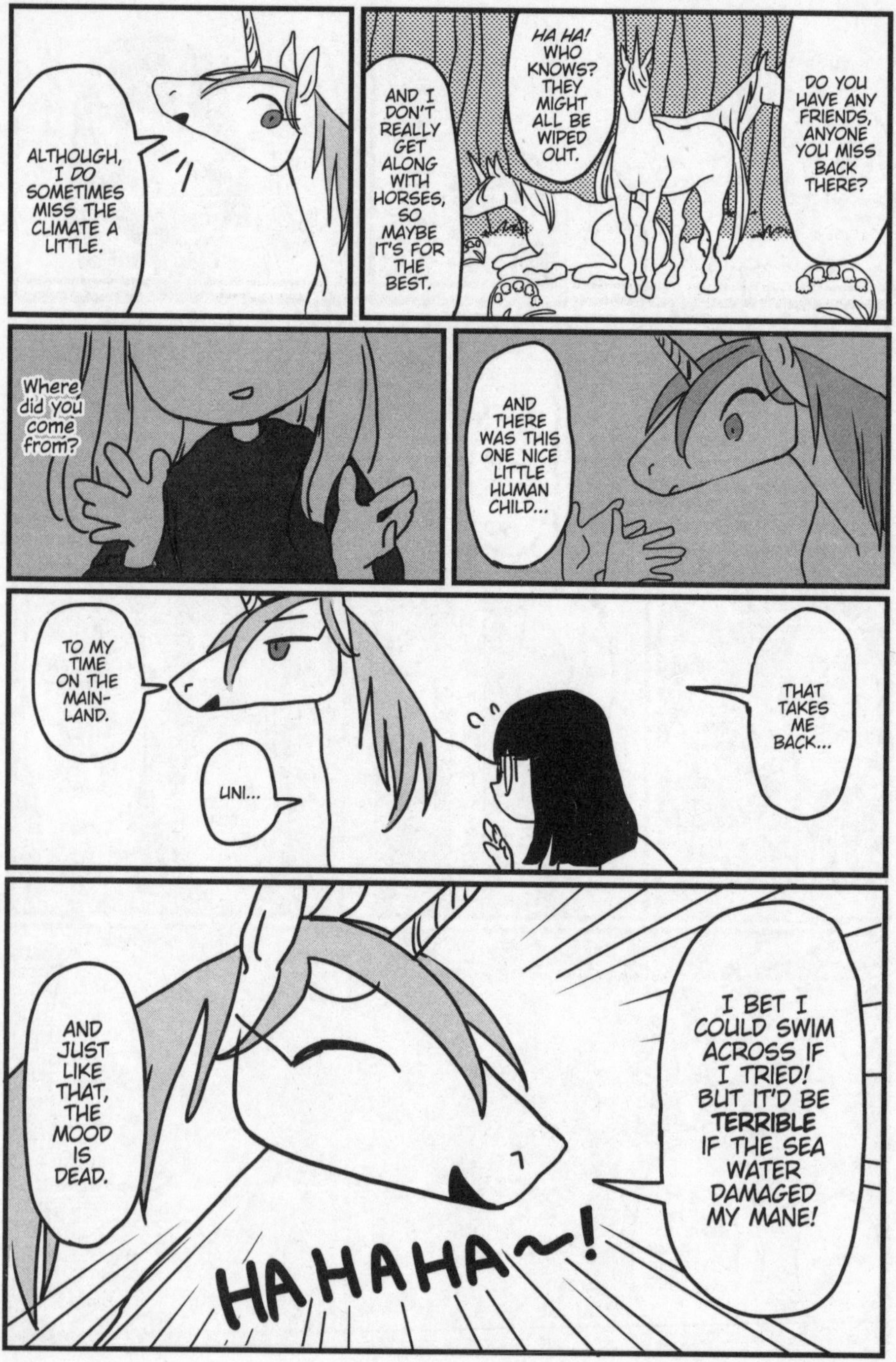
DO YOU HAVE ANY FRIENDS, ANYONE YOU MISS BACK THERE?
HA HA! WHO KNOWS? THEY MIGHT ALL BE WIPED OUT.
AND I DON'T REALLY GET ALONG WITH HORSES, SO MAYBE IT'S FOR THE BEST.
ALTHOUGH, I *DO* SOMETIMES MISS THE CLIMATE A LITTLE.
AND THERE WAS THIS ONE NICE LITTLE HUMAN CHILD...
Where did you come from?
THAT TAKES ME BACK...
TO MY TIME ON THE MAIN-LAND.
UNI...
I BET I COULD SWIM ACROSS IF I TRIED! BUT IT'D BE **TERRIBLE** IF THE SEA WATER DAMAGED MY MANE!
HAHAHA~!
AND JUST LIKE THAT, THE MOOD IS DEAD.

UNICORNS, UNICORNS EVERYWHERE

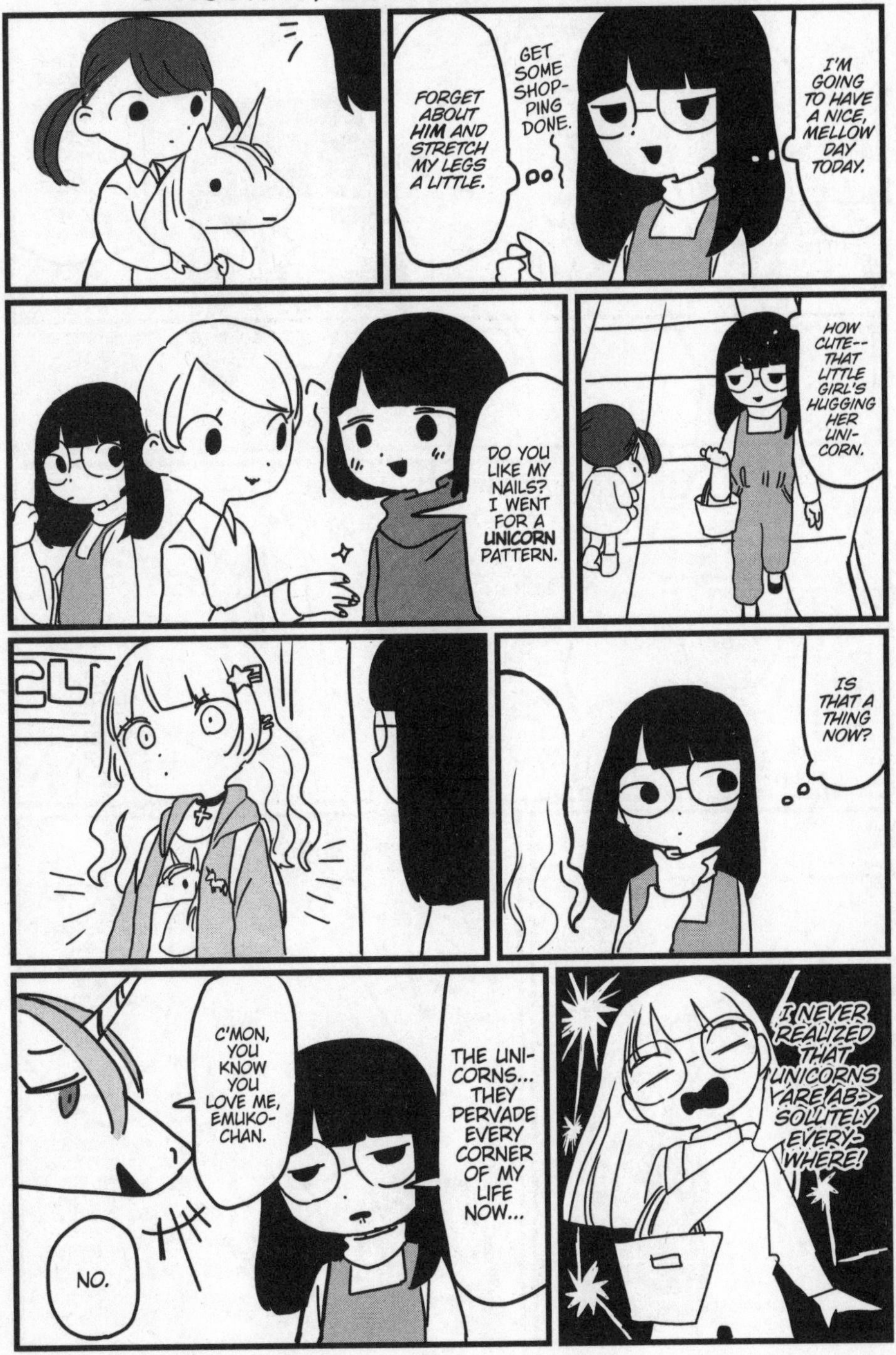

I'M GOING TO HAVE A NICE, MELLOW DAY TODAY.
GET SOME SHOP-PING DONE.
FORGET ABOUT HIM AND STRETCH MY LEGS A LITTLE.
HOW CUTE--THAT LITTLE GIRL'S HUGGING HER UNI-CORN.
DO YOU LIKE MY NAILS? I WENT FOR A UNICORN PATTERN.
IS THAT A THING NOW?
I NEVER REALIZED THAT UNICORNS ARE ABSOLUTELY EVERY-WHERE!
THE UNI-CORNS... THEY PERVADE EVERY CORNER OF MY LIFE NOW...
C'MON, YOU KNOW YOU LOVE ME, EMUKO-CHAN.
NO.

DISSATISFIED

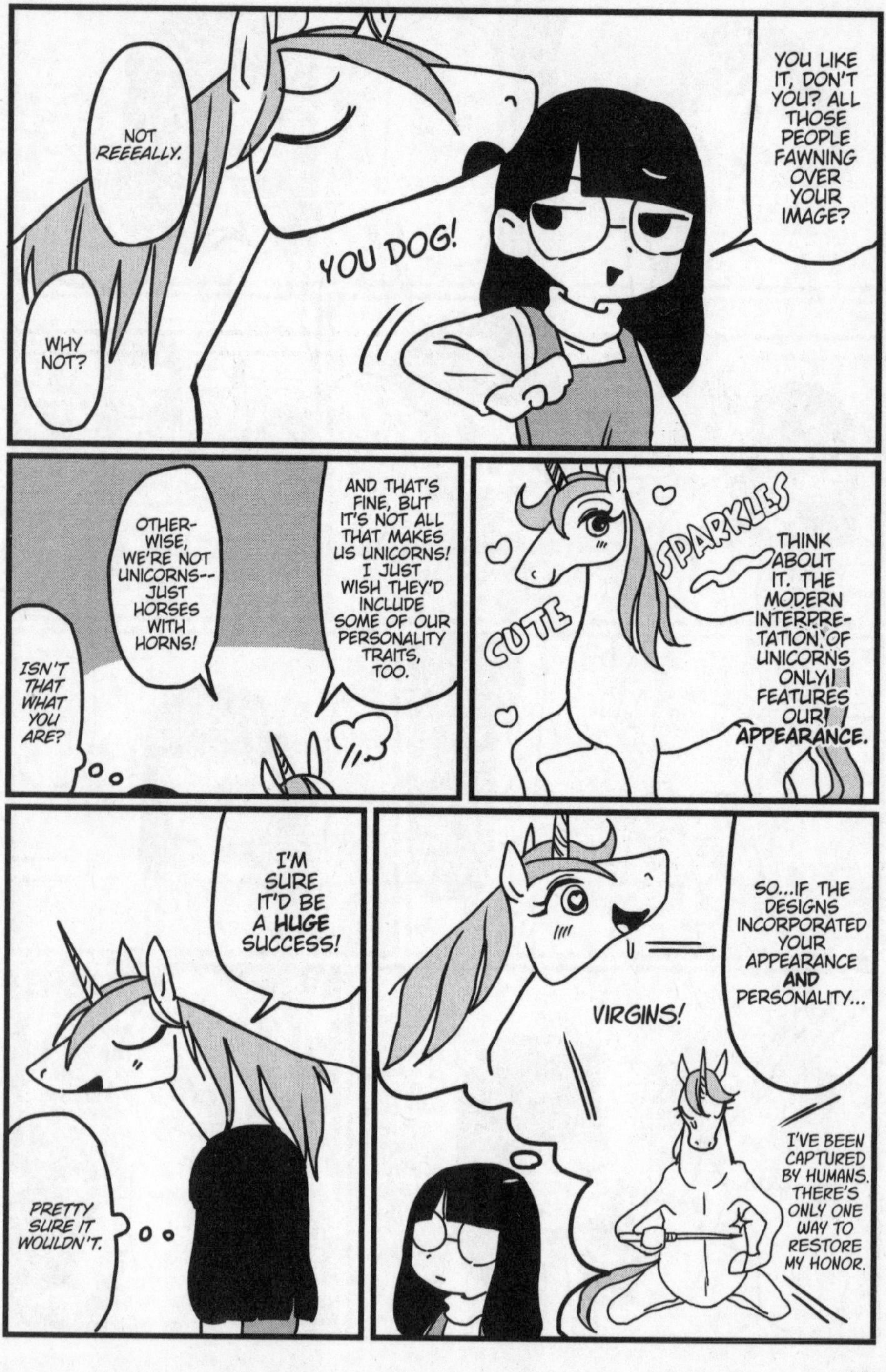
YOU LIKE IT, DON'T YOU? ALL THOSE PEOPLE FAWNING OVER YOUR IMAGE?
YOU DOG!
NOT REEEALLY.
WHY NOT?
THINK ABOUT IT. THE MODERN INTERPRE-TATION OF UNICORNS ONLY FEATURES OUR **APPEARANCE.**
SPARKLES
CUTE
AND THAT'S FINE, BUT IT'S NOT ALL THAT MAKES US UNICORNS! I JUST WISH THEY'D INCLUDE SOME OF OUR PERSONALITY TRAITS, TOO.
OTHER-WISE, WE'RE NOT UNICORNS--JUST HORSES WITH HORNS!
ISN'T THAT WHAT YOU ARE?
SO...IF THE DESIGNS INCORPORATED YOUR APPEARANCE **AND** PERSONALITY...
VIRGINS!
I'VE BEEN CAPTURED BY HUMANS. THERE'S ONLY ONE WAY TO RESTORE MY HONOR.
I'M SURE IT'D BE A **HUGE** SUCCESS!
PRETTY SURE IT WOULDN'T.

CHAPTER 4 CLEANING DAY

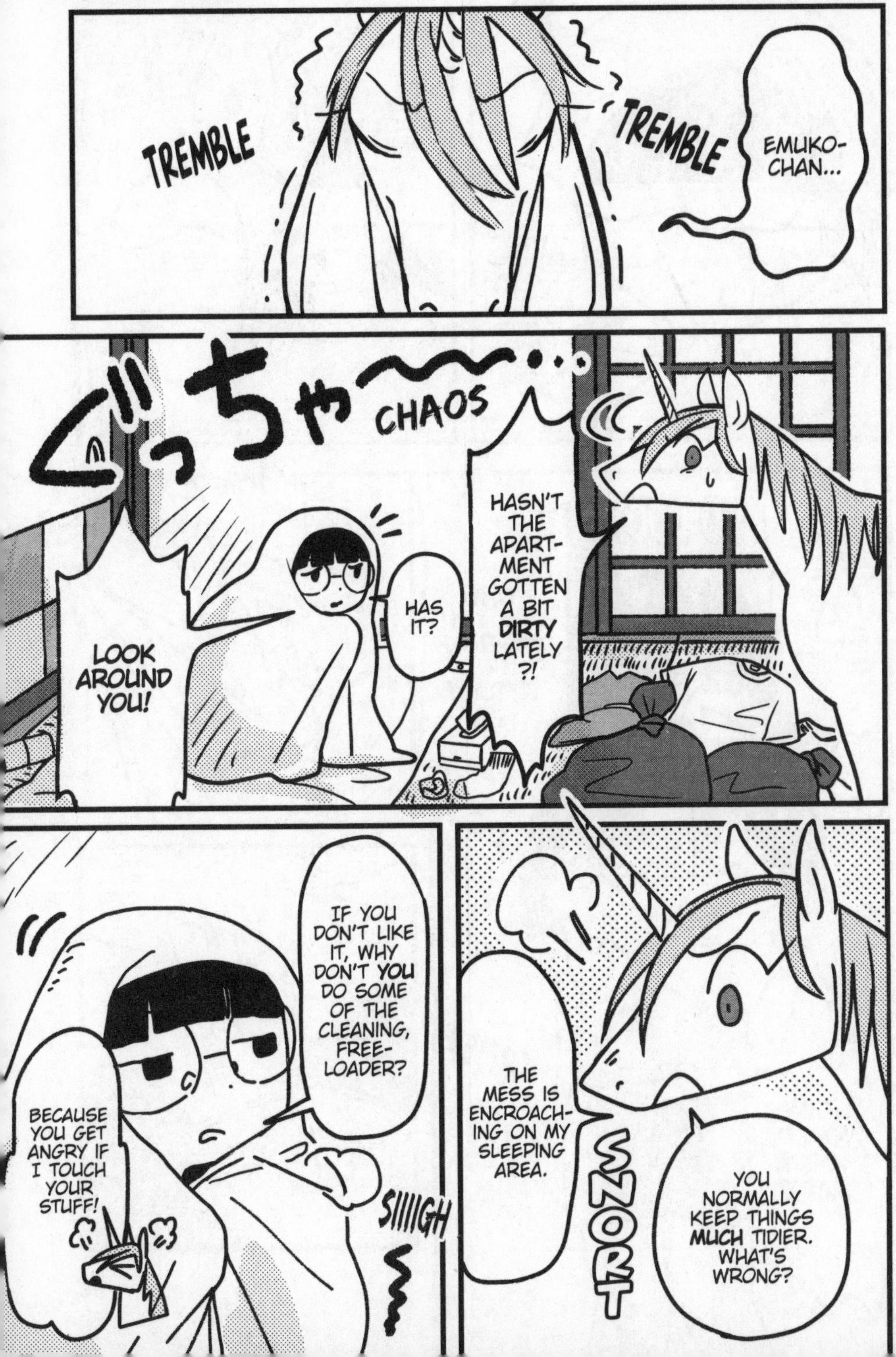
EMUKO-CHAN...
TREMBLE
TREMBLE
ぐっちゃ〜〜…
CHAOS
HASN'T THE APARTMENT GOTTEN A BIT DIRTY LATELY?!
HAS IT?
LOOK AROUND YOU!
THE MESS IS ENCROACHING ON MY SLEEPING AREA.
SNORT
YOU NORMALLY KEEP THINGS MUCH TIDIER. WHAT'S WRONG?
IF YOU DON'T LIKE IT, WHY DON'T YOU DO SOME OF THE CLEANING, FREE-LOADER?
SIIIIGH
BECAUSE YOU GET ANGRY IF I TOUCH YOUR STUFF!

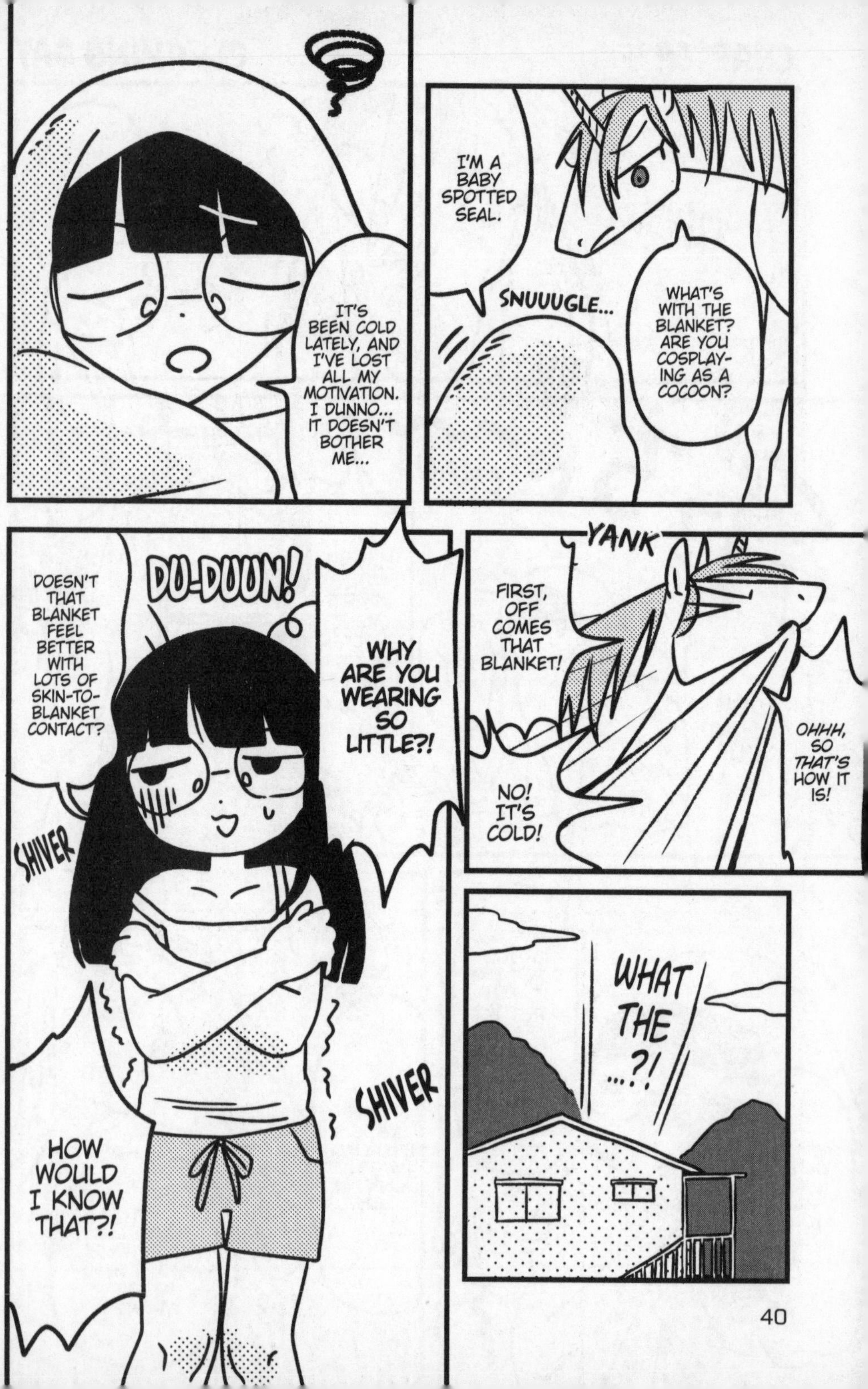
WHAT'S WITH THE BLANKET? ARE YOU COSPLAYING AS A COCOON?
SNUUUGLE...
I'M A BABY SPOTTED SEAL.
IT'S BEEN COLD LATELY, AND I'VE LOST ALL MY MOTIVATION. I DUNNO... IT DOESN'T BOTHER ME...
YANK
OHHH, SO THAT'S HOW IT IS!
FIRST, OFF COMES THAT BLANKET!
NO! IT'S COLD!
WHAT THE ...?!
DU-DUUN!
WHY ARE YOU WEARING SO LITTLE?!
DOESN'T THAT BLANKET FEEL BETTER WITH LOTS OF SKIN-TO-BLANKET CONTACT?
SHIVER
SHIVER
IDIOT!
HOW WOULD I KNOW THAT?!

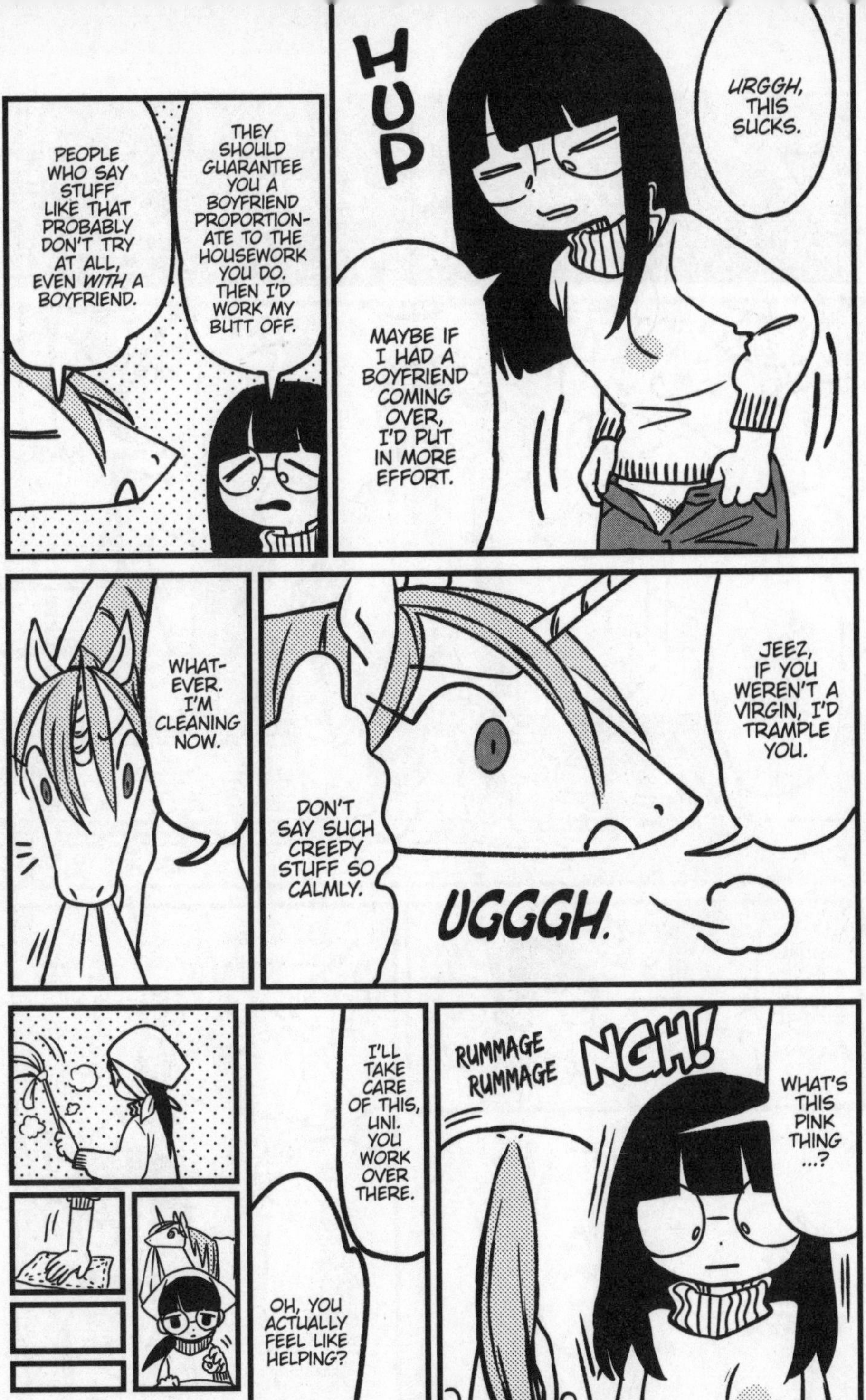
URGGH, THIS SUCKS.
HUP
MAYBE IF I HAD A BOYFRIEND COMING OVER, I'D PUT IN MORE EFFORT.
THEY SHOULD GUARANTEE YOU A BOYFRIEND PROPORTION-ATE TO THE HOUSEWORK YOU DO. THEN I'D WORK MY BUTT OFF.
PEOPLE WHO SAY STUFF LIKE THAT PROBABLY DON'T TRY AT ALL, EVEN *WITH* A BOYFRIEND.
JEEZ, IF YOU WEREN'T A VIRGIN, I'D TRAMPLE YOU.
DON'T SAY SUCH CREEPY STUFF SO CALMLY.
UGGGH.
WHAT-EVER. I'M CLEANING NOW.
NGH!
RUMMAGE RUMMAGE
WHAT'S THIS PINK THING ...?
I'LL TAKE CARE OF THIS, UNI. YOU WORK OVER THERE.
OH, YOU ACTUALLY FEEL LIKE HELPING?

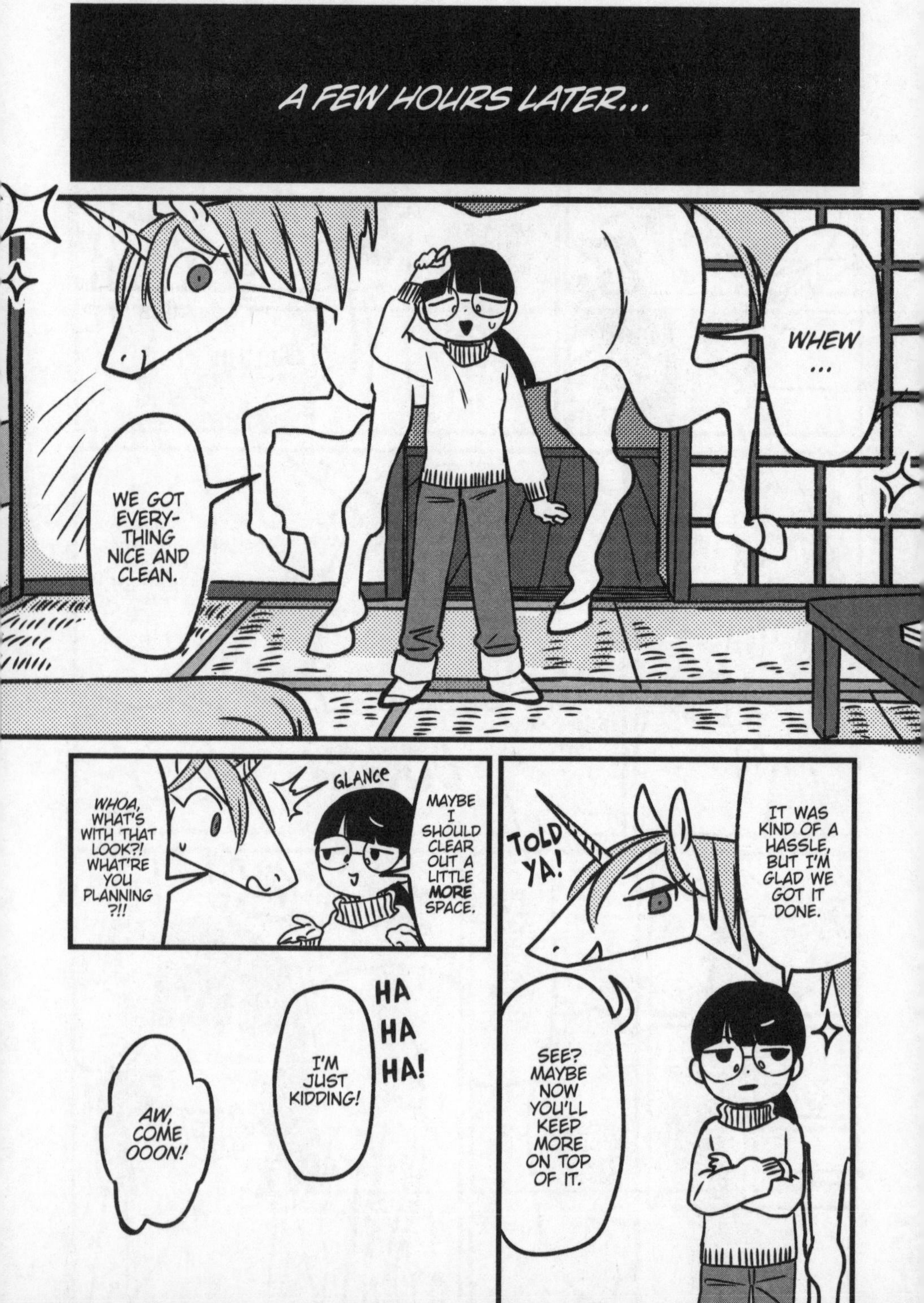
A FEW HOURS LATER...
WHEW ...
WE GOT EVERYTHING NICE AND CLEAN.
IT WAS KIND OF A HASSLE, BUT I'M GLAD WE GOT IT DONE.
TOLD YA!
SEE? MAYBE NOW YOU'LL KEEP MORE ON TOP OF IT.
MAYBE I SHOULD CLEAR OUT A LITTLE MORE SPACE.
GLANCE
WHOA, WHAT'S WITH THAT LOOK?! WHAT'RE YOU PLANNING ?!!
HA HA HA!
I'M JUST KIDDING!
AW, COME OOON!

CHRISTMAS EVE

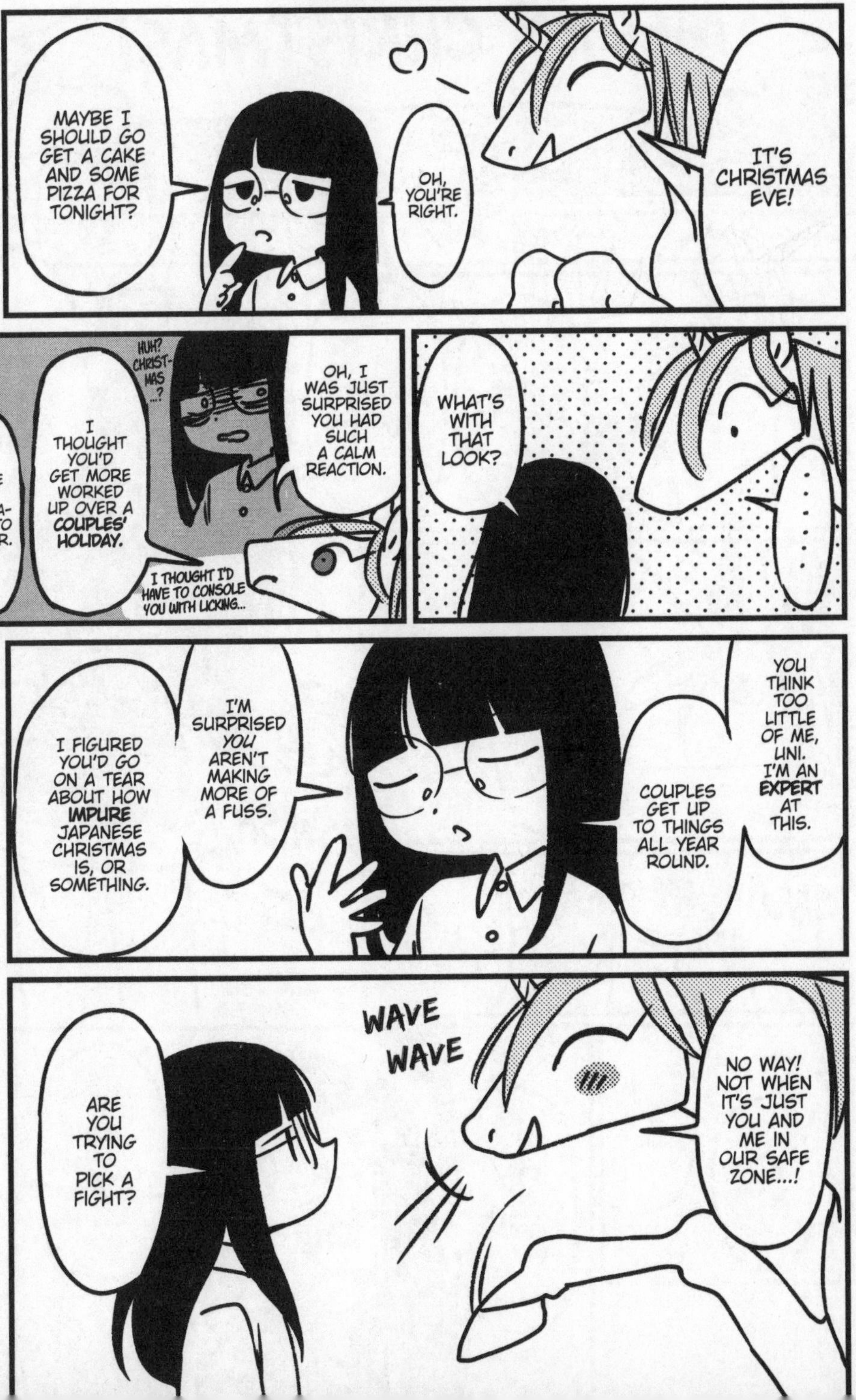
IT'S CHRISTMAS EVE!
OH, YOU'RE RIGHT.
MAYBE I SHOULD GO GET A CAKE AND SOME PIZZA FOR TONIGHT?
.....
WHAT'S WITH THAT LOOK?
OH, I WAS JUST SURPRISED YOU HAD SUCH A CALM REACTION.
HUH? CHRISTMAS ...?
I THOUGHT YOU'D GET MORE WORKED UP OVER A **COUPLES' HOLIDAY.**
I THOUGHT I'D HAVE TO CONSOLE YOU WITH LICKING...
I HAVE NO EXPECTATIONS TO SHATTER.
YOU THINK TOO LITTLE OF ME, UNI. I'M AN **EXPERT** AT THIS.
COUPLES GET UP TO THINGS ALL YEAR ROUND.
I'M SURPRISED *YOU* AREN'T MAKING MORE OF A FUSS.
I FIGURED YOU'D GO ON A TEAR ABOUT HOW **IMPURE** JAPANESE CHRISTMAS IS, OR SOMETHING.
NO WAY! NOT WHEN IT'S JUST YOU AND ME IN OUR SAFE ZONE...!
WAVE WAVE
ARE YOU TRYING TO PICK A FIGHT?

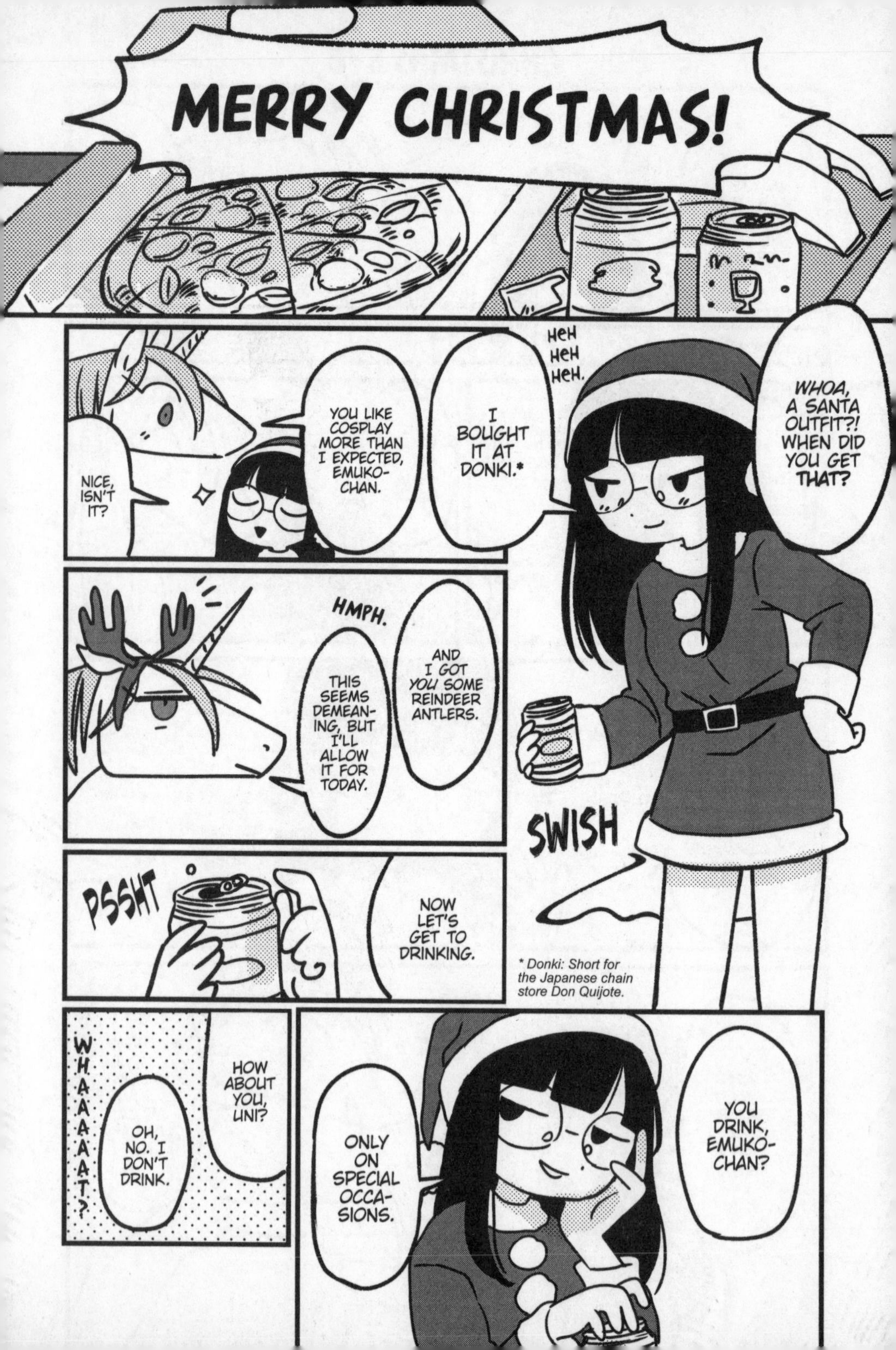

MERRY CHRISTMAS!
WHOA, A SANTA OUTFIT?! WHEN DID YOU GET THAT?
HEH HEH HEH.
I BOUGHT IT AT DONKI.*
SWISH
YOU LIKE COSPLAY MORE THAN I EXPECTED, EMUKO-CHAN.
NICE, ISN'T IT?
AND I GOT *YOU* SOME REINDEER ANTLERS.
HMPH.
THIS SEEMS DEMEANING, BUT I'LL ALLOW IT FOR TODAY.
NOW LET'S GET TO DRINKING.
PSSHT
YOU DRINK, EMUKO-CHAN?
ONLY ON SPECIAL OCCASIONS.
HOW ABOUT YOU, UNI?
OH, NO. I DON'T DRINK.
WHAAAAAAT?

** Donki: Short for the Japanese chain store Don Quijote.*

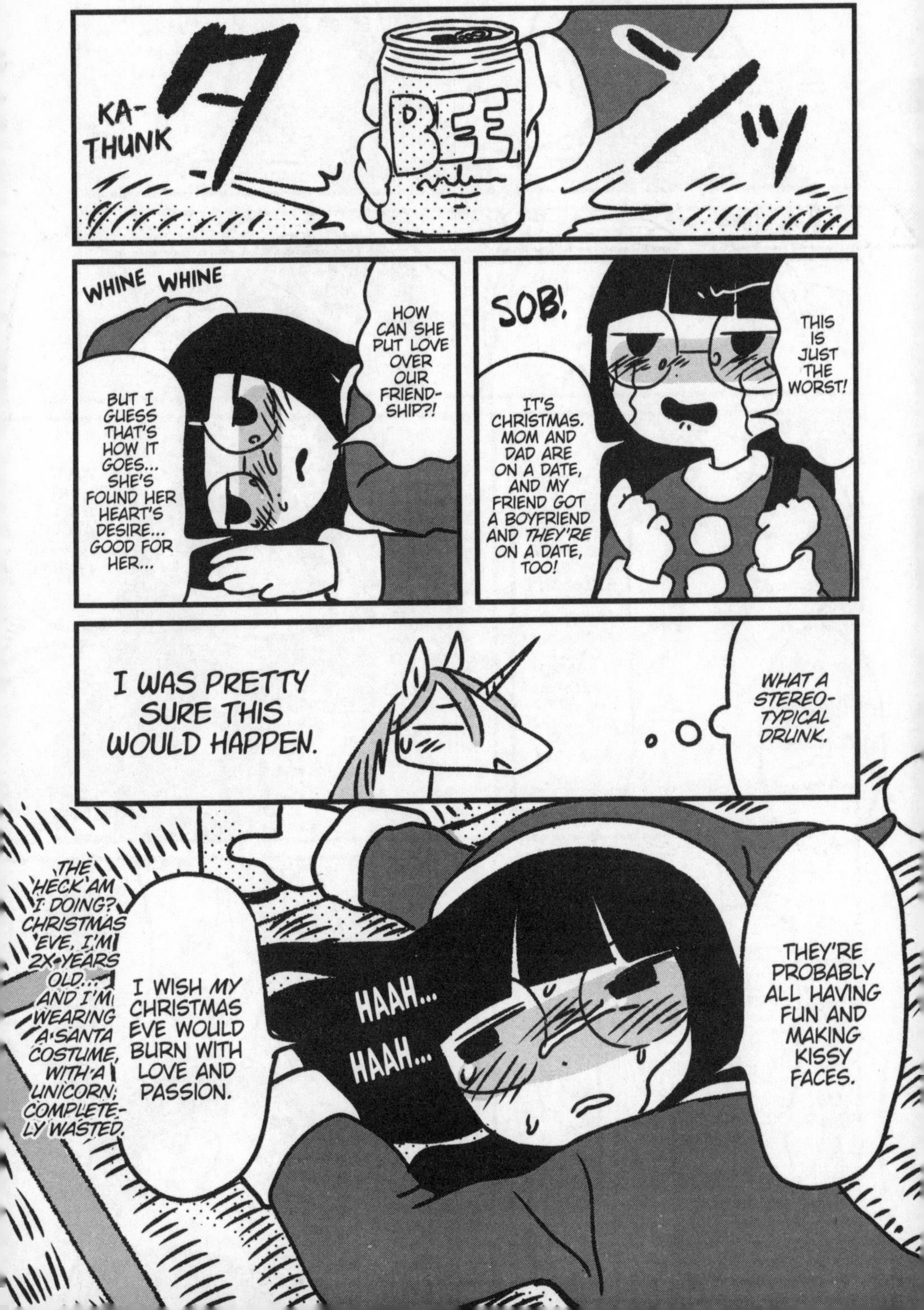
KA-THUNK
THIS IS JUST THE WORST!
SOB!
IT'S CHRISTMAS. MOM AND DAD ARE ON A DATE, AND MY FRIEND GOT A BOYFRIEND AND *THEY'RE* ON A DATE, TOO!
HOW CAN SHE PUT LOVE OVER OUR FRIENDSHIP?!
WHINE WHINE
BUT I GUESS THAT'S HOW IT GOES... SHE'S FOUND HER HEART'S DESIRE... GOOD FOR HER...
WHAT A STEREOTYPICAL DRUNK.
I WAS PRETTY SURE THIS WOULD HAPPEN.
THEY'RE PROBABLY ALL HAVING FUN AND MAKING KISSY FACES.
HAAH... HAAH...
I WISH *MY* CHRISTMAS EVE WOULD BURN WITH LOVE AND PASSION.
THE HECK AM I DOING? CHRISTMAS EVE, I'M 2X-YEARS OLD... AND I'M WEARING A SANTA COSTUME, WITH A UNICORN, COMPLETELY WASTED.

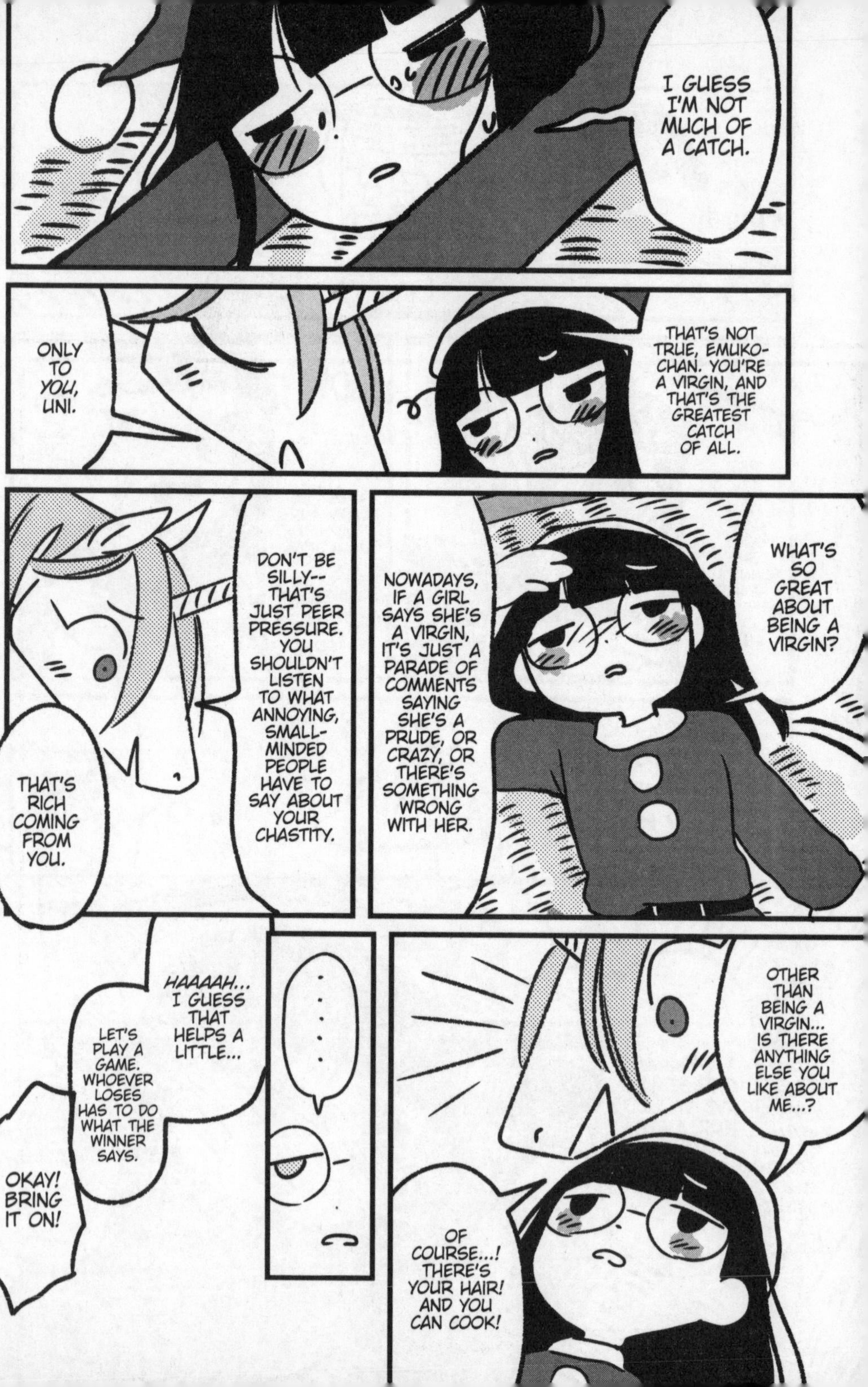
I GUESS I'M NOT MUCH OF A CATCH.
THAT'S NOT TRUE, EMUKO-CHAN. YOU'RE A VIRGIN, AND THAT'S THE GREATEST CATCH OF ALL.
ONLY TO *YOU*, UNI.
WHAT'S SO GREAT ABOUT BEING A VIRGIN?
NOWADAYS, IF A GIRL SAYS SHE'S A VIRGIN, IT'S JUST A PARADE OF COMMENTS SAYING SHE'S A PRUDE, OR CRAZY, OR THERE'S SOMETHING WRONG WITH HER.
DON'T BE SILLY-- THAT'S JUST PEER PRESSURE. YOU SHOULDN'T LISTEN TO WHAT ANNOYING, SMALL-MINDED PEOPLE HAVE TO SAY ABOUT YOUR CHASTITY.
THAT'S RICH COMING FROM YOU.
OTHER THAN BEING A VIRGIN... IS THERE ANYTHING ELSE YOU LIKE ABOUT ME...?
OF COURSE...! THERE'S YOUR HAIR! AND YOU CAN COOK!
......
HAAAAH... I GUESS THAT HELPS A LITTLE...
LET'S PLAY A GAME. WHOEVER LOSES HAS TO DO WHAT THE WINNER SAYS.
OKAY! BRING IT ON!

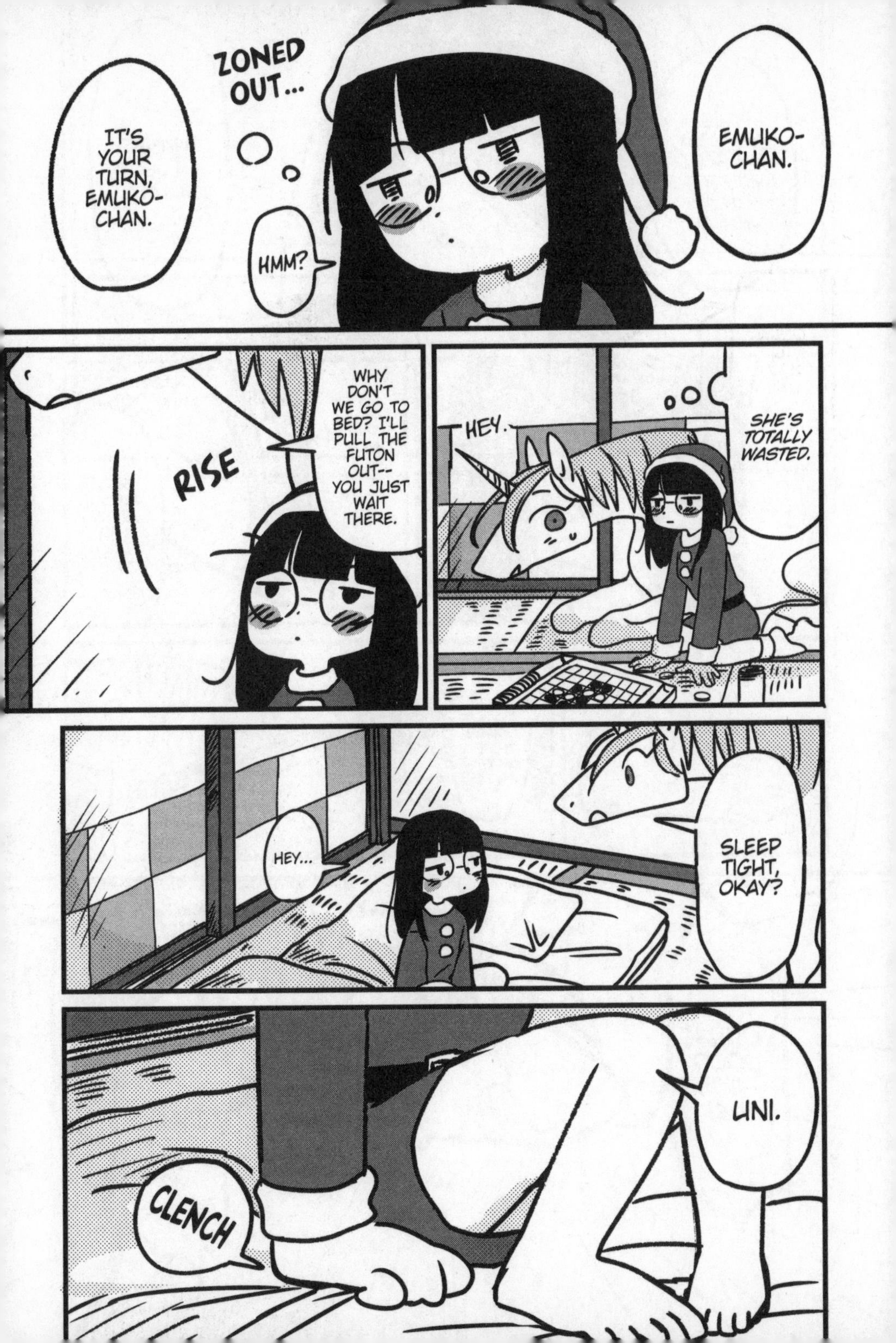
EMUKO-CHAN.
ZONED OUT...
IT'S YOUR TURN, EMUKO-CHAN.
HMM?
SHE'S TOTALLY WASTED.
HEY.
WHY DON'T WE GO TO BED? I'LL PULL THE FUTON OUT-- YOU JUST WAIT THERE.
RISE
SLEEP TIGHT, OKAY?
HEY...
UNI.
CLENCH

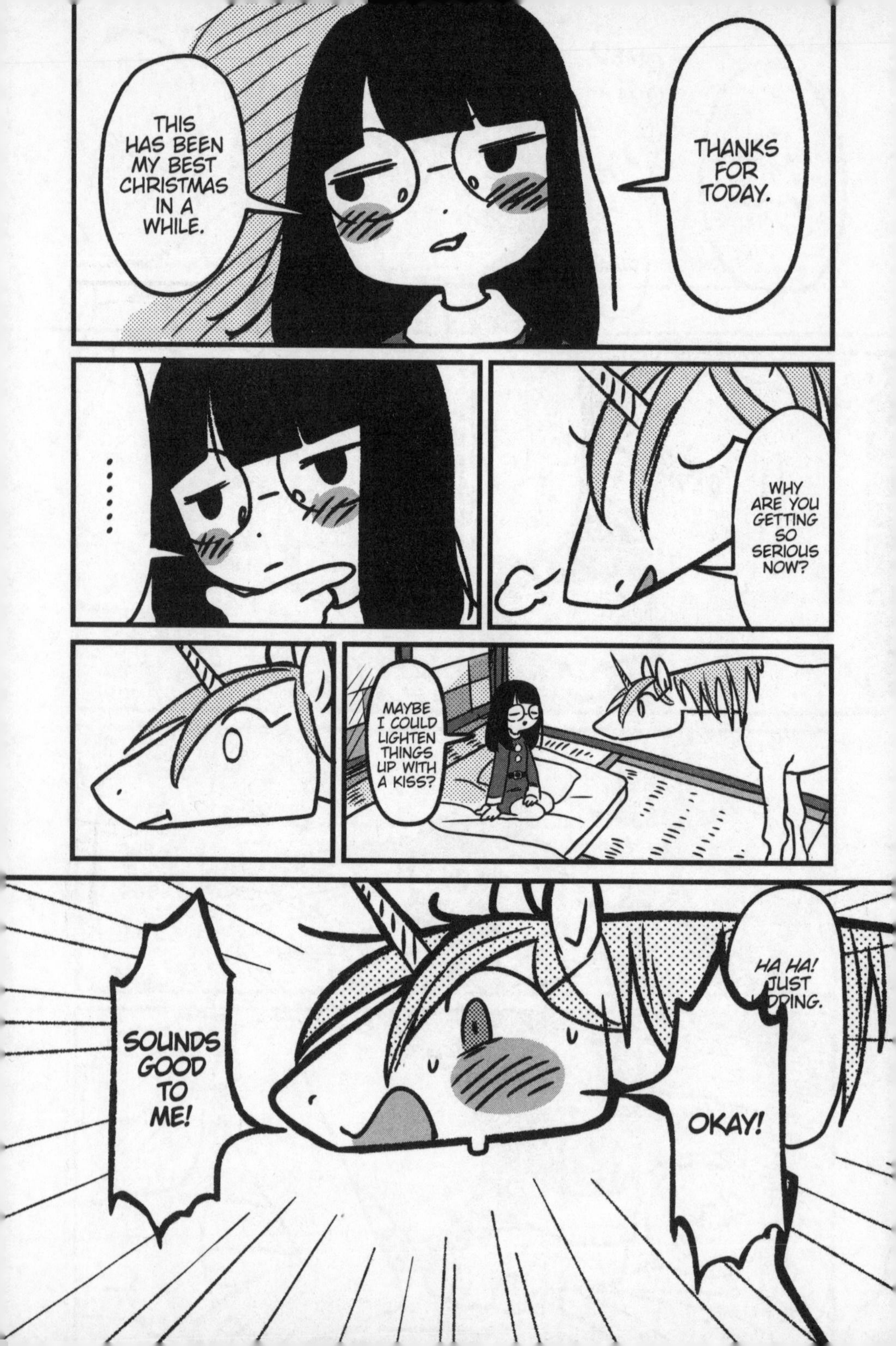
THANKS FOR TODAY.
THIS HAS BEEN MY BEST CHRISTMAS IN A WHILE.
WHY ARE YOU GETTING SO SERIOUS NOW?
......
MAYBE I COULD LIGHTEN THINGS UP WITH A KISS?
HA HA! JUST DDING.
OKAY!
SOUNDS GOOD TO ME!

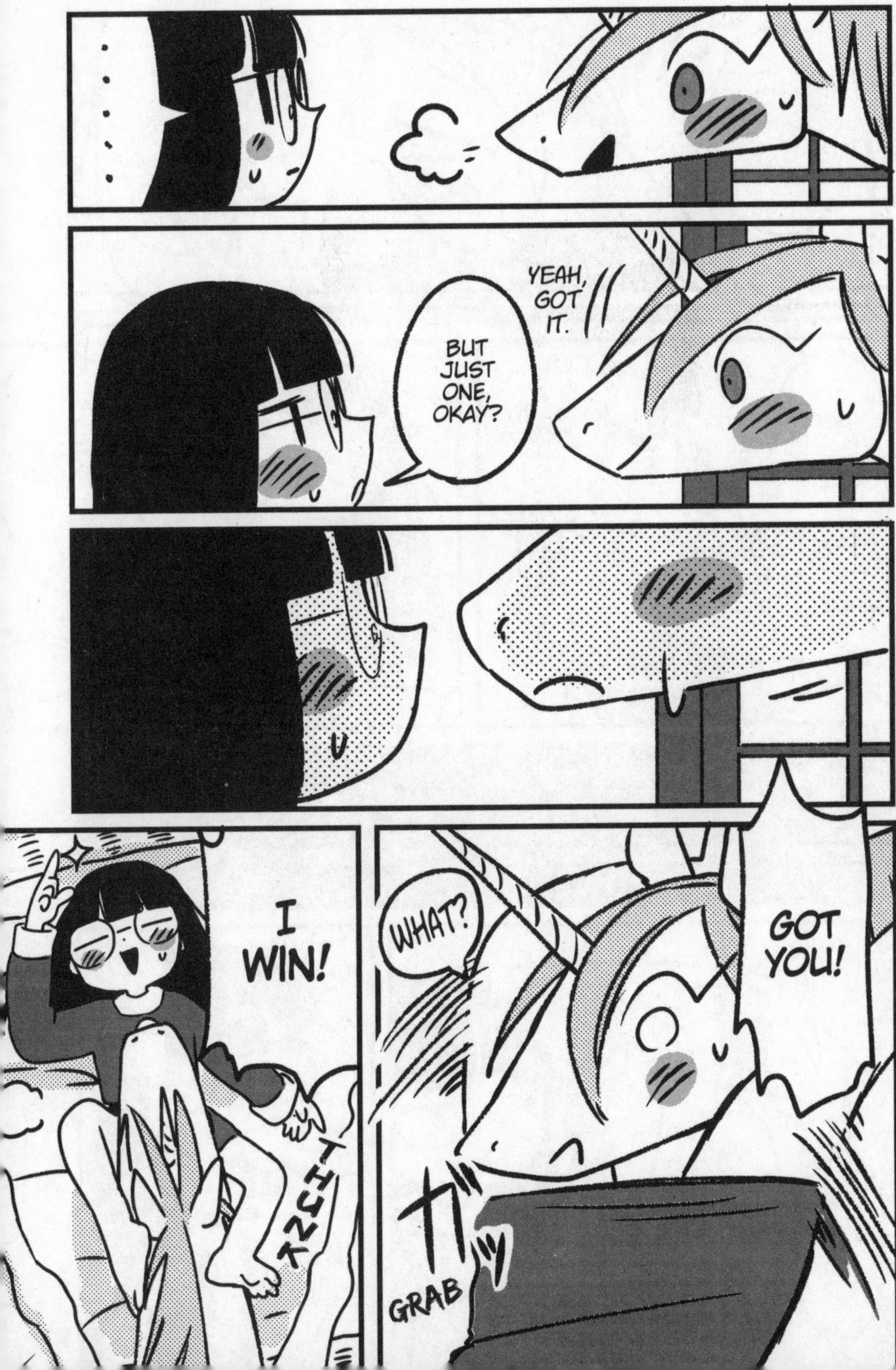
YEAH, GOT IT.
BUT JUST ONE, OKAY?
GOT YOU!
WHAT?
GRAB
I WIN!
THUNK

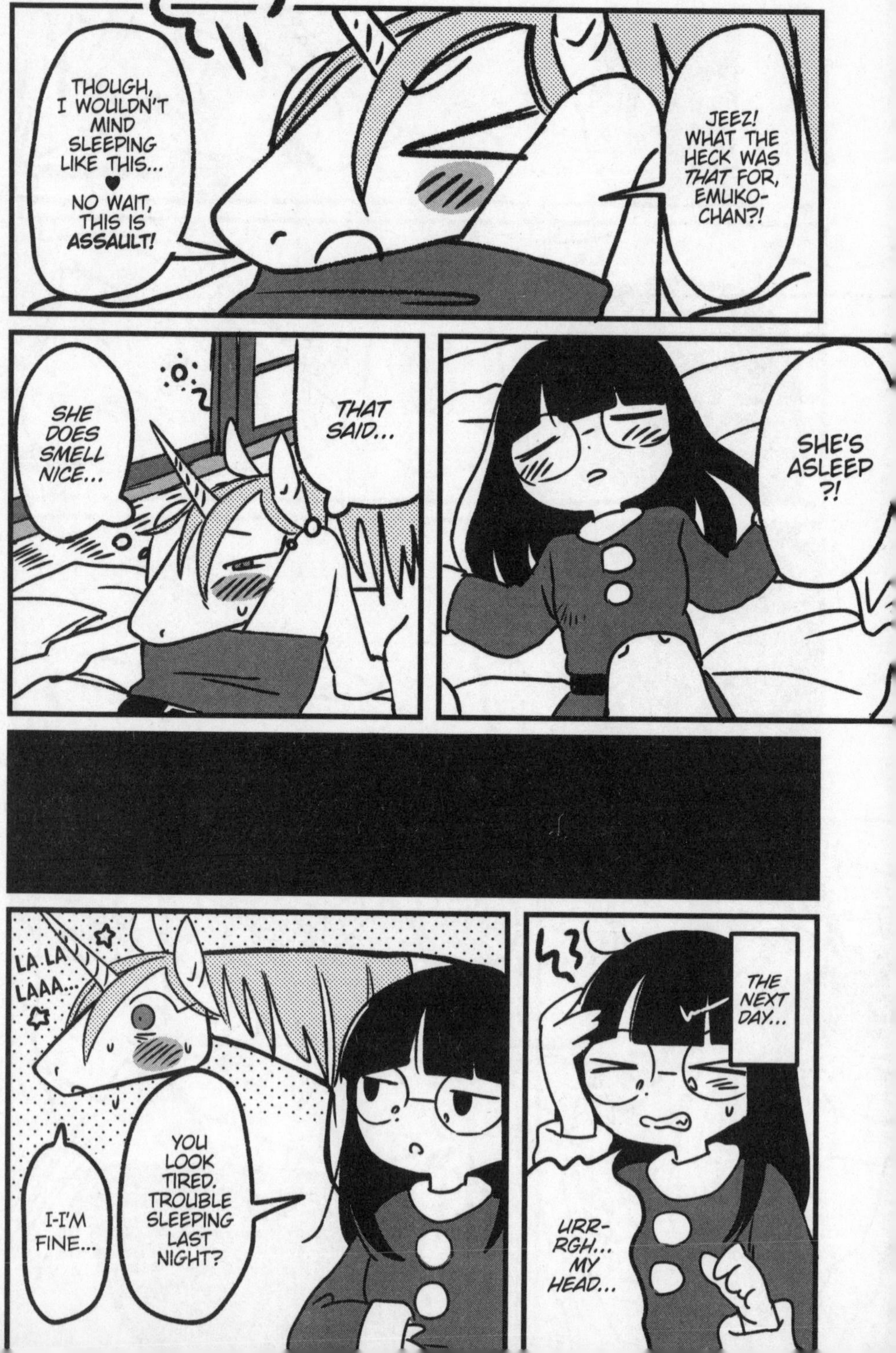
JEEZ! WHAT THE HECK WAS *THAT* FOR, EMUKO-CHAN?!
THOUGH, I WOULDN'T MIND SLEEPING LIKE THIS... ♥ NO WAIT, THIS IS ASSAULT!
SHE'S ASLEEP?!
THAT SAID...
SHE DOES SMELL NICE...
THE NEXT DAY...
URR-RGH... MY HEAD...
LA LA LAAA...
YOU LOOK TIRED. TROUBLE SLEEPING LAST NIGHT?
I-I'M FINE...

THE TAMING OF THE BEAST

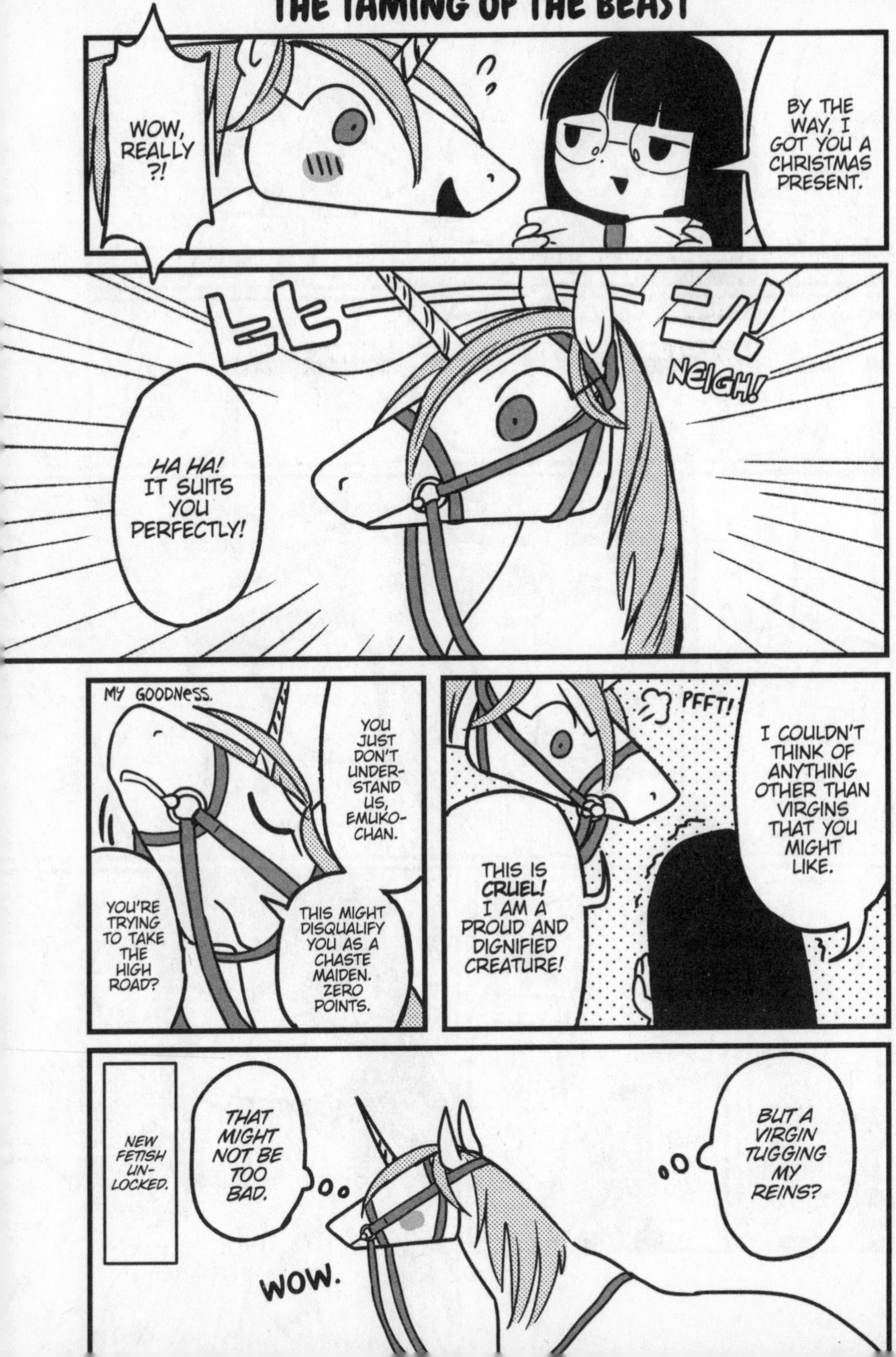

BY THE WAY, I GOT YOU A CHRISTMAS PRESENT.
WOW, REALLY?!
ヒヒーン!
NEIGH!
HA HA! IT SUITS YOU PERFECTLY!
PFFT!
I COULDN'T THINK OF ANYTHING OTHER THAN VIRGINS THAT YOU MIGHT LIKE.
THIS IS CRUEL! I AM A PROUD AND DIGNIFIED CREATURE!
MY GOODNESS.
YOU JUST DON'T UNDERSTAND US, EMUKO-CHAN.
YOU'RE TRYING TO TAKE THE HIGH ROAD?
THIS MIGHT DISQUALIFY YOU AS A CHASTE MAIDEN. ZERO POINTS.
BUT A VIRGIN TUGGING MY REINS?
THAT MIGHT NOT BE TOO BAD.
NEW FETISH UN-LOCKED.
WOW.

A LADY'S MODESTY

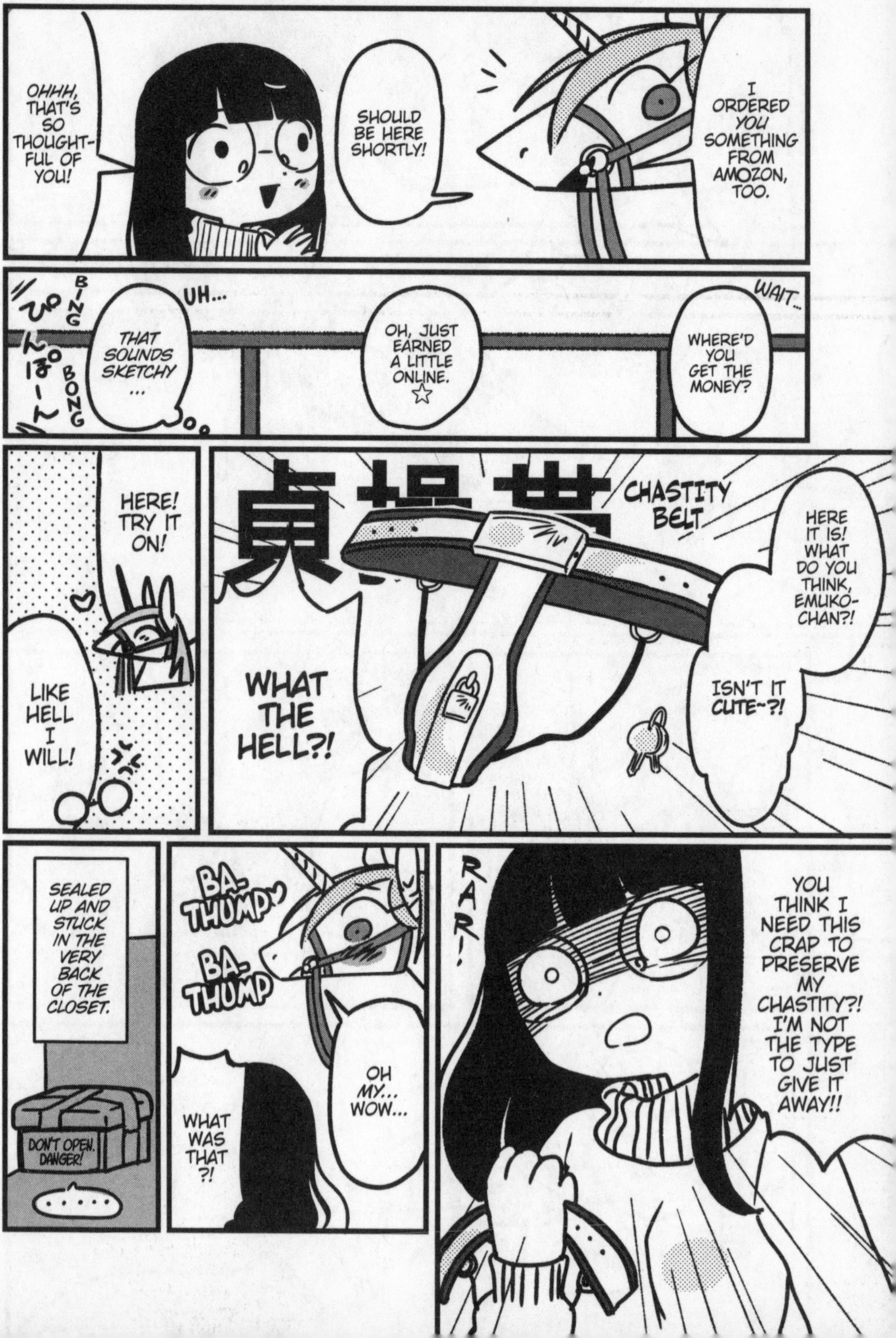

I ORDERED YOU SOMETHING FROM AMOZON, TOO.
SHOULD BE HERE SHORTLY!
OHHH, THAT'S SO THOUGHTFUL OF YOU!
WAIT...
WHERE'D YOU GET THE MONEY?
OH, JUST EARNED A LITTLE ONLINE. ☆
UH...
THAT SOUNDS SKETCHY...
ぴんぽーん
BING BONG
貞操帯
CHASTITY BELT
HERE IT IS! WHAT DO YOU THINK, EMUKO-CHAN?!
ISN'T IT CUTE~?!
WHAT THE HELL?!
HERE! TRY IT ON!
LIKE HELL I WILL!
RAR!
YOU THINK I NEED THIS CRAP TO PRESERVE MY CHASTITY?! I'M NOT THE TYPE TO JUST GIVE IT AWAY!!
BA-THUMP
BA-THUMP
OH MY... WOW...
WHAT WAS THAT?!
SEALED UP AND STUCK IN THE VERY BACK OF THE CLOSET.
DON'T OPEN. DANGER!
.....

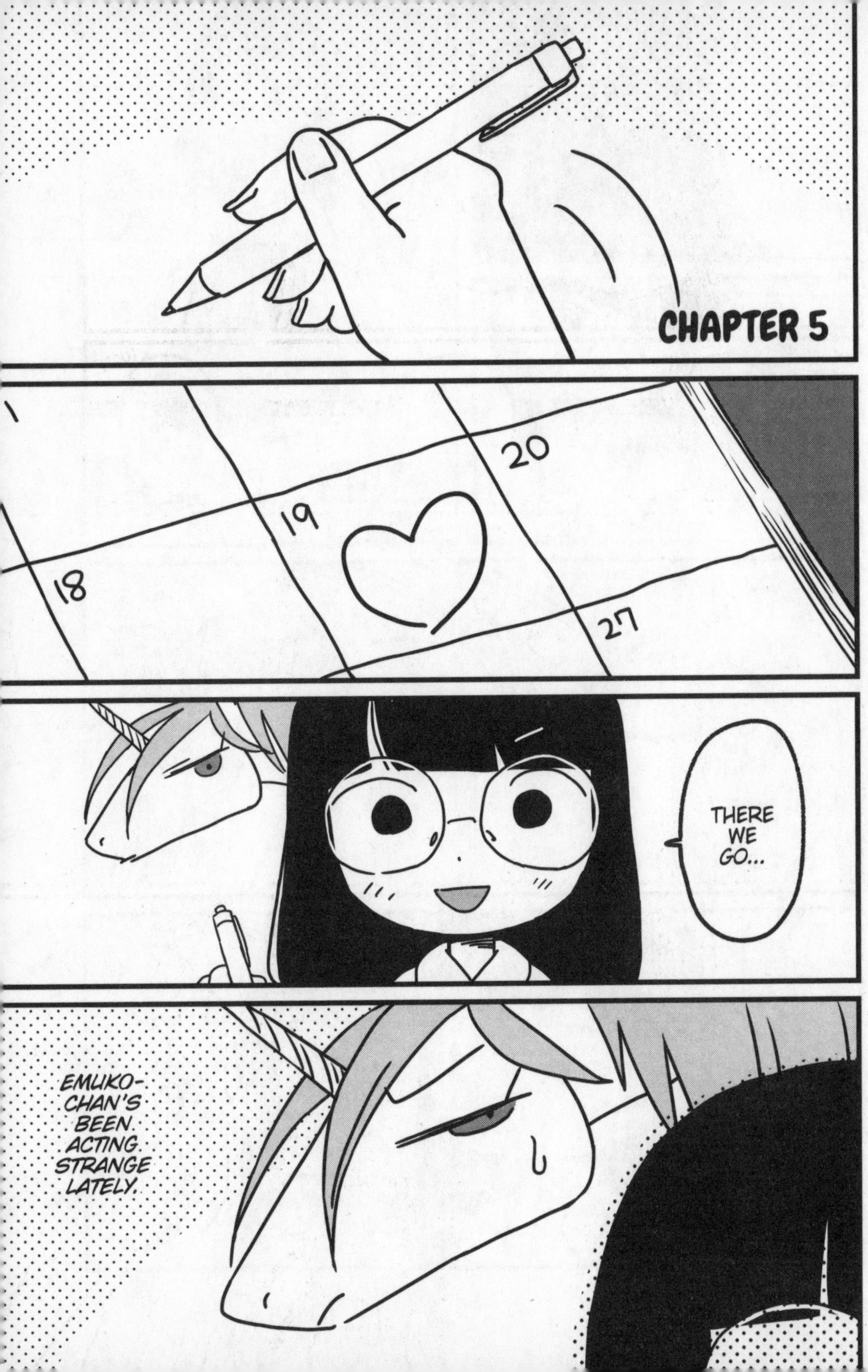
CHAPTER 5
20
19
18
27
THERE WE GO...
EMUKO-CHAN'S BEEN ACTING STRANGE LATELY.

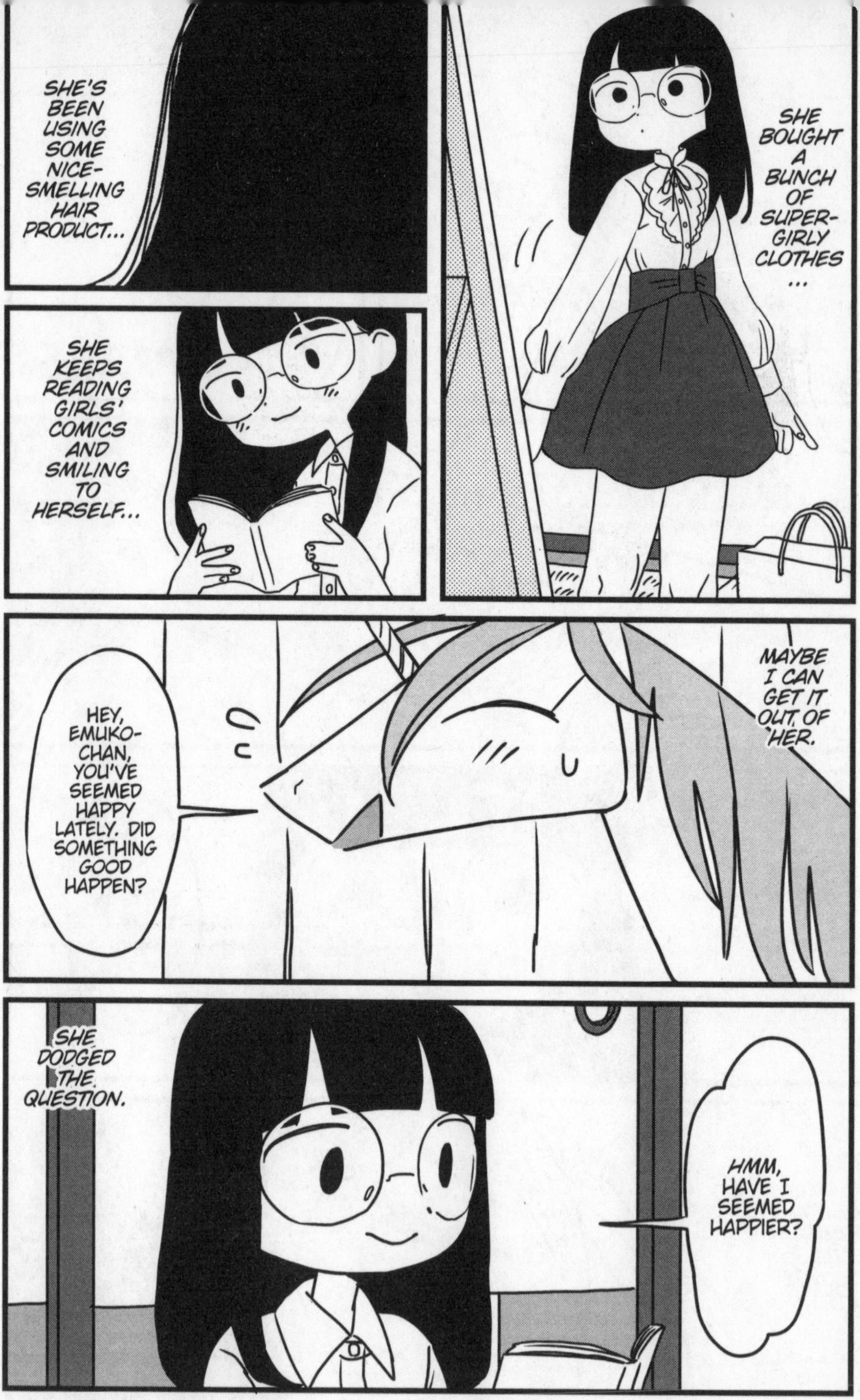
SHE BOUGHT A BUNCH OF SUPER-GIRLY CLOTHES...
SHE'S BEEN USING SOME NICE-SMELLING HAIR PRODUCT...
SHE KEEPS READING GIRLS' COMICS AND SMILING TO HERSELF...
MAYBE I CAN GET IT OUT OF HER.
HEY, EMUKO-CHAN, YOU'VE SEEMED HAPPY LATELY. DID SOMETHING GOOD HAPPEN?
HMM, HAVE I SEEMED HAPPIER?
SHE DODGED THE QUESTION.

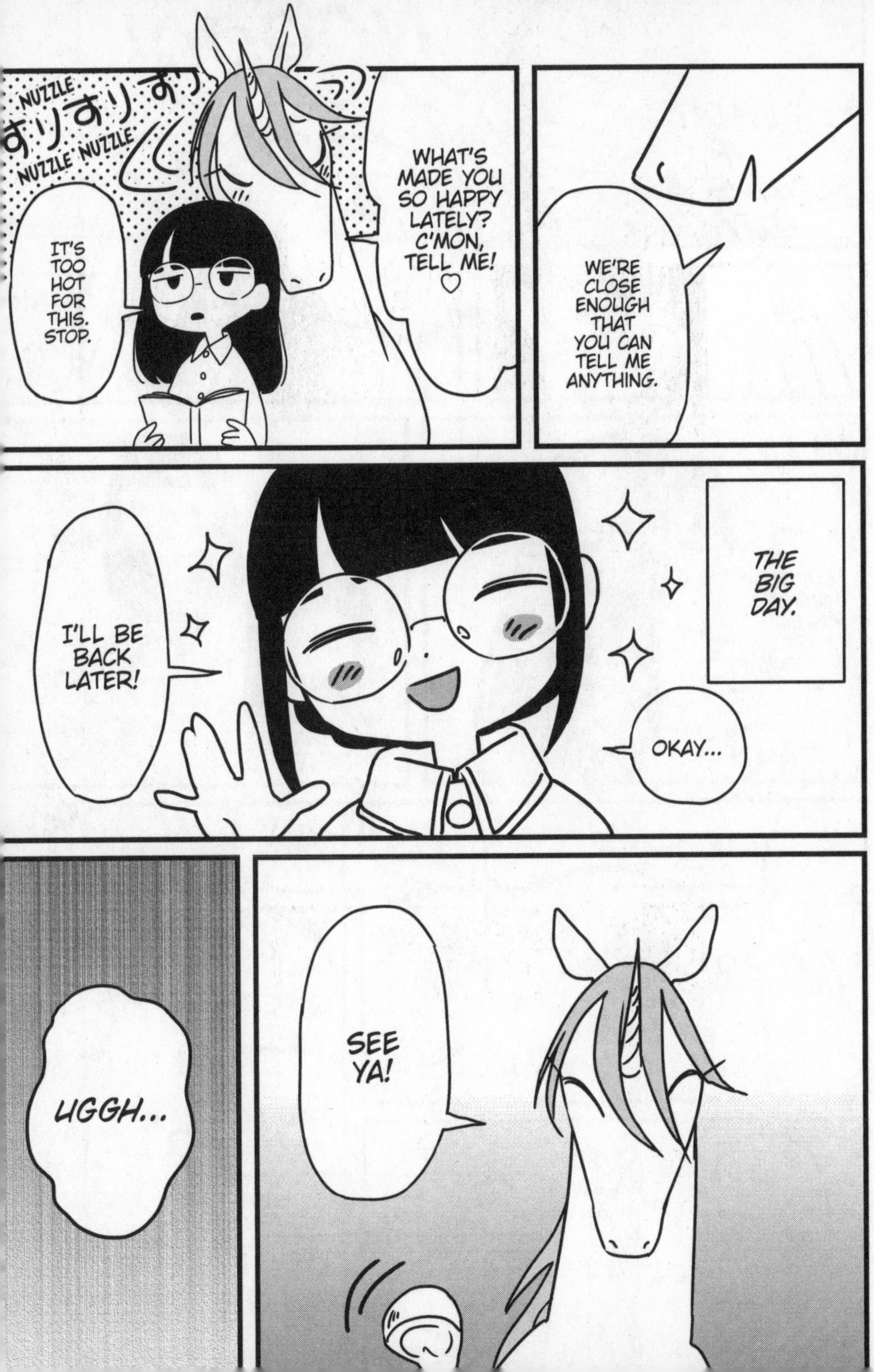
WE'RE CLOSE ENOUGH THAT YOU CAN TELL ME ANYTHING.
WHAT'S MADE YOU SO HAPPY LATELY? C'MON, TELL ME! ♡
すりすりすり
NUZZLE NUZZLE NUZZLE
IT'S TOO HOT FOR THIS. STOP.
THE BIG DAY.
OKAY...
I'LL BE BACK LATER!
SEE YA!
UGGH...

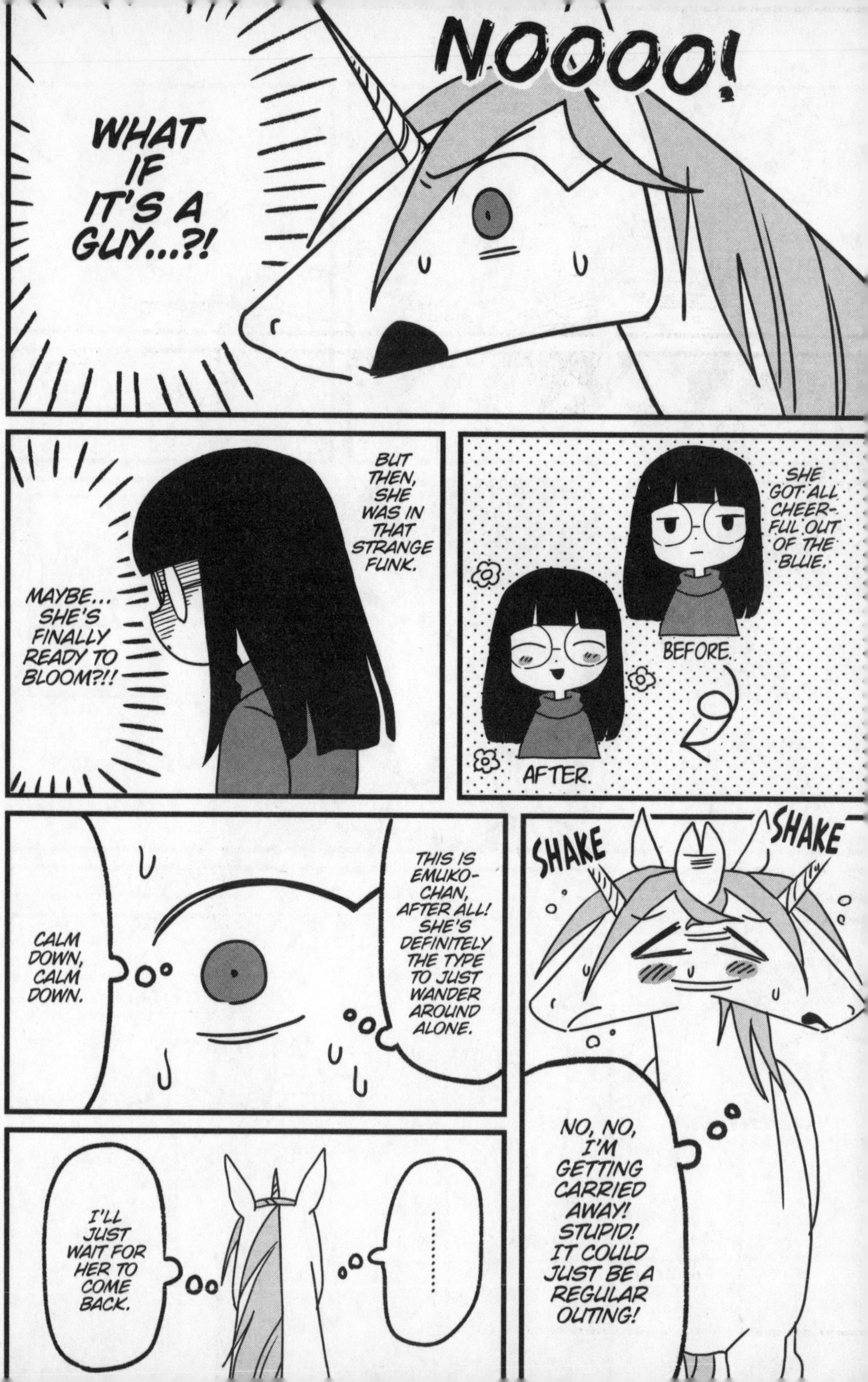
NOOOO!
WHAT IF IT'S A GUY...?!
SHE GOT ALL CHEERFUL OUT OF THE BLUE.
BEFORE.
AFTER.
BUT THEN, SHE WAS IN THAT STRANGE FUNK.
MAYBE... SHE'S FINALLY READY TO BLOOM?!!
SHAKE
SHAKE
NO, NO, I'M GETTING CARRIED AWAY! STUPID! IT COULD JUST BE A REGULAR OUTING!
THIS IS EMUKO-CHAN, AFTER ALL! SHE'S DEFINITELY THE TYPE TO JUST WANDER AROUND ALONE.
CALM DOWN, CALM DOWN.
......
I'LL JUST WAIT FOR HER TO COME BACK.

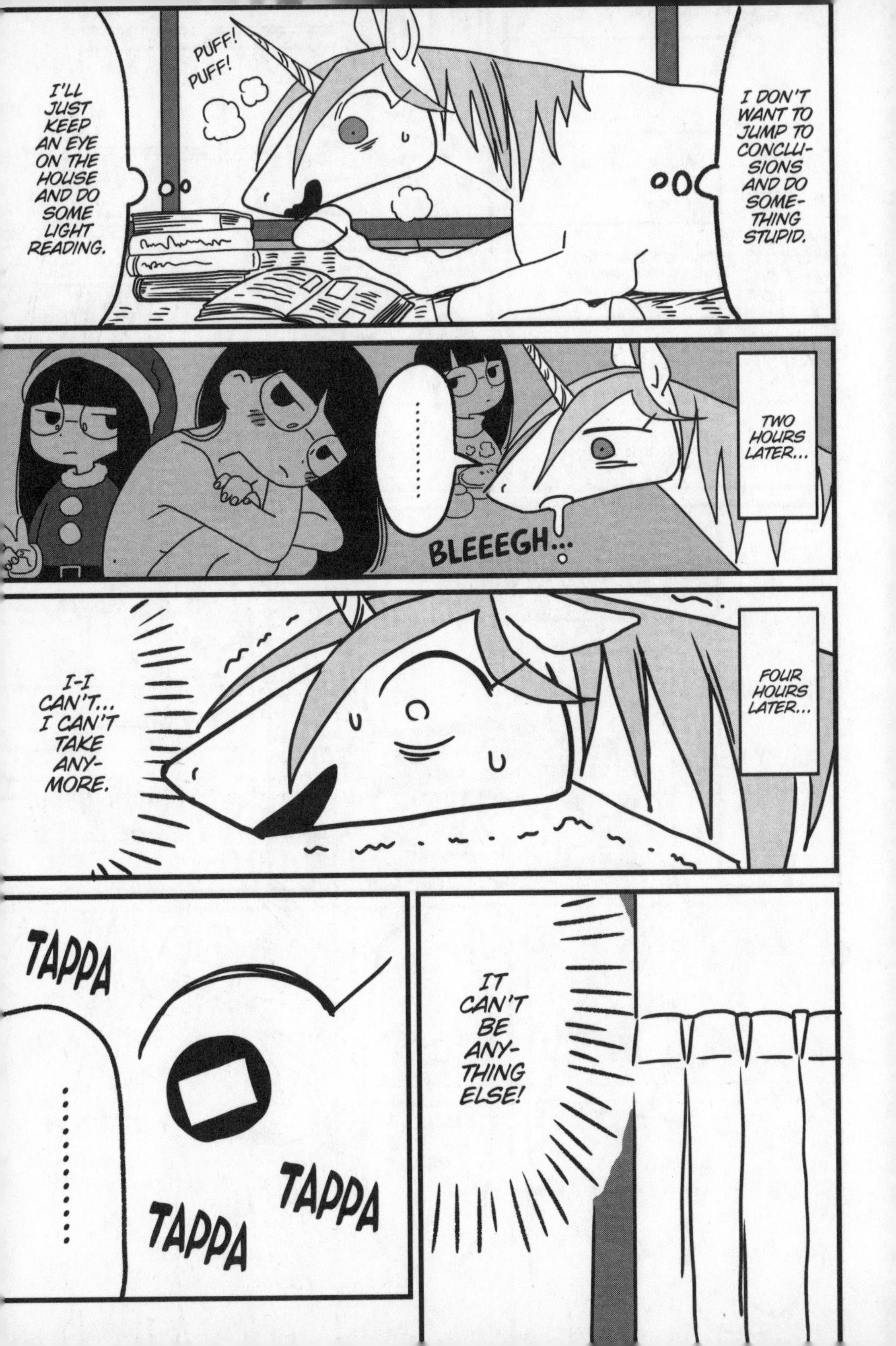
I DON'T WANT TO JUMP TO CONCLUSIONS AND DO SOMETHING STUPID.
PUFF! PUFF!
I'LL JUST KEEP AN EYE ON THE HOUSE AND DO SOME LIGHT READING.
TWO HOURS LATER...
......
BLEEEGH...
FOUR HOURS LATER...
I-I CAN'T... I CAN'T TAKE ANYMORE.
IT CAN'T BE ANYTHING ELSE!
TAPPA
....
TAPPA
TAPPA

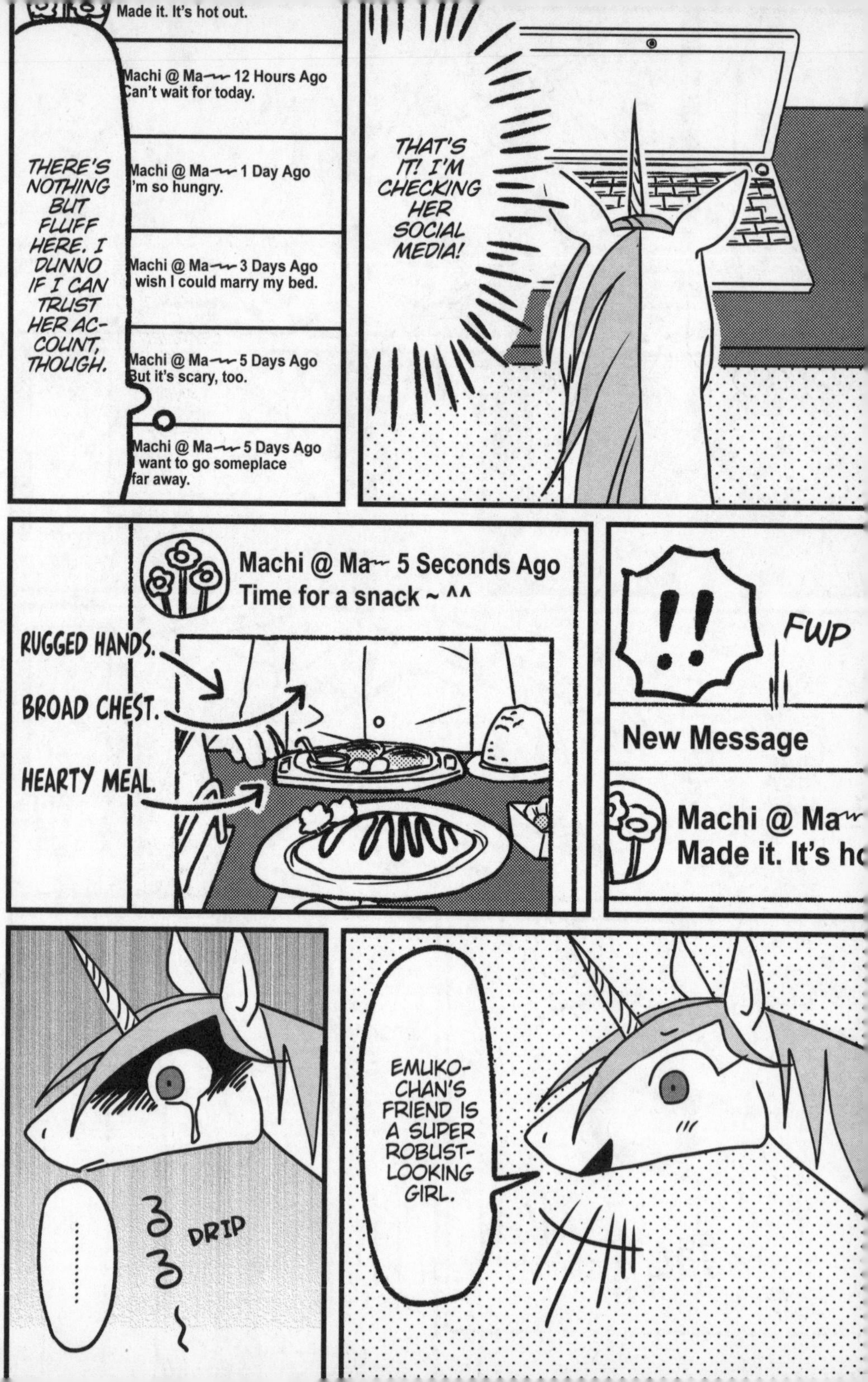
THAT'S IT! I'M CHECKING HER SOCIAL MEDIA!
Made it. It's hot out.
Machi @ Ma~ 12 Hours Ago
Can't wait for today.
Machi @ Ma~ 1 Day Ago
I'm so hungry.
Machi @ Ma~ 3 Days Ago
I wish I could marry my bed.
Machi @ Ma~ 5 Days Ago
But it's scary, too.
Machi @ Ma~ 5 Days Ago
I want to go someplace far away.
THERE'S NOTHING BUT FLUFF HERE. I DUNNO IF I CAN TRUST HER ACCOUNT, THOUGH.
!!
FWP
New Message
Machi @ Ma~
Made it. It's ho
Machi @ Ma~ 5 Seconds Ago
Time for a snack ~ ^^
RUGGED HANDS.
BROAD CHEST.
HEARTY MEAL.
EMUKO-CHAN'S FRIEND IS A SUPER ROBUST-LOOKING GIRL.
……
DRIP

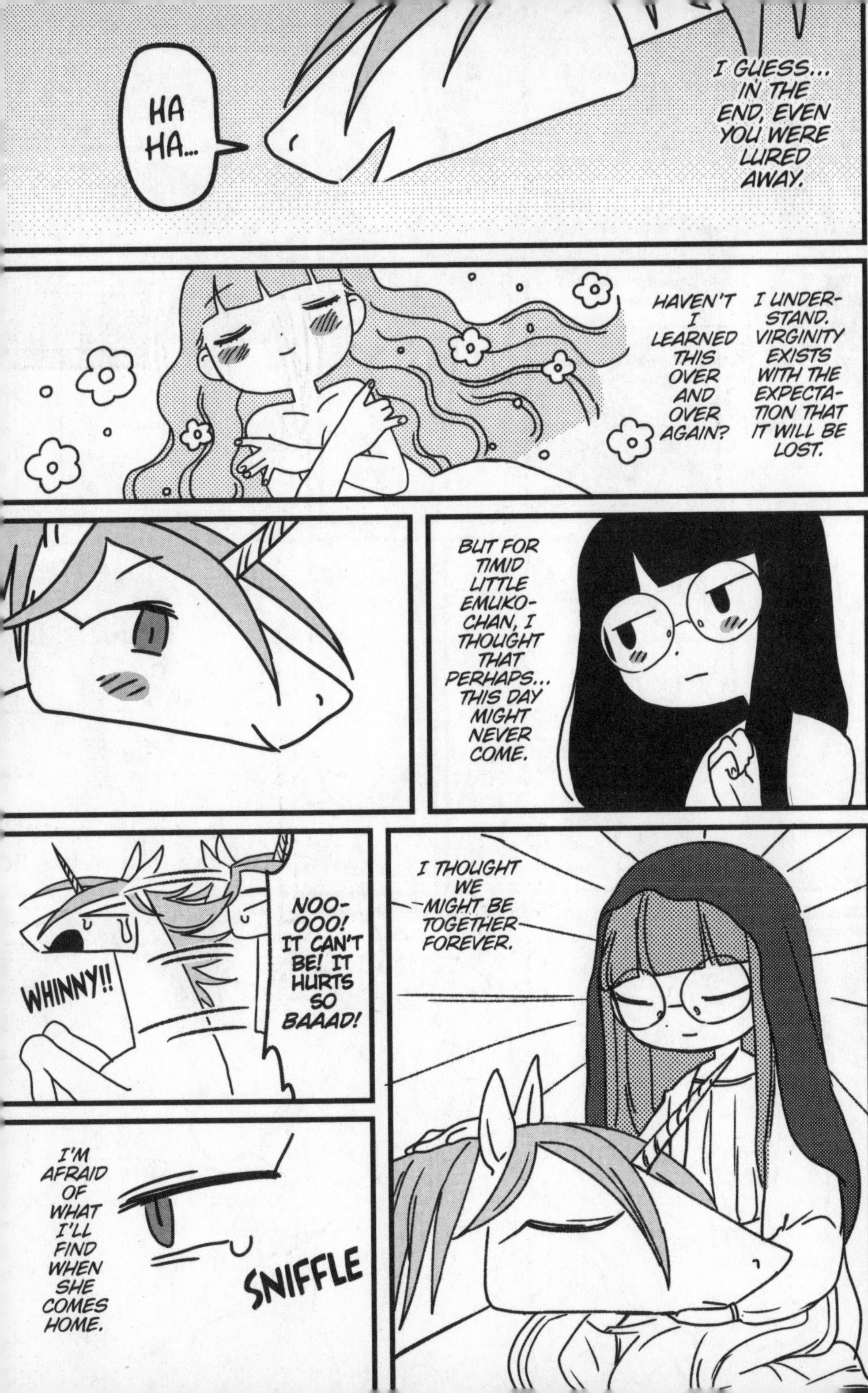
I GUESS... IN THE END, EVEN YOU WERE LURED AWAY.
HA HA...
I UNDER-STAND. VIRGINITY EXISTS WITH THE EXPECTA-TION THAT IT WILL BE LOST.
HAVEN'T I LEARNED THIS OVER AND OVER AGAIN?
BUT FOR TIMID LITTLE EMUKO-CHAN, I THOUGHT THAT PERHAPS... THIS DAY MIGHT NEVER COME.
I THOUGHT WE MIGHT BE TOGETHER FOREVER.
NOO-OOO! IT CAN'T BE! IT HURTS SO BAAAD!
WHINNY!!
I'M AFRAID OF WHAT I'LL FIND WHEN SHE COMES HOME.
SNIFFLE

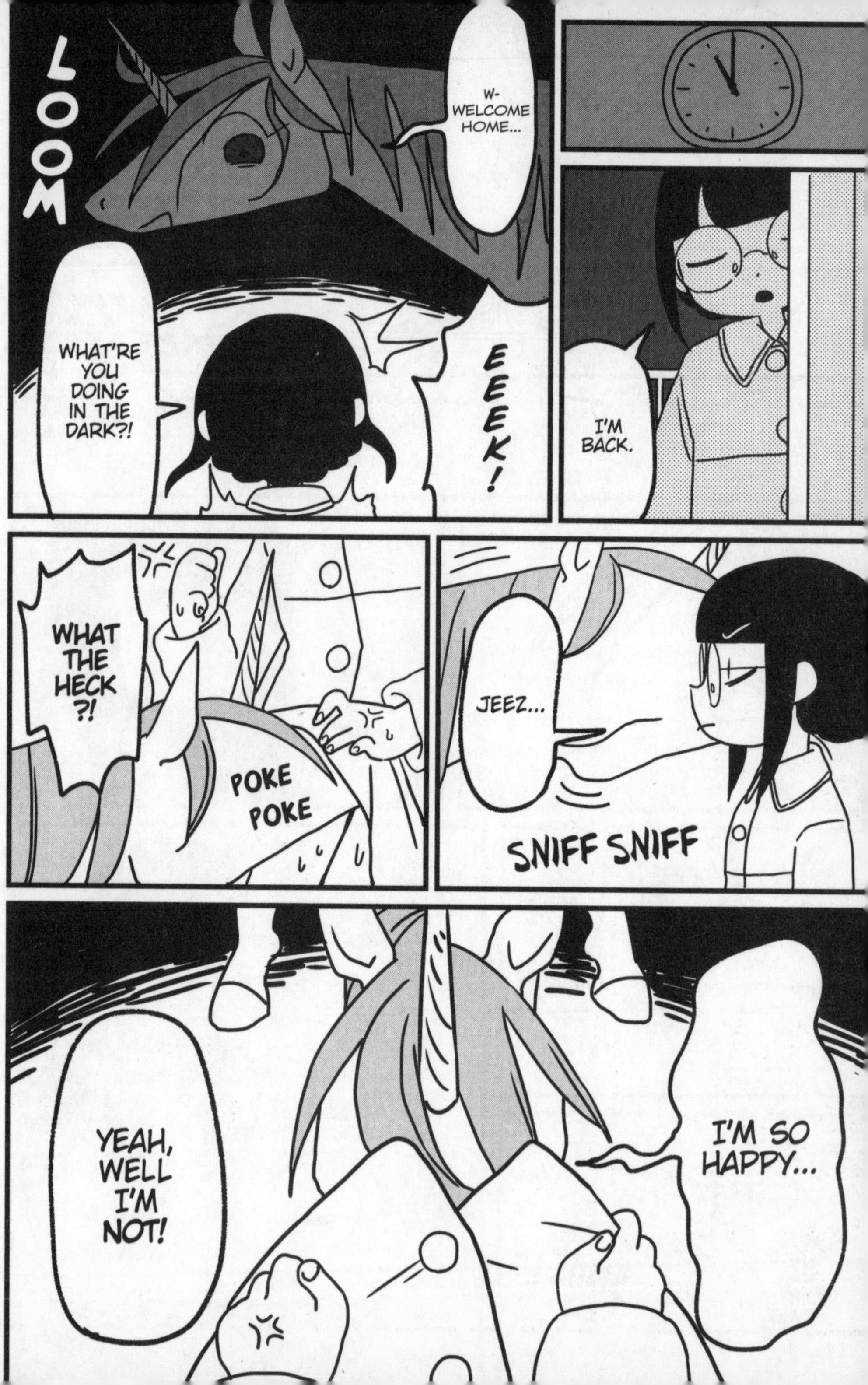
I'M BACK.
W- WELCOME HOME...
LOOM
EEEK!
WHAT'RE YOU DOING IN THE DARK?!
JEEZ...
SNIFF SNIFF
WHAT THE HECK?!
POKE POKE
I'M SO HAPPY...
YEAH, WELL I'M NOT!

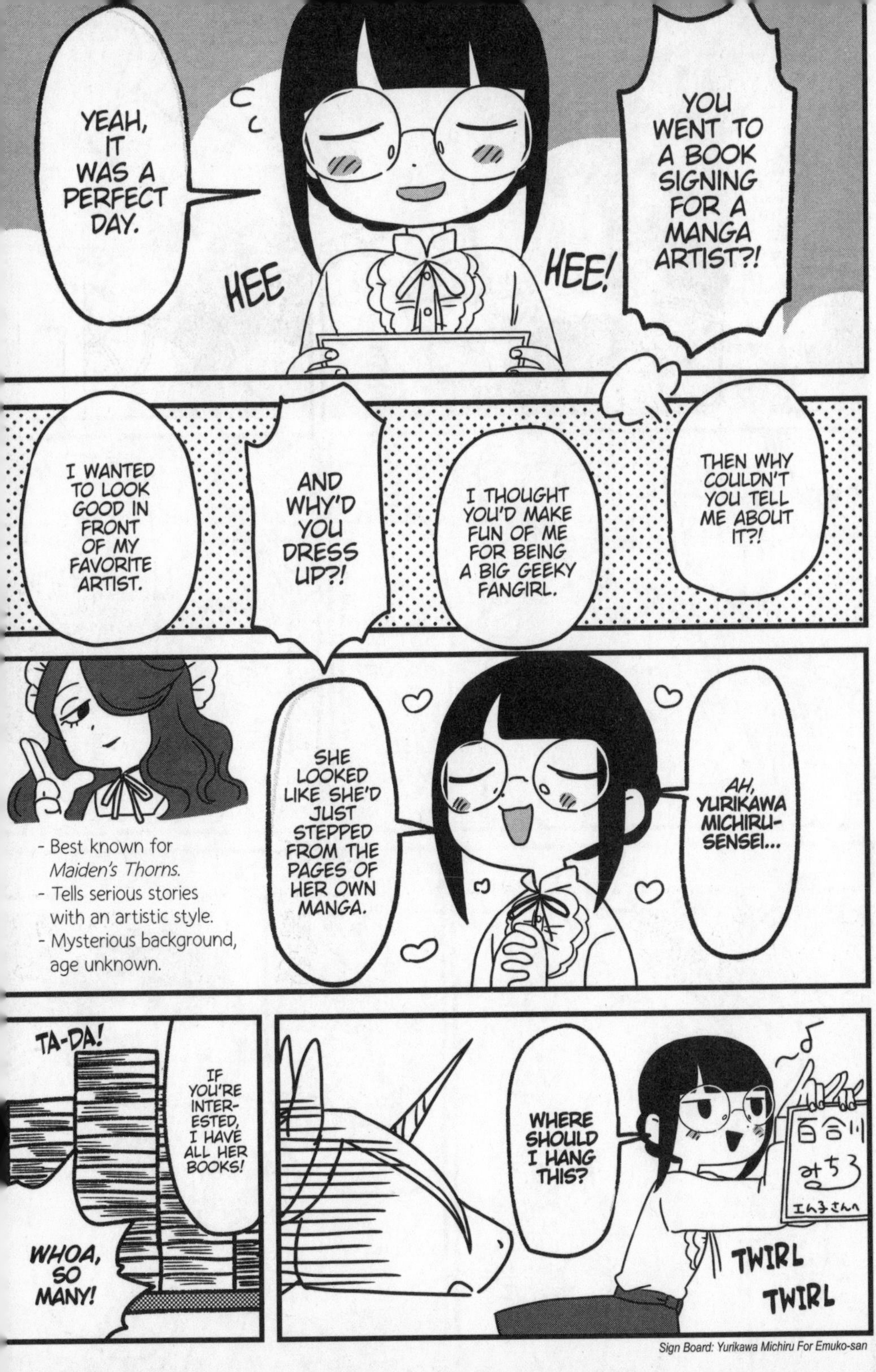
YOU WENT TO A BOOK SIGNING FOR A MANGA ARTIST?!
YEAH, IT WAS A PERFECT DAY.
HEE HEE!
THEN WHY COULDN'T YOU TELL ME ABOUT IT?!
I THOUGHT YOU'D MAKE FUN OF ME FOR BEING A BIG GEEKY FANGIRL.
AND WHY'D YOU DRESS UP?!
I WANTED TO LOOK GOOD IN FRONT OF MY FAVORITE ARTIST.
AH, YURIKAWA MICHIRU-SENSEI...
SHE LOOKED LIKE SHE'D JUST STEPPED FROM THE PAGES OF HER OWN MANGA.
- Best known for *Maiden's Thorns*.
- Tells serious stories with an artistic style.
- Mysterious background, age unknown.
WHERE SHOULD I HANG THIS?
百合川 みちる
エム子さんへ
TWIRL TWIRL
TA-DA!
IF YOU'RE INTERESTED, I HAVE ALL HER BOOKS!
WHOA, SO MANY!
Sign Board: Yurikawa Michiru For Emuko-san

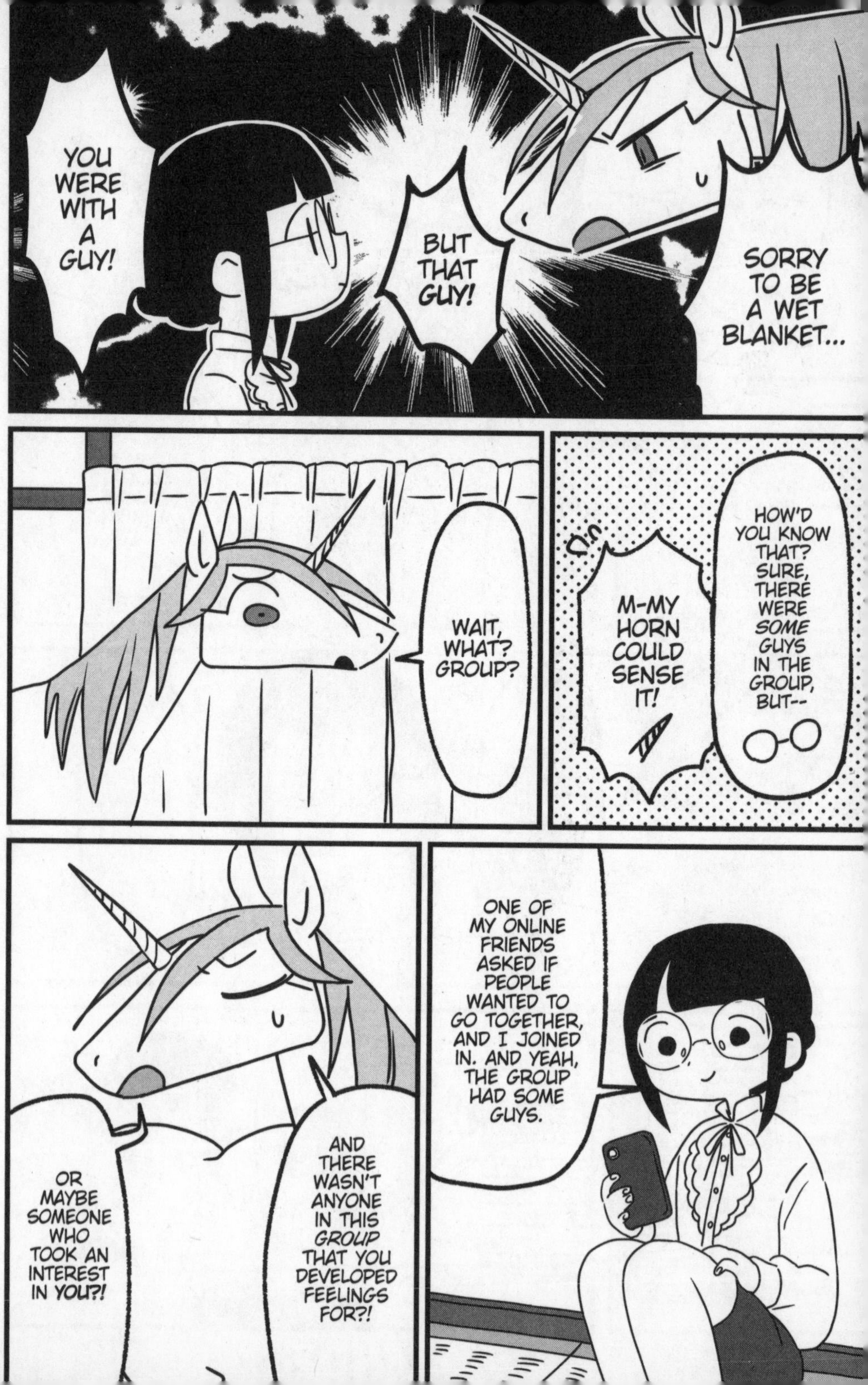
SORRY TO BE A WET BLANKET...
BUT THAT GUY!
YOU WERE WITH A GUY!
HOW'D YOU KNOW THAT? SURE, THERE WERE *SOME* GUYS IN THE GROUP, BUT--
M-MY HORN COULD SENSE IT!
WAIT, WHAT? GROUP?
ONE OF MY ONLINE FRIENDS ASKED IF PEOPLE WANTED TO GO TOGETHER, AND I JOINED IN. AND YEAH, THE GROUP HAD SOME GUYS.
AND THERE WASN'T ANYONE IN THIS *GROUP* THAT YOU DEVELOPED FEELINGS FOR?!
OR MAYBE SOMEONE WHO TOOK AN INTEREST IN *YOU*?!

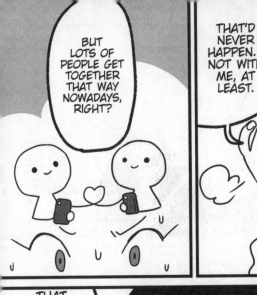

NO WAY.
THAT'D NEVER HAPPEN... NOT WITH ME, AT LEAST.
BUT LOTS OF PEOPLE GET TOGETHER THAT WAY NOWADAYS, RIGHT?
THAT MIGHT BE TRUE FOR SOME PEOPLE, BUT I'M SIMPLY UNINTERESTED. FOR STARTERS, I WOULD *NEVER* WANT TO MIX SUCH IMPURE FEELINGS WITH THE *PURE ADMIRATION* THAT I FEEL FOR YURIKAWA-SENSEI. SURE, SOME MAY BELIEVE
BLAH
THAT WHENEVER GIRLS AND BOYS GET TOGETHER IT ALWAYS ENDS IN ROMANCE, BUT PERSONALLY I TREAT THIS HOBBY FAR MORE SERI-OUSLY AND WOULDN'T WANT TO DILUTE IT WITH ROMANCE. NOW, I CAN'T SPEAK FOR ANYONE BUT MYSELF, HOWEVER
BLAH
OH CRAP ...
SHE'S ONE OF **THOSE** GEEKS.
IT'S KIND OF CUTE, THOUGH ...

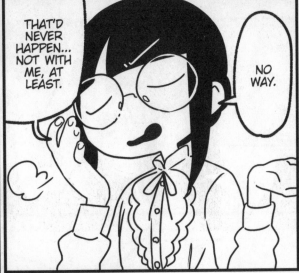

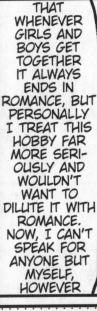

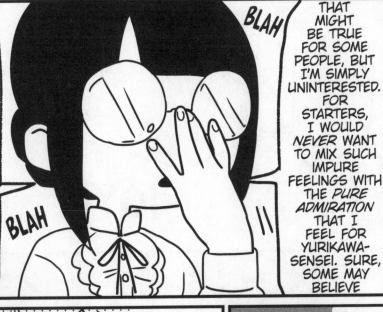

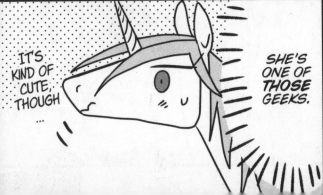

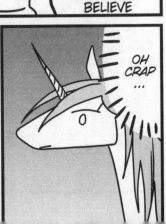

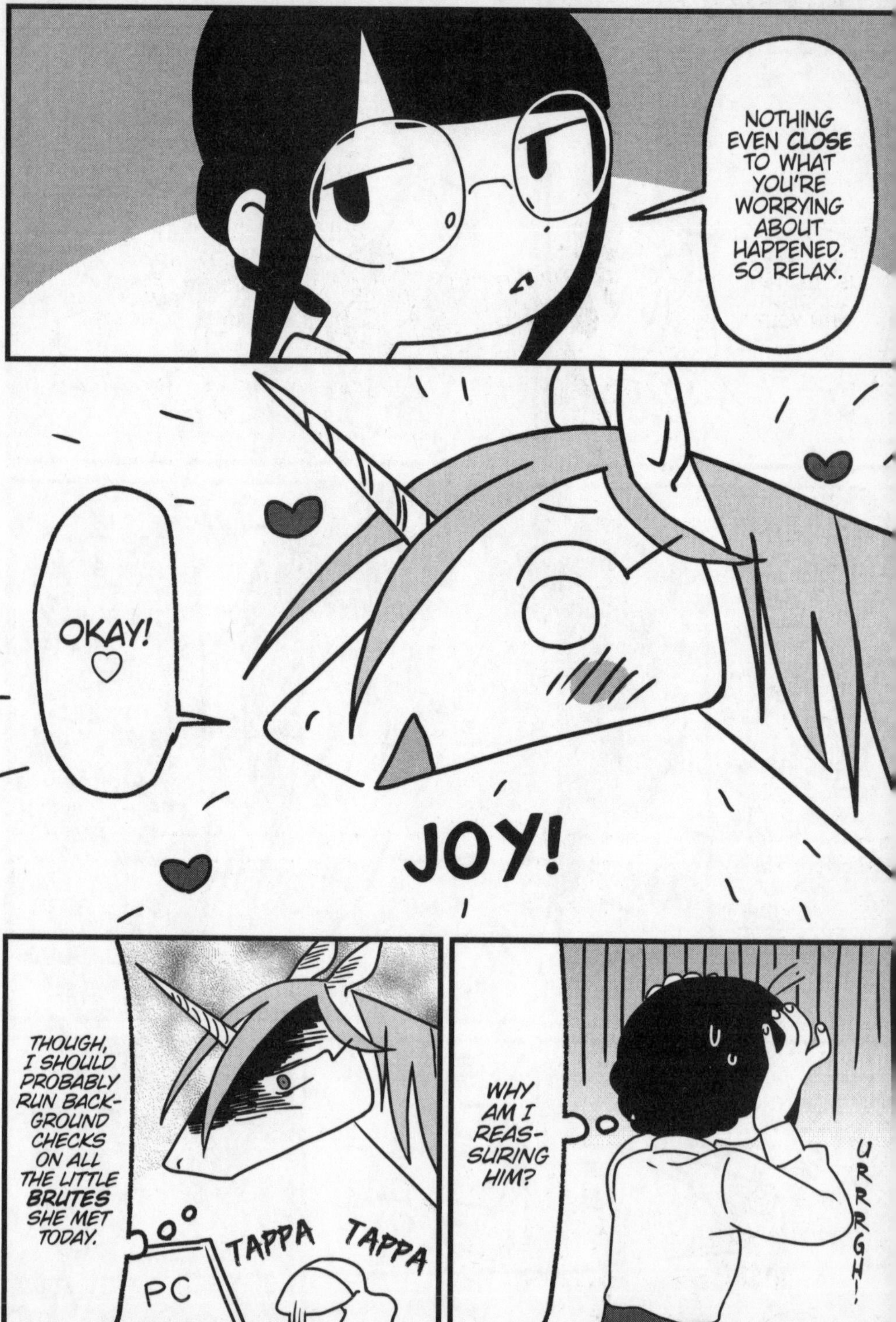
NOTHING EVEN CLOSE TO WHAT YOU'RE WORRYING ABOUT HAPPENED. SO RELAX.
OKAY! ♡
JOY!
WHY AM I REAS-SURING HIM?
URRRGH!
THOUGH, I SHOULD PROBABLY RUN BACK-GROUND CHECKS ON ALL THE LITTLE BRUTES SHE MET TODAY.
TAPPA TAPPA
PC

CHAPTER 6 SETSUBUN

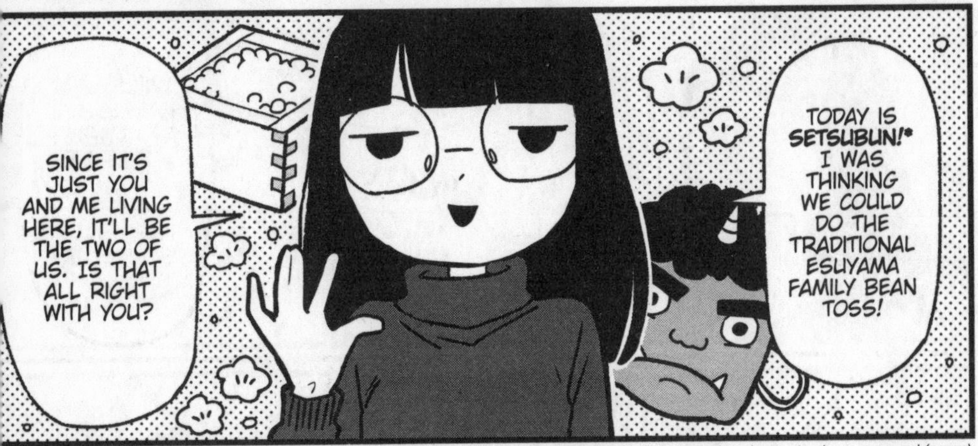
TODAY IS SETSUBUN!* I WAS THINKING WE COULD DO THE TRADITIONAL ESUYAMA FAMILY BEAN TOSS!
SINCE IT'S JUST YOU AND ME LIVING HERE, IT'LL BE THE TWO OF US. IS THAT ALL RIGHT WITH YOU?

*Setsubun: A Japanese festival celebrated by throwing roasted soybeans to chase away oni (ogres).

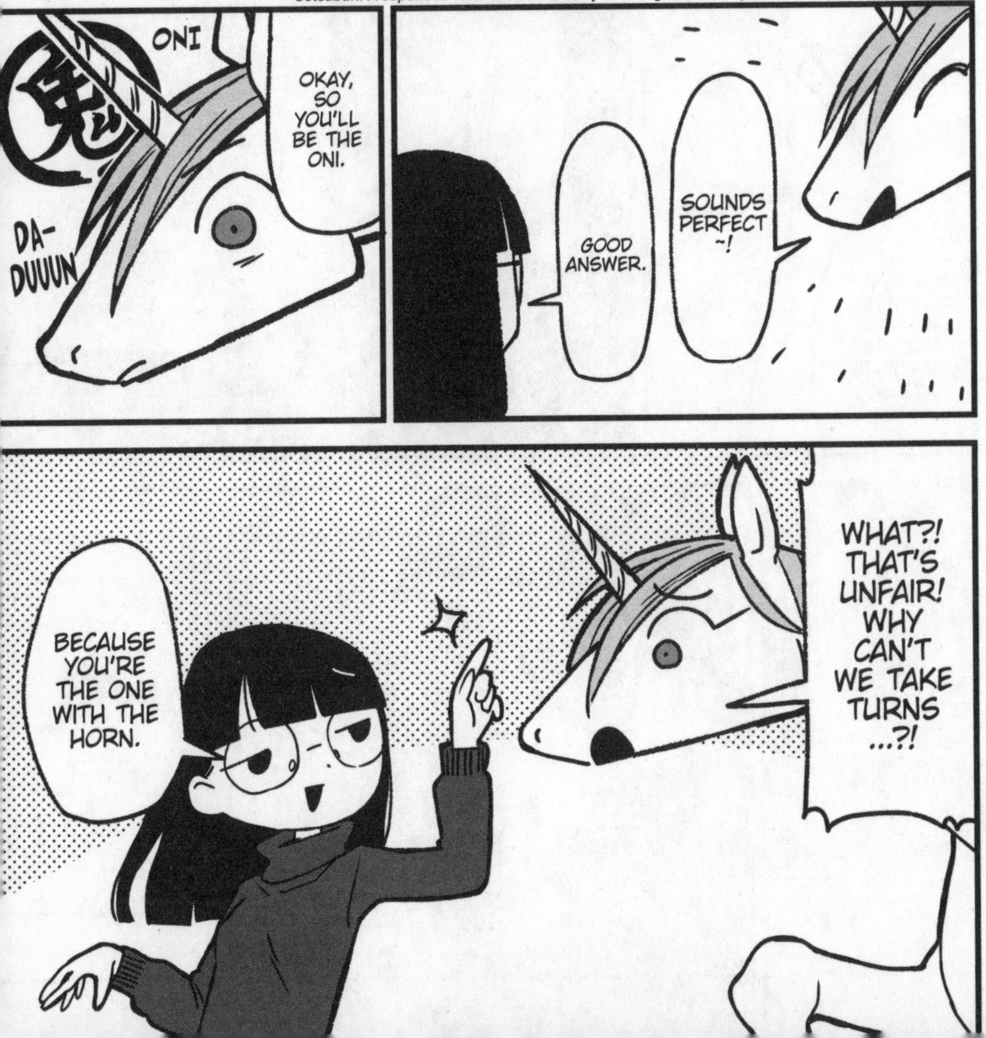
SOUNDS PERFECT ~!
GOOD ANSWER.
OKAY, SO YOU'LL BE THE ONI.
ONI
DA-DUUUN
WHAT?! THAT'S UNFAIR! WHY CAN'T WE TAKE TURNS ...?!
BECAUSE YOU'RE THE ONE WITH THE HORN.

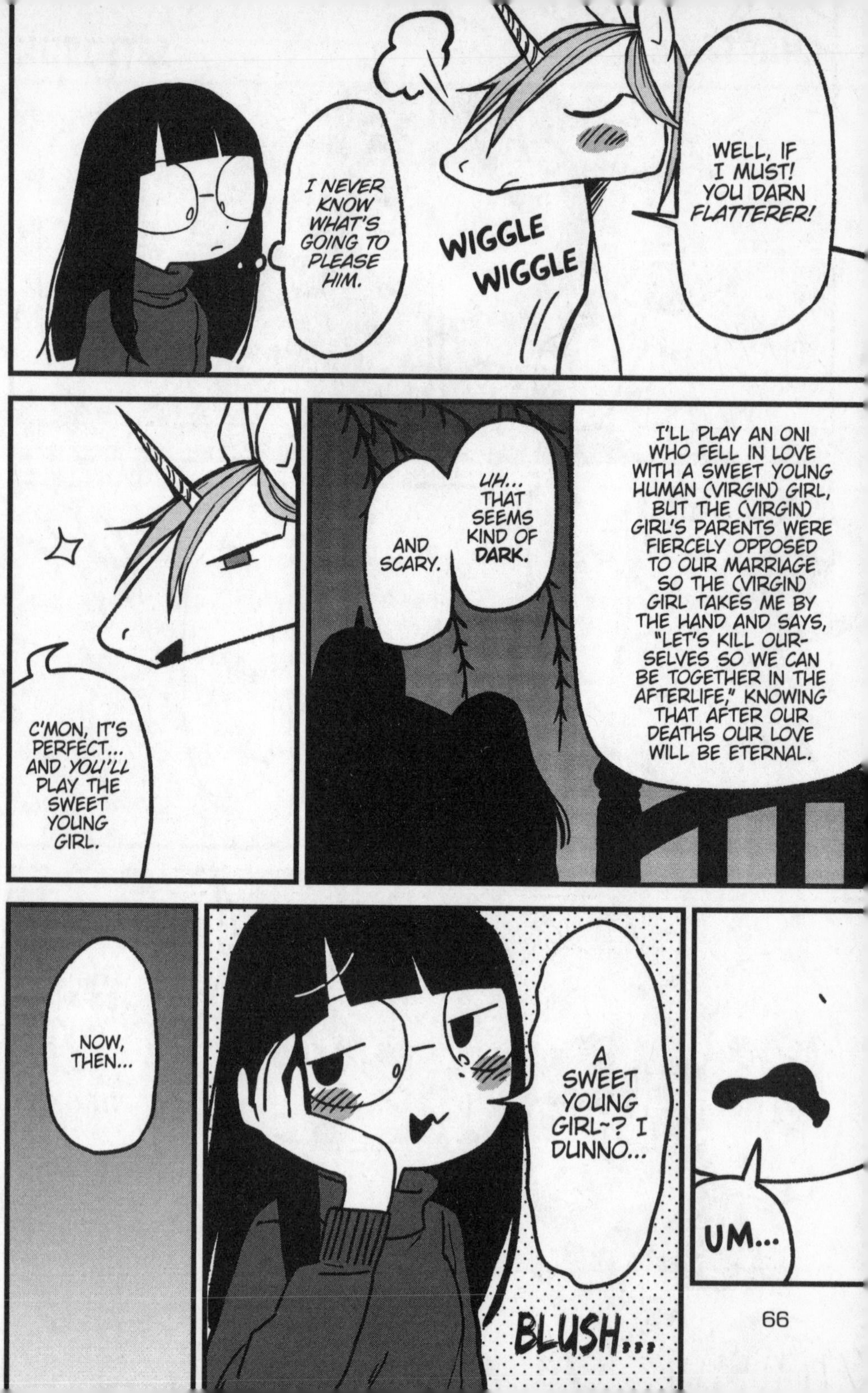

WELL, IF I MUST! YOU DARN FLATTERER!
WIGGLE WIGGLE
I NEVER KNOW WHAT'S GOING TO PLEASE HIM.
I'LL PLAY AN ONI WHO FELL IN LOVE WITH A SWEET YOUNG HUMAN (VIRGIN) GIRL, BUT THE (VIRGIN) GIRL'S PARENTS WERE FIERCELY OPPOSED TO OUR MARRIAGE SO THE (VIRGIN) GIRL TAKES ME BY THE HAND AND SAYS, "LET'S KILL OURSELVES SO WE CAN BE TOGETHER IN THE AFTERLIFE," KNOWING THAT AFTER OUR DEATHS OUR LOVE WILL BE ETERNAL.
UH... THAT SEEMS KIND OF DARK.
AND SCARY.
C'MON, IT'S PERFECT... AND YOU'LL PLAY THE SWEET YOUNG GIRL.
UM...
A SWEET YOUNG GIRL~? I DUNNO...
BLUSH...
NOW, THEN...

MORNING VIEW

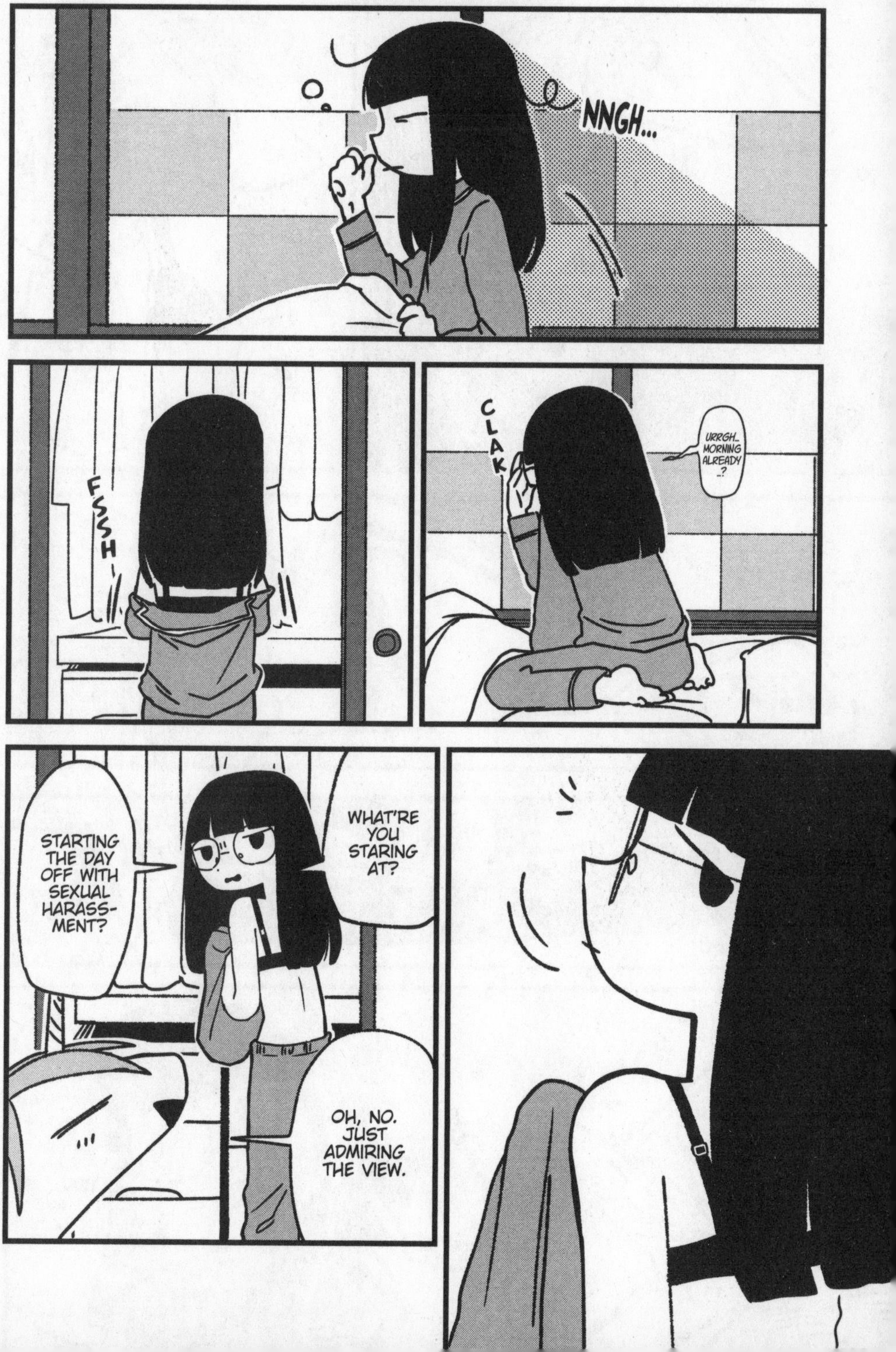
NNGH...
CLAK
URRGH... MORNING ALREADY ...?
FSSH
WHAT'RE YOU STARING AT?
STARTING THE DAY OFF WITH SEXUAL HARASS-MENT?
OH, NO. JUST ADMIRING THE VIEW.

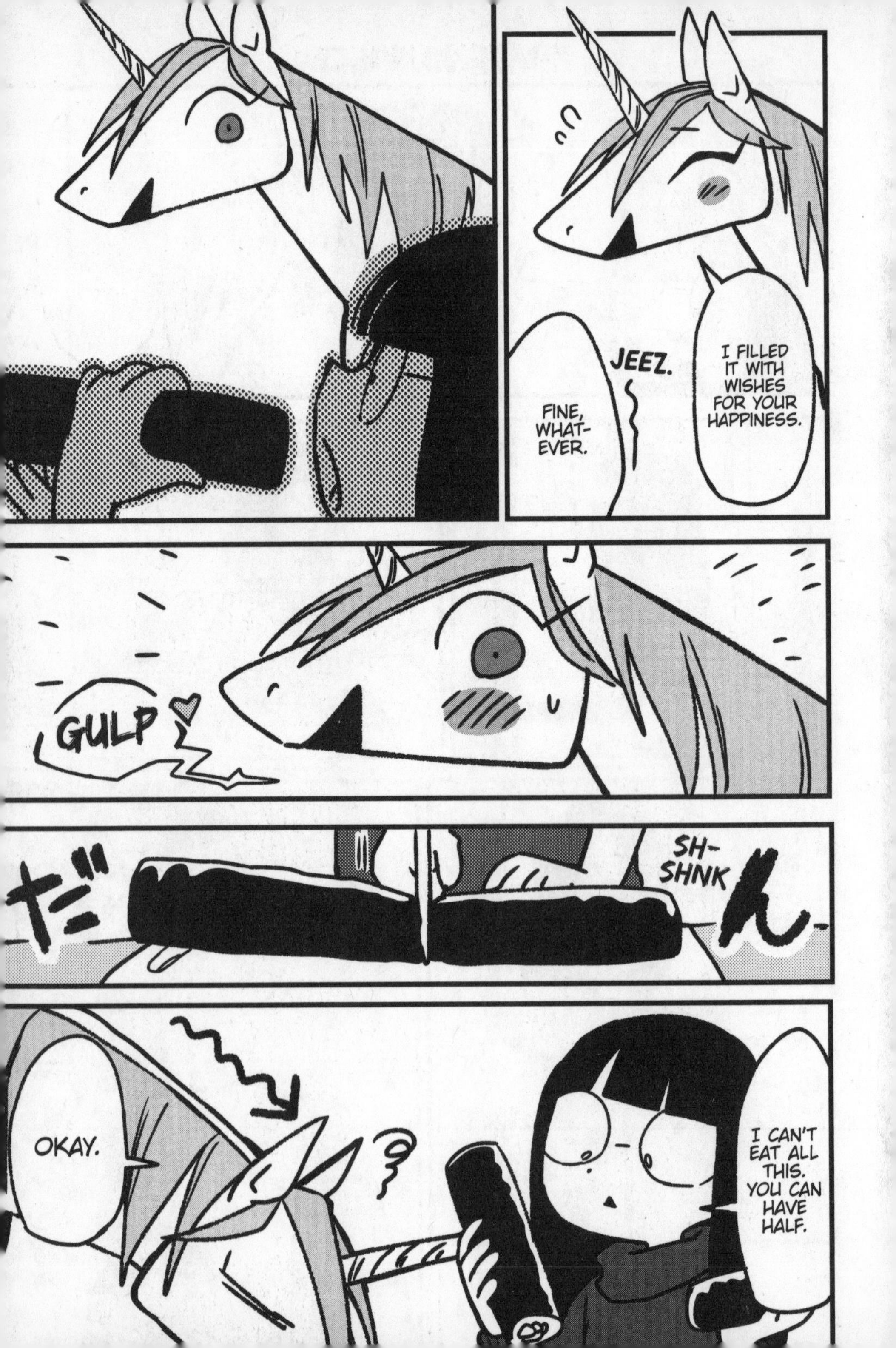
I FILLED IT WITH WISHES FOR YOUR HAPPINESS.
JEEZ.
FINE, WHATEVER.
GULP
SH-SHNK
I CAN'T EAT ALL THIS. YOU CAN HAVE HALF.
OKAY.

HARD TO SWALLOW

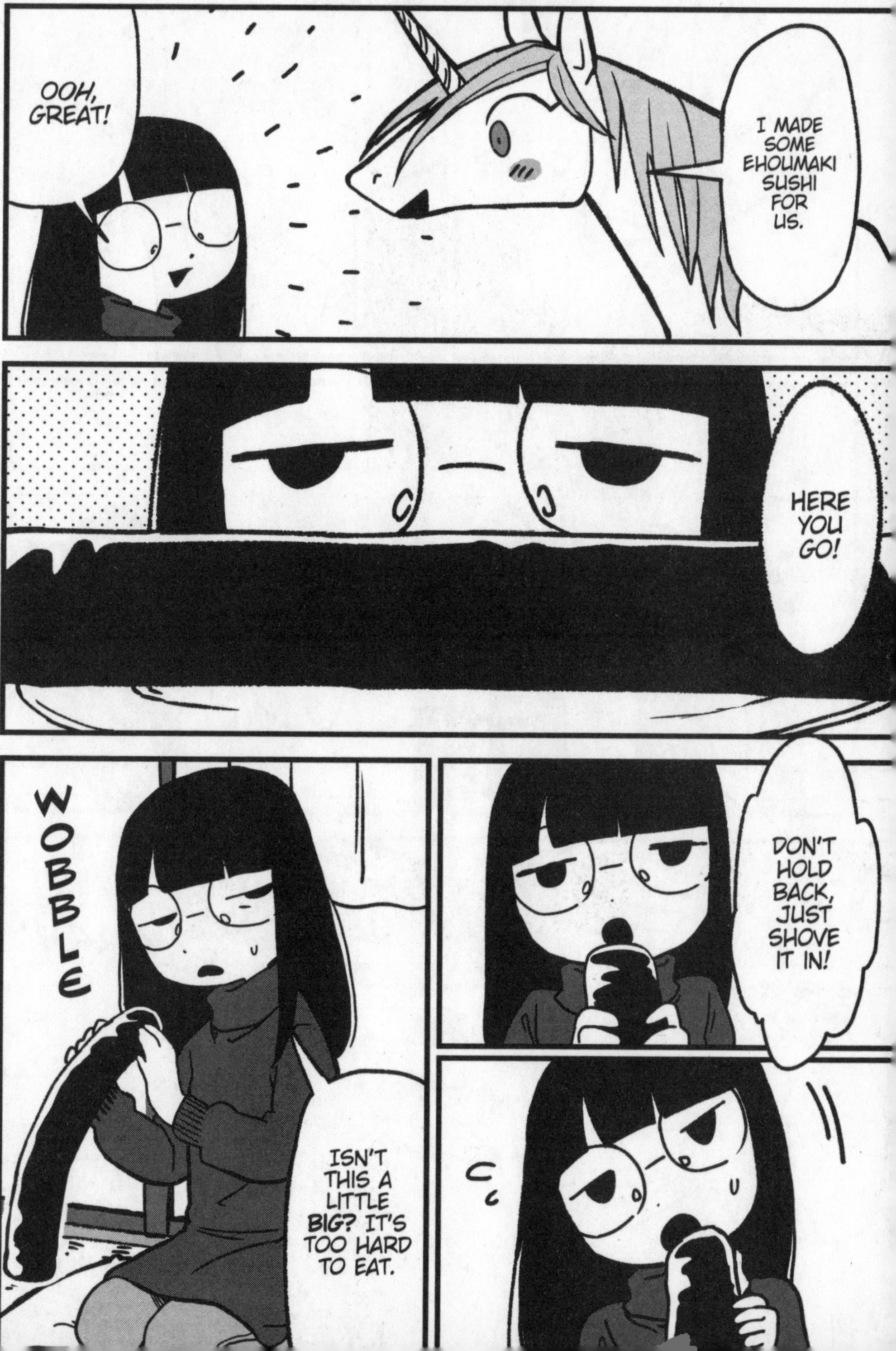
I MADE SOME EHOUMAKI SUSHI FOR US.
OOH, GREAT!
HERE YOU GO!
DON'T HOLD BACK, JUST SHOVE IT IN!
WOBBLE
ISN'T THIS A LITTLE BIG? IT'S TOO HARD TO EAT.

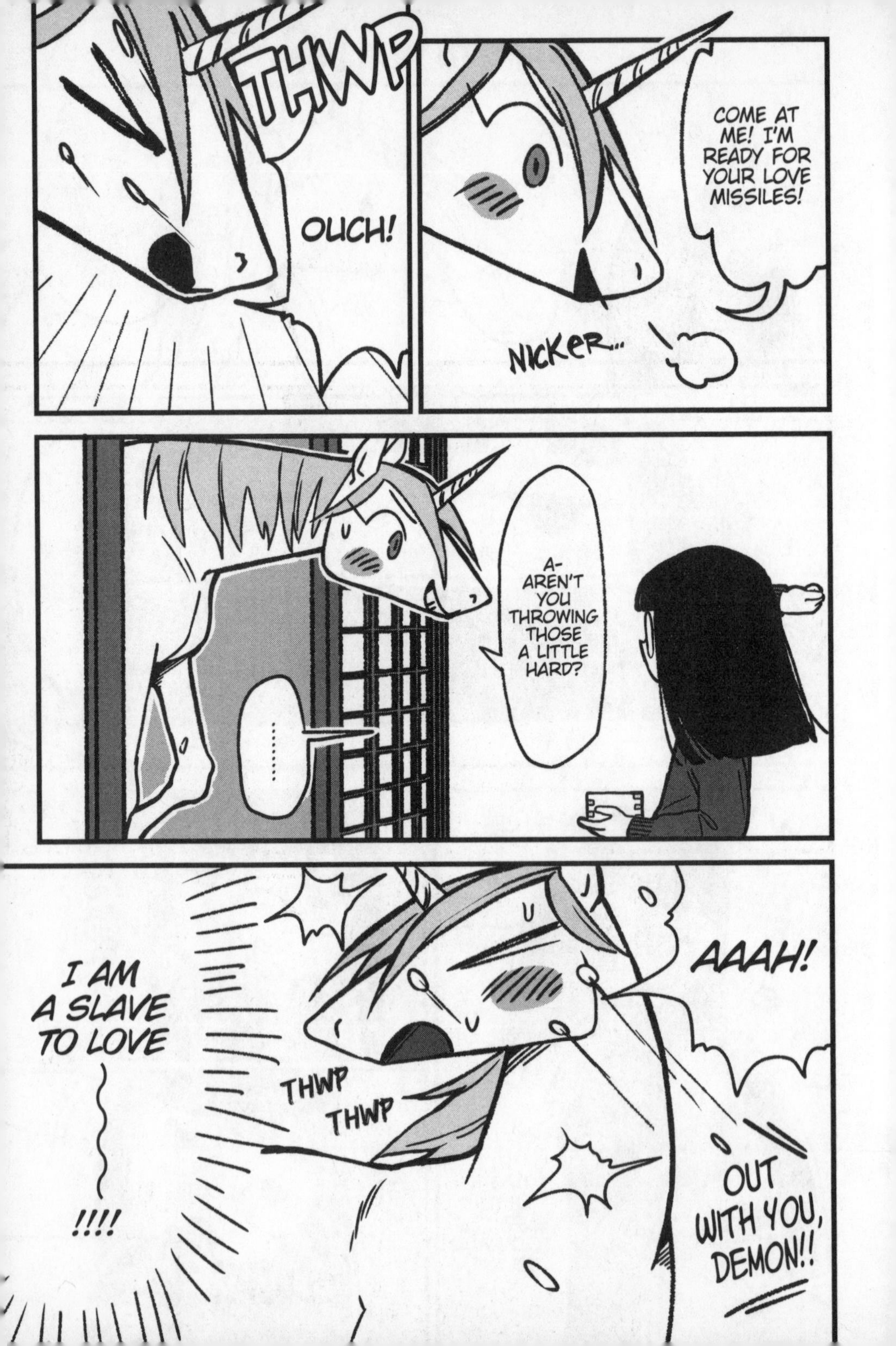
COME AT ME! I'M READY FOR YOUR LOVE MISSILES!
NICKER...
THWP
OUCH!
A- AREN'T YOU THROWING THOSE A LITTLE HARD?
......
AAAH!
OUT WITH YOU, DEMON!!
THWP THWP
I AM A SLAVE TO LOVE
!!!!

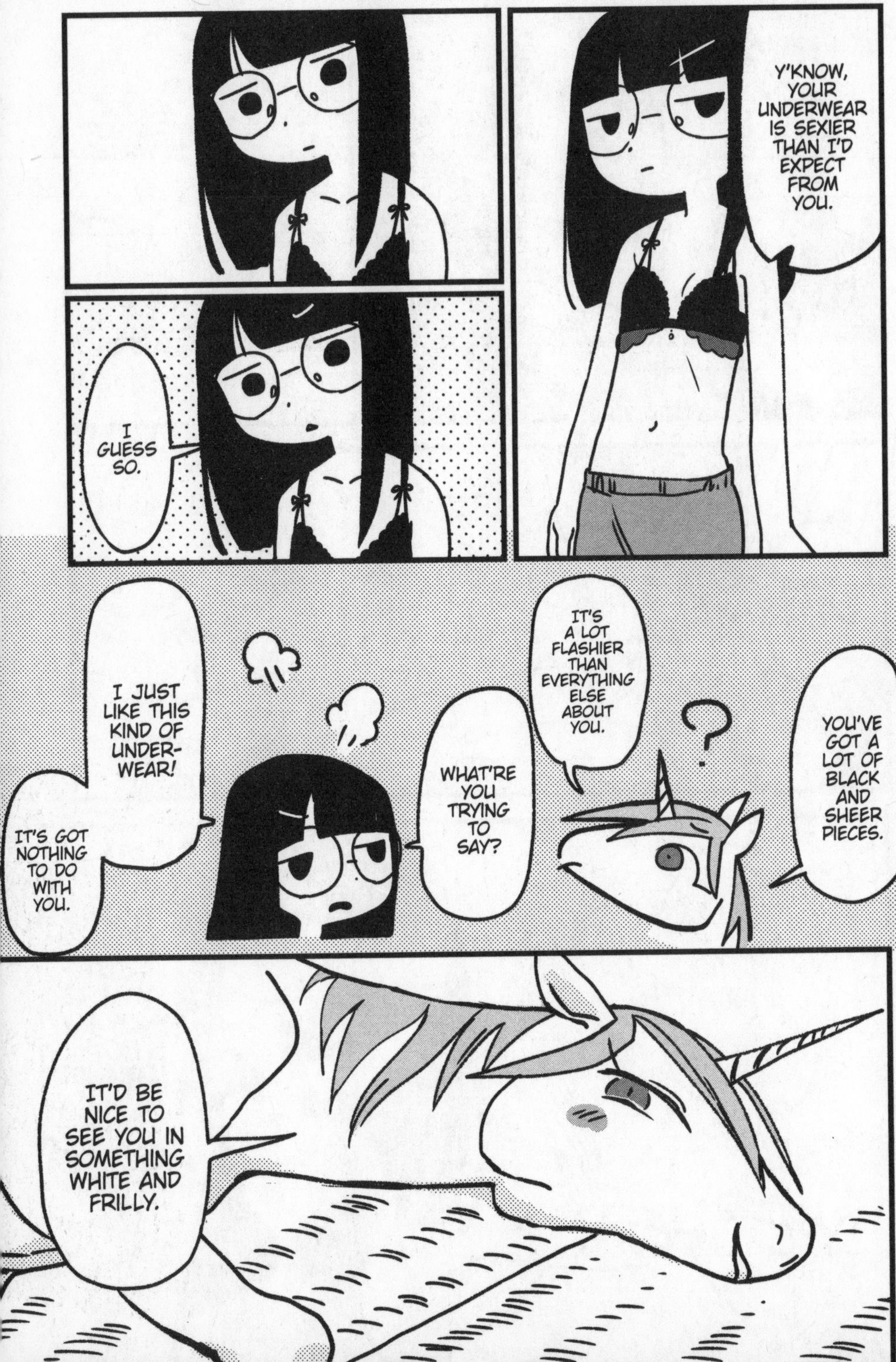
Y'KNOW, YOUR UNDERWEAR IS SEXIER THAN I'D EXPECT FROM YOU.
I GUESS SO.
YOU'VE GOT A LOT OF BLACK AND SHEER PIECES.
IT'S A LOT FLASHIER THAN EVERYTHING ELSE ABOUT YOU.
?
WHAT'RE YOU TRYING TO SAY?
I JUST LIKE THIS KIND OF UNDER-WEAR!
IT'S GOT NOTHING TO DO WITH YOU.
IT'D BE NICE TO SEE YOU IN SOMETHING WHITE AND FRILLY.

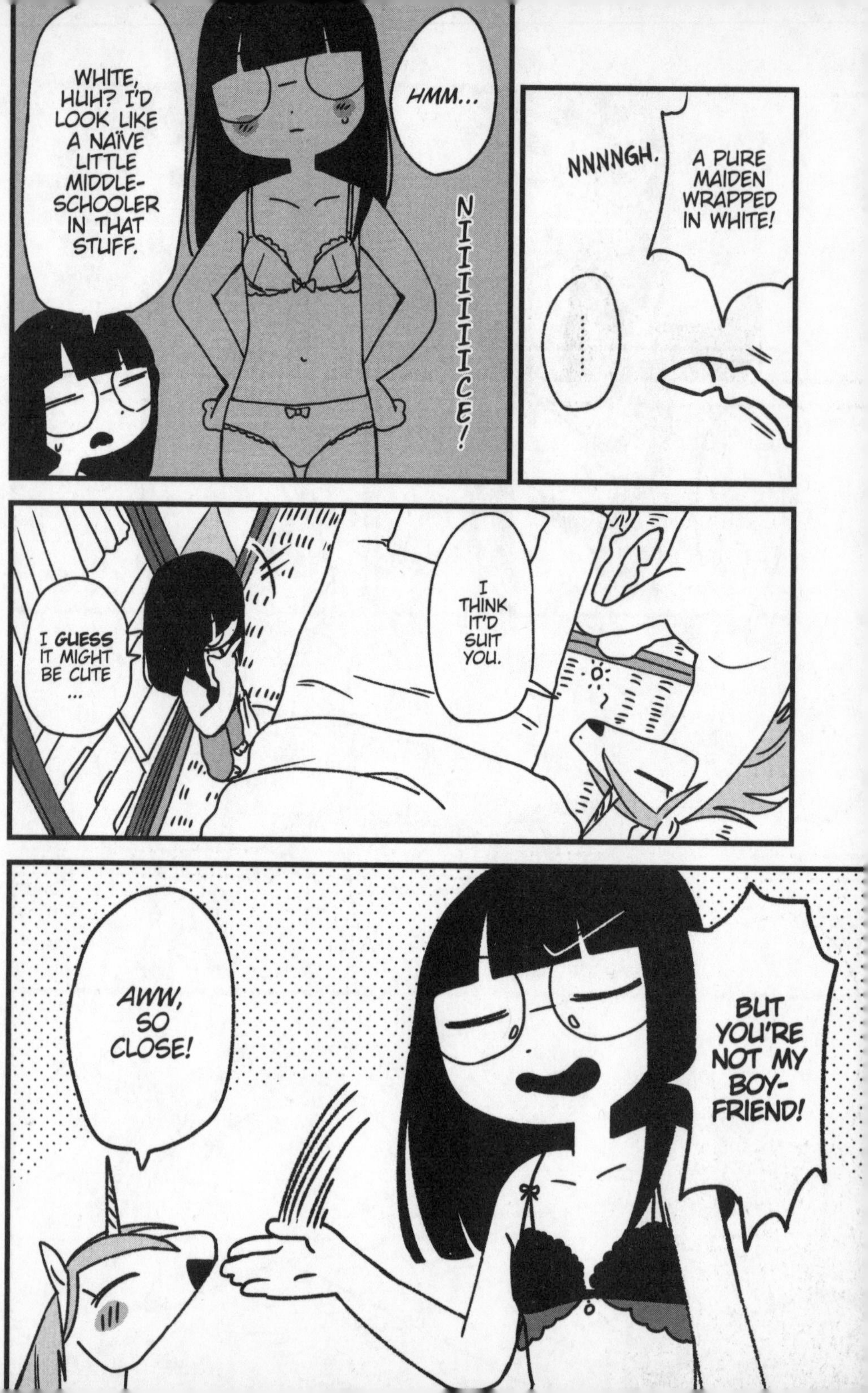
A PURE MAIDEN WRAPPED IN WHITE!
NNNNGH.
...
HMM...
NIIIIIIICE!
WHITE, HUH? I'D LOOK LIKE A NAÏVE LITTLE MIDDLE-SCHOOLER IN THAT STUFF.
I THINK IT'D SUIT YOU.
I GUESS IT MIGHT BE CUTE ...
BUT YOU'RE NOT MY BOY-FRIEND!
AWW, SO CLOSE!

SWEET TEMPTATION

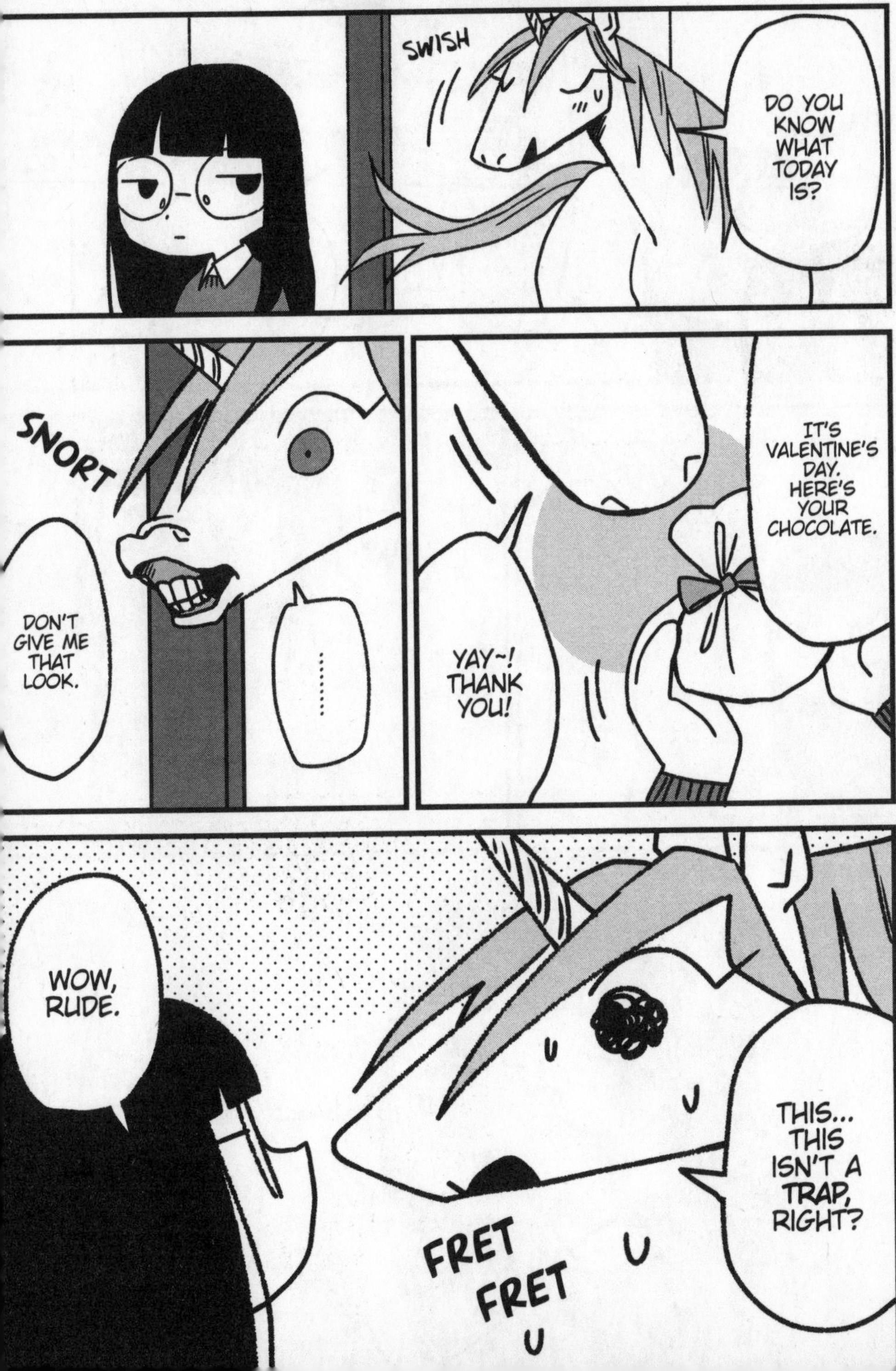
SWISH
DO YOU KNOW WHAT TODAY IS?
IT'S VALENTINE'S DAY. HERE'S YOUR CHOCOLATE.
YAY~! THANK YOU!
......
SNORT
DON'T GIVE ME THAT LOOK.
THIS... THIS ISN'T A TRAP, RIGHT?
FRET FRET
WOW, RUDE.

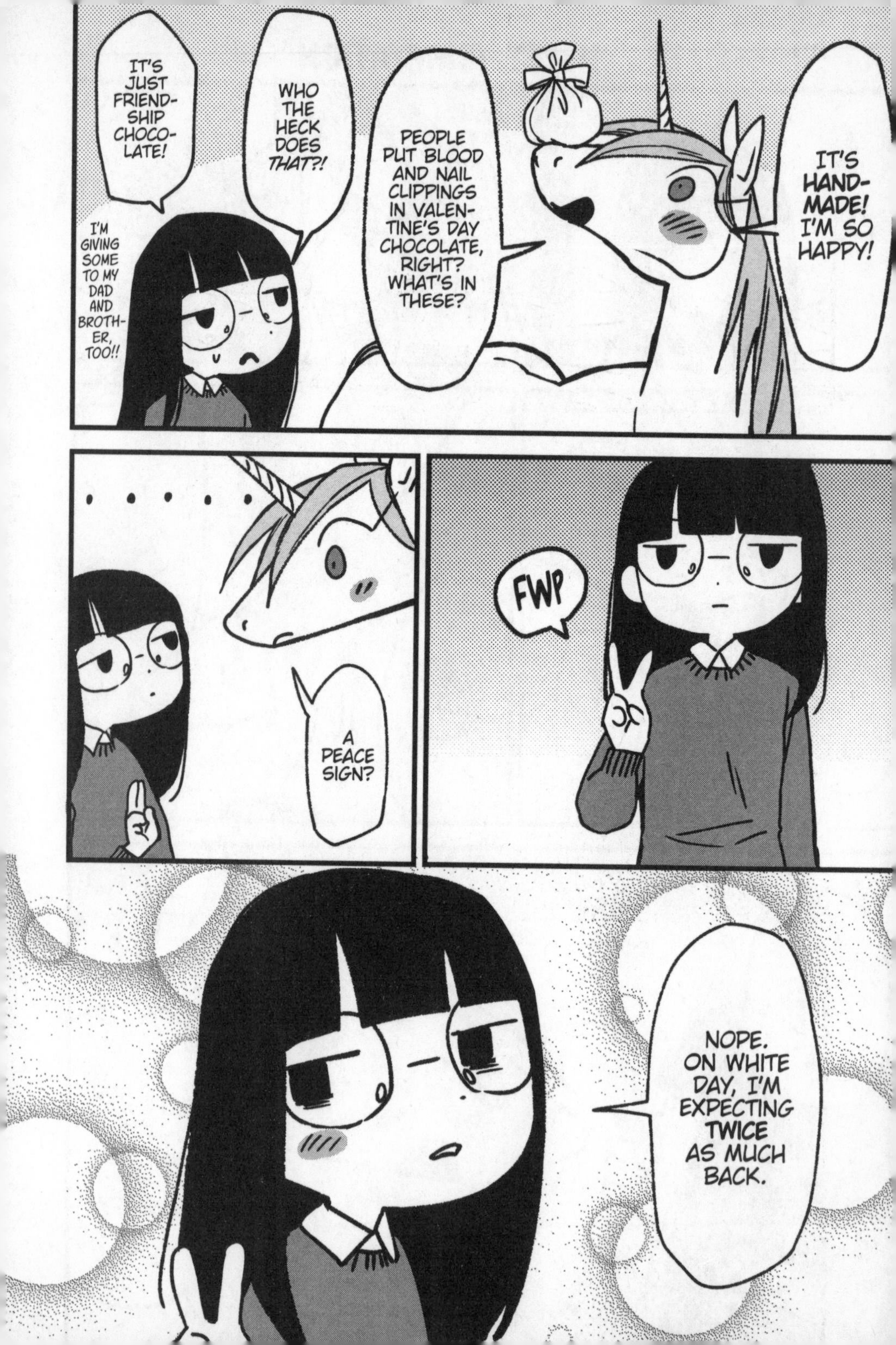
IT'S HAND-MADE! I'M SO HAPPY!
PEOPLE PUT BLOOD AND NAIL CLIPPINGS IN VALEN-TINE'S DAY CHOCOLATE, RIGHT? WHAT'S IN THESE?
WHO THE HECK DOES THAT?!
IT'S JUST FRIEND-SHIP CHOCO-LATE!
I'M GIVING SOME TO MY DAD AND BROTH-ER, TOO!!
FWP
.....
A PEACE SIGN?
NOPE. ON WHITE DAY, I'M EXPECTING TWICE AS MUCH BACK.

CHAPTER 7 FANTASY AND REALITY

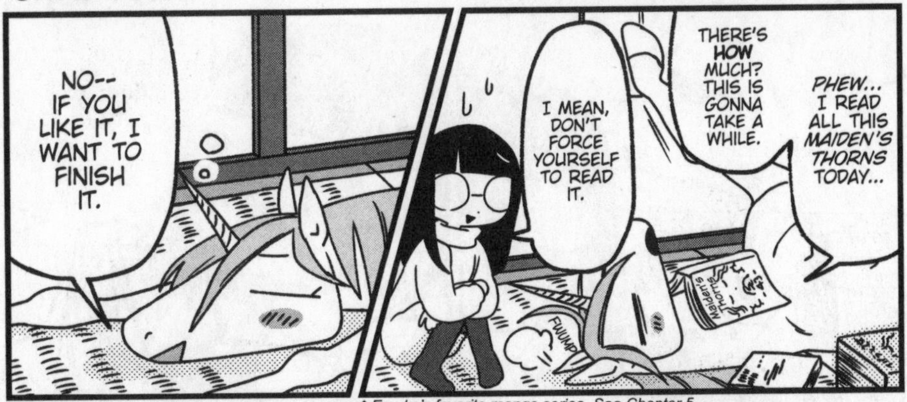
PHEW... I READ ALL THIS MAIDEN'S THORNS TODAY...
THERE'S HOW MUCH? THIS IS GONNA TAKE A WHILE.
I MEAN, DON'T FORCE YOURSELF TO READ IT.
Maiden's Thorns
FWUMP
NO-- IF YOU LIKE IT, I WANT TO FINISH IT.

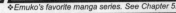

❖Emuko's favorite manga series. See Chapter 5.

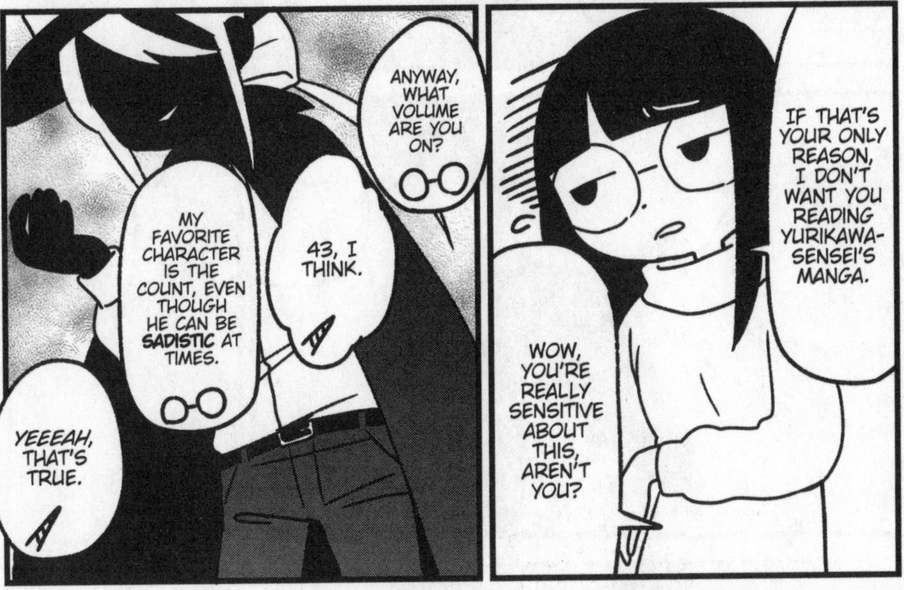
IF THAT'S YOUR ONLY REASON, I DON'T WANT YOU READING YURIKAWA-SENSEI'S MANGA.
WOW, YOU'RE REALLY SENSITIVE ABOUT THIS, AREN'T YOU?
ANYWAY, WHAT VOLUME ARE YOU ON?
43, I THINK.
MY FAVORITE CHARACTER IS THE COUNT, EVEN THOUGH HE CAN BE SADISTIC AT TIMES.
YEEEAH, THAT'S TRUE.

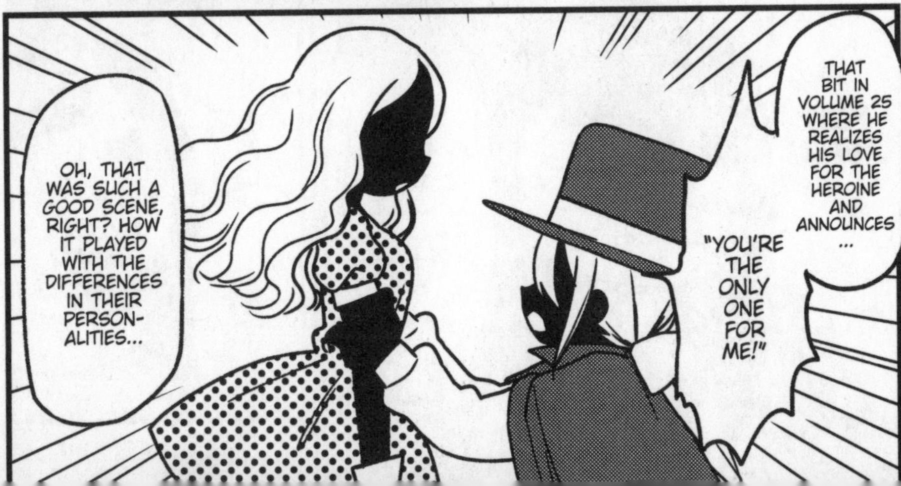
THAT BIT IN VOLUME 25 WHERE HE REALIZES HIS LOVE FOR THE HEROINE AND ANNOUNCES ...
"YOU'RE THE ONLY ONE FOR ME!"
OH, THAT WAS SUCH A GOOD SCENE, RIGHT? HOW IT PLAYED WITH THE DIFFERENCES IN THEIR PERSON-ALITIES...

HMMM...

SQUEE! ♡

I WISH SOMEONE WOULD SAY THAT TO ME, EVEN JUST ONCE.

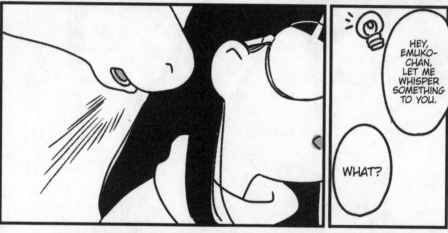

HEY, EMUKO-CHAN, LET ME WHISPER SOMETHING TO YOU.

WHAT?

YOU JERK!

IT ACTUALLY DOESN'T SOUND THAT NICE IN REAL LIFE.

EWWW.

A VISITOR

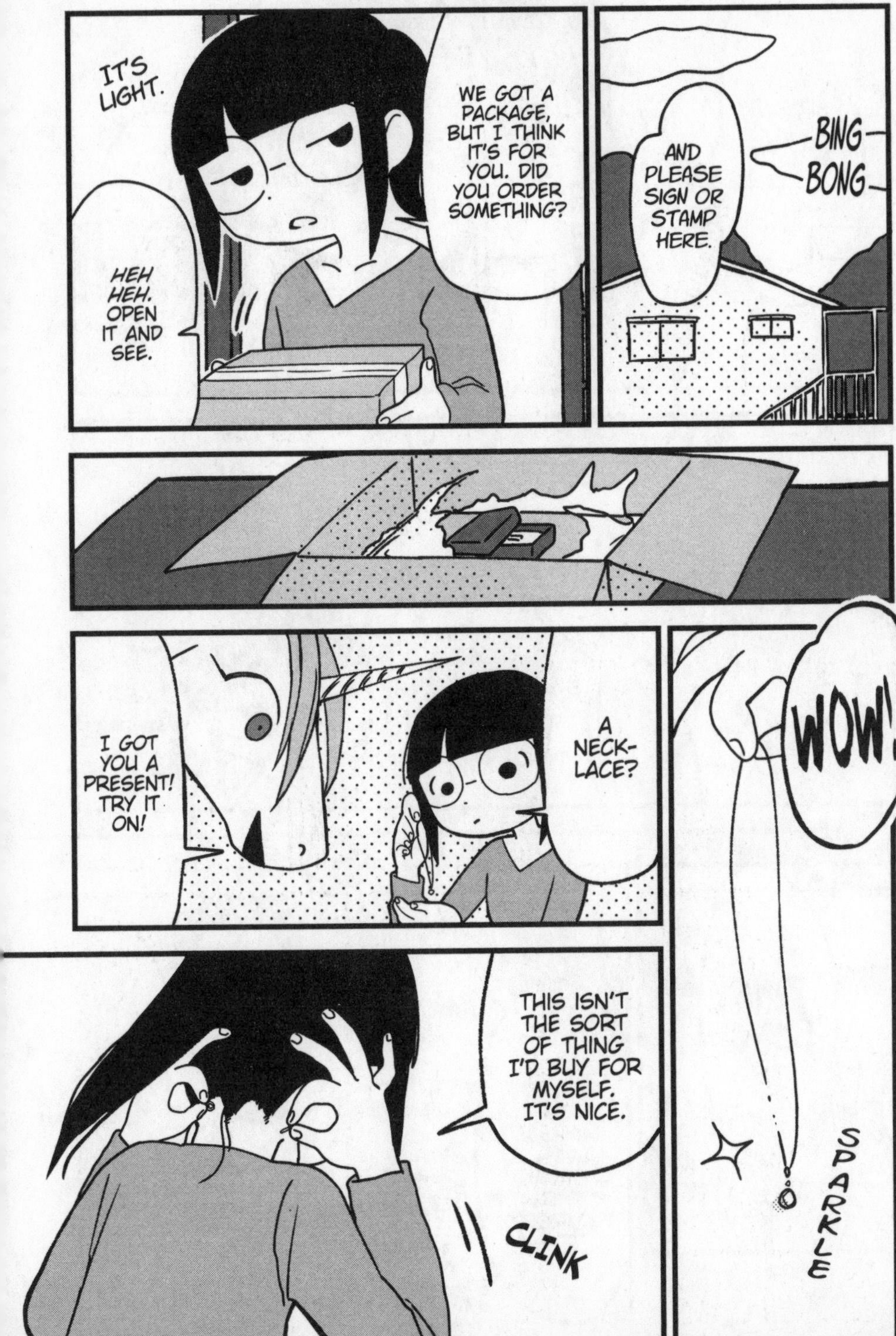
BING BONG
AND PLEASE SIGN OR STAMP HERE.
WE GOT A PACKAGE, BUT I THINK IT'S FOR YOU. DID YOU ORDER SOMETHING?
IT'S LIGHT.
HEH HEH. OPEN IT AND SEE.
WOW!
SPARKLE
A NECKLACE?
I GOT YOU A PRESENT! TRY IT ON!
THIS ISN'T THE SORT OF THING I'D BUY FOR MYSELF. IT'S NICE.
CLINK

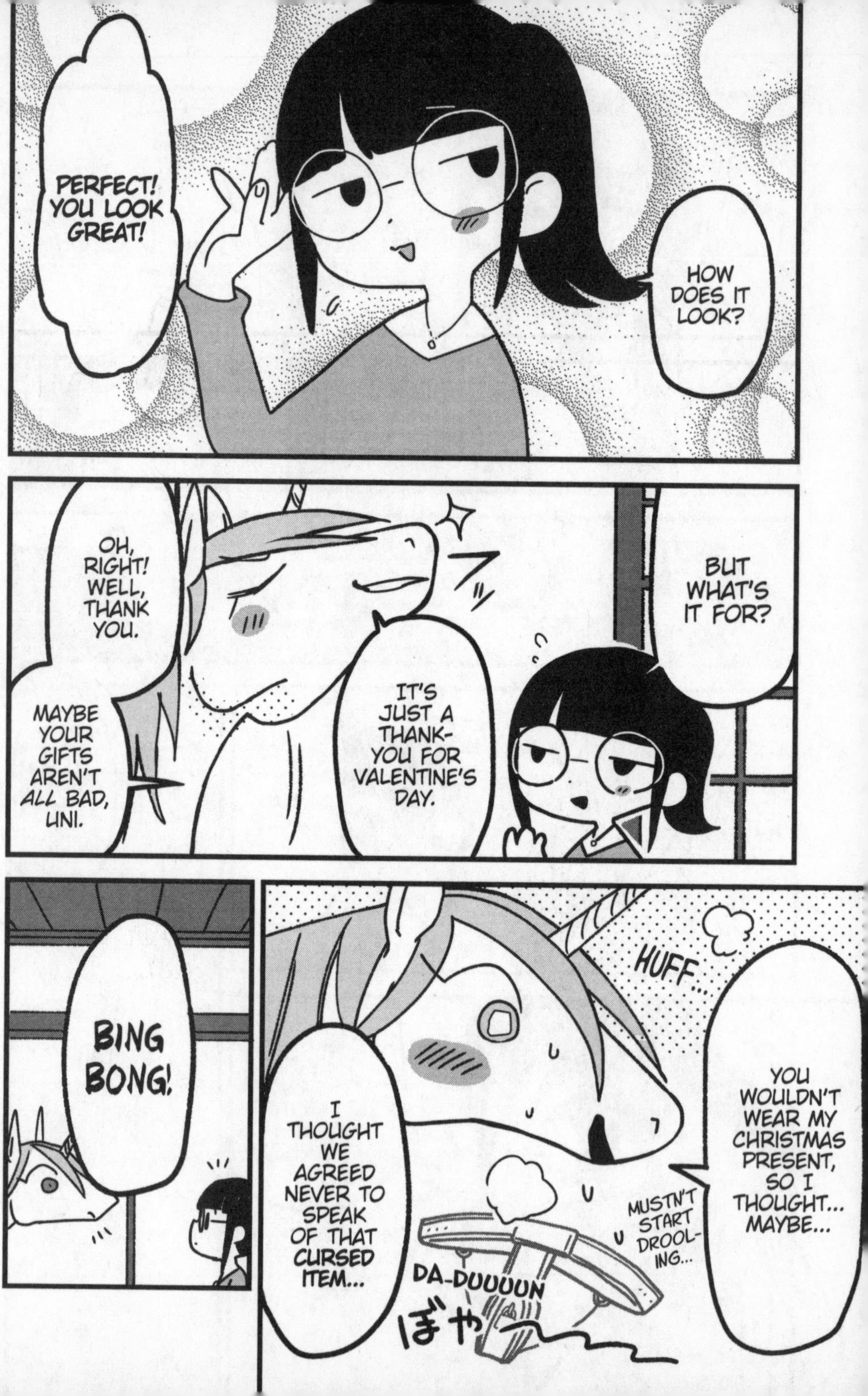
HOW DOES IT LOOK?
PERFECT! YOU LOOK GREAT!
BUT WHAT'S IT FOR?
IT'S JUST A THANK-YOU FOR VALENTINE'S DAY.
OH, RIGHT! WELL, THANK YOU.
MAYBE YOUR GIFTS AREN'T ALL BAD, UNI.
HUFF...
YOU WOULDN'T WEAR MY CHRISTMAS PRESENT, SO I THOUGHT... MAYBE...
MUSTN'T START DROOLING...
I THOUGHT WE AGREED NEVER TO SPEAK OF THAT CURSED ITEM...
DA-DUUUUN
ぼやー
BING BONG!

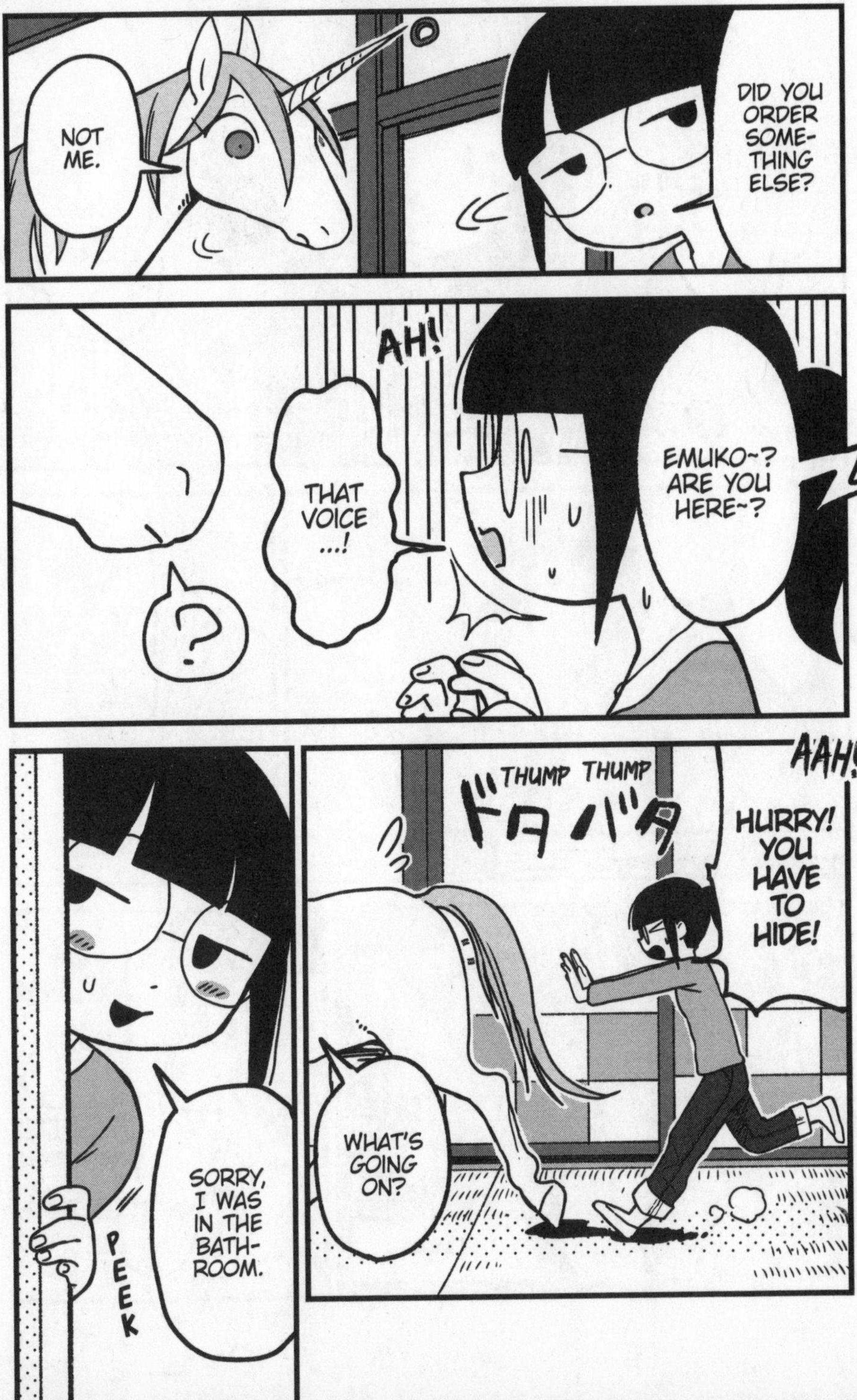
DID YOU ORDER SOME-THING ELSE?
NOT ME.
EMUKO~? ARE YOU HERE~?
AH!
THAT VOICE ...!
?
AAH!
HURRY! YOU HAVE TO HIDE!
THUMP THUMP
ドタバタ
WHAT'S GOING ON?
SORRY, I WAS IN THE BATH-ROOM.
PEEK

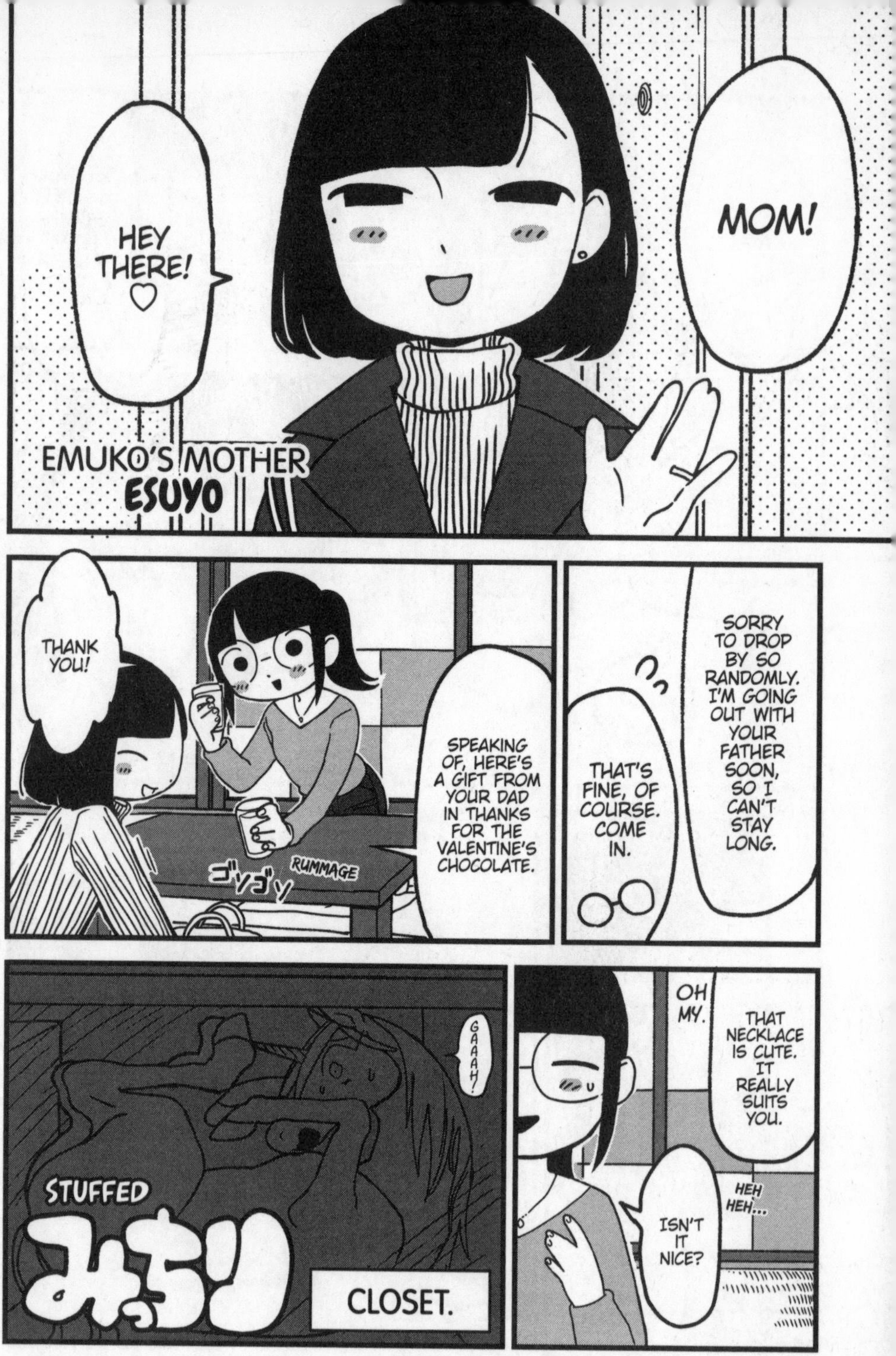
MOM!
HEY THERE! ♡
EMUKO'S MOTHER
ESUYO
SORRY TO DROP BY SO RANDOMLY. I'M GOING OUT WITH YOUR FATHER SOON, SO I CAN'T STAY LONG.
THAT'S FINE, OF COURSE. COME IN.
SPEAKING OF, HERE'S A GIFT FROM YOUR DAD IN THANKS FOR THE VALENTINE'S CHOCOLATE.
ゴソゴソ
RUMMAGE
THANK YOU!
OH MY.
THAT NECKLACE IS CUTE. IT REALLY SUITS YOU.
HEH HEH...
ISN'T IT NICE?
GAAAH!
STUFFED
みっちり
CLOSET.

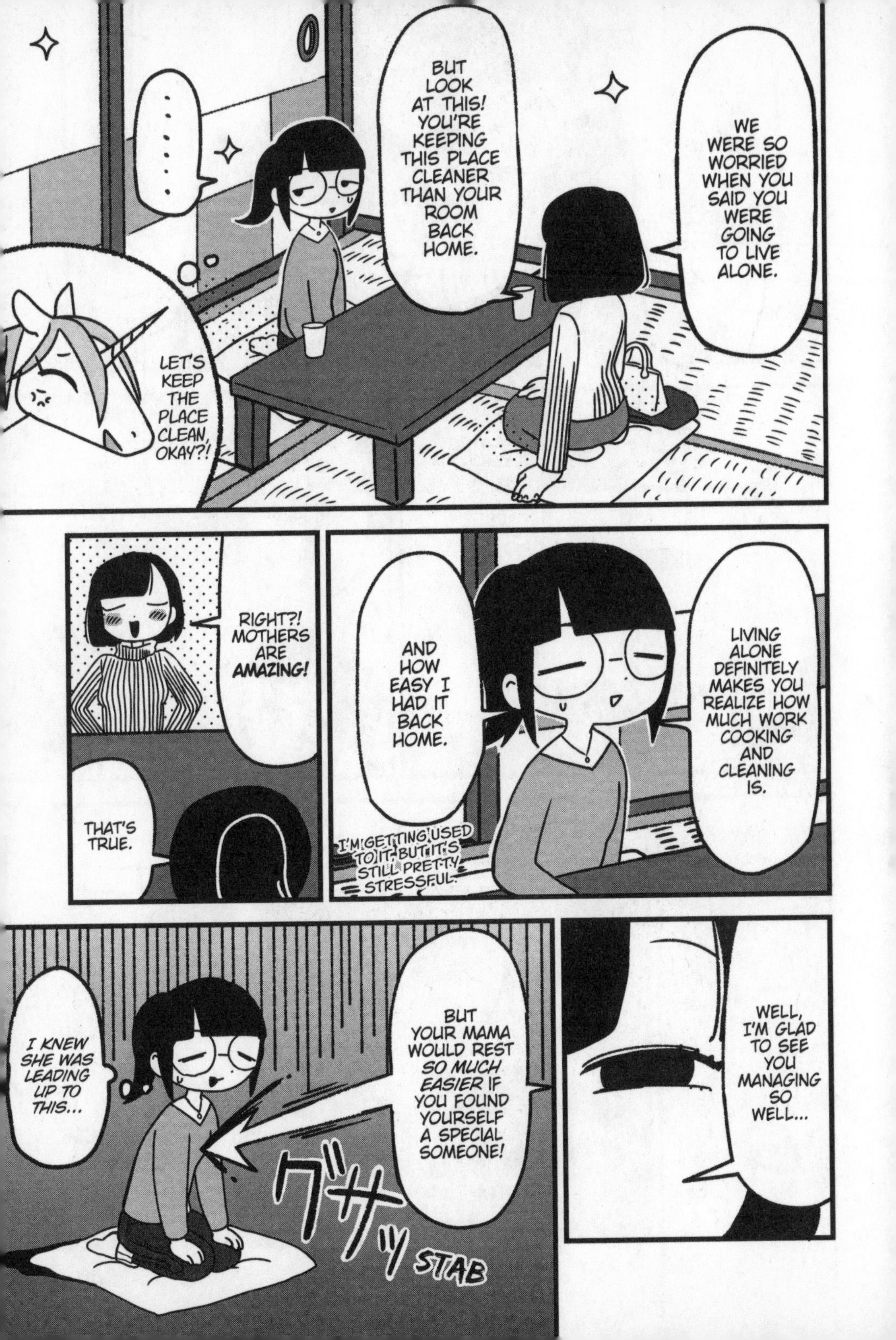
WE WERE SO WORRIED WHEN YOU SAID YOU WERE GOING TO LIVE ALONE.
BUT LOOK AT THIS! YOU'RE KEEPING THIS PLACE CLEANER THAN YOUR ROOM BACK HOME.
......
LET'S KEEP THE PLACE CLEAN, OKAY?!
LIVING ALONE DEFINITELY MAKES YOU REALIZE HOW MUCH WORK COOKING AND CLEANING IS.
AND HOW EASY I HAD IT BACK HOME.
I'M GETTING USED TO IT, BUT IT'S STILL PRETTY STRESSFUL.
RIGHT?! MOTHERS ARE **AMAZING!**
THAT'S TRUE.
WELL, I'M GLAD TO SEE YOU MANAGING SO WELL...
BUT YOUR MAMA WOULD REST *SO MUCH EASIER* IF YOU FOUND YOURSELF A SPECIAL SOMEONE!
I KNEW SHE WAS LEADING UP TO THIS...
グサッ
STAB

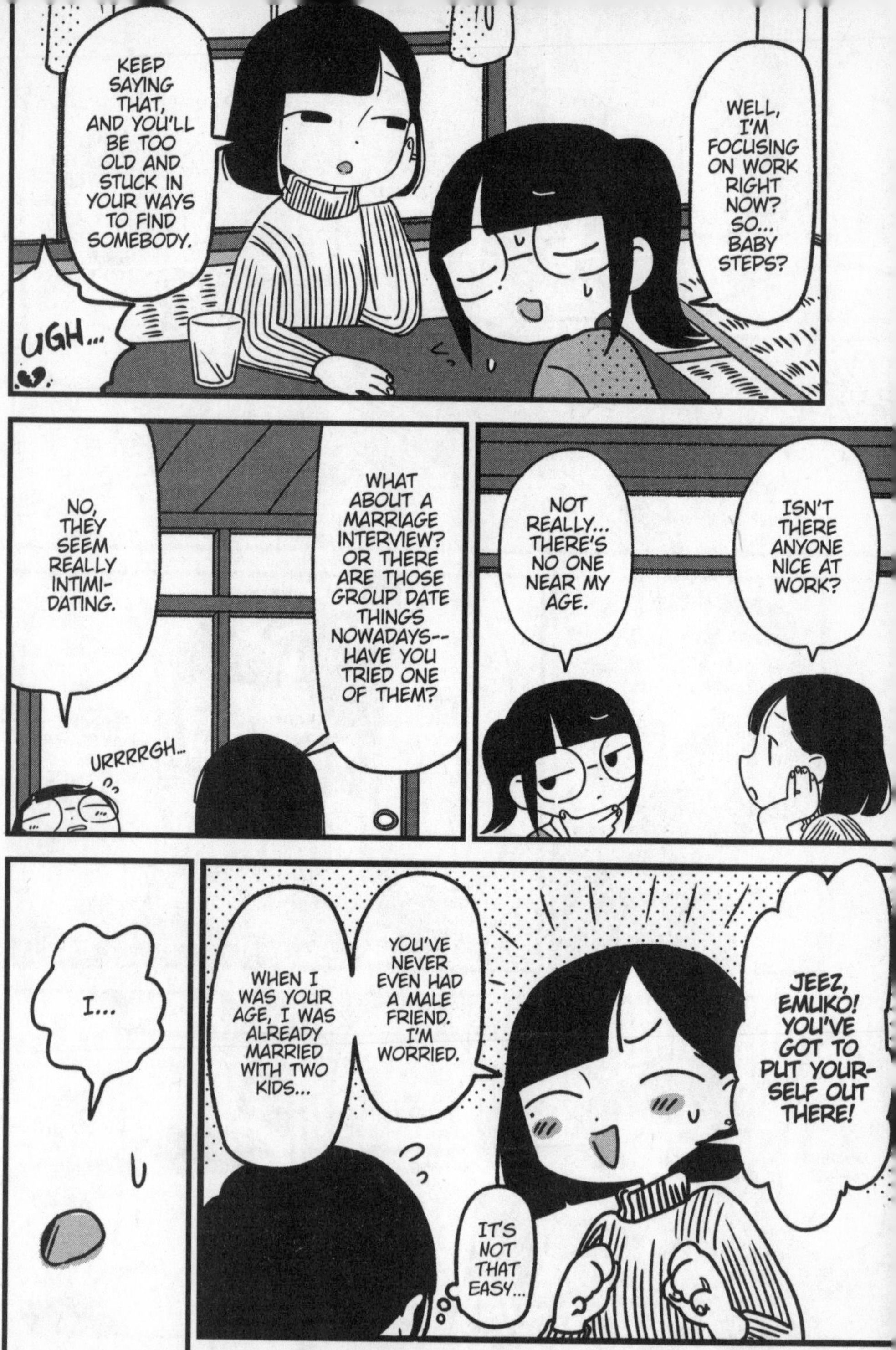
WELL, I'M FOCUSING ON WORK RIGHT NOW? SO... BABY STEPS?
KEEP SAYING THAT, AND YOU'LL BE TOO OLD AND STUCK IN YOUR WAYS TO FIND SOMEBODY.
UGH...
ISN'T THERE ANYONE NICE AT WORK?
NOT REALLY... THERE'S NO ONE NEAR MY AGE.
WHAT ABOUT A MARRIAGE INTERVIEW? OR THERE ARE THOSE GROUP DATE THINGS NOWADAYS--HAVE YOU TRIED ONE OF THEM?
NO, THEY SEEM REALLY INTIMI-DATING.
URRRRGH...
JEEZ, EMUKO! YOU'VE GOT TO PUT YOUR-SELF OUT THERE!
YOU'VE NEVER EVEN HAD A MALE FRIEND. I'M WORRIED.
WHEN I WAS YOUR AGE, I WAS ALREADY MARRIED WITH TWO KIDS...
IT'S NOT THAT EASY...
I...

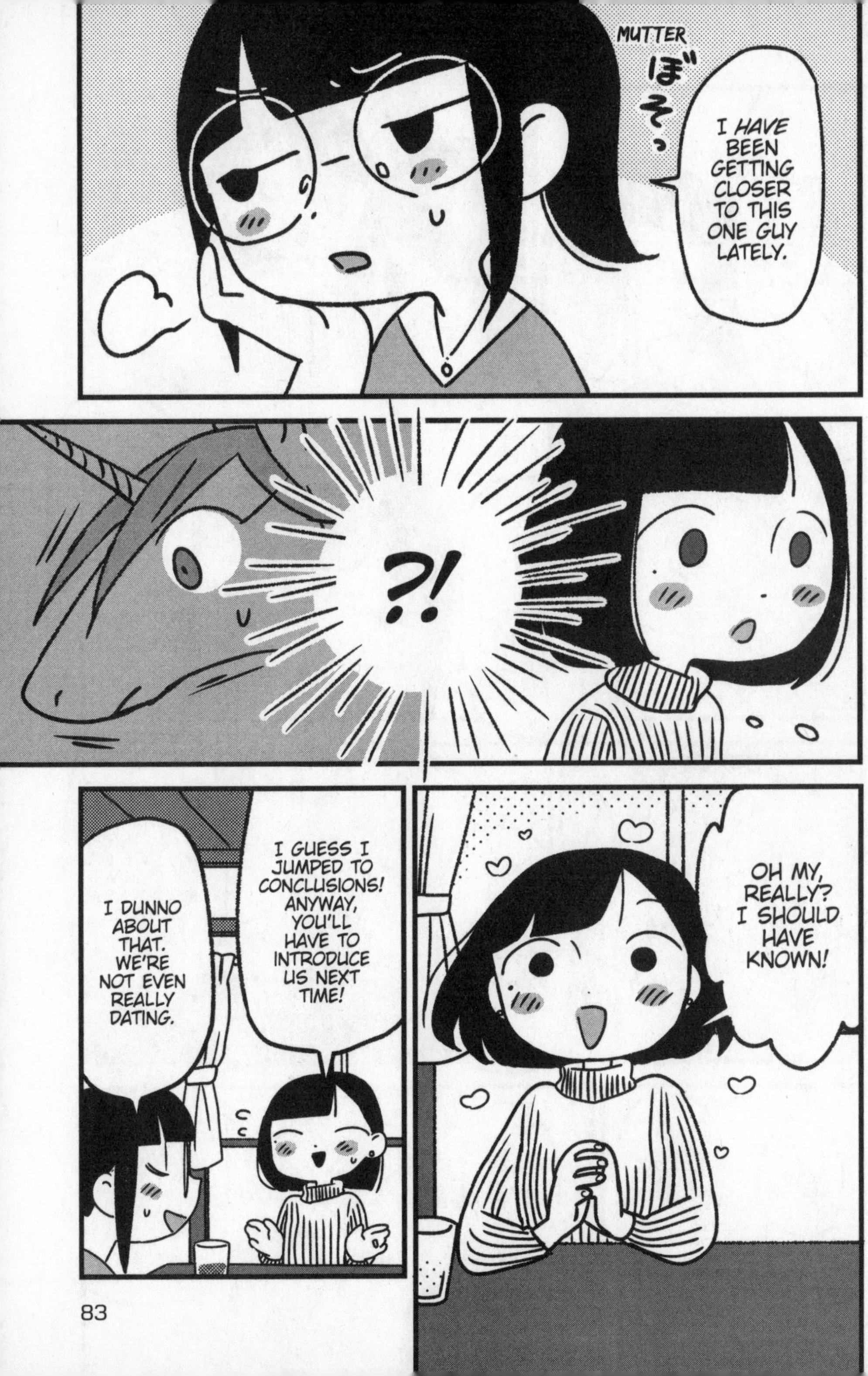
MUTTER
ぼそっ
I HAVE BEEN GETTING CLOSER TO THIS ONE GUY LATELY.
?!
OH MY, REALLY? I SHOULD HAVE KNOWN!
I GUESS I JUMPED TO CONCLUSIONS! ANYWAY, YOU'LL HAVE TO INTRODUCE US NEXT TIME!
I DUNNO ABOUT THAT. WE'RE NOT EVEN REALLY DATING.

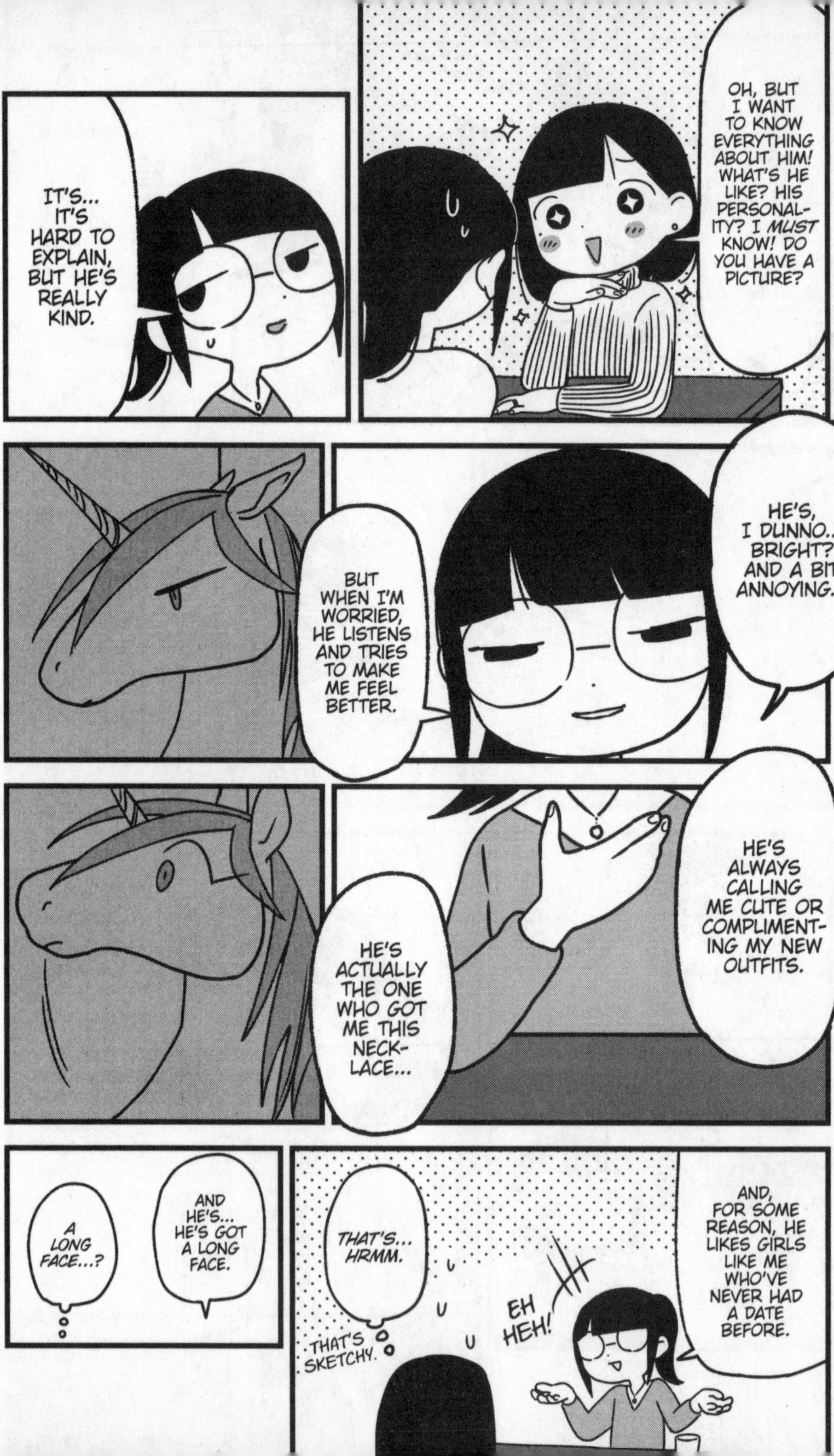
OH, BUT I WANT TO KNOW EVERYTHING ABOUT HIM! WHAT'S HE LIKE? HIS PERSONALITY? I *MUST* KNOW! DO YOU HAVE A PICTURE?
IT'S... IT'S HARD TO EXPLAIN, BUT HE'S REALLY KIND.
HE'S, I DUNNO... BRIGHT? AND A BIT ANNOYING...
BUT WHEN I'M WORRIED, HE LISTENS AND TRIES TO MAKE ME FEEL BETTER.
HE'S ALWAYS CALLING ME CUTE OR COMPLIMENTING MY NEW OUTFITS.
HE'S ACTUALLY THE ONE WHO GOT ME THIS NECKLACE...
AND, FOR SOME REASON, HE LIKES GIRLS LIKE ME WHO'VE NEVER HAD A DATE BEFORE.
EH HEH!
THAT'S... HRMM.
THAT'S SKETCHY.
AND HE'S... HE'S GOT A LONG FACE.
A LONG FACE...?

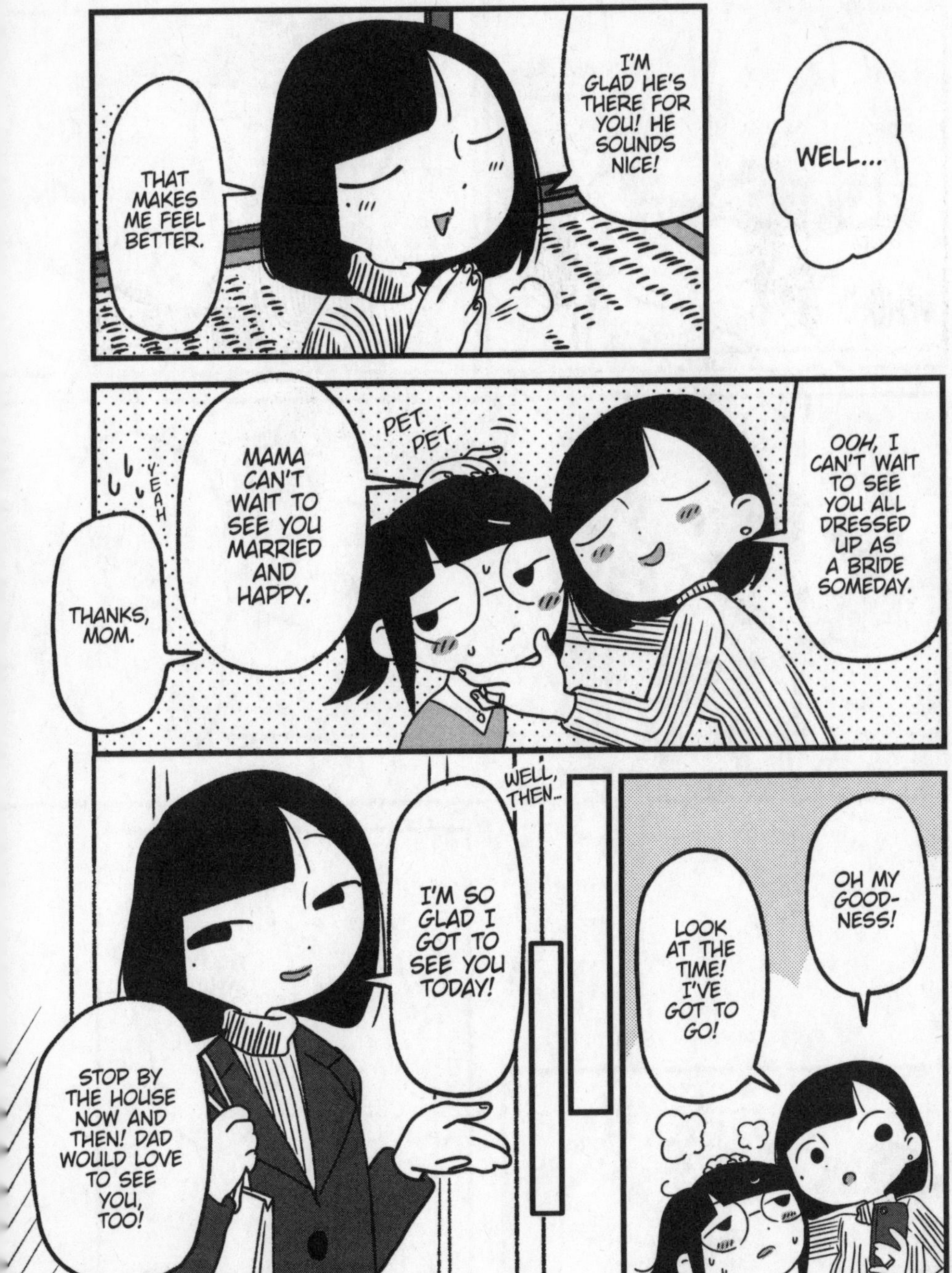
WELL...
I'M GLAD HE'S THERE FOR YOU! HE SOUNDS NICE!
THAT MAKES ME FEEL BETTER.
OOH, I CAN'T WAIT TO SEE YOU ALL DRESSED UP AS A BRIDE SOMEDAY.
PET PET
MAMA CAN'T WAIT TO SEE YOU MARRIED AND HAPPY.
YEAH
THANKS, MOM.
OH MY GOODNESS!
LOOK AT THE TIME! I'VE GOT TO GO!
WELL, THEN...
I'M SO GLAD I GOT TO SEE YOU TODAY!
STOP BY THE HOUSE NOW AND THEN! DAD WOULD LOVE TO SEE YOU, TOO!

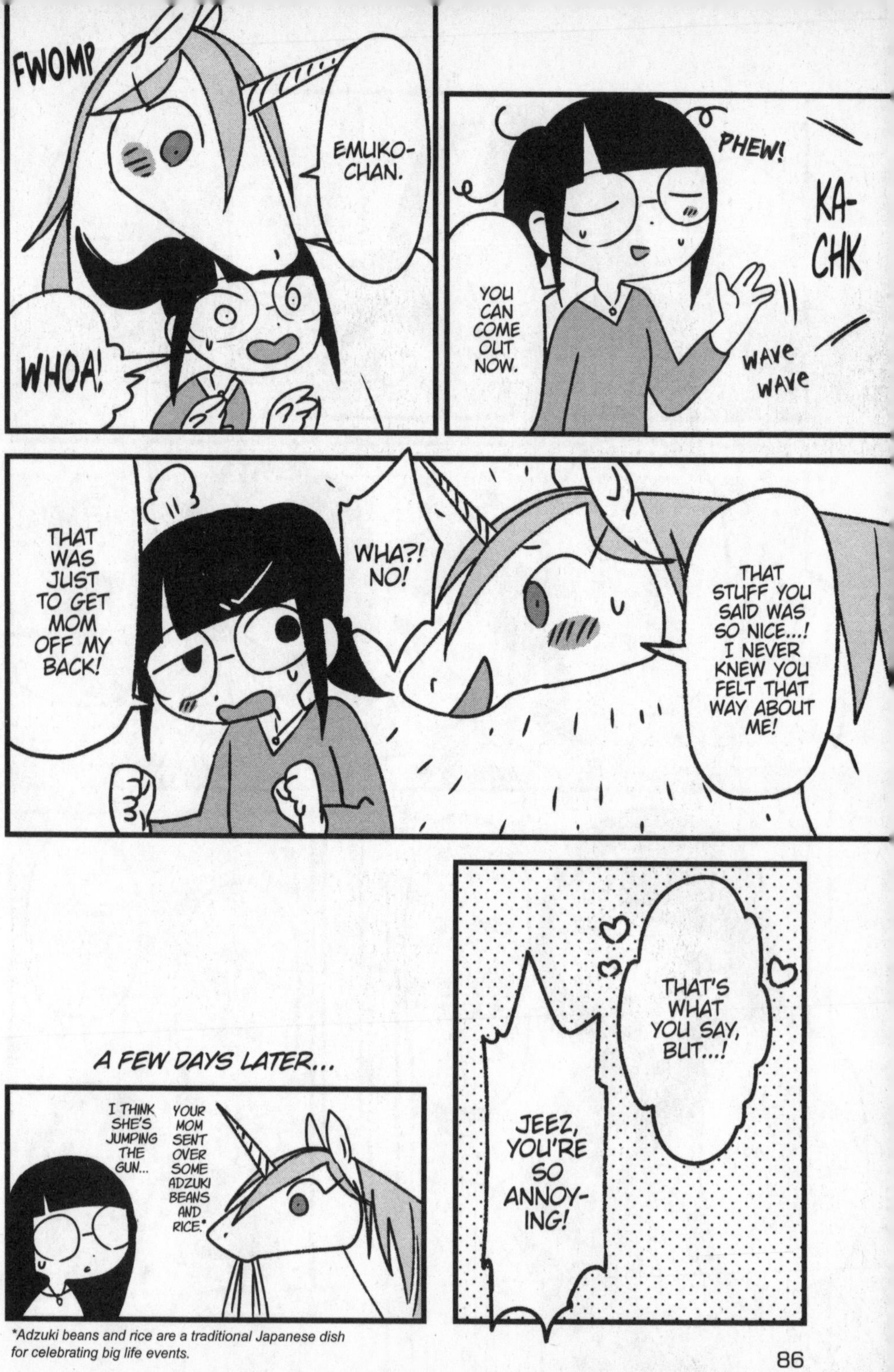
PHEW!
KA-CHK
YOU CAN COME OUT NOW.
wave wave
FWOMP
EMUKO-CHAN.
WHOA!
THAT STUFF YOU SAID WAS SO NICE...! I NEVER KNEW YOU FELT THAT WAY ABOUT ME!
WHA?! NO!
THAT WAS JUST TO GET MOM OFF MY BACK!
THAT'S WHAT YOU SAY, BUT...!
JEEZ, YOU'RE SO ANNOY-ING!
A FEW DAYS LATER...
YOUR MOM SENT OVER SOME ADZUKI BEANS AND RICE.*
I THINK SHE'S JUMPING THE GUN...

*Adzuki beans and rice are a traditional Japanese dish for celebrating big life events.

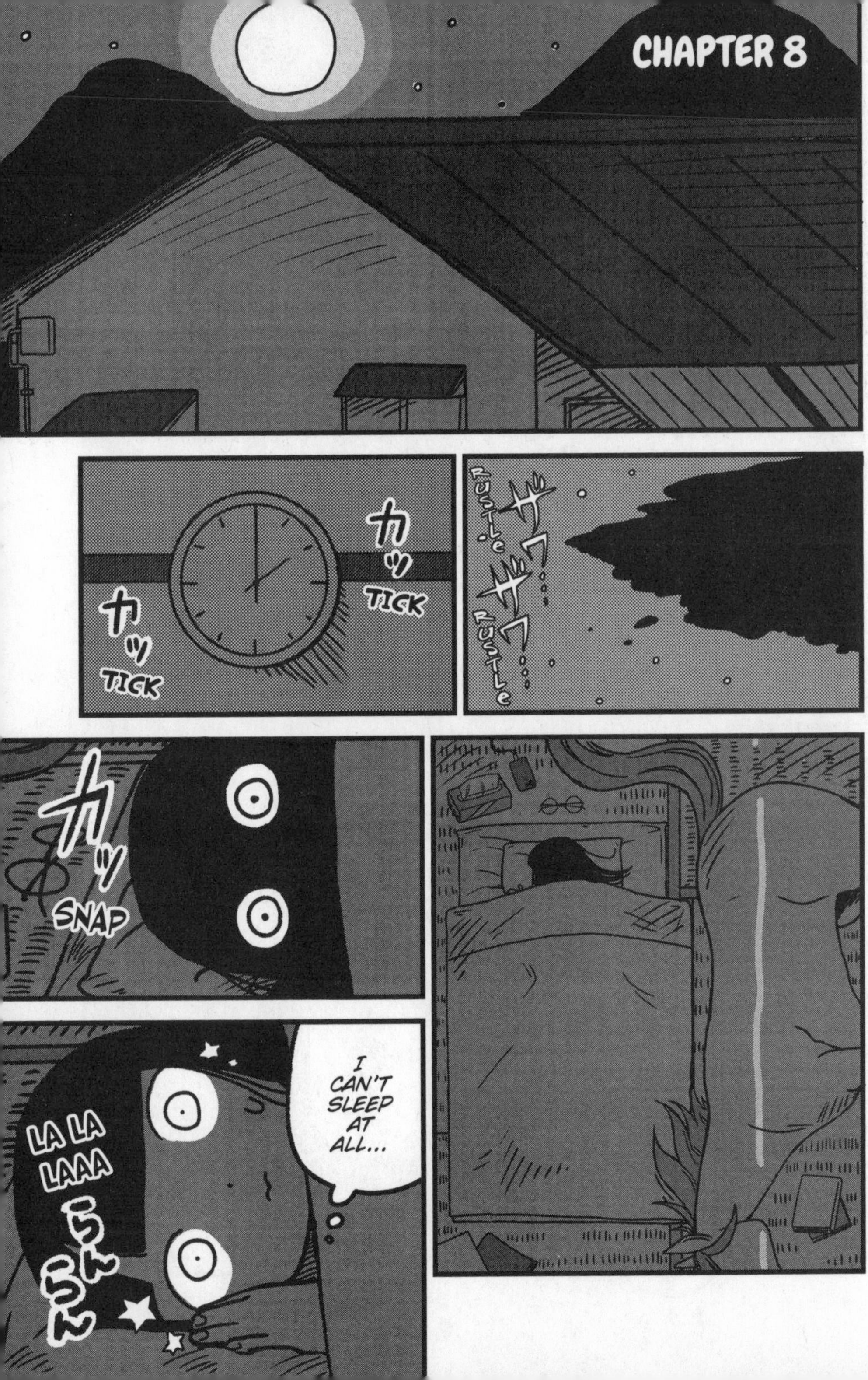
CHAPTER 8
ザワ… ザワ…
RUSTLE RUSTLE
カッ
TICK
カッ
TICK
カッ
SNAP
I CAN'T SLEEP AT ALL…
LA LA LAAA
らん らん

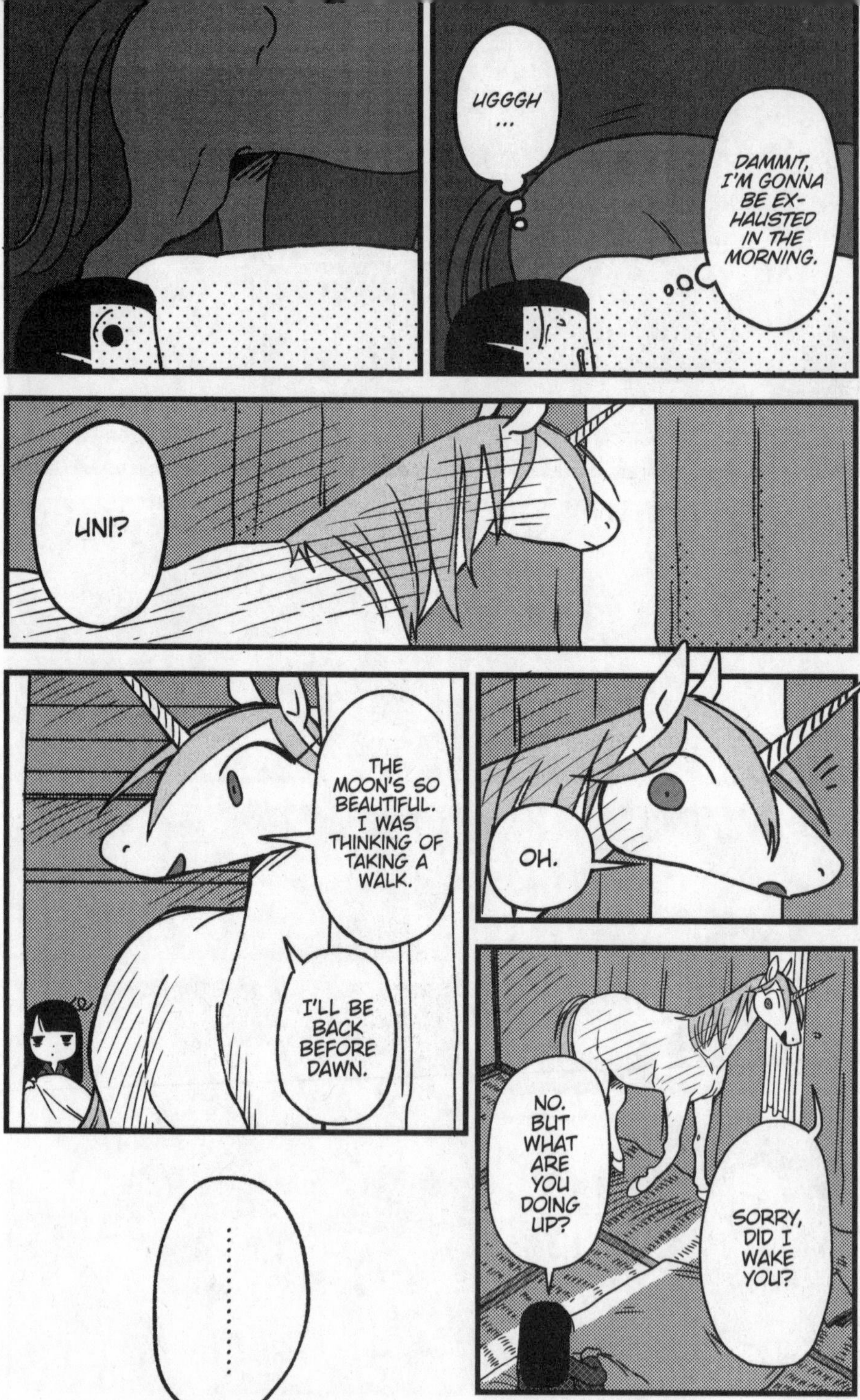
UGGGH ...
DAMMIT, I'M GONNA BE EX-HAUSTED IN THE MORNING.
UNI?
OH.
SORRY, DID I WAKE YOU?
NO. BUT WHAT ARE YOU DOING UP?
THE MOON'S SO BEAUTIFUL. I WAS THINKING OF TAKING A WALK.
I'LL BE BACK BEFORE DAWN.
......

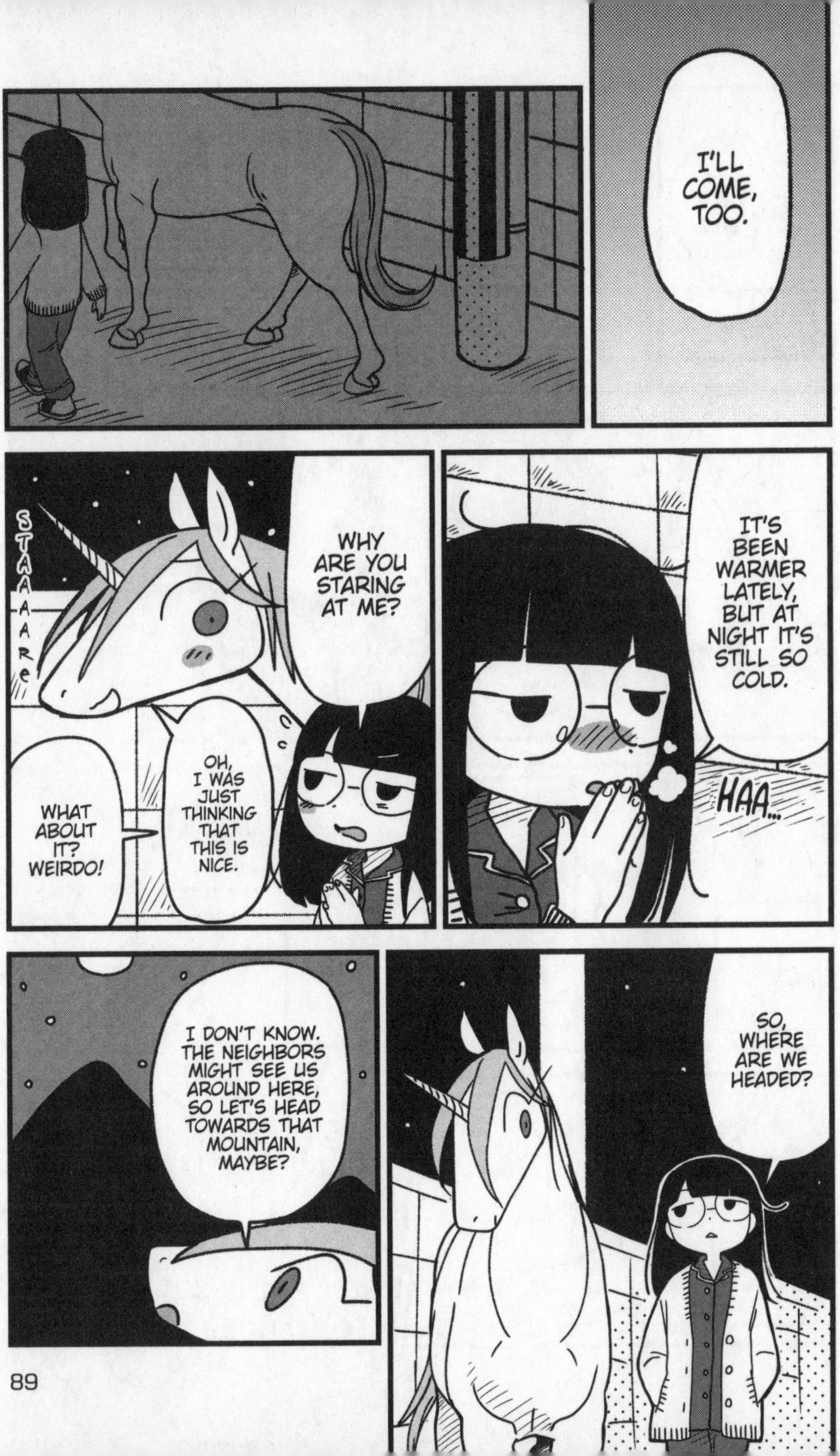

I'LL COME, TOO.
IT'S BEEN WARMER LATELY, BUT AT NIGHT IT'S STILL SO COLD.
HAA...
WHY ARE YOU STARING AT ME?
STAAAAARE
OH, I WAS JUST THINKING THAT THIS IS NICE.
WHAT ABOUT IT? WEIRDO!
SO, WHERE ARE WE HEADED?
I DON'T KNOW. THE NEIGHBORS MIGHT SEE US AROUND HERE, SO LET'S HEAD TOWARDS THAT MOUNTAIN, MAYBE?

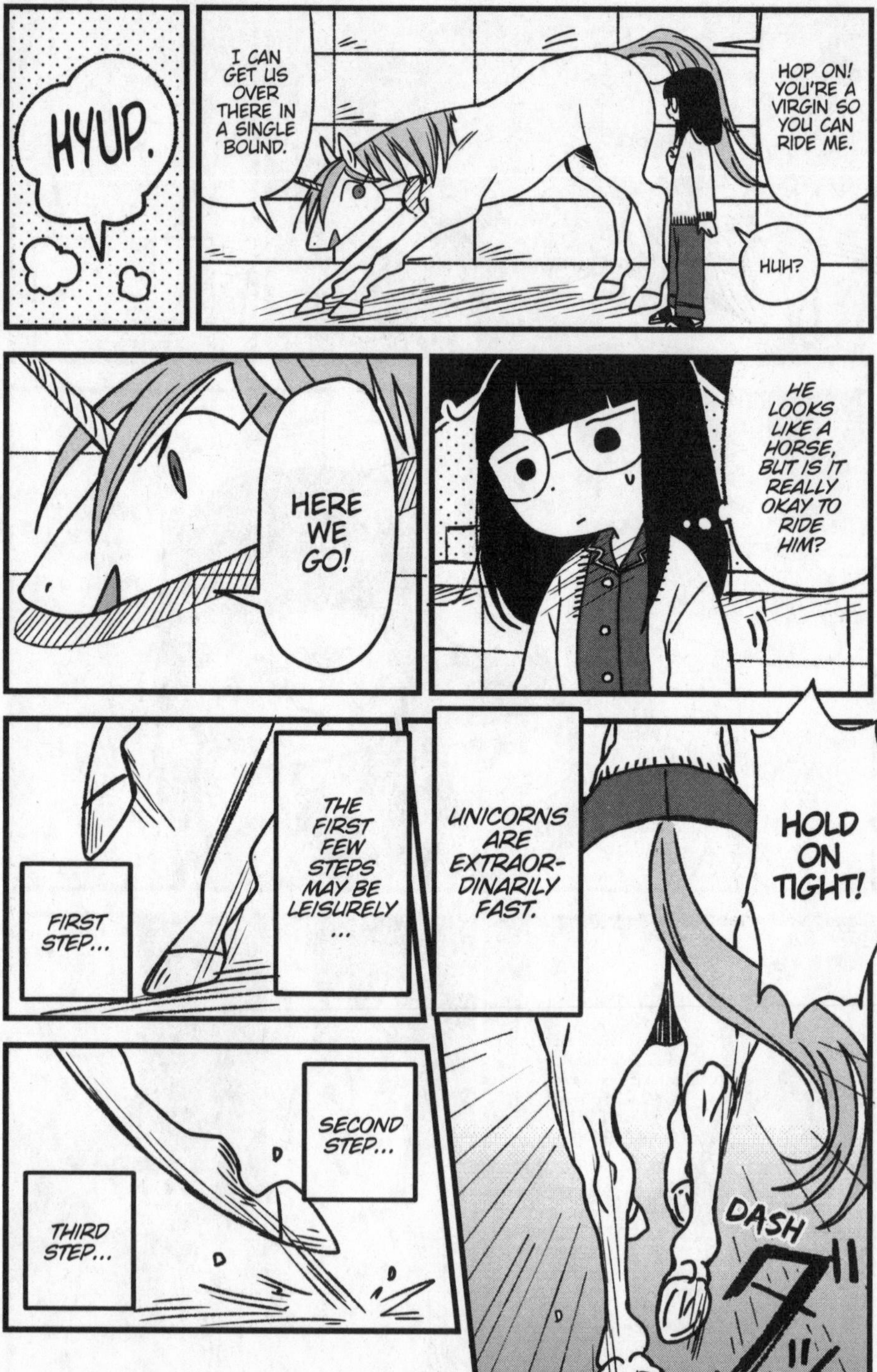

HOP ON! YOU'RE A VIRGIN SO YOU CAN RIDE ME.
I CAN GET US OVER THERE IN A SINGLE BOUND.
HUH?
HYUP.
HE LOOKS LIKE A HORSE, BUT IS IT REALLY OKAY TO RIDE HIM?
HERE WE GO!
HOLD ON TIGHT!
UNICORNS ARE EXTRAOR-DINARILY FAST.
DASH
THE FIRST FEW STEPS MAY BE LEISURELY ...
FIRST STEP...
SECOND STEP...
THIRD STEP...

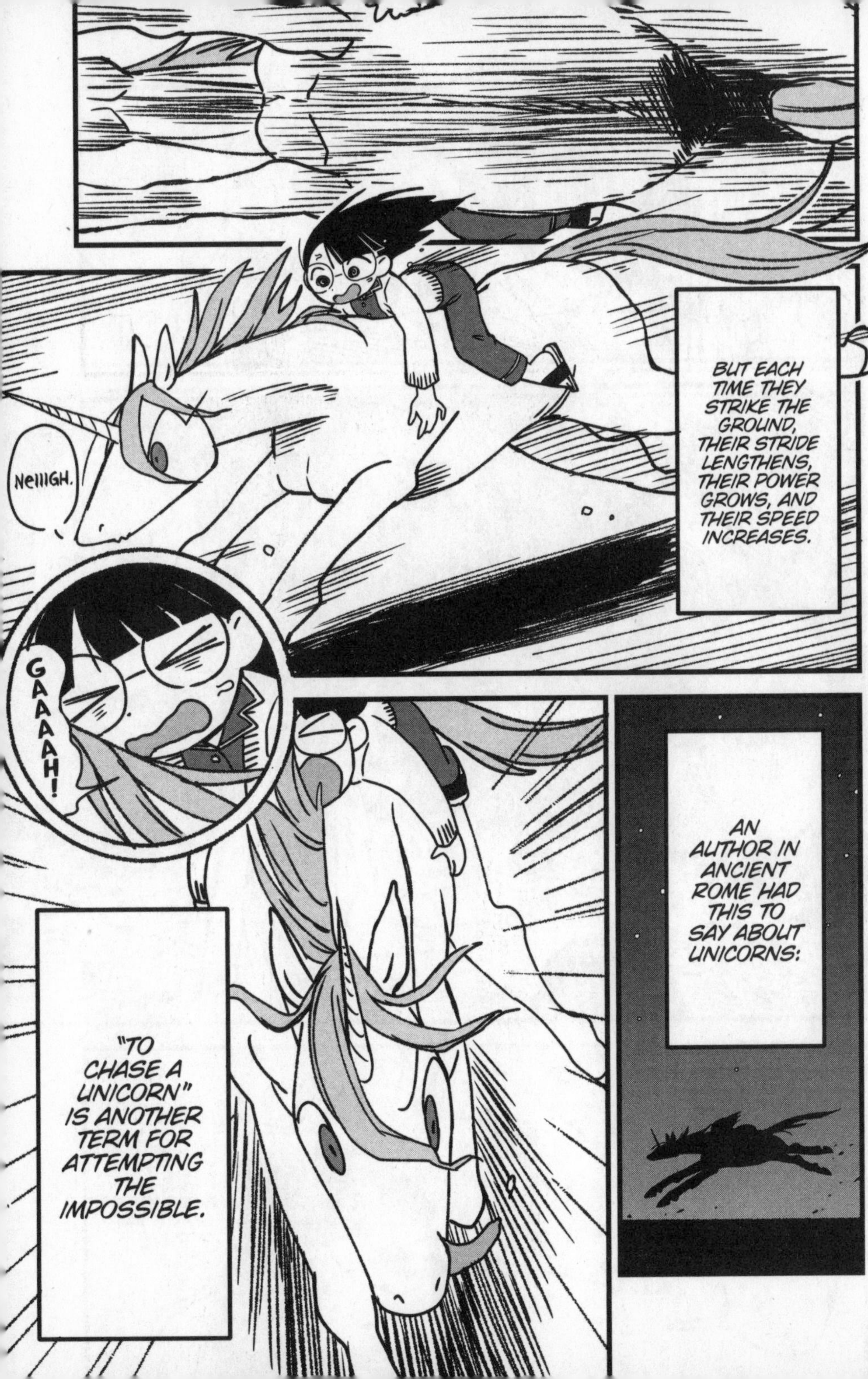
BUT EACH TIME THEY STRIKE THE GROUND, THEIR STRIDE LENGTHENS, THEIR POWER GROWS, AND THEIR SPEED INCREASES.
NEIIIGH.
AN AUTHOR IN ANCIENT ROME HAD THIS TO SAY ABOUT UNICORNS:
GAAAAH!
"TO CHASE A UNICORN" IS ANOTHER TERM FOR ATTEMPTING THE IMPOSSIBLE.

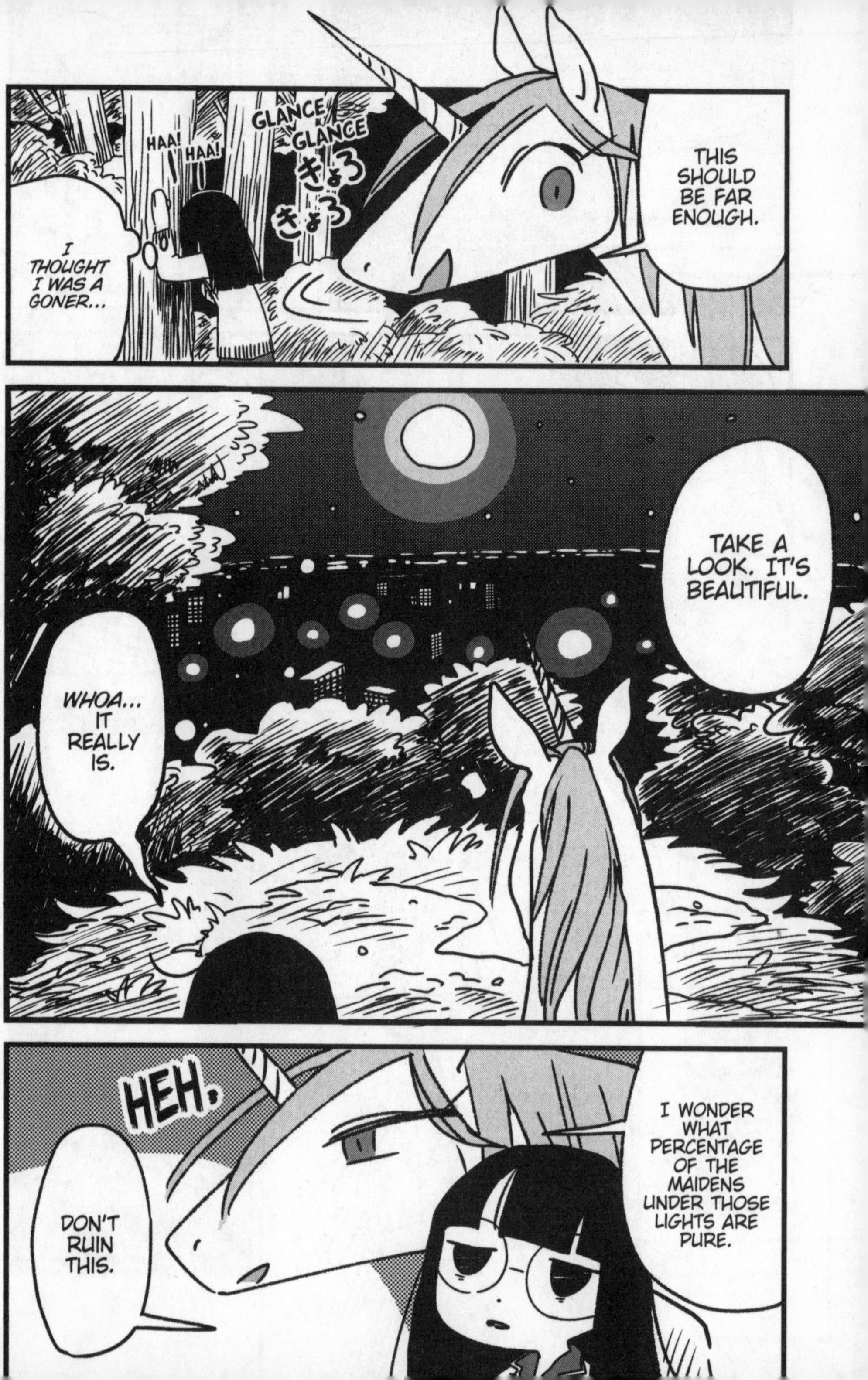
THIS SHOULD BE FAR ENOUGH.
GLANCE GLANCE
きょろきょろ
HAA! HAA!
I THOUGHT I WAS A GONER...
TAKE A LOOK. IT'S BEAUTIFUL.
WHOA... IT REALLY IS.
I WONDER WHAT PERCENTAGE OF THE MAIDENS UNDER THOSE LIGHTS ARE PURE.
HEH.
DON'T RUIN THIS.

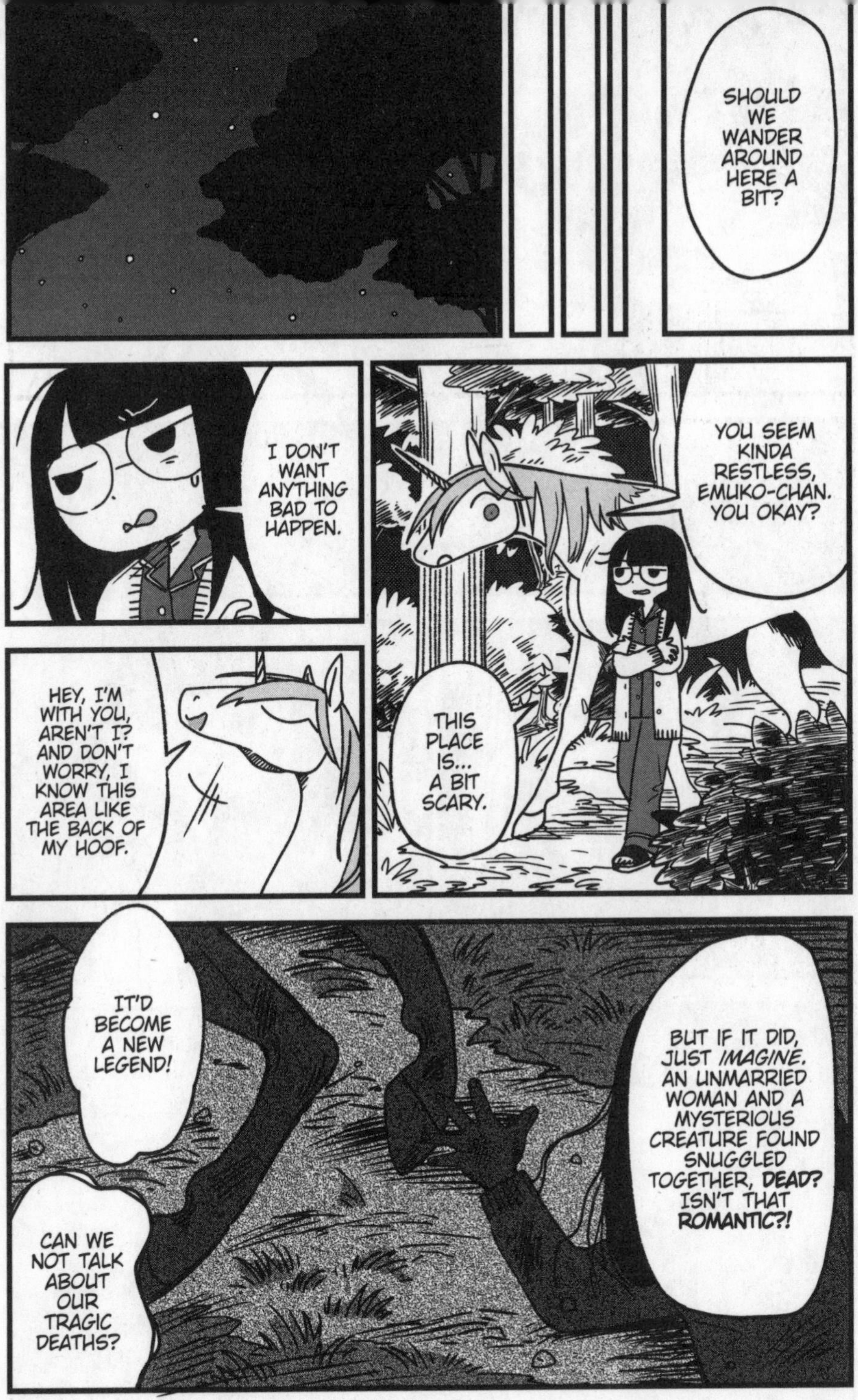
SHOULD WE WANDER AROUND HERE A BIT?
YOU SEEM KINDA RESTLESS, EMUKO-CHAN. YOU OKAY?
THIS PLACE IS... A BIT SCARY.
I DON'T WANT ANYTHING BAD TO HAPPEN.
HEY, I'M WITH YOU, AREN'T I? AND DON'T WORRY, I KNOW THIS AREA LIKE THE BACK OF MY HOOF.
BUT IF IT DID, JUST *IMAGINE*. AN UNMARRIED WOMAN AND A MYSTERIOUS CREATURE FOUND SNUGGLED TOGETHER, **DEAD?** ISN'T THAT **ROMANTIC?!**
IT'D BECOME A NEW LEGEND!
CAN WE NOT TALK ABOUT OUR TRAGIC DEATHS?

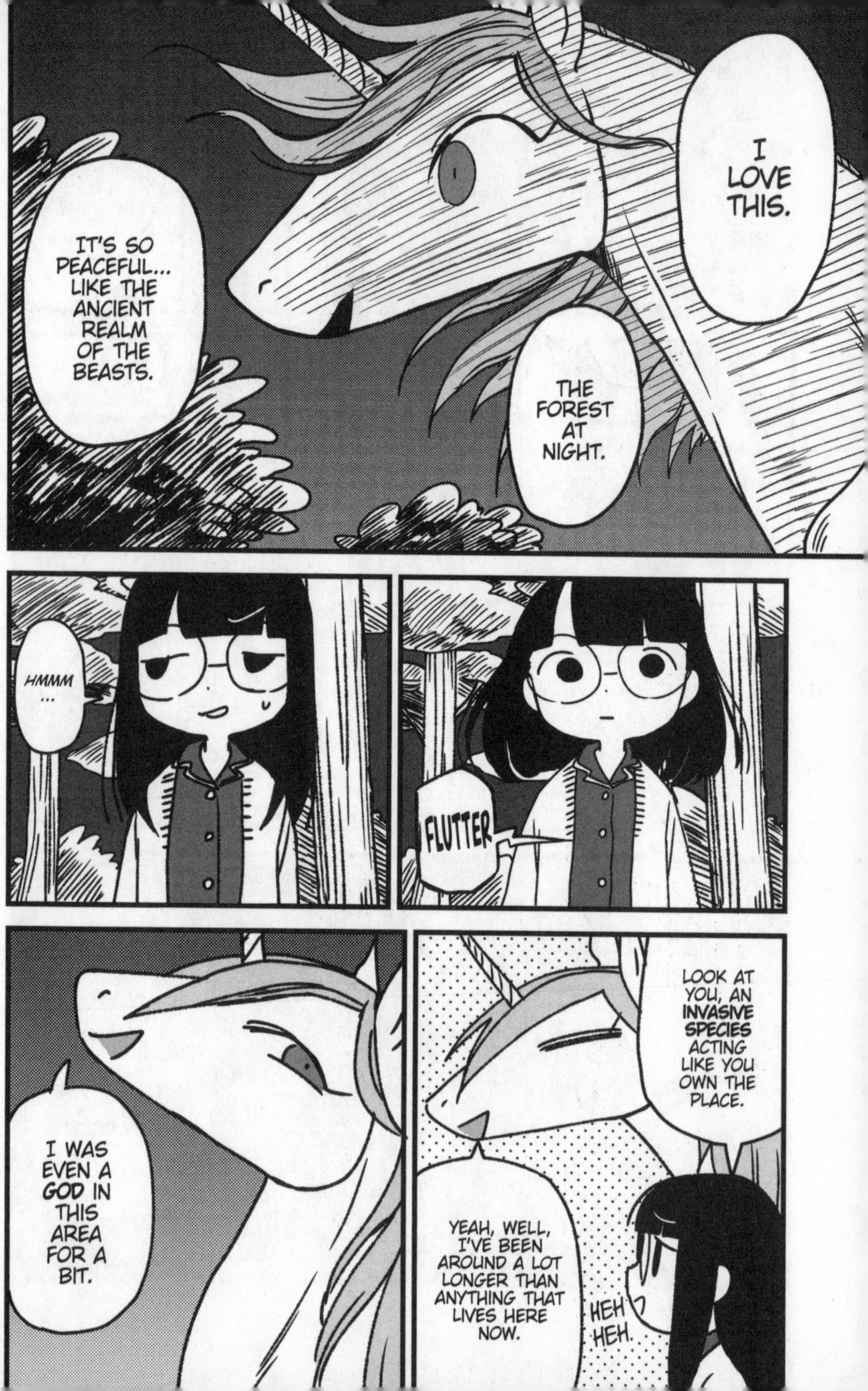
I LOVE THIS.
THE FOREST AT NIGHT.
IT'S SO PEACEFUL... LIKE THE ANCIENT REALM OF THE BEASTS.
FLUTTER
HMMM...
LOOK AT YOU, AN **INVASIVE SPECIES** ACTING LIKE YOU OWN THE PLACE.
YEAH, WELL, I'VE BEEN AROUND A LOT LONGER THAN ANYTHING THAT LIVES HERE NOW.
HEH HEH.
I WAS EVEN A **GOD** IN THIS AREA FOR A BIT.

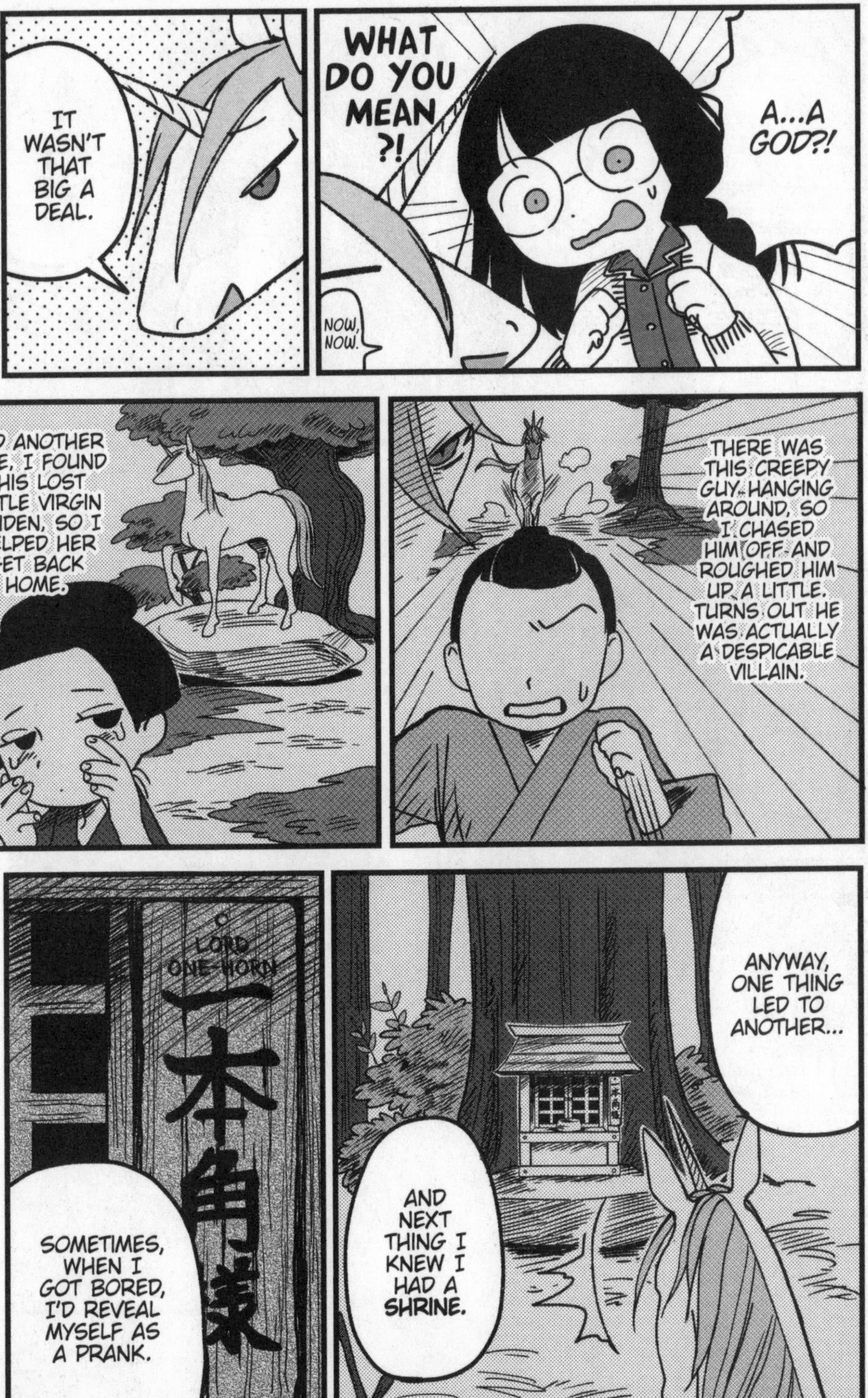
A...A GOD?!
WHAT DO YOU MEAN?!
NOW, NOW.
IT WASN'T THAT BIG A DEAL.
THERE WAS THIS CREEPY GUY HANGING AROUND, SO I CHASED HIM OFF AND ROUGHED HIM UP A LITTLE. TURNS OUT HE WAS ACTUALLY A DESPICABLE VILLAIN.
AND ANOTHER TIME, I FOUND THIS LOST LITTLE VIRGIN MAIDEN, SO I HELPED HER GET BACK HOME.
ANYWAY, ONE THING LED TO ANOTHER...
AND NEXT THING I KNEW I HAD A SHRINE.
LORD ONE-HORN
一本角様
SOMETIMES, WHEN I GOT BORED, I'D REVEAL MYSELF AS A PRANK.

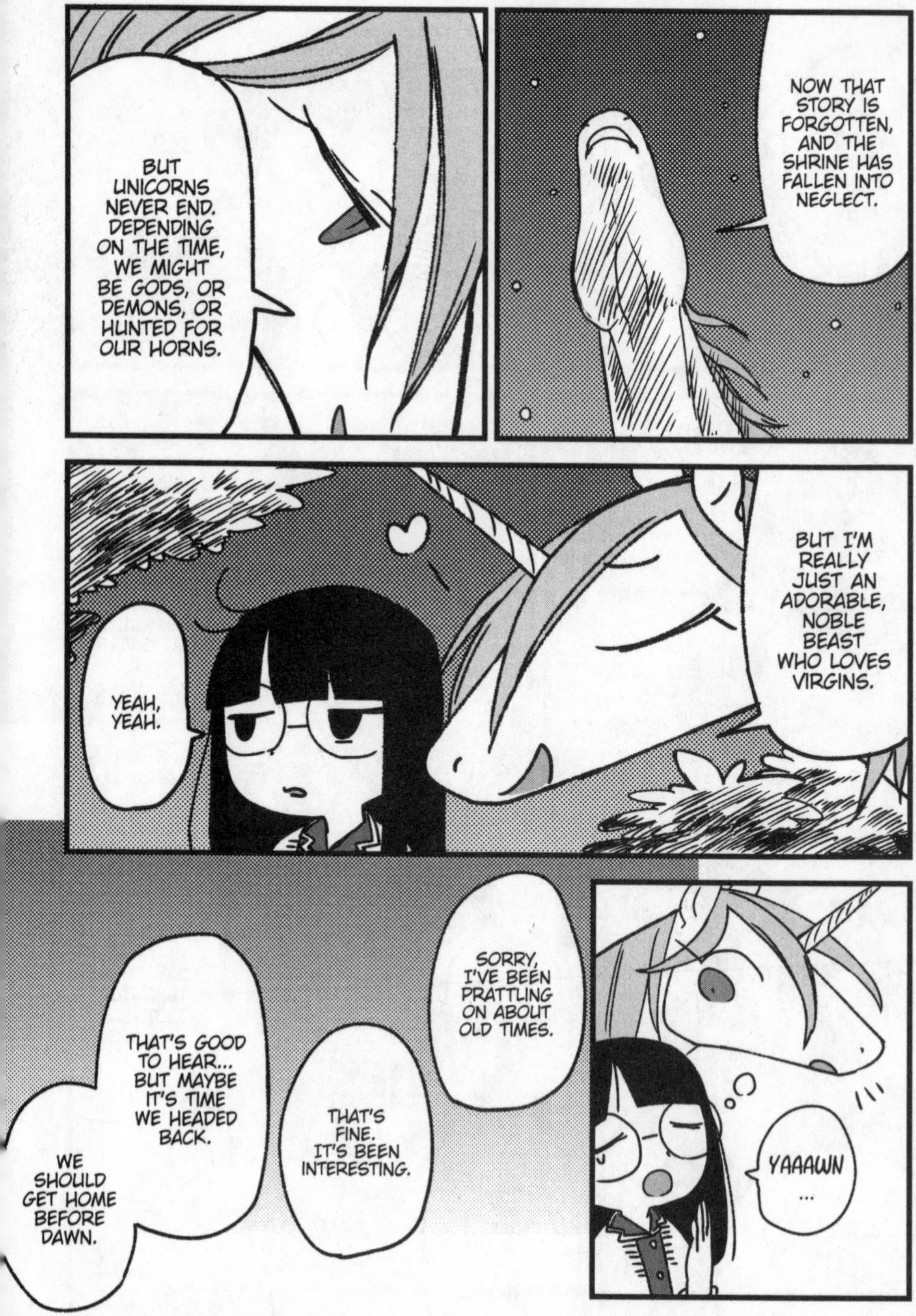
NOW THAT STORY IS FORGOTTEN, AND THE SHRINE HAS FALLEN INTO NEGLECT.
BUT UNICORNS NEVER END. DEPENDING ON THE TIME, WE MIGHT BE GODS, OR DEMONS, OR HUNTED FOR OUR HORNS.
BUT I'M REALLY JUST AN ADORABLE, NOBLE BEAST WHO LOVES VIRGINS.
YEAH, YEAH.
YAAAWN ...
SORRY, I'VE BEEN PRATTLING ON ABOUT OLD TIMES.
THAT'S FINE. IT'S BEEN INTERESTING.
THAT'S GOOD TO HEAR... BUT MAYBE IT'S TIME WE HEADED BACK.
WE SHOULD GET HOME BEFORE DAWN.

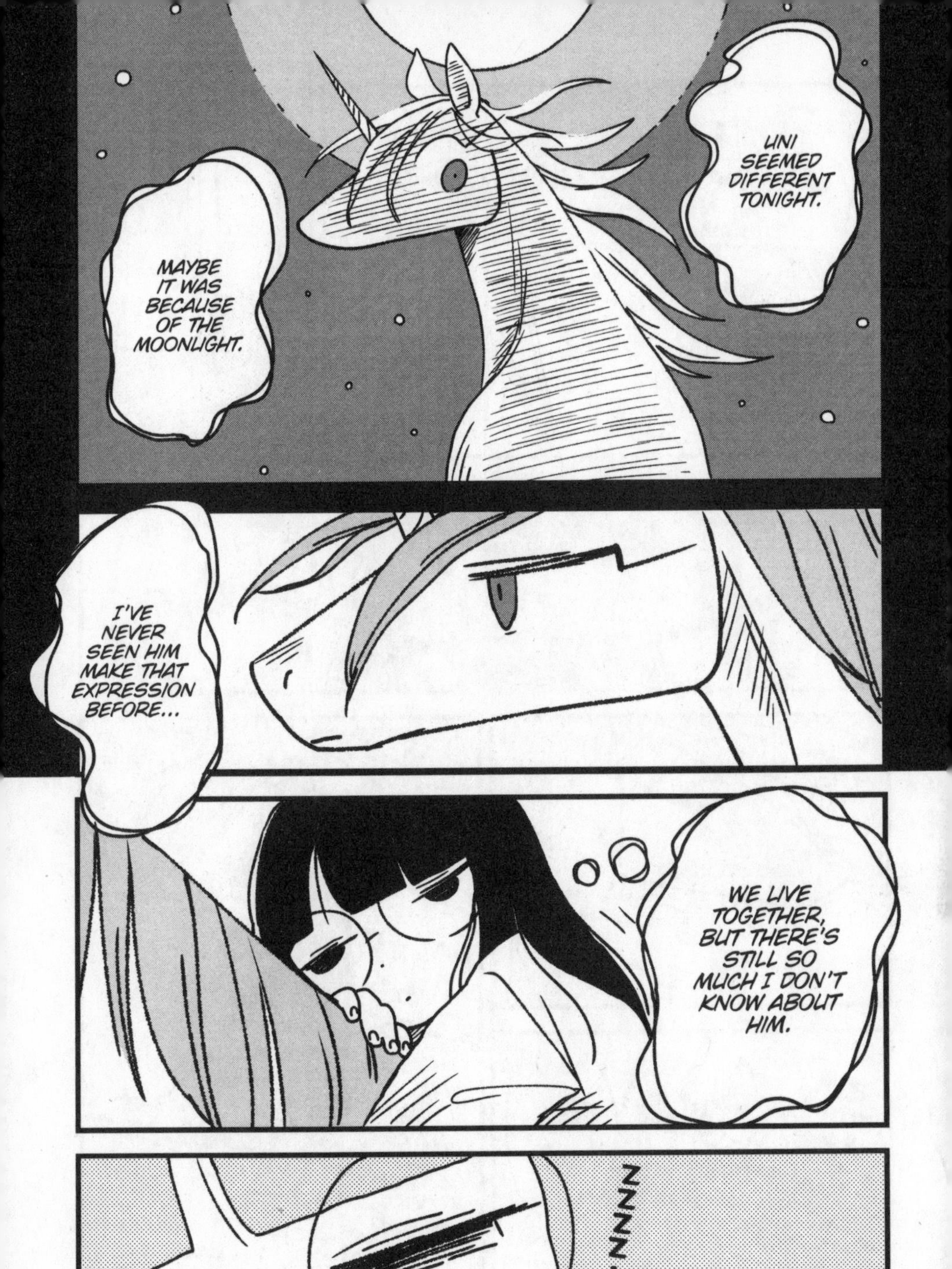
UNI SEEMED DIFFERENT TONIGHT.
MAYBE IT WAS BECAUSE OF THE MOONLIGHT.
I'VE NEVER SEEN HIM MAKE THAT EXPRESSION BEFORE...
WE LIVE TOGETHER, BUT THERE'S STILL SO MUCH I DON'T KNOW ABOUT HIM.
ZZZZ...

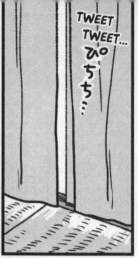

TWEET
TWEET...
ぴ
ち
ち...

GUUH
...

WHEN
DID I FALL
ASLEEP...?

ZZZZ...
ZZZZ...

・・・・・・・

AND
THIS
GUY
SNUCK
INTO
MY BED
AGAIN.

Z Z
Z
Z Z

OH
WELL.

MAYBE
JUST
THIS
ONCE.

CHAPTER 9 A MAIDEN'S BANGS

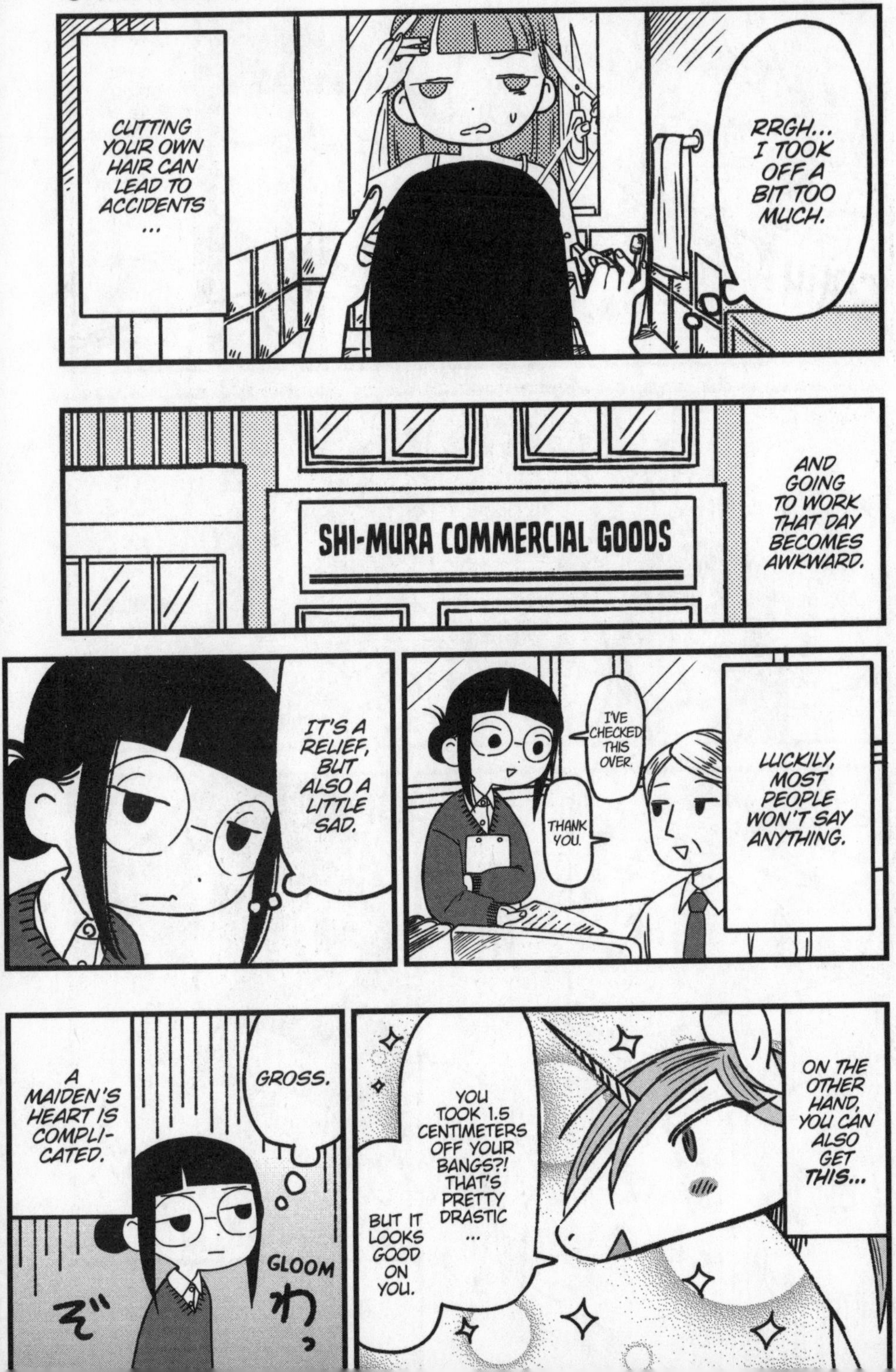
RRGH... I TOOK OFF A BIT TOO MUCH.
CUTTING YOUR OWN HAIR CAN LEAD TO ACCIDENTS ...
AND GOING TO WORK THAT DAY BECOMES AWKWARD.
SHI-MURA COMMERCIAL GOODS
LUCKILY, MOST PEOPLE WON'T SAY ANYTHING.
I'VE CHECKED THIS OVER.
THANK YOU.
IT'S A RELIEF, BUT ALSO A LITTLE SAD.
ON THE OTHER HAND, YOU CAN ALSO GET THIS...
YOU TOOK 1.5 CENTIMETERS OFF YOUR BANGS?! THAT'S PRETTY DRASTIC ...
BUT IT LOOKS GOOD ON YOU.
GROSS.
A MAIDEN'S HEART IS COMPLI-CATED.
GLOOM
ぞわっ

MAKEOVER

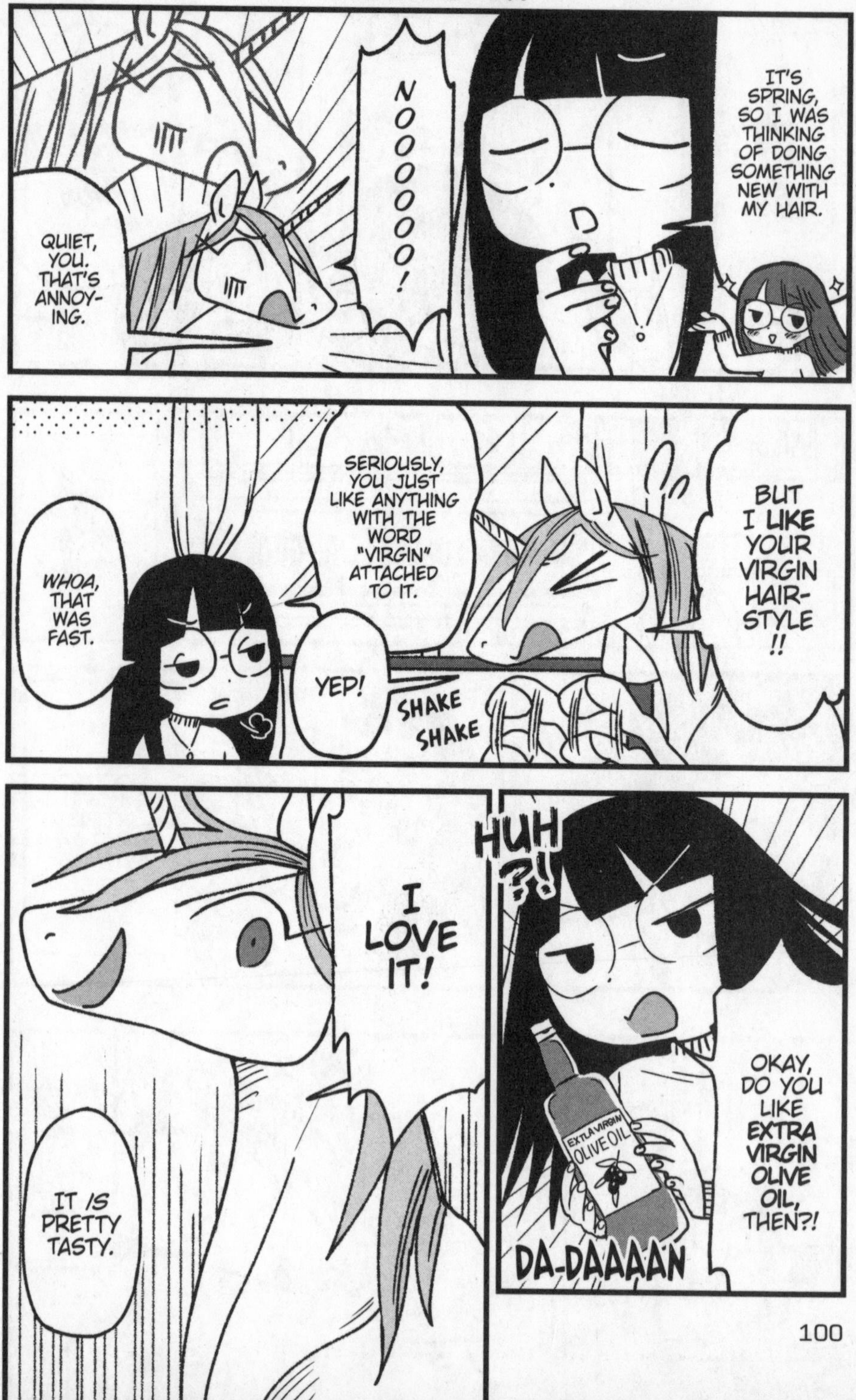
IT'S SPRING, SO I WAS THINKING OF DOING SOMETHING NEW WITH MY HAIR.
NOOOOOOOO!
QUIET, YOU. THAT'S ANNOY-ING.
BUT I LIKE YOUR VIRGIN HAIR-STYLE!!
SHAKE SHAKE
SERIOUSLY, YOU JUST LIKE ANYTHING WITH THE WORD "VIRGIN" ATTACHED TO IT.
YEP!
WHOA, THAT WAS FAST.
HUH?!
OKAY, DO YOU LIKE EXTRA VIRGIN OLIVE OIL, THEN?!
EXTLA VIRGIN OLIVE OIL
DA-DAAAAN
I LOVE IT!
IT IS PRETTY TASTY.

MANE ATTRACTION

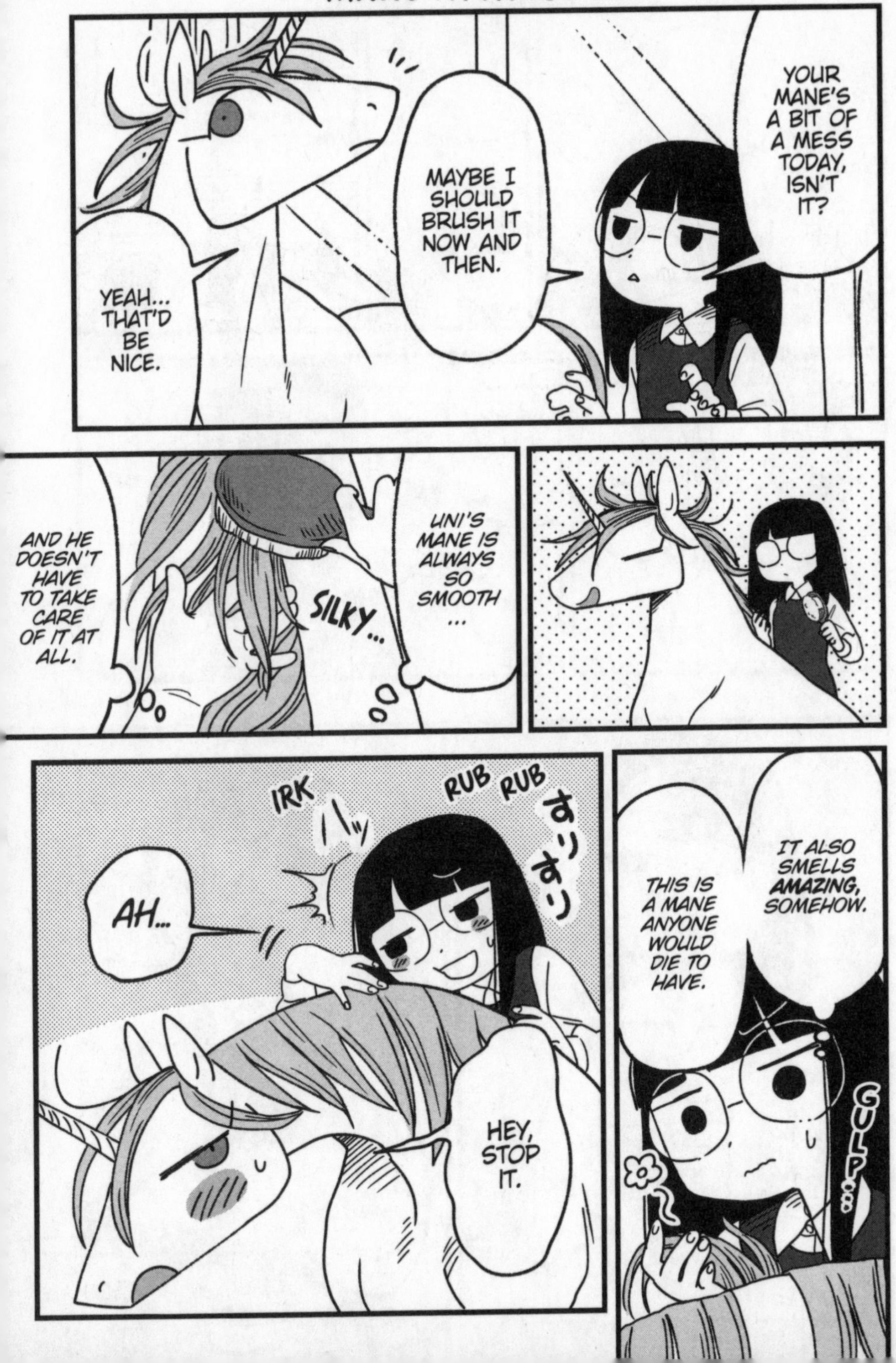
YOUR MANE'S A BIT OF A MESS TODAY, ISN'T IT?
MAYBE I SHOULD BRUSH IT NOW AND THEN.
YEAH... THAT'D BE NICE.
UNI'S MANE IS ALWAYS SO SMOOTH ...
SILKY...
AND HE DOESN'T HAVE TO TAKE CARE OF IT AT ALL.
IT ALSO SMELLS **AMAZING**, SOMEHOW.
THIS IS A MANE ANYONE WOULD DIE TO HAVE.
GULP...
RUB RUB
すりすり
IRK
ハッ
AH...
HEY, STOP IT.

PUPPY LOVE

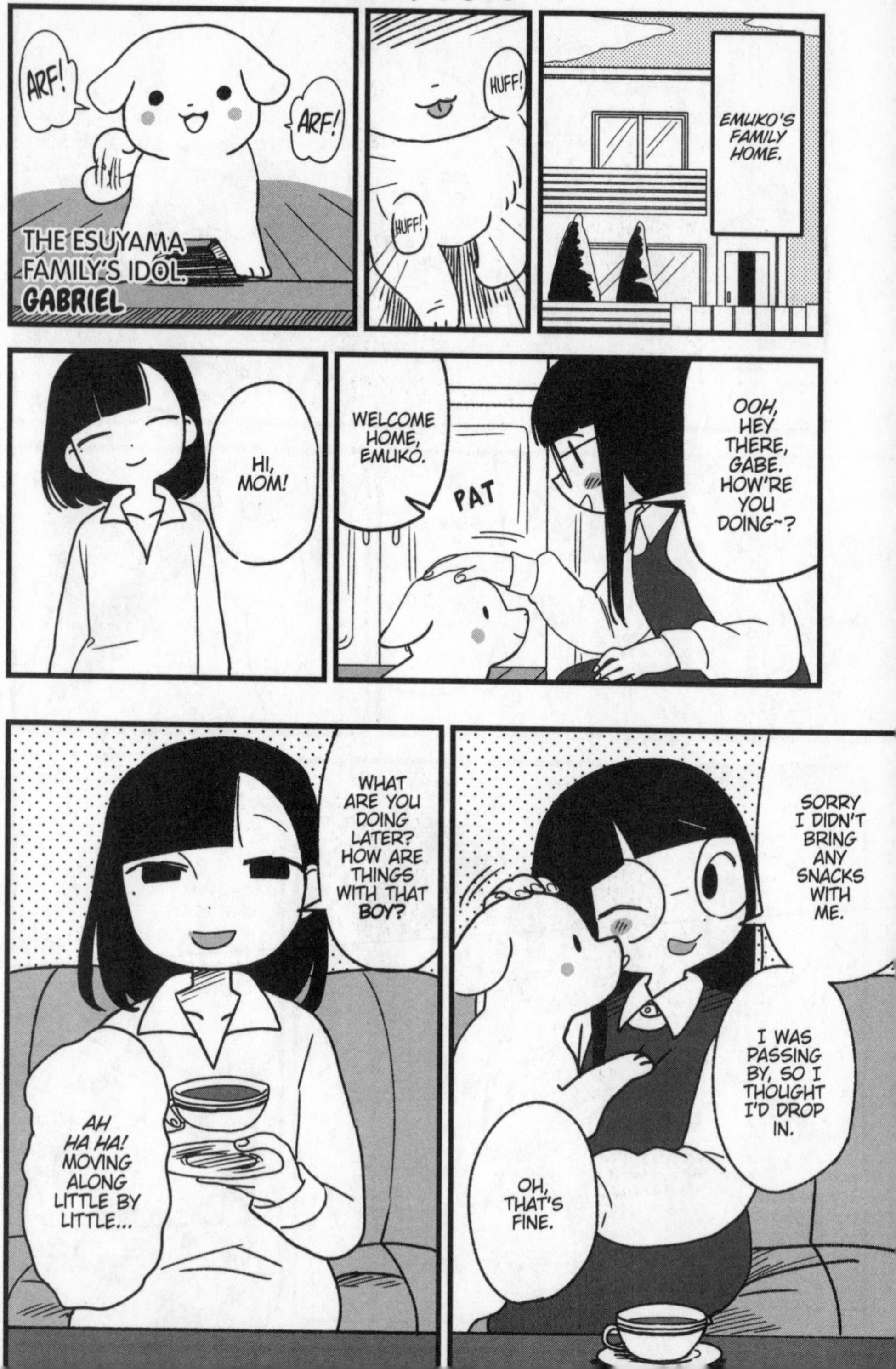
EMUKO'S FAMILY HOME.
HUFF!
HUFF!
ARF!
ARF!
THE ESUYAMA FAMILY'S IDOL. GABRIEL
OOH, HEY THERE, GABE. HOW'RE YOU DOING~?
WELCOME HOME, EMUKO.
PAT
HI, MOM!
SORRY I DIDN'T BRING ANY SNACKS WITH ME.
I WAS PASSING BY, SO I THOUGHT I'D DROP IN.
OH, THAT'S FINE.
WHAT ARE YOU DOING LATER? HOW ARE THINGS WITH THAT BOY?
AH HA HA! MOVING ALONG LITTLE BY LITTLE...

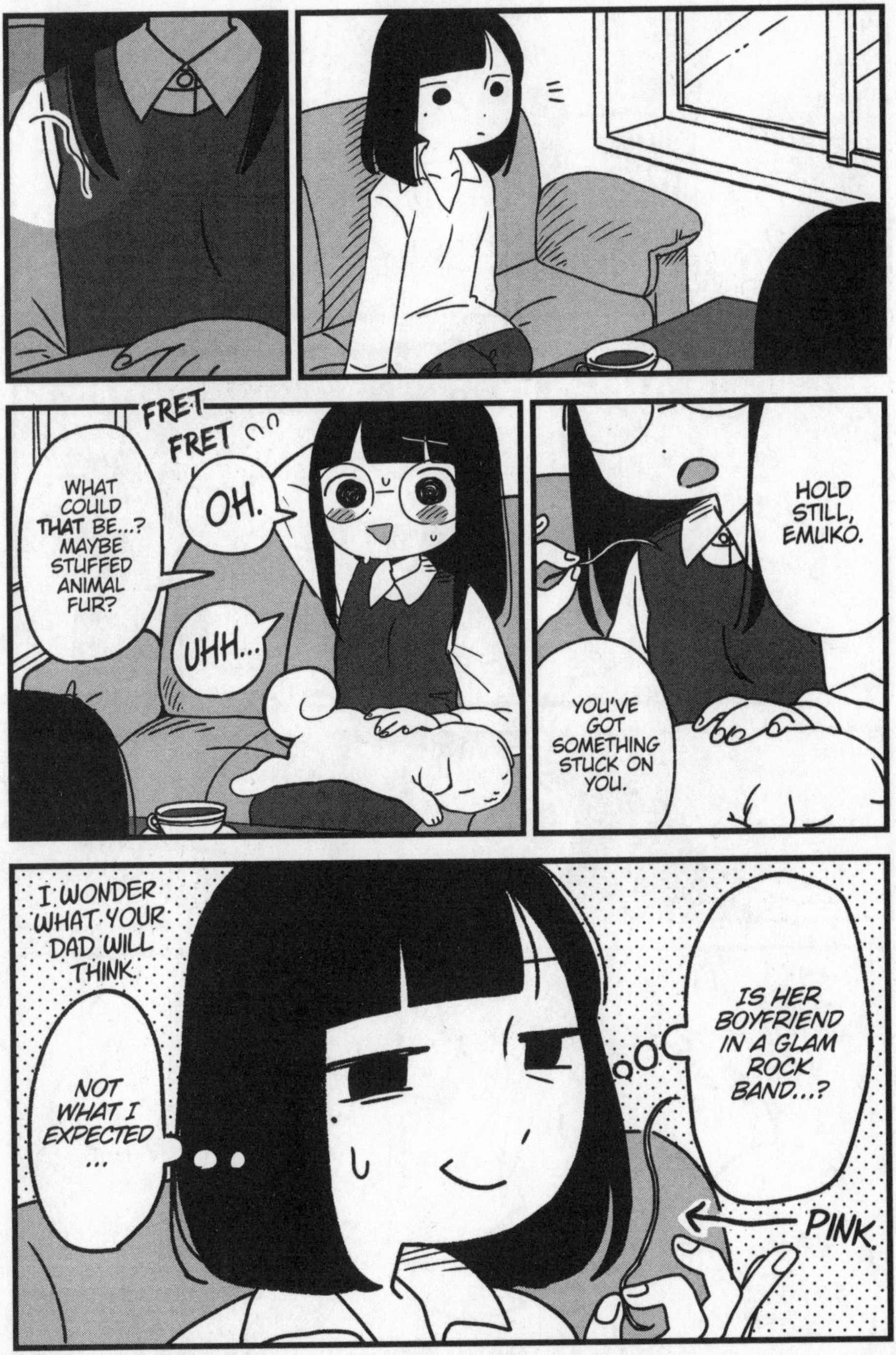
HOLD STILL, EMUKO.
YOU'VE GOT SOMETHING STUCK ON YOU.
FRET FRET
OH.
WHAT COULD THAT BE...? MAYBE STUFFED ANIMAL FUR?
UHH...
IS HER BOYFRIEND IN A GLAM ROCK BAND...?
PINK.
I WONDER WHAT YOUR DAD WILL THINK.
NOT WHAT I EXPECTED ...

PET FRIENDLY

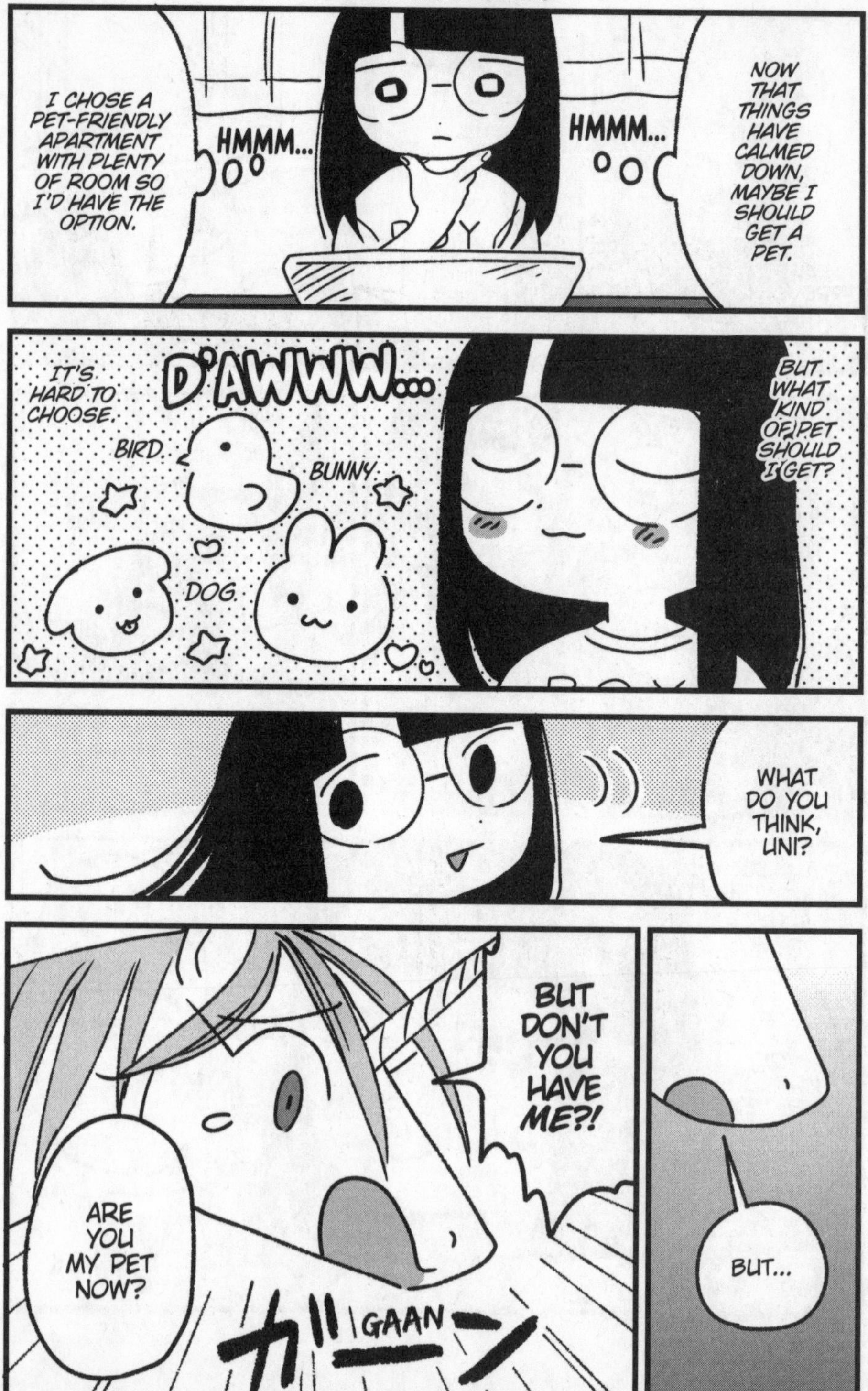

NOW THAT THINGS HAVE CALMED DOWN, MAYBE I SHOULD GET A PET.
HMMM...
HMMM...
I CHOSE A PET-FRIENDLY APARTMENT WITH PLENTY OF ROOM SO I'D HAVE THE OPTION.
BUT. WHAT KIND OF PET SHOULD I GET?
D'AWWW...
IT'S HARD TO CHOOSE.
BIRD.
BUNNY.
DOG.
WHAT DO YOU THINK, UNI?
BUT...
BUT DON'T YOU HAVE *ME*?!
ARE YOU MY PET NOW?
GAAN

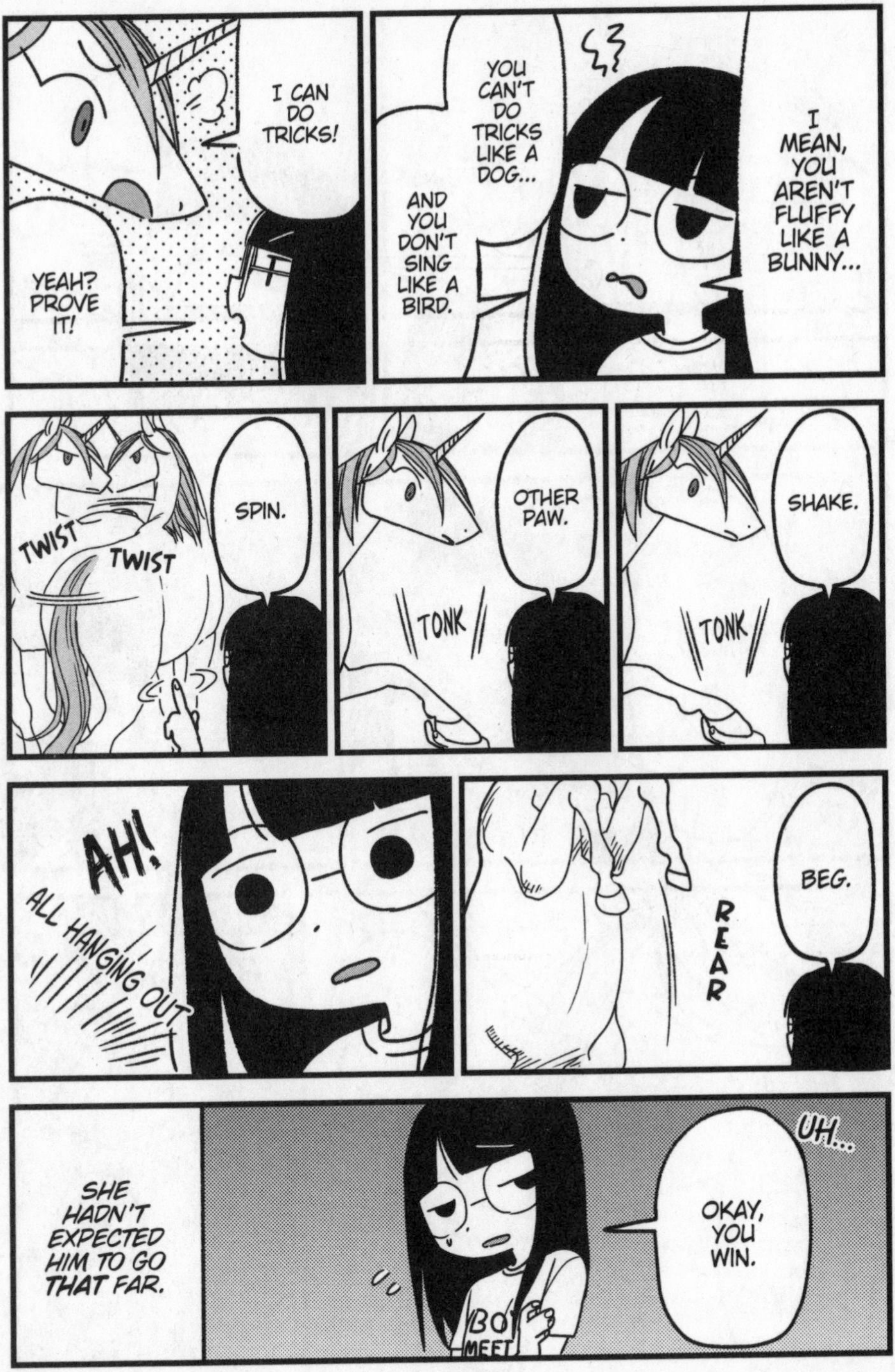
I MEAN, YOU AREN'T FLUFFY LIKE A BUNNY...
YOU CAN'T DO TRICKS LIKE A DOG...
AND YOU DON'T SING LIKE A BIRD.
I CAN DO TRICKS!
YEAH? PROVE IT!
SHAKE.
TONK
OTHER PAW.
TONK
SPIN.
TWIST
TWIST
BEG.
REAR
AH!
ALL HANGING OUT
UH...
OKAY, YOU WIN.
SHE HADN'T EXPECTED HIM TO GO THAT FAR.

FAVORITE ANIMALS

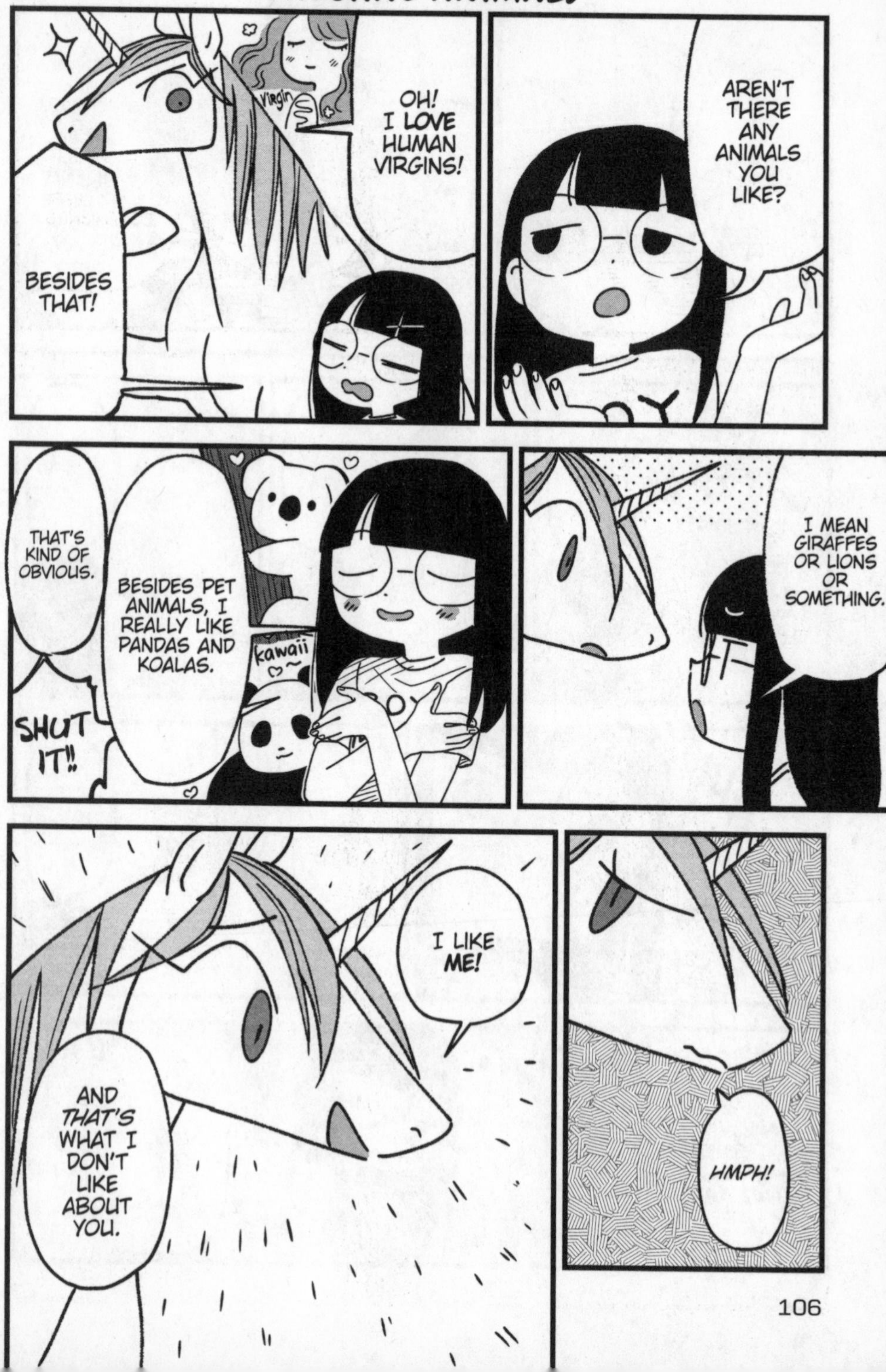

AREN'T THERE ANY ANIMALS YOU LIKE?
OH! I LOVE HUMAN VIRGINS!
Virgin
BESIDES THAT!
I MEAN GIRAFFES OR LIONS OR SOMETHING.
BESIDES PET ANIMALS, I REALLY LIKE PANDAS AND KOALAS.
kawaii ~
THAT'S KIND OF OBVIOUS.
SHUT IT!!
HMPH!
I LIKE ME!
AND *THAT'S* WHAT I DON'T LIKE ABOUT YOU.

DATING

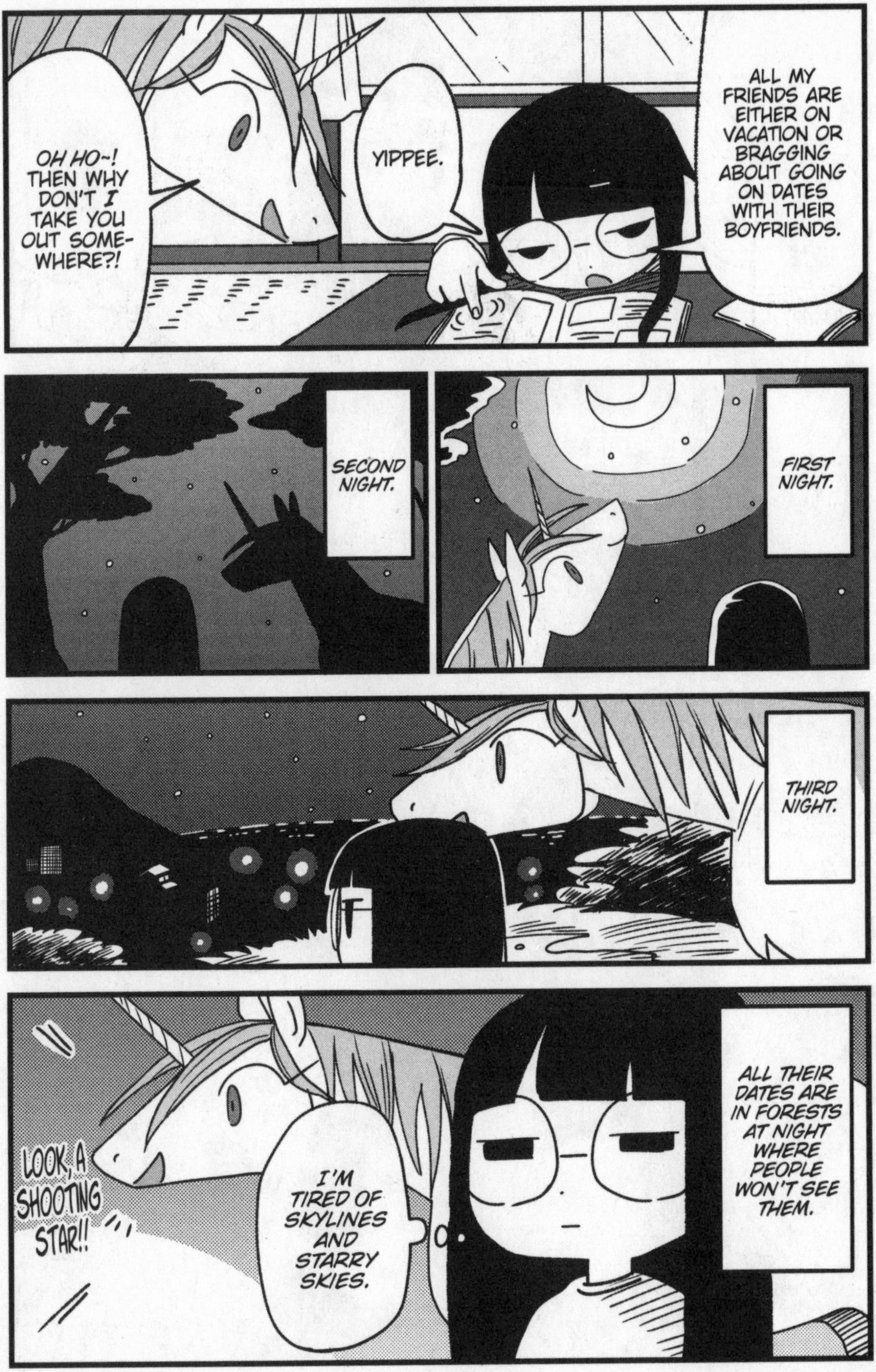
ALL MY FRIENDS ARE EITHER ON VACATION OR BRAGGING ABOUT GOING ON DATES WITH THEIR BOYFRIENDS.
YIPPEE.
OH HO~! THEN WHY DON'T *I* TAKE YOU OUT SOME-WHERE?!
FIRST NIGHT.
SECOND NIGHT.
THIRD NIGHT.
ALL THEIR DATES ARE IN FORESTS AT NIGHT WHERE PEOPLE WON'T SEE THEM.
I'M TIRED OF SKYLINES AND STARRY SKIES.
LOOK, A SHOOTING STAR!!

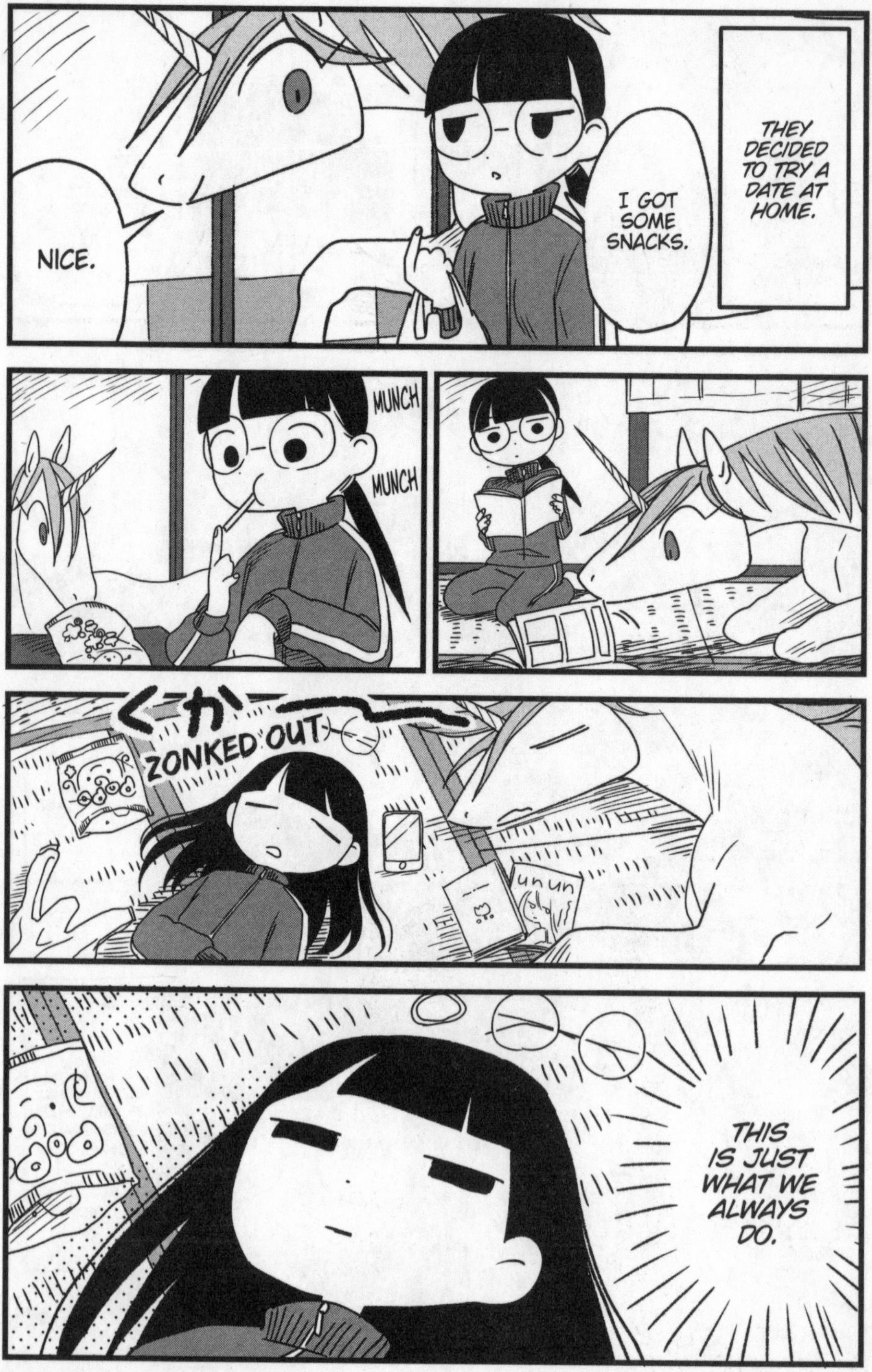
THEY DECIDED TO TRY A DATE AT HOME.
I GOT SOME SNACKS.
NICE.
MUNCH
MUNCH
くかー
ZONKED OUT
un un
THIS IS JUST WHAT WE ALWAYS DO.

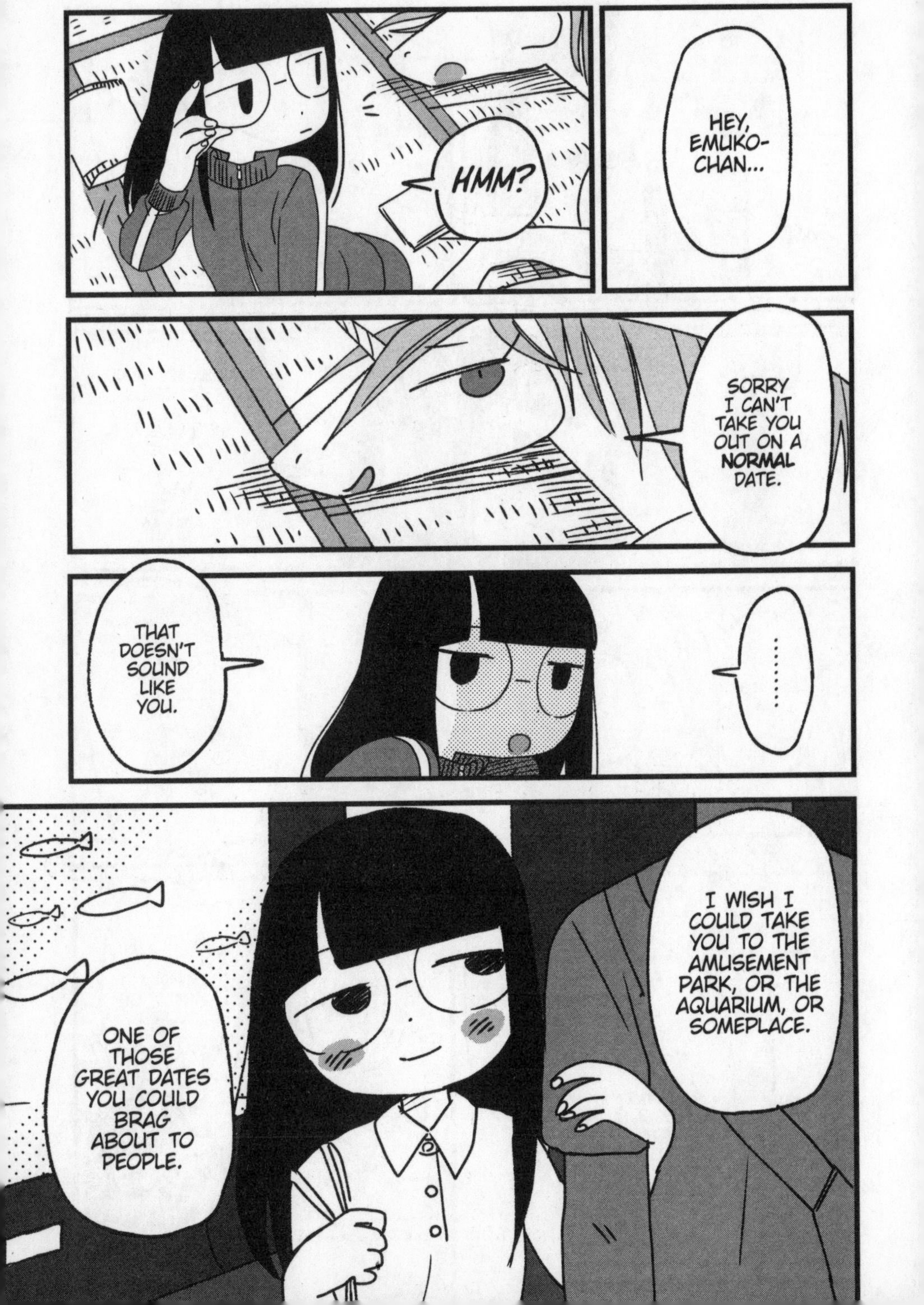
HEY, EMUKO-CHAN...
HMM?
SORRY I CAN'T TAKE YOU OUT ON A NORMAL DATE.
......
THAT DOESN'T SOUND LIKE YOU.
I WISH I COULD TAKE YOU TO THE AMUSEMENT PARK, OR THE AQUARIUM, OR SOMEPLACE.
ONE OF THOSE GREAT DATES YOU COULD BRAG ABOUT TO PEOPLE.

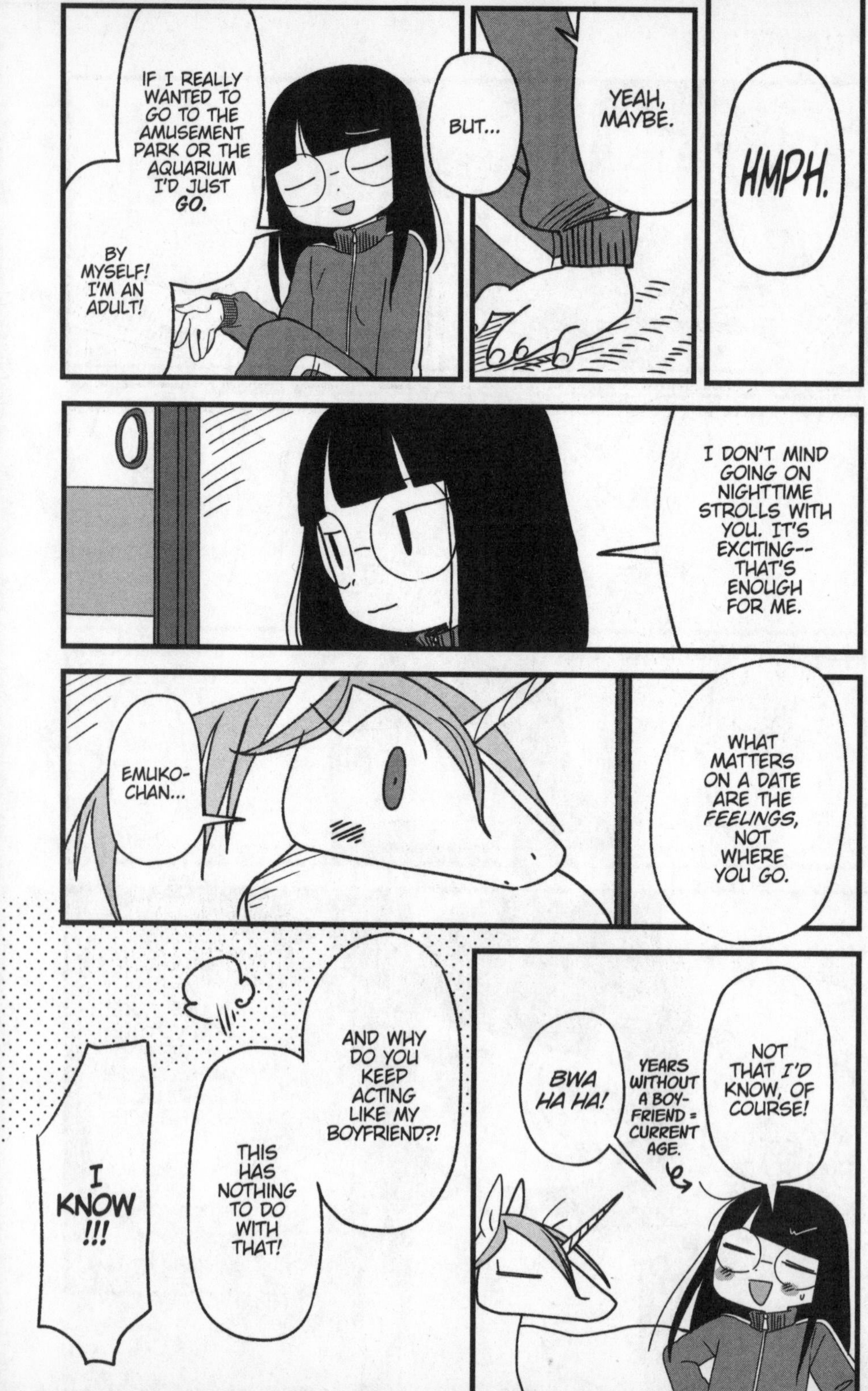
HMPH.
YEAH, MAYBE.
BUT...
IF I REALLY WANTED TO GO TO THE AMUSEMENT PARK OR THE AQUARIUM I'D JUST GO.
BY MYSELF! I'M AN ADULT!
I DON'T MIND GOING ON NIGHTTIME STROLLS WITH YOU. IT'S EXCITING--THAT'S ENOUGH FOR ME.
WHAT MATTERS ON A DATE ARE THE FEELINGS, NOT WHERE YOU GO.
EMUKO-CHAN...
NOT THAT I'D KNOW, OF COURSE!
YEARS WITHOUT A BOY-FRIEND = CURRENT AGE.
BWA HA HA!
AND WHY DO YOU KEEP ACTING LIKE MY BOYFRIEND?!
THIS HAS NOTHING TO DO WITH THAT!
I KNOW!!!

CHAPTER 10

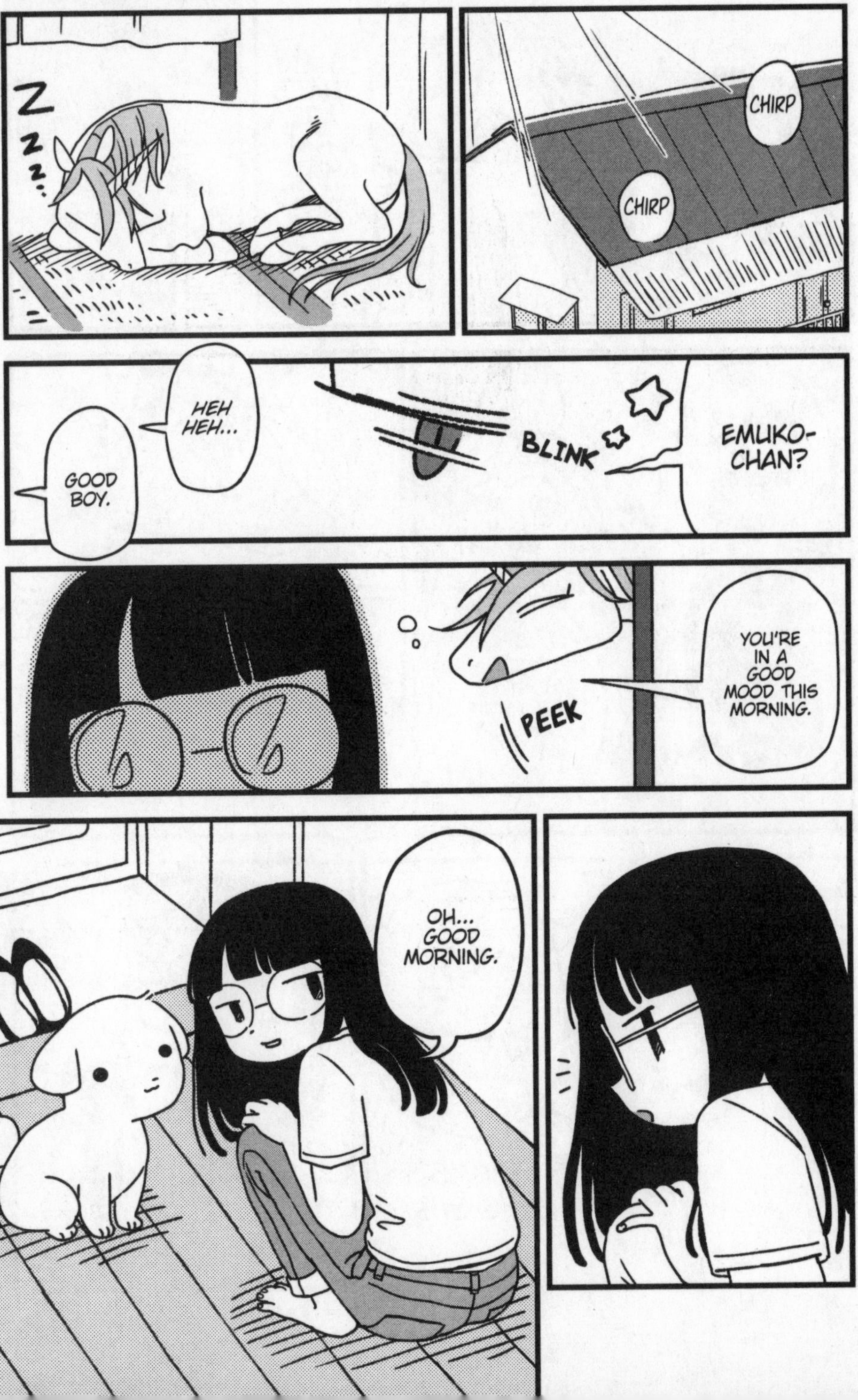
CHIRP
CHIRP
Z Z Z...
EMUKO-CHAN?
BLINK
HEH HEH...
GOOD BOY.
YOU'RE IN A GOOD MOOD THIS MORNING.
PEEK
OH... GOOD MORNING.

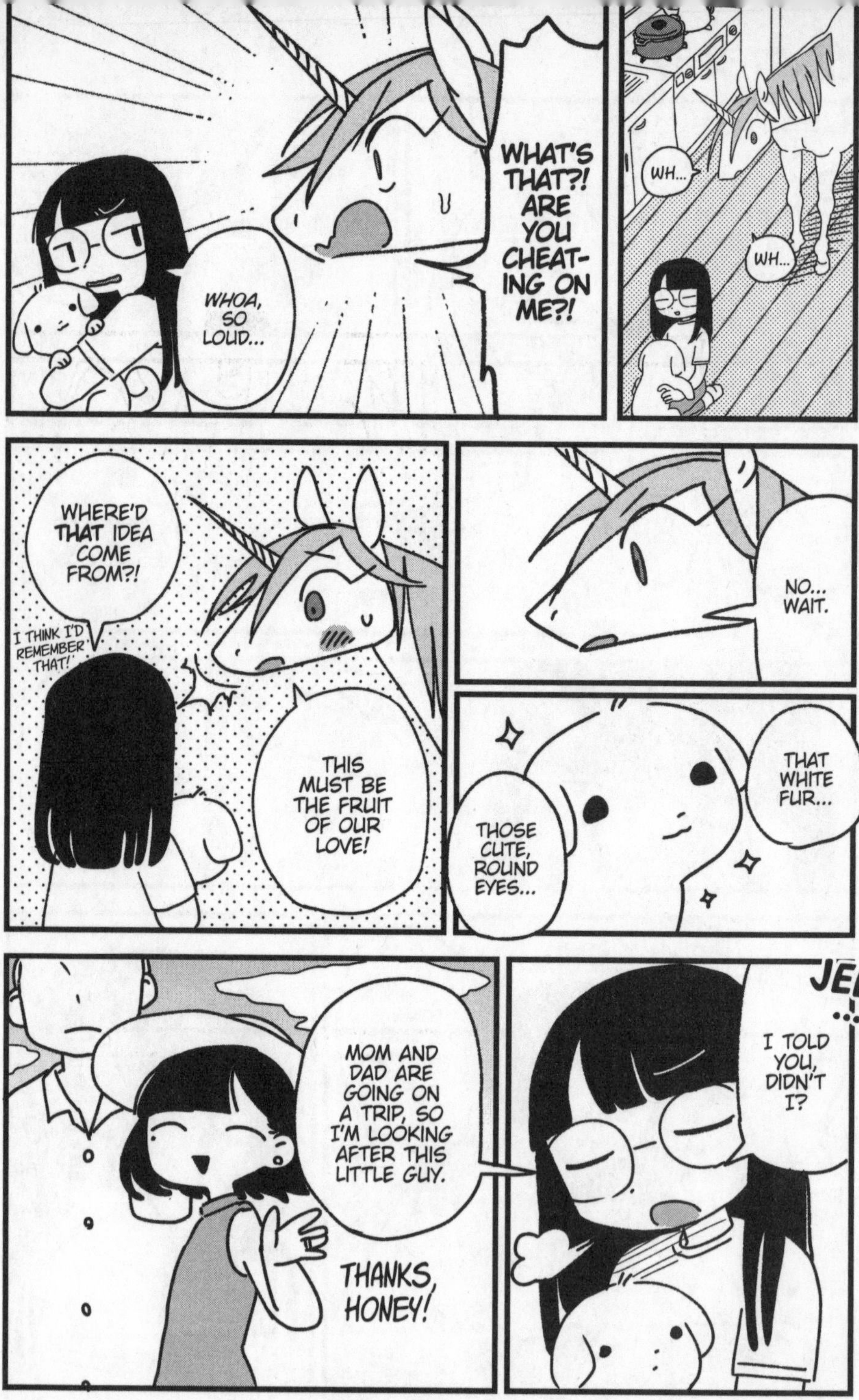
WH...
WH...
WHAT'S THAT?! ARE YOU CHEAT-ING ON ME?!
WHOA, SO LOUD...
NO... WAIT.
THAT WHITE FUR...
THOSE CUTE, ROUND EYES...
THIS MUST BE THE FRUIT OF OUR LOVE!
WHERE'D THAT IDEA COME FROM?!
I THINK I'D REMEMBER THAT!
JEEZ...
I TOLD YOU, DIDN'T I?
MOM AND DAD ARE GOING ON A TRIP, SO I'M LOOKING AFTER THIS LITTLE GUY.
THANKS, HONEY!

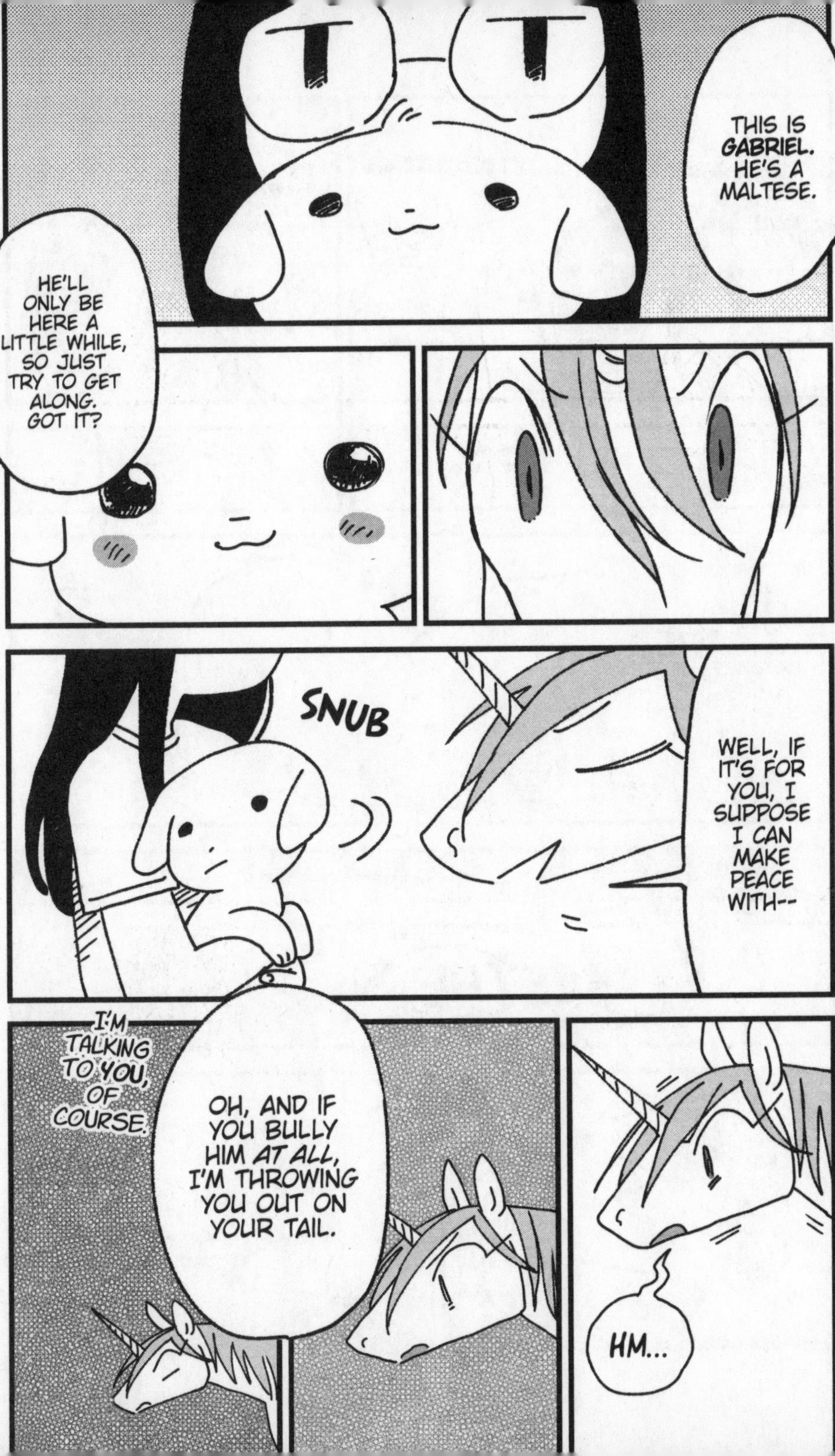
THIS IS GABRIEL. HE'S A MALTESE.
HE'LL ONLY BE HERE A LITTLE WHILE, SO JUST TRY TO GET ALONG. GOT IT?
WELL, IF IT'S FOR YOU, I SUPPOSE I CAN MAKE PEACE WITH--
SNUB
HM...
OH, AND IF YOU BULLY HIM AT ALL, I'M THROWING YOU OUT ON YOUR TAIL.
I'M TALKING TO YOU, OF COURSE.

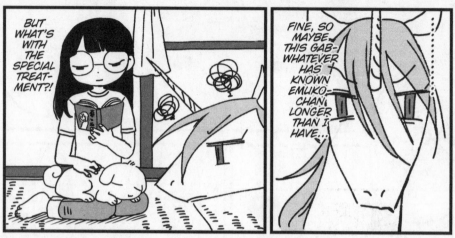

FINE, SO MAYBE THIS GAB-WHATEVER HAS KNOWN EMUKO-CHAN LONGER THAN I HAVE...
BUT WHAT'S WITH THE SPECIAL TREATMENT?!
SHE LETS IT SLEEP IN HER LAP!
IT'S JUST A DOG!
UNICORNS ARE SUPPOSED TO LIE ACROSS A MAIDEN'S LAP!
SEETHE...
PEEK
WHAT'S IT LOOKING AT ME FOR?
?

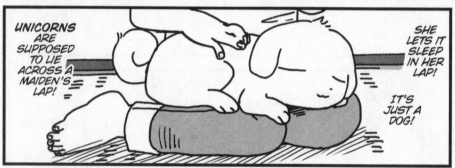

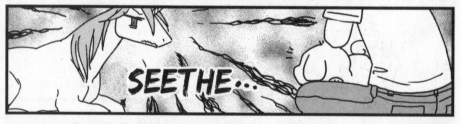

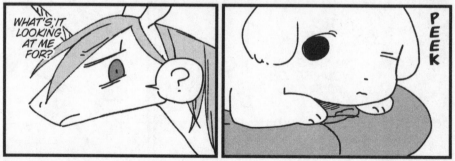

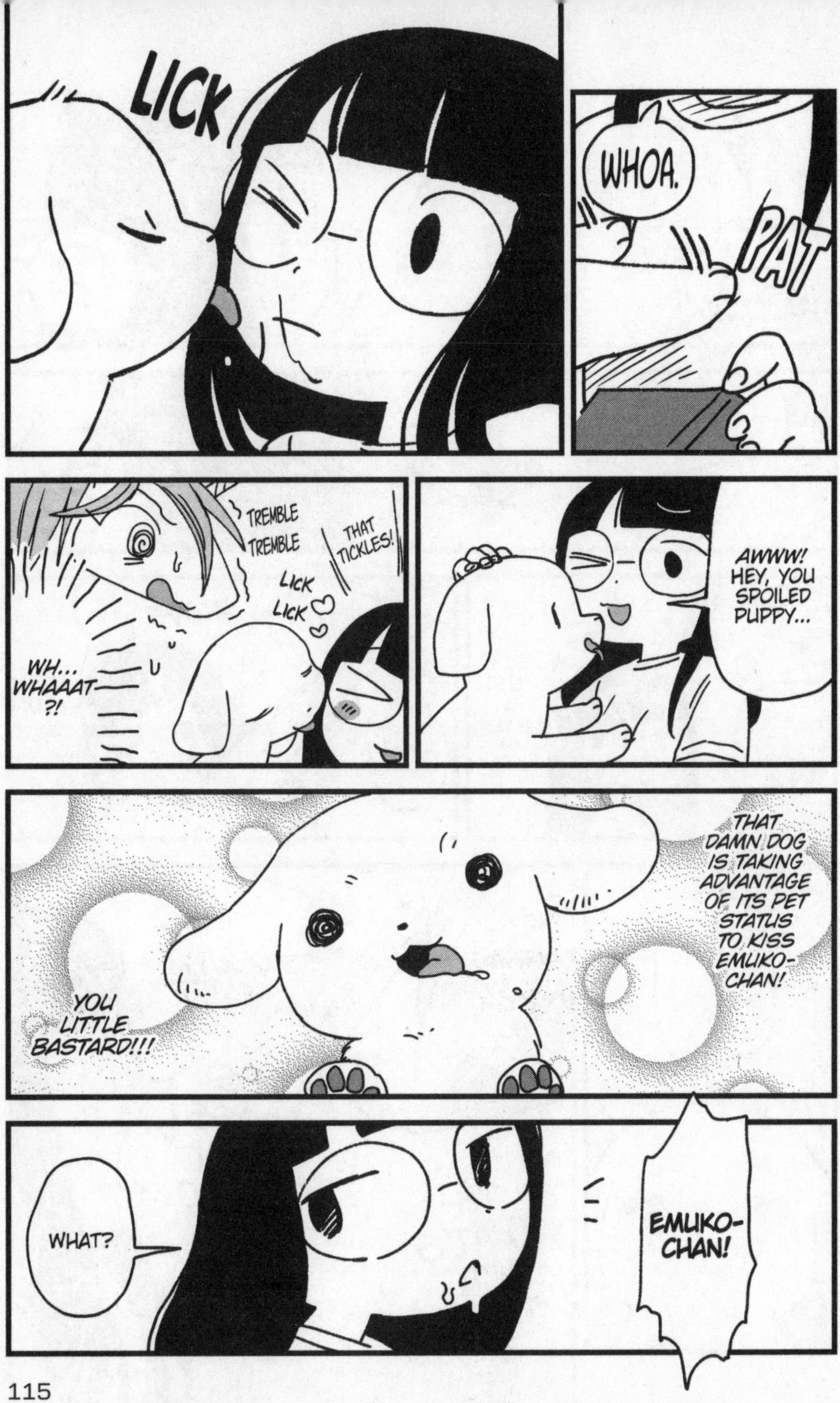
WHOA.
PAT
LICK
AWWW! HEY, YOU SPOILED PUPPY...
THAT TICKLES!
TREMBLE TREMBLE
LICK LICK
WH... WHAAAT?!
THAT DAMN DOG IS TAKING ADVANTAGE OF ITS PET STATUS TO KISS EMUKO-CHAN!
YOU LITTLE BASTARD!!!
EMUKO-CHAN!
WHAT?

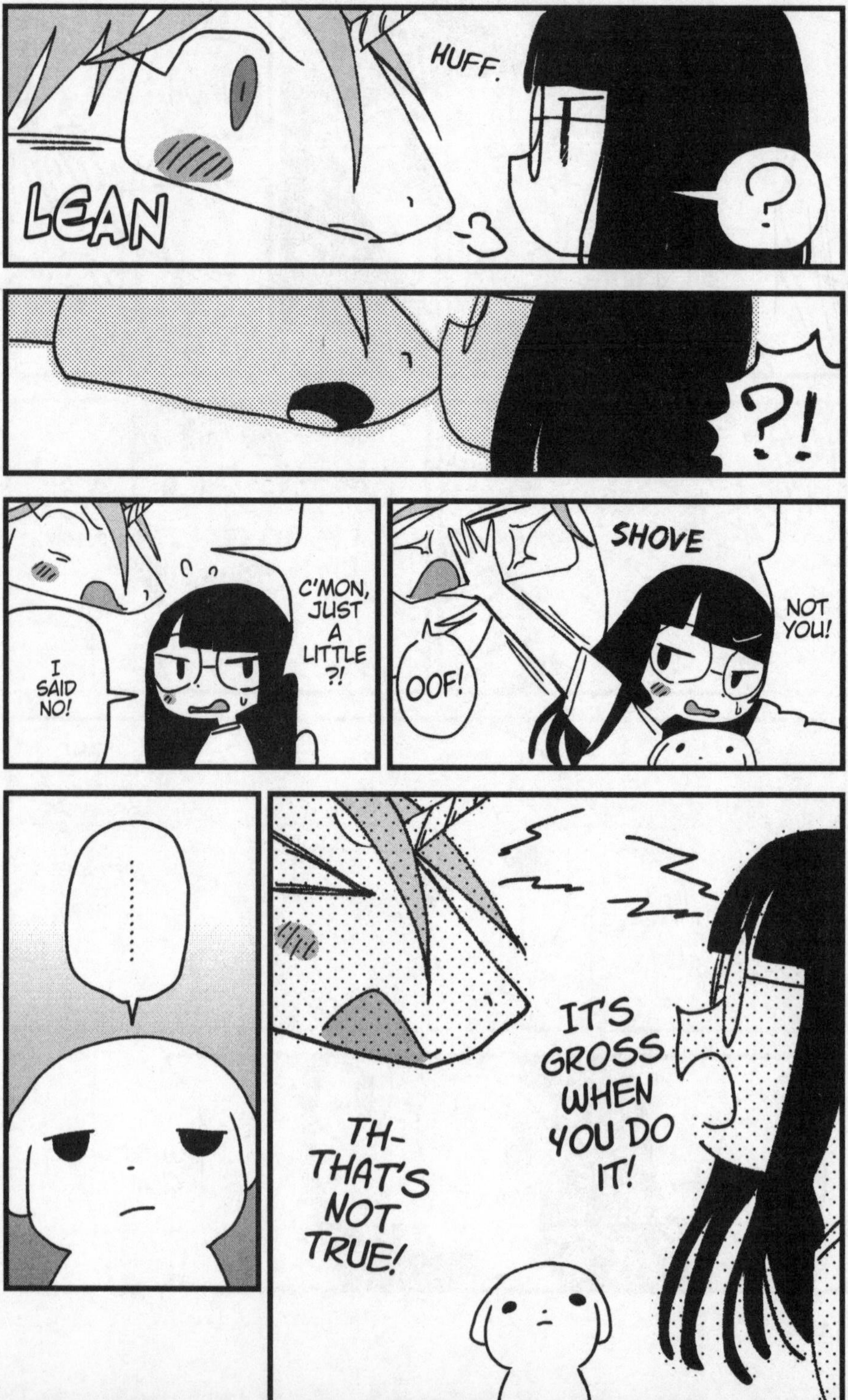
HUFF.
?
LEAN
?!
SHOVE
NOT YOU!
OOF!
C'MON, JUST A LITTLE ?!
I SAID NO!
IT'S GROSS WHEN YOU DO IT!
TH-THAT'S NOT TRUE!
......

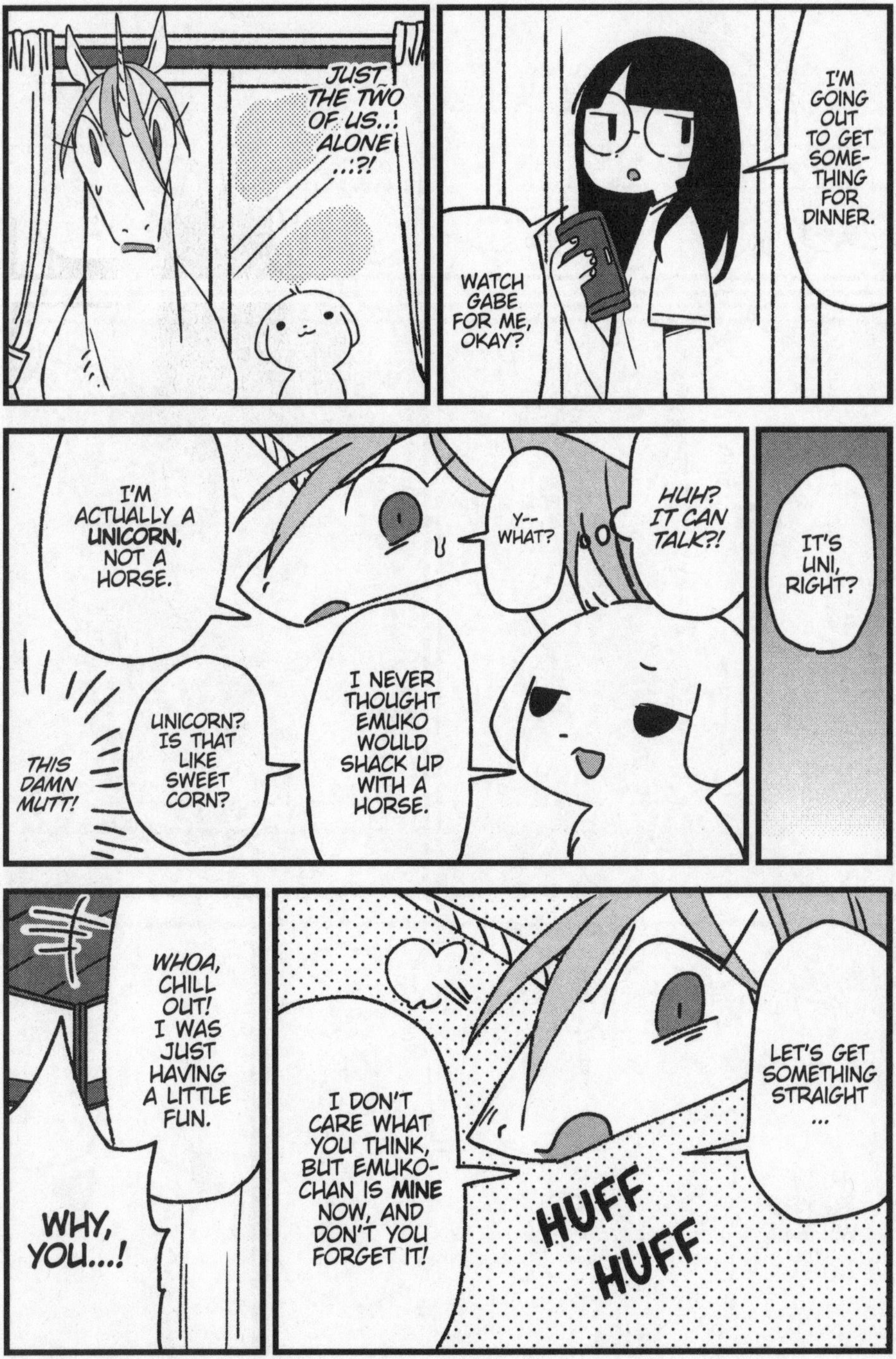
I'M GOING OUT TO GET SOMETHING FOR DINNER.
WATCH GABE FOR ME, OKAY?
JUST THE TWO OF US... ALONE ...?!
IT'S UNI, RIGHT?
HUH? IT CAN TALK?!
Y-- WHAT?
I NEVER THOUGHT EMUKO WOULD SHACK UP WITH A HORSE.
I'M ACTUALLY A **UNICORN,** NOT A HORSE.
UNICORN? IS THAT LIKE SWEET CORN?
THIS DAMN MUTT!
LET'S GET SOMETHING STRAIGHT ...
HUFF HUFF
I DON'T CARE WHAT YOU THINK, BUT EMUKO-CHAN IS **MINE** NOW, AND DON'T YOU FORGET IT!
WHOA, CHILL OUT! I WAS JUST HAVING A LITTLE FUN.
WHY, YOU...!

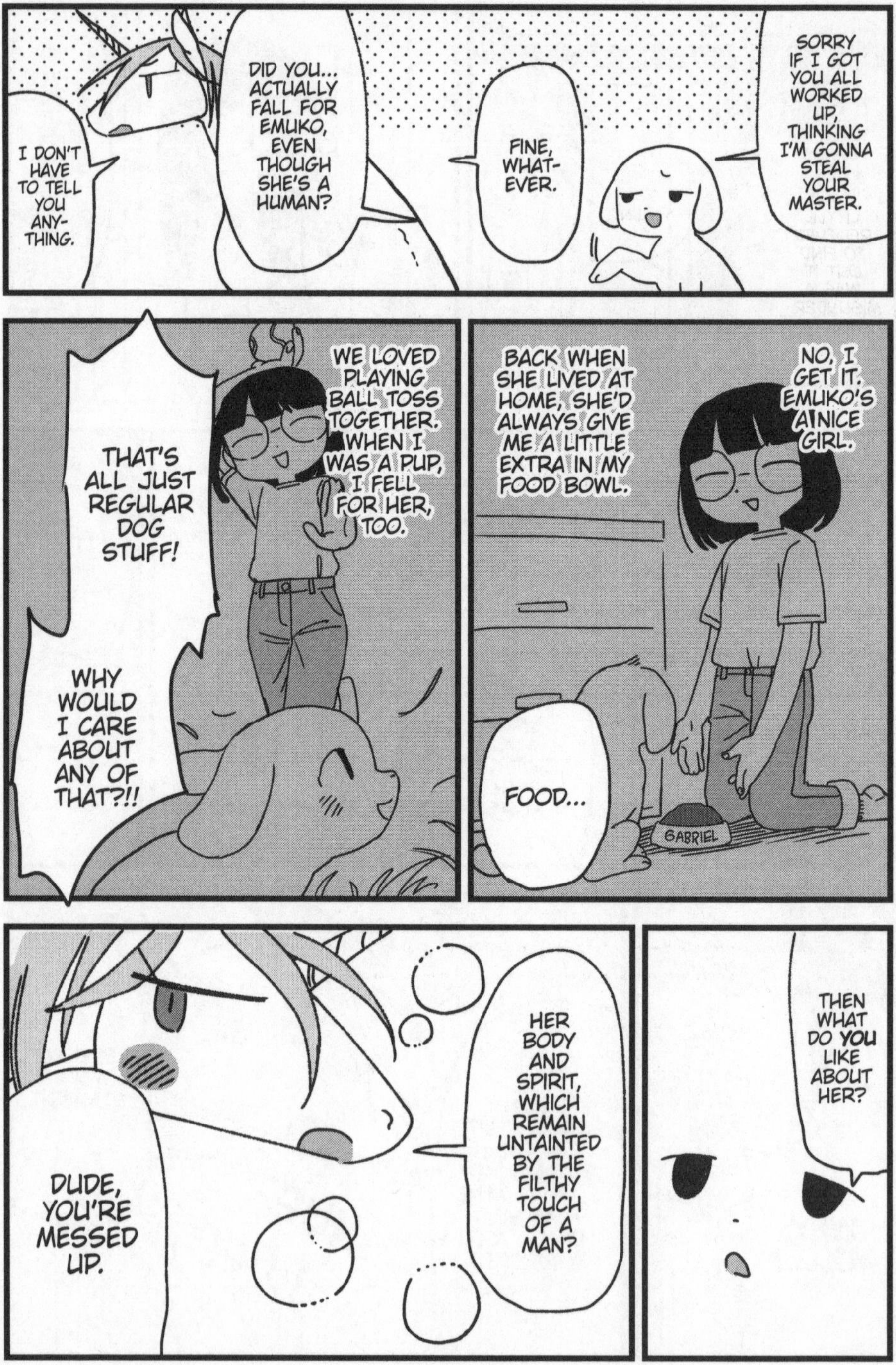
SORRY IF I GOT YOU ALL WORKED UP, THINKING I'M GONNA STEAL YOUR MASTER.
FINE, WHATEVER.
DID YOU... ACTUALLY FALL FOR EMUKO, EVEN THOUGH SHE'S A HUMAN?
I DON'T HAVE TO TELL YOU ANYTHING.
NO, I GET IT. EMUKO'S A NICE GIRL.
BACK WHEN SHE LIVED AT HOME, SHE'D ALWAYS GIVE ME A LITTLE EXTRA IN MY FOOD BOWL.
FOOD...
GABRIEL
WE LOVED PLAYING BALL TOSS TOGETHER. WHEN I WAS A PUP, I FELL FOR HER, TOO.
THAT'S ALL JUST REGULAR DOG STUFF!
WHY WOULD I CARE ABOUT ANY OF THAT?!!
THEN WHAT DO **YOU** LIKE ABOUT HER?
HER BODY AND SPIRIT, WHICH REMAIN UNTAINTED BY THE FILTHY TOUCH OF A MAN?
DUDE, YOU'RE MESSED UP.

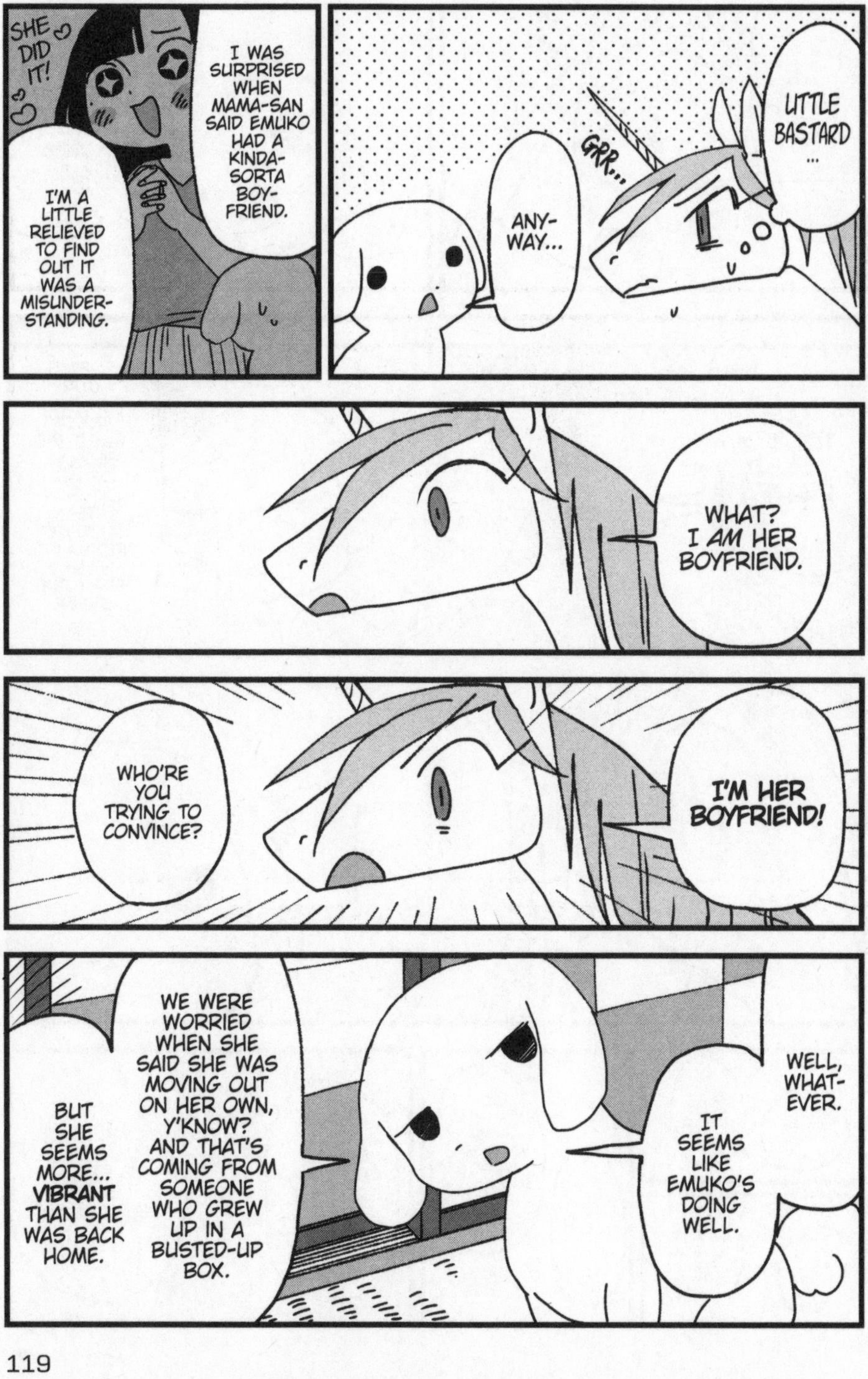
LITTLE BASTARD ...
GRR...
ANYWAY...
I WAS SURPRISED WHEN MAMA-SAN SAID EMUKO HAD A KINDA-SORTA BOYFRIEND.
SHE DID IT!
I'M A LITTLE RELIEVED TO FIND OUT IT WAS A MISUNDERSTANDING.
WHAT? I *AM* HER BOYFRIEND.
I'M HER BOYFRIEND!
WHO'RE YOU TRYING TO CONVINCE?
WELL, WHATEVER.
IT SEEMS LIKE EMUKO'S DOING WELL.
WE WERE WORRIED WHEN SHE SAID SHE WAS MOVING OUT ON HER OWN, Y'KNOW? AND THAT'S COMING FROM SOMEONE WHO GREW UP IN A BUSTED-UP BOX.
BUT SHE SEEMS MORE... **VIBRANT** THAN SHE WAS BACK HOME.

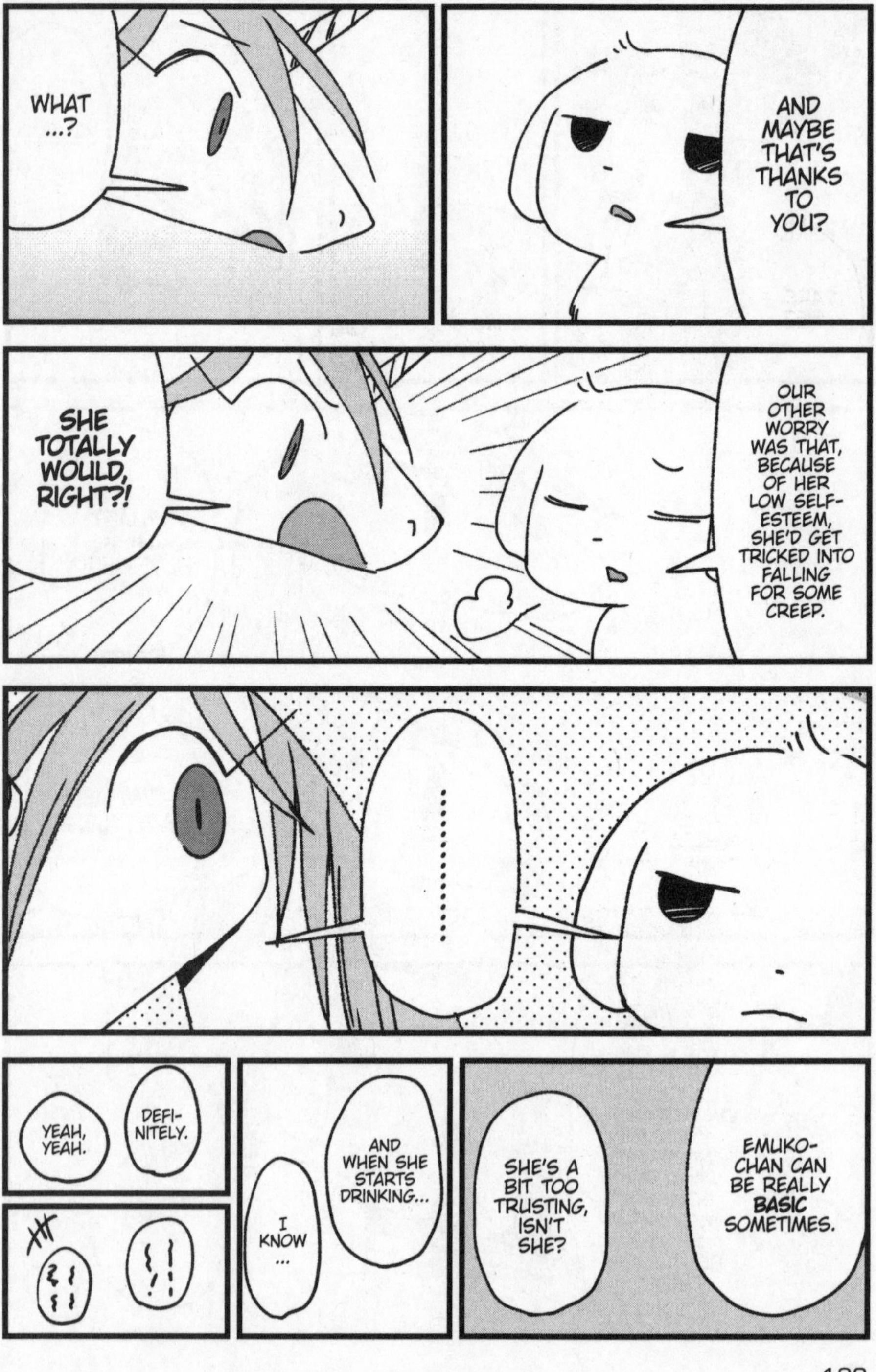
AND MAYBE THAT'S THANKS TO YOU?
WHAT ...?
OUR OTHER WORRY WAS THAT, BECAUSE OF HER LOW SELF-ESTEEM, SHE'D GET TRICKED INTO FALLING FOR SOME CREEP.
SHE TOTALLY WOULD, RIGHT?!
......
EMUKO-CHAN CAN BE REALLY **BASIC** SOMETIMES.
SHE'S A BIT TOO TRUSTING, ISN'T SHE?
AND WHEN SHE STARTS DRINKING...
I KNOW ...
DEFI-NITELY.
YEAH, YEAH.

HUNH.

ARE WE?

HMM? WHEN DID YOU TWO GET SO FRIENDLY?

CHATTER CHATTER

I'M HOME.

UGGGH...

IT'S SO HOT...

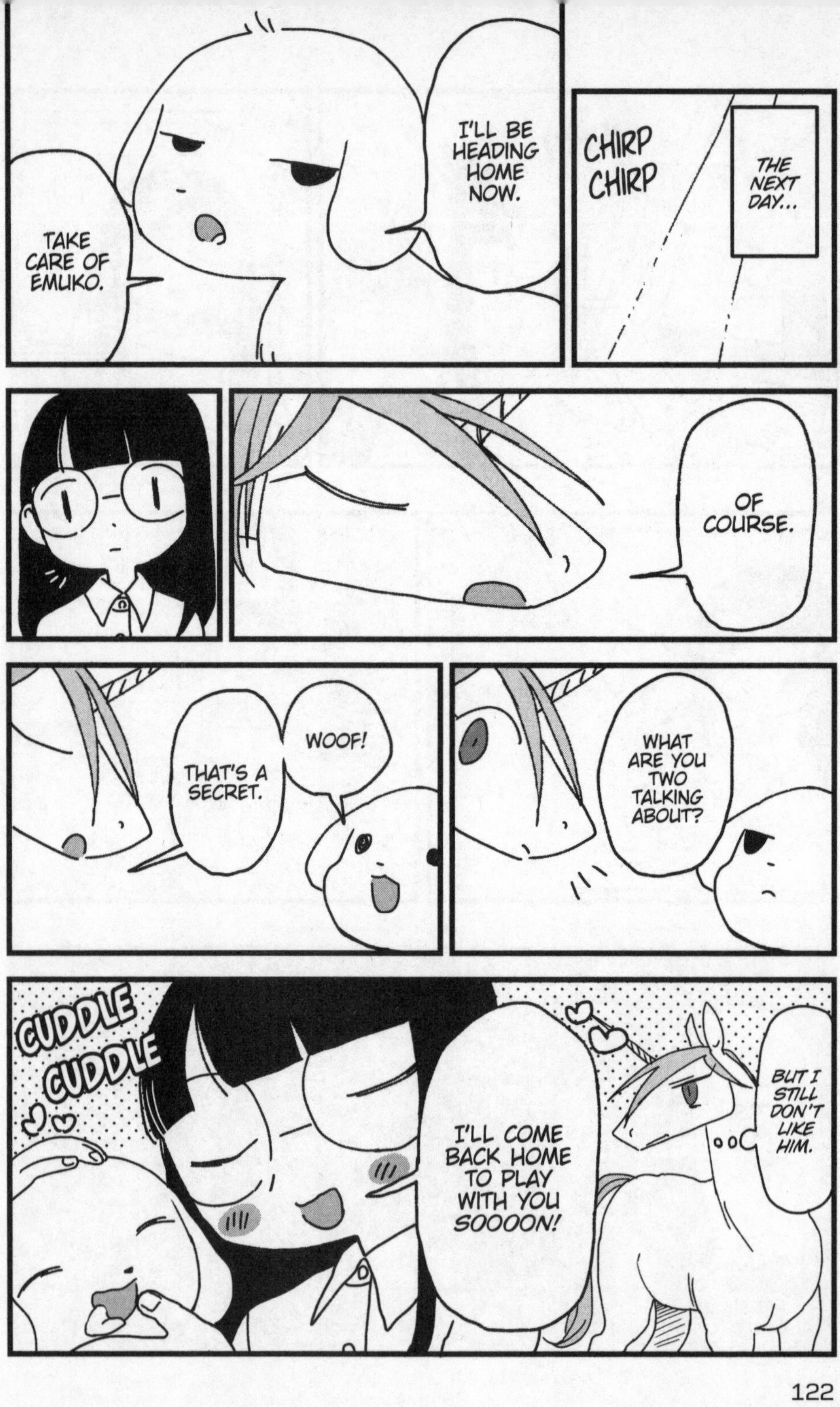
THE NEXT DAY...
CHIRP CHIRP
I'LL BE HEADING HOME NOW.
TAKE CARE OF EMUKO.
OF COURSE.
WHAT ARE YOU TWO TALKING ABOUT?
WOOF!
THAT'S A SECRET.
BUT I STILL DON'T LIKE HIM.
I'LL COME BACK HOME TO PLAY WITH YOU SOOOON!
CUDDLE CUDDLE

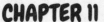

CHAPTER 11 PERSONALITY TEST

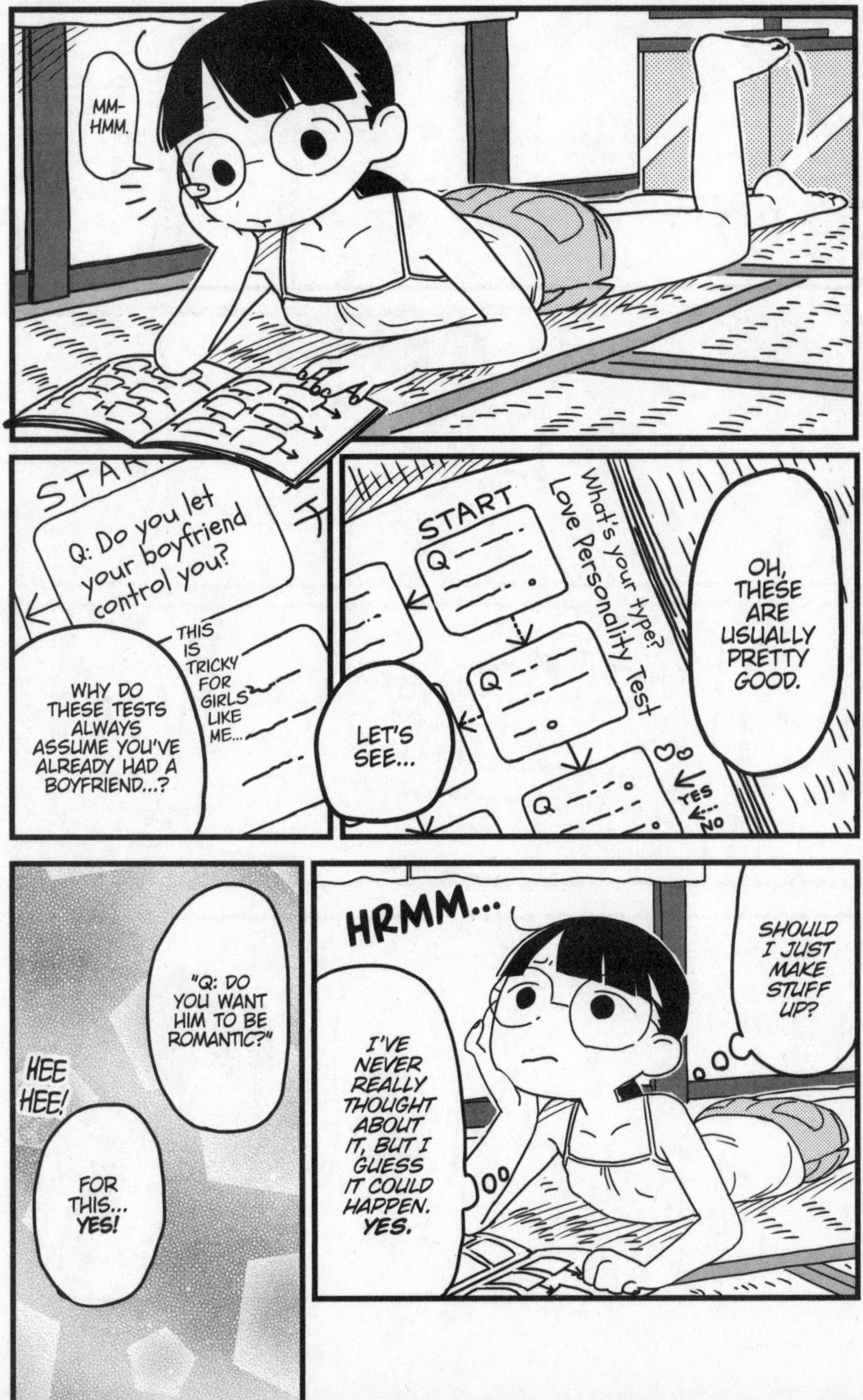
MM-HMM.
OH, THESE ARE USUALLY PRETTY GOOD.
What's your type? Love Personality Test
START
LET'S SEE...
YES
NO
START
Q: Do you let your boyfriend control you?
THIS IS TRICKY FOR GIRLS LIKE ME...
WHY DO THESE TESTS ALWAYS ASSUME YOU'VE ALREADY HAD A BOYFRIEND...?
SHOULD I JUST MAKE STUFF UP?
HRMM...
I'VE NEVER REALLY THOUGHT ABOUT IT, BUT I GUESS IT COULD HAPPEN. YES.
"Q: DO YOU WANT HIM TO BE ROMANTIC?"
HEE HEE!
FOR THIS... YES!

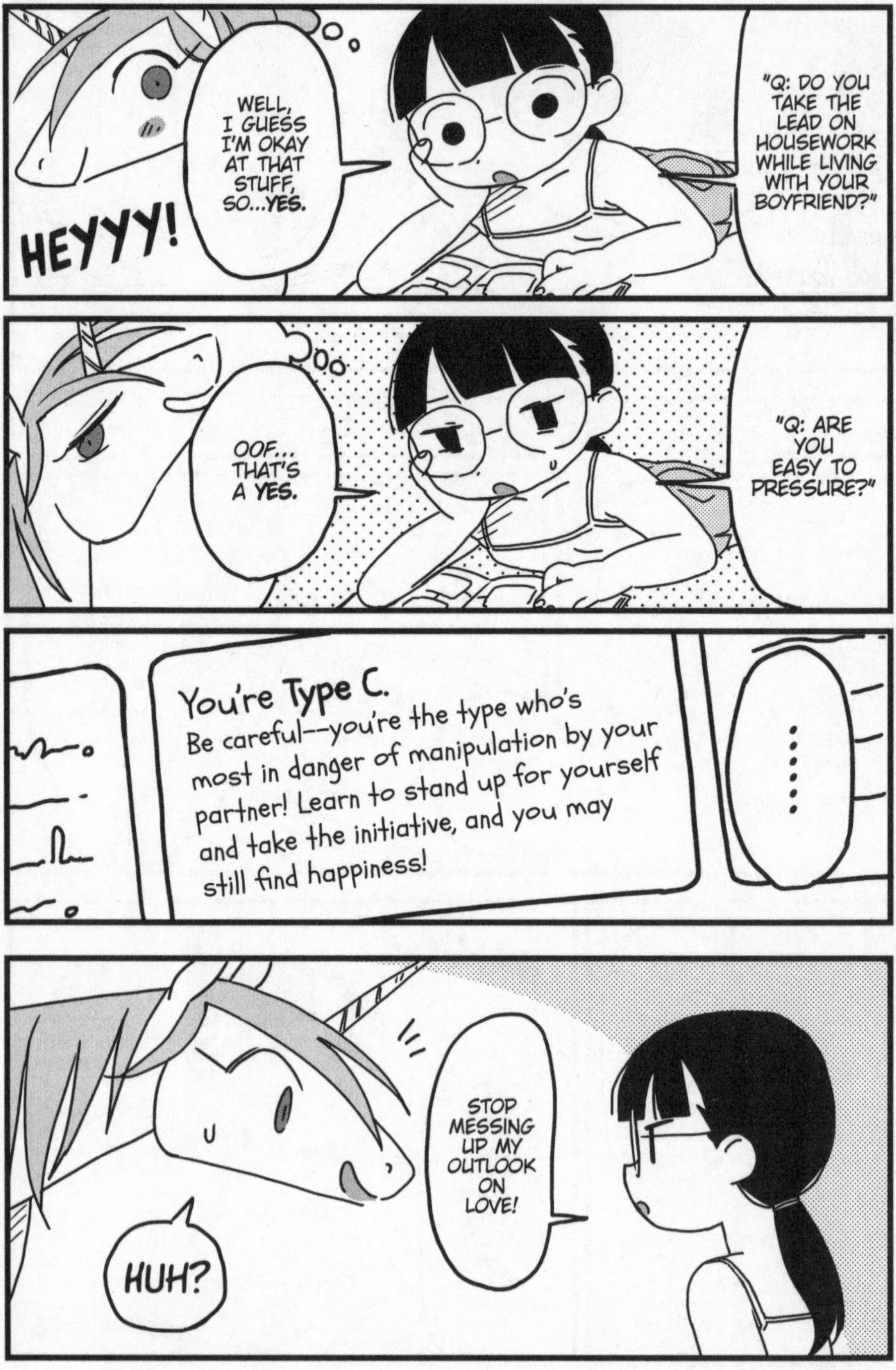

"Q: DO YOU TAKE THE LEAD ON HOUSEWORK WHILE LIVING WITH YOUR BOYFRIEND?"
WELL, I GUESS I'M OKAY AT THAT STUFF, SO...YES.
HEYYY!
"Q: ARE YOU EASY TO PRESSURE?"
OOF... THAT'S A YES.
......
You're Type C. Be careful--you're the type who's most in danger of manipulation by your partner! Learn to stand up for yourself and take the initiative, and you may still find happiness!
STOP MESSING UP MY OUTLOOK ON LOVE!
HUH?

ASTROLOGY

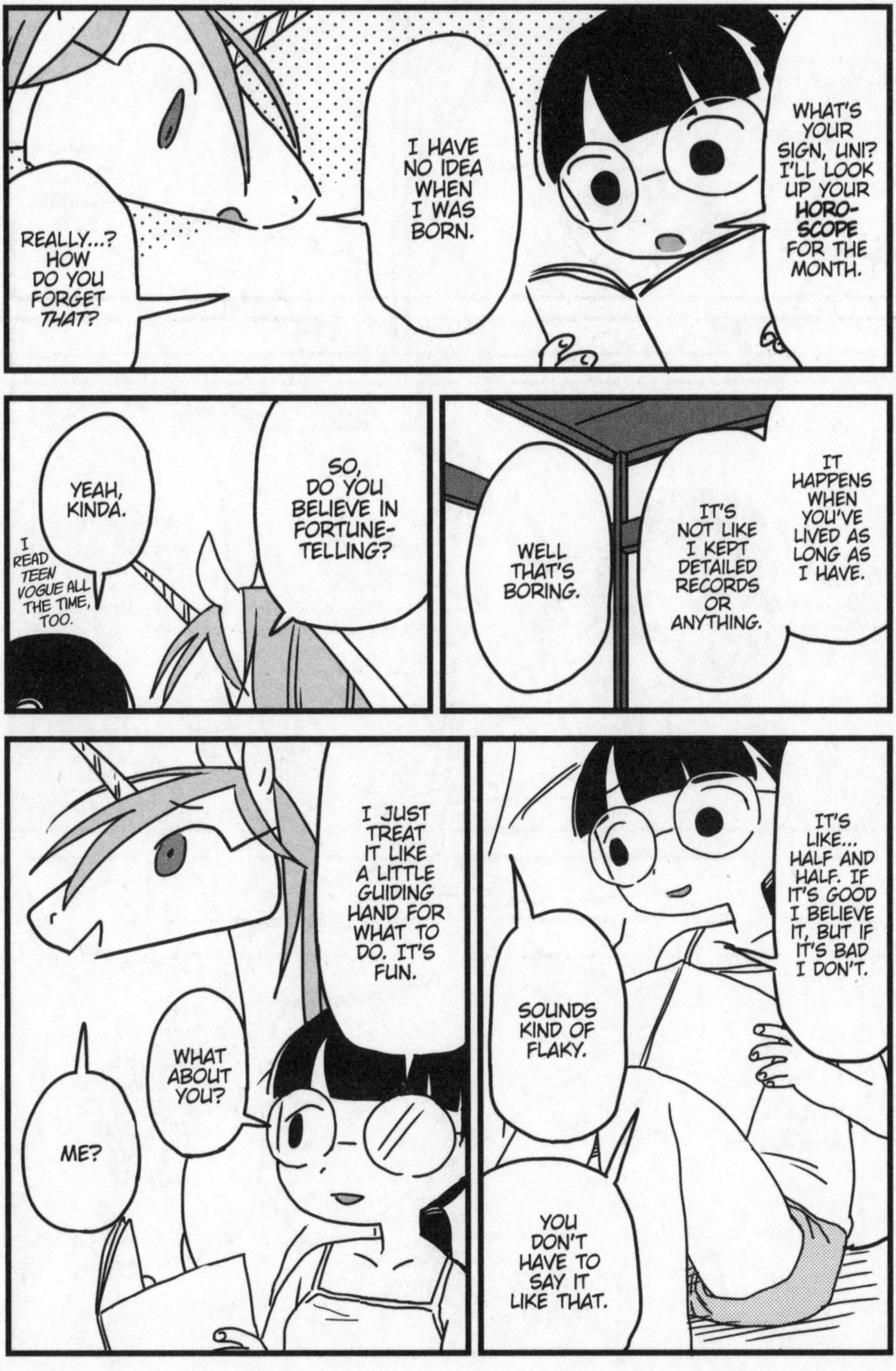
WHAT'S YOUR SIGN, UNI? I'LL LOOK UP YOUR **HOROSCOPE** FOR THE MONTH.
I HAVE NO IDEA WHEN I WAS BORN.
REALLY...? HOW DO YOU FORGET *THAT?*
IT HAPPENS WHEN YOU'VE LIVED AS LONG AS I HAVE.
IT'S NOT LIKE I KEPT DETAILED RECORDS OR ANYTHING.
WELL THAT'S BORING.
SO, DO YOU BELIEVE IN FORTUNE-TELLING?
YEAH, KINDA.
I READ *TEEN VOGUE* ALL THE TIME, TOO.
IT'S LIKE... HALF AND HALF. IF IT'S GOOD I BELIEVE IT, BUT IF IT'S BAD I DON'T.
SOUNDS KIND OF FLAKY.
YOU DON'T HAVE TO SAY IT LIKE THAT.
I JUST TREAT IT LIKE A LITTLE GUIDING HAND FOR WHAT TO DO. IT'S FUN.
WHAT ABOUT YOU?
ME?

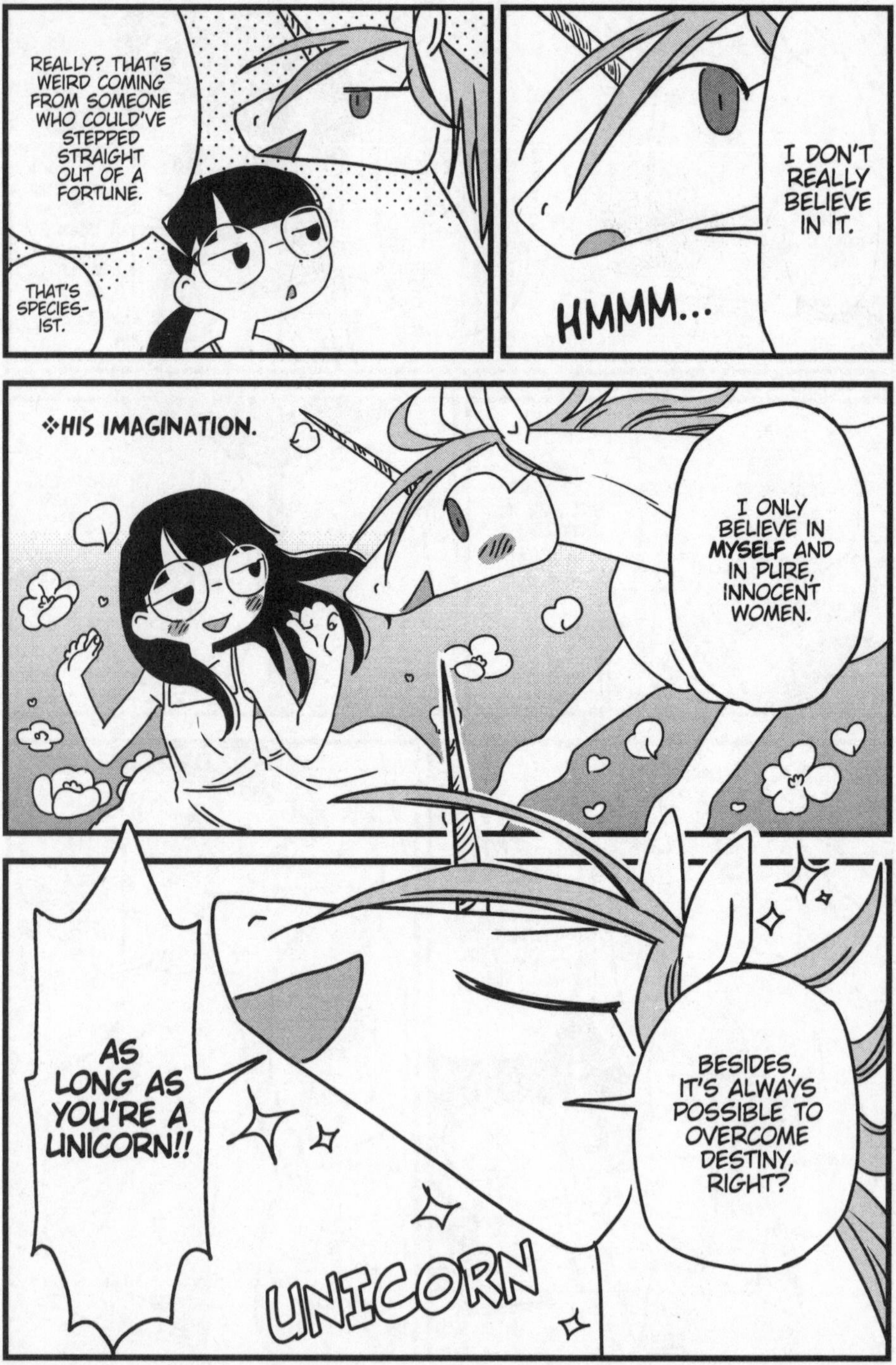

I DON'T REALLY BELIEVE IN IT.
HMMM...
REALLY? THAT'S WEIRD COMING FROM SOMEONE WHO COULD'VE STEPPED STRAIGHT OUT OF A FORTUNE.
THAT'S SPECIES-IST.
I ONLY BELIEVE IN MYSELF AND IN PURE, INNOCENT WOMEN.
❖HIS IMAGINATION.
BESIDES, IT'S ALWAYS POSSIBLE TO OVERCOME DESTINY, RIGHT?
AS LONG AS YOU'RE A UNICORN!!
UNICORN

TODAY'S FORTUNE

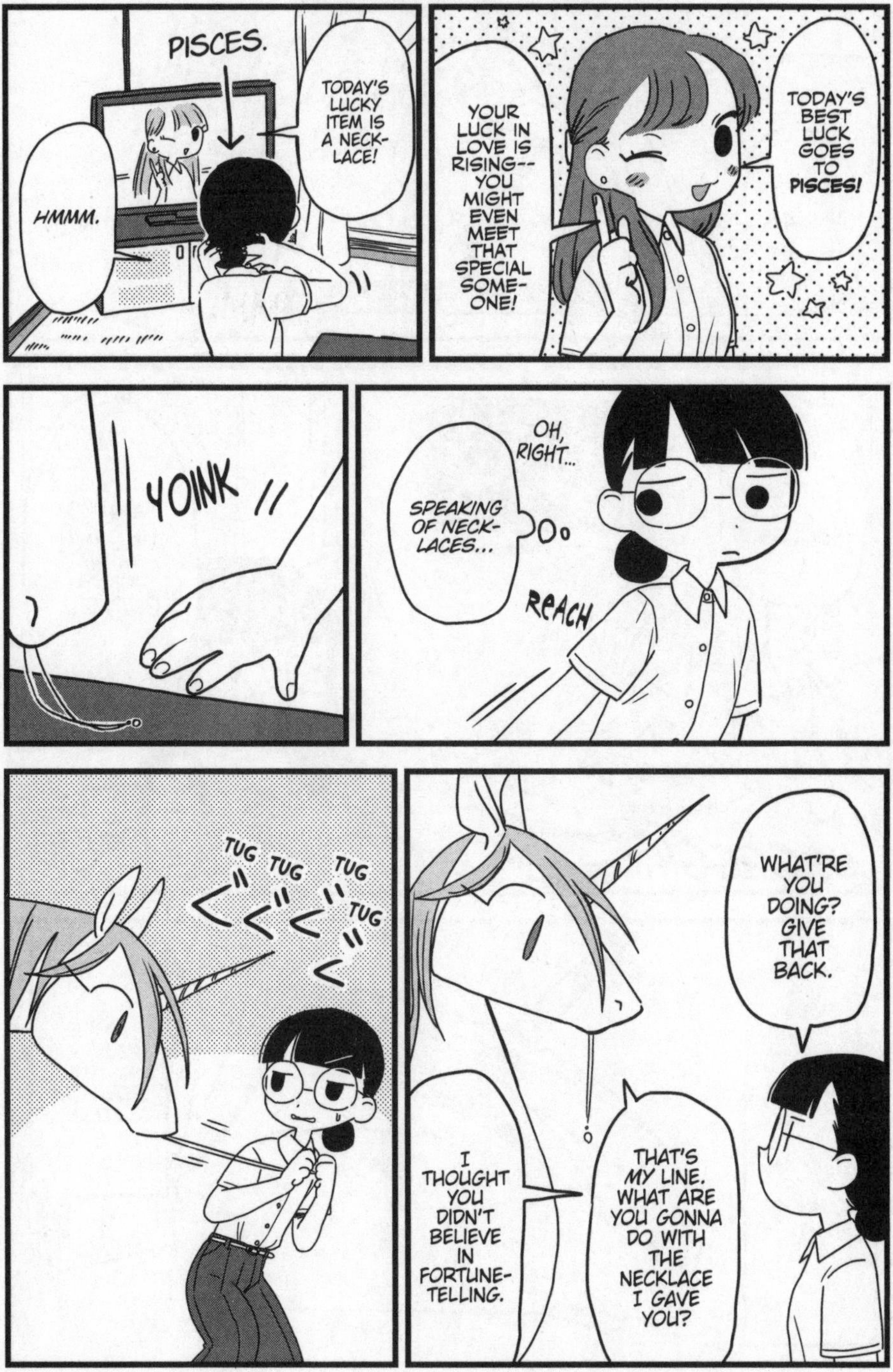
TODAY'S BEST LUCK GOES TO PISCES!
YOUR LUCK IN LOVE IS RISING--YOU MIGHT EVEN MEET THAT SPECIAL SOMEONE!
PISCES.
TODAY'S LUCKY ITEM IS A NECKLACE!
HMMM.
OH, RIGHT...
SPEAKING OF NECKLACES...
REACH
YOINK
WHAT'RE YOU DOING? GIVE THAT BACK.
THAT'S MY LINE. WHAT ARE YOU GONNA DO WITH THE NECKLACE I GAVE YOU?
I THOUGHT YOU DIDN'T BELIEVE IN FORTUNE-TELLING.
TUG TUG TUG TUG

A UNICORN'S MELANCHOLY

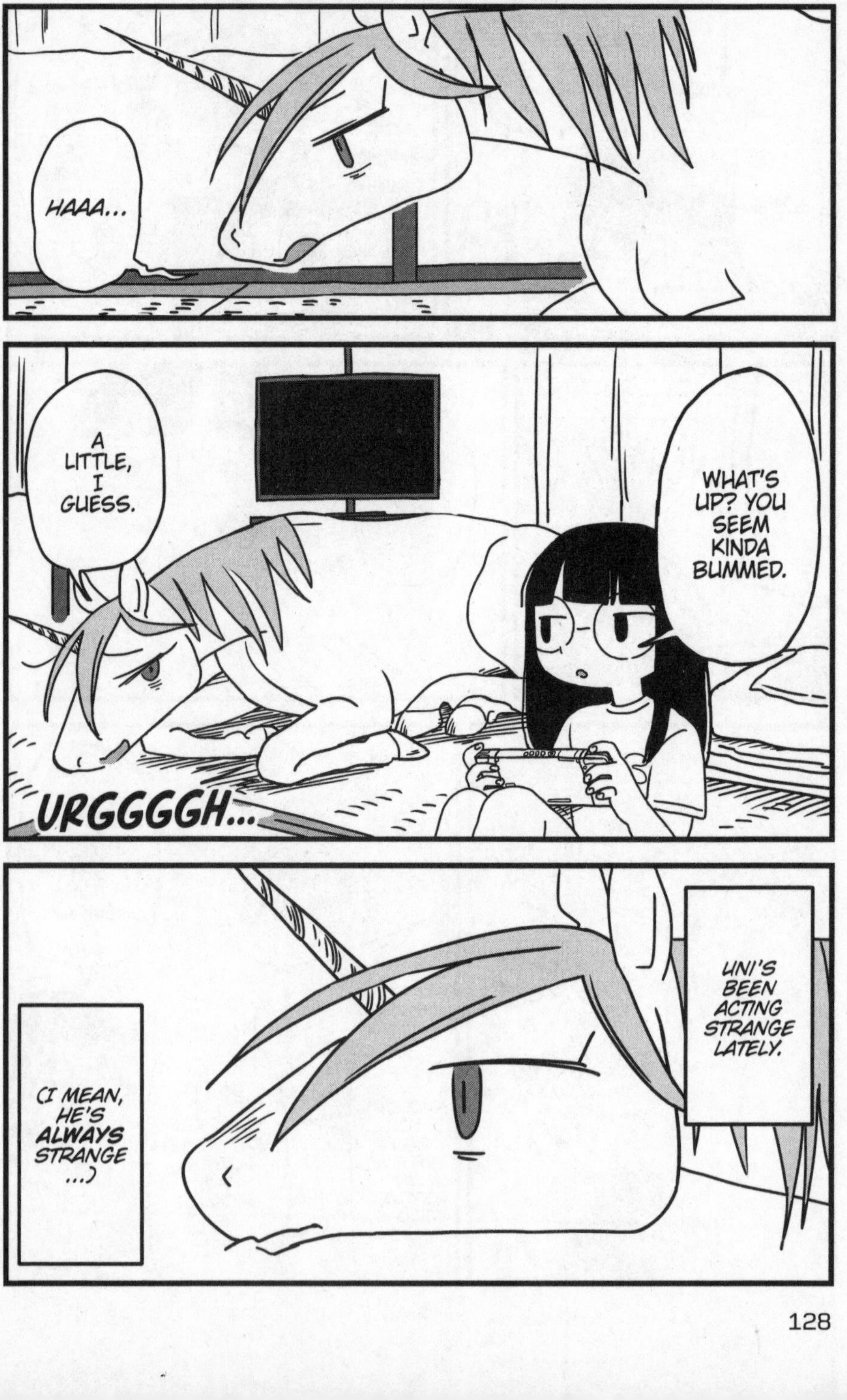
HAAA...
WHAT'S UP? YOU SEEM KINDA BUMMED.
A LITTLE, I GUESS.
URGGGGH...
UNI'S BEEN ACTING STRANGE LATELY.
(I MEAN, HE'S **ALWAYS** STRANGE ...)

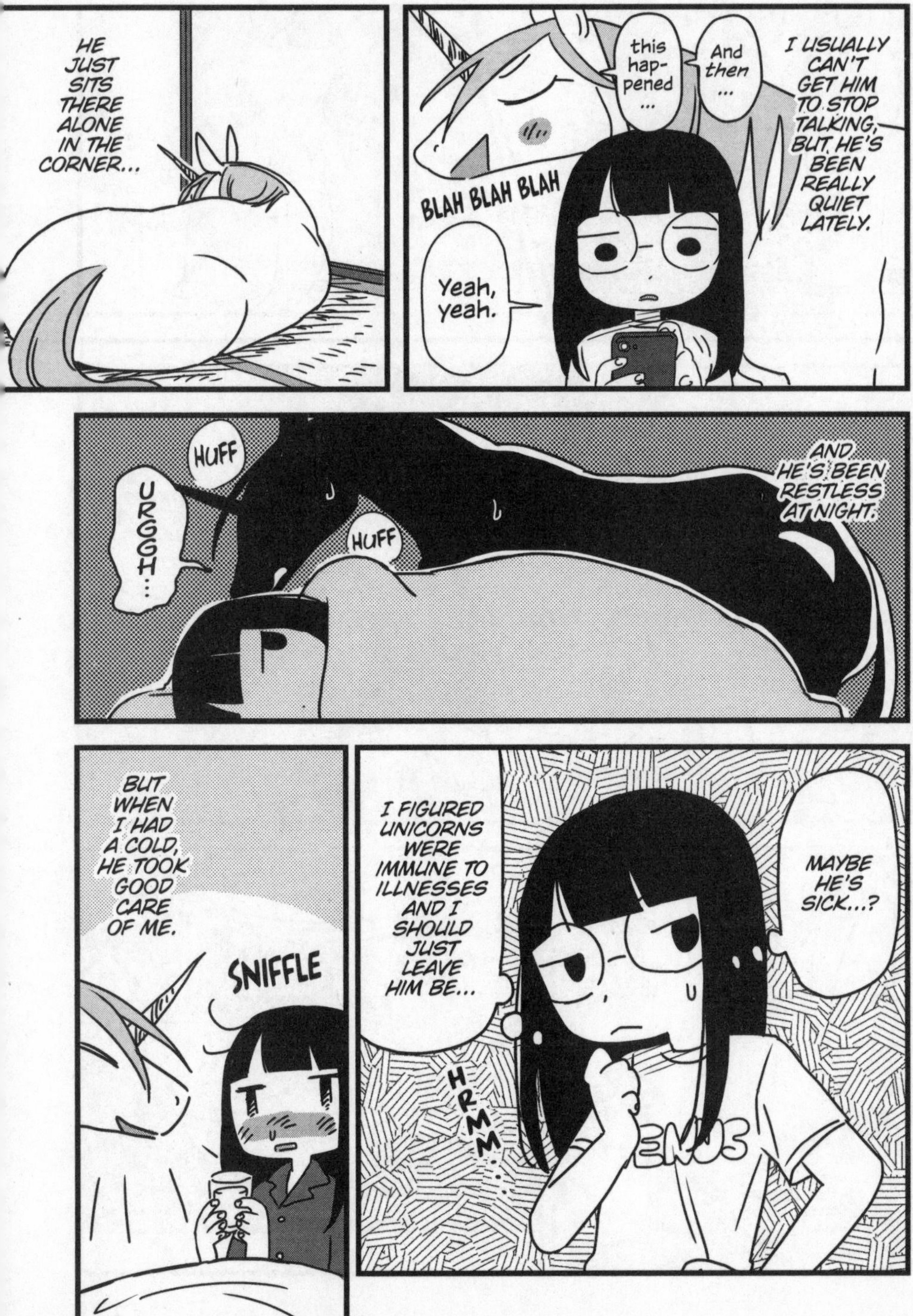
I USUALLY CAN'T GET HIM TO STOP TALKING, BUT HE'S BEEN REALLY QUIET LATELY.
And then ...
this hap-pened ...
BLAH BLAH BLAH
Yeah, yeah.
HE JUST SITS THERE ALONE IN THE CORNER...
AND HE'S BEEN RESTLESS AT NIGHT.
HUFF
URGGH...
HUFF
MAYBE HE'S SICK...?
I FIGURED UNICORNS WERE IMMUNE TO ILLNESSES AND I SHOULD JUST LEAVE HIM BE...
HRMM...
BUT WHEN I HAD A COLD, HE TOOK GOOD CARE OF ME.
SNIFFLE

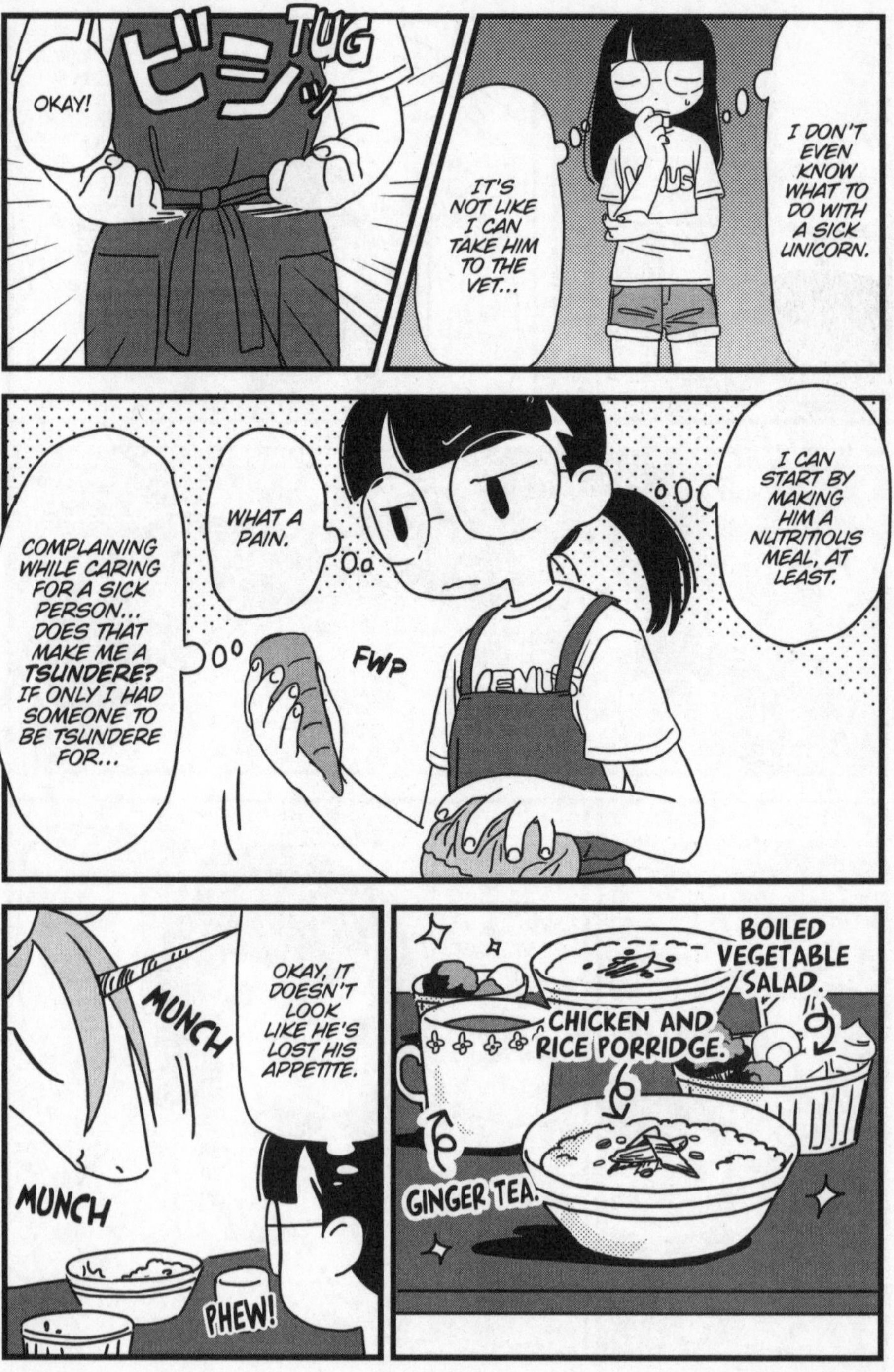
I DON'T EVEN KNOW WHAT TO DO WITH A SICK UNICORN.
IT'S NOT LIKE I CAN TAKE HIM TO THE VET...
TUG
OKAY!
I CAN START BY MAKING HIM A NUTRITIOUS MEAL, AT LEAST.
WHAT A PAIN.
COMPLAINING WHILE CARING FOR A SICK PERSON... DOES THAT MAKE ME A TSUNDERE? IF ONLY I HAD SOMEONE TO BE TSUNDERE FOR...
FWP
BOILED VEGETABLE SALAD.
CHICKEN AND RICE PORRIDGE.
GINGER TEA.
OKAY, IT DOESN'T LOOK LIKE HE'S LOST HIS APPETITE.
MUNCH
MUNCH
PHEW!

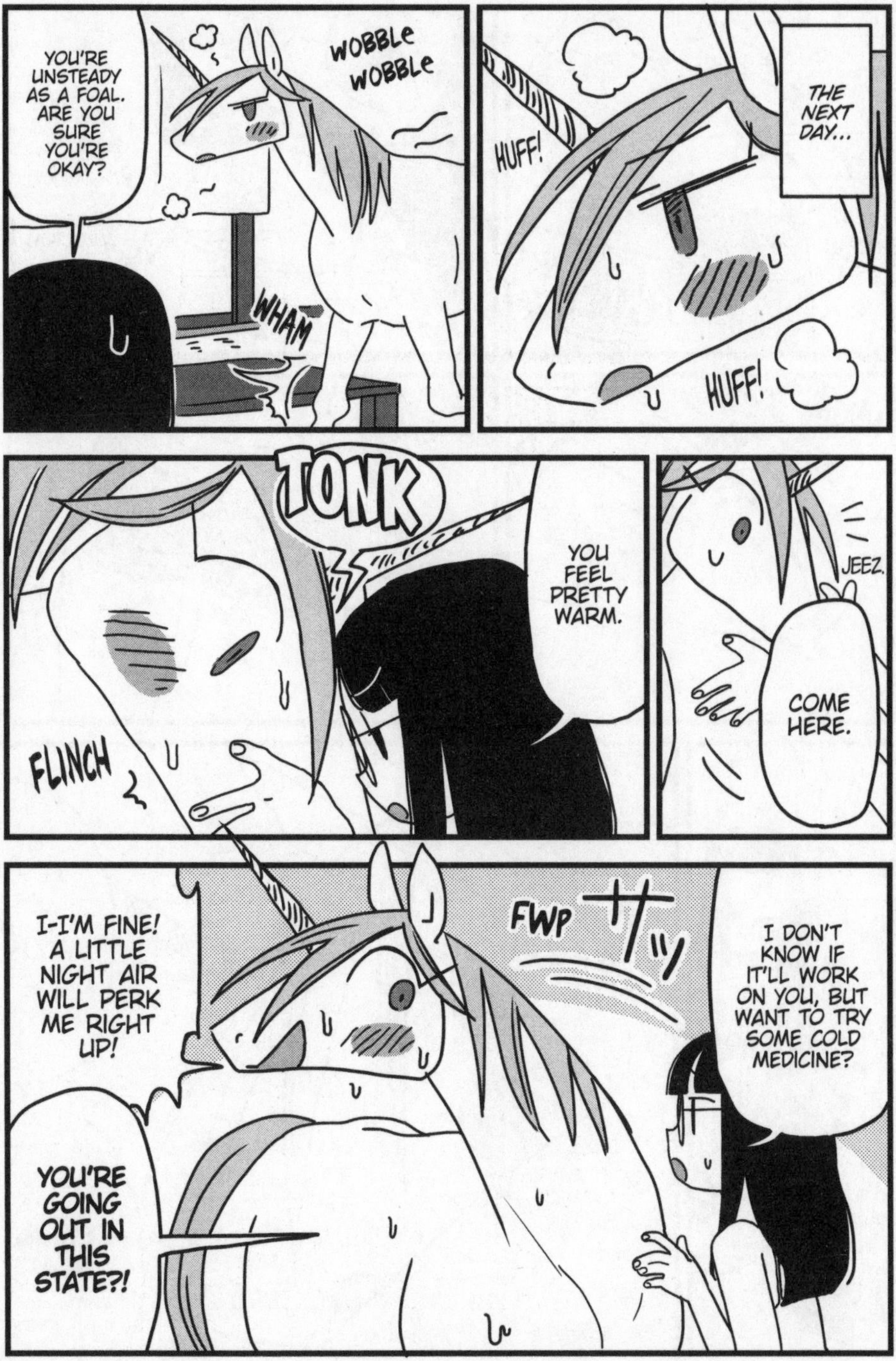
THE NEXT DAY...
HUFF!
HUFF!
WOBBLE WOBBLE
YOU'RE UNSTEADY AS A FOAL. ARE YOU SURE YOU'RE OKAY?
WHAM
JEEZ.
COME HERE.
TONK
YOU FEEL PRETTY WARM.
FLINCH
I DON'T KNOW IF IT'LL WORK ON YOU, BUT WANT TO TRY SOME COLD MEDICINE?
FWP サッ
I-I'M FINE! A LITTLE NIGHT AIR WILL PERK ME RIGHT UP!
YOU'RE GOING OUT IN THIS STATE?!

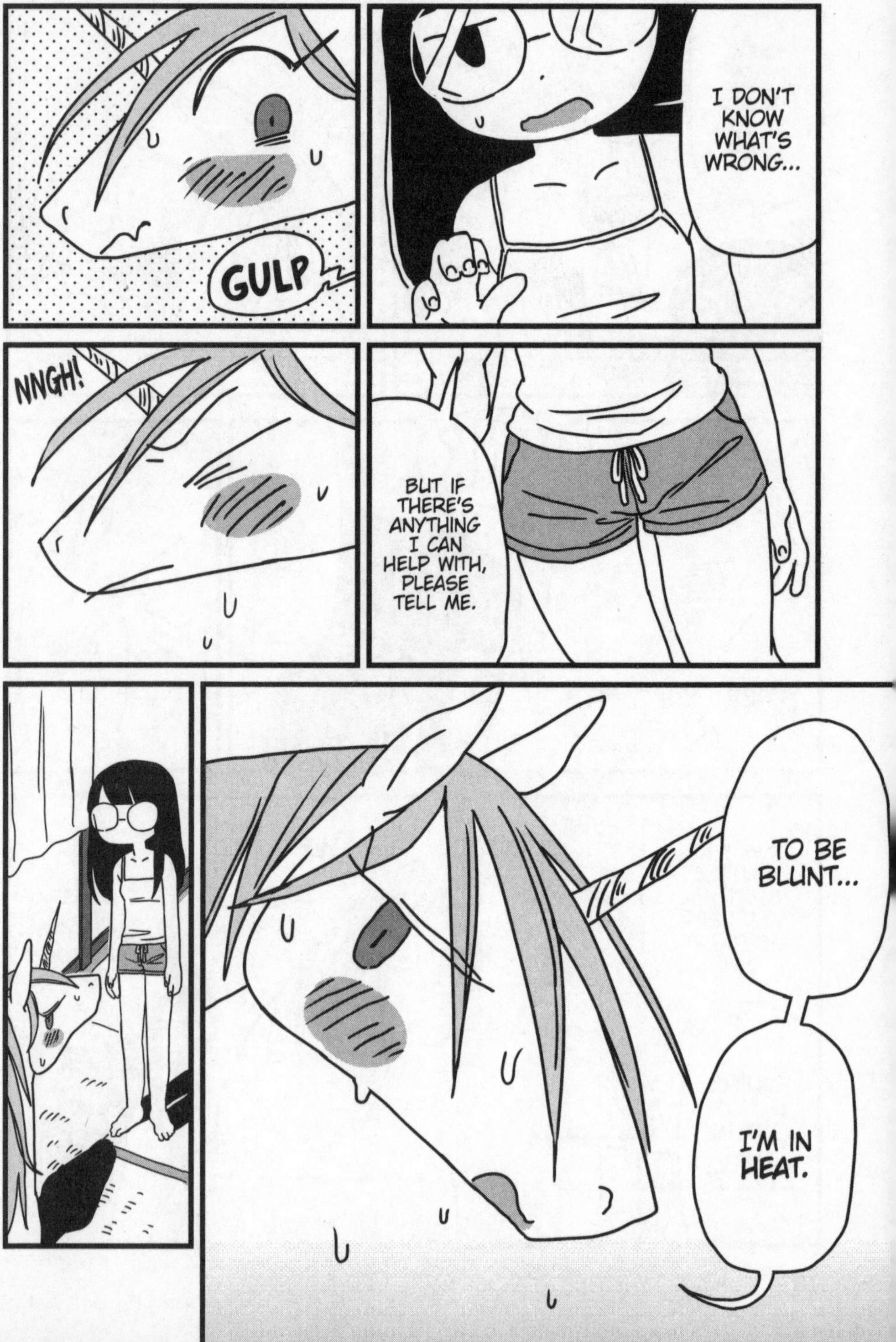
I DON'T KNOW WHAT'S WRONG...
GULP
BUT IF THERE'S ANYTHING I CAN HELP WITH, PLEASE TELL ME.
NNGH!
TO BE BLUNT...
I'M IN HEAT.

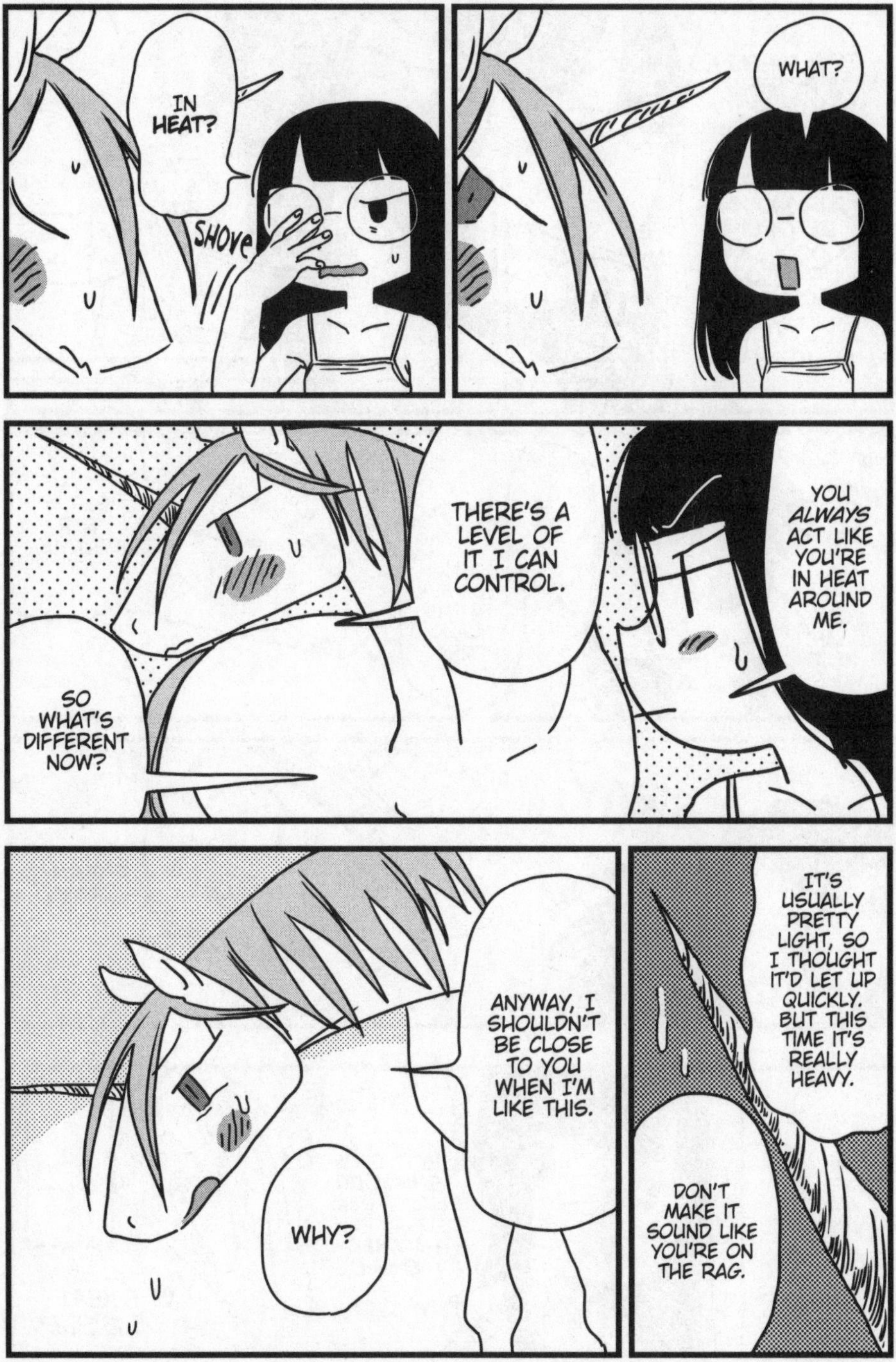
WHAT?
IN HEAT?
SHOVE
YOU ALWAYS ACT LIKE YOU'RE IN HEAT AROUND ME.
THERE'S A LEVEL OF IT I CAN CONTROL.
SO WHAT'S DIFFERENT NOW?
IT'S USUALLY PRETTY LIGHT, SO I THOUGHT IT'D LET UP QUICKLY. BUT THIS TIME IT'S REALLY HEAVY.
DON'T MAKE IT SOUND LIKE YOU'RE ON THE RAG.
ANYWAY, I SHOULDN'T BE CLOSE TO YOU WHEN I'M LIKE THIS.
WHY?

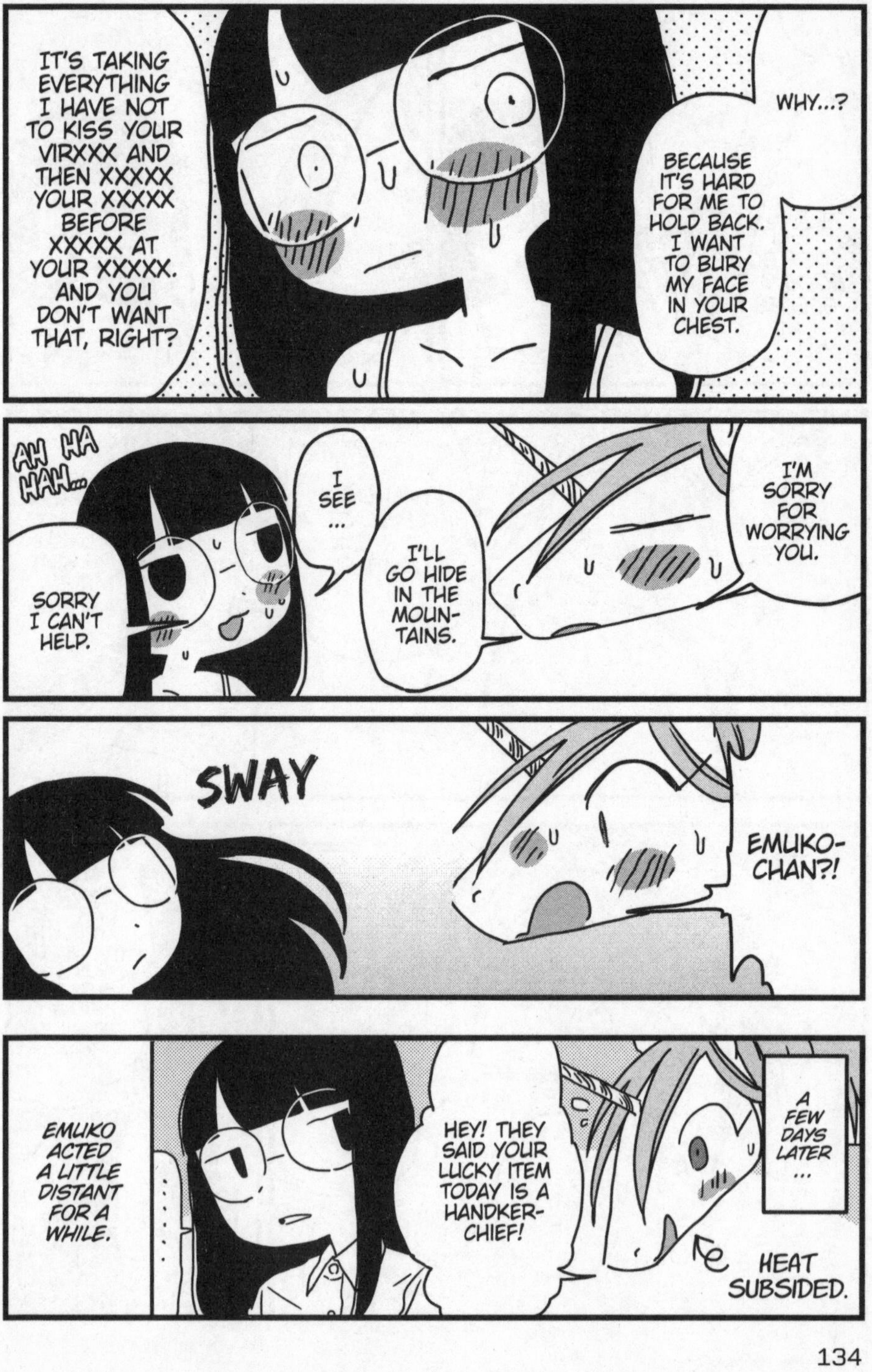
WHY...?
BECAUSE IT'S HARD FOR ME TO HOLD BACK. I WANT TO BURY MY FACE IN YOUR CHEST.
IT'S TAKING EVERYTHING I HAVE NOT TO KISS YOUR VIRXXX AND THEN XXXXX YOUR XXXXX BEFORE XXXXX AT YOUR XXXXX. AND YOU DON'T WANT THAT, RIGHT?
I'M SORRY FOR WORRYING YOU.
I'LL GO HIDE IN THE MOUNTAINS.
I SEE ...
SORRY I CAN'T HELP.
AH HA HAH...
EMUKO-CHAN?!
SWAY
A FEW DAYS LATER ...
HEAT SUBSIDED.
HEY! THEY SAID YOUR LUCKY ITEM TODAY IS A HANDKERCHIEF!
EMUKO ACTED A LITTLE DISTANT FOR A WHILE.

CHAPTER 12

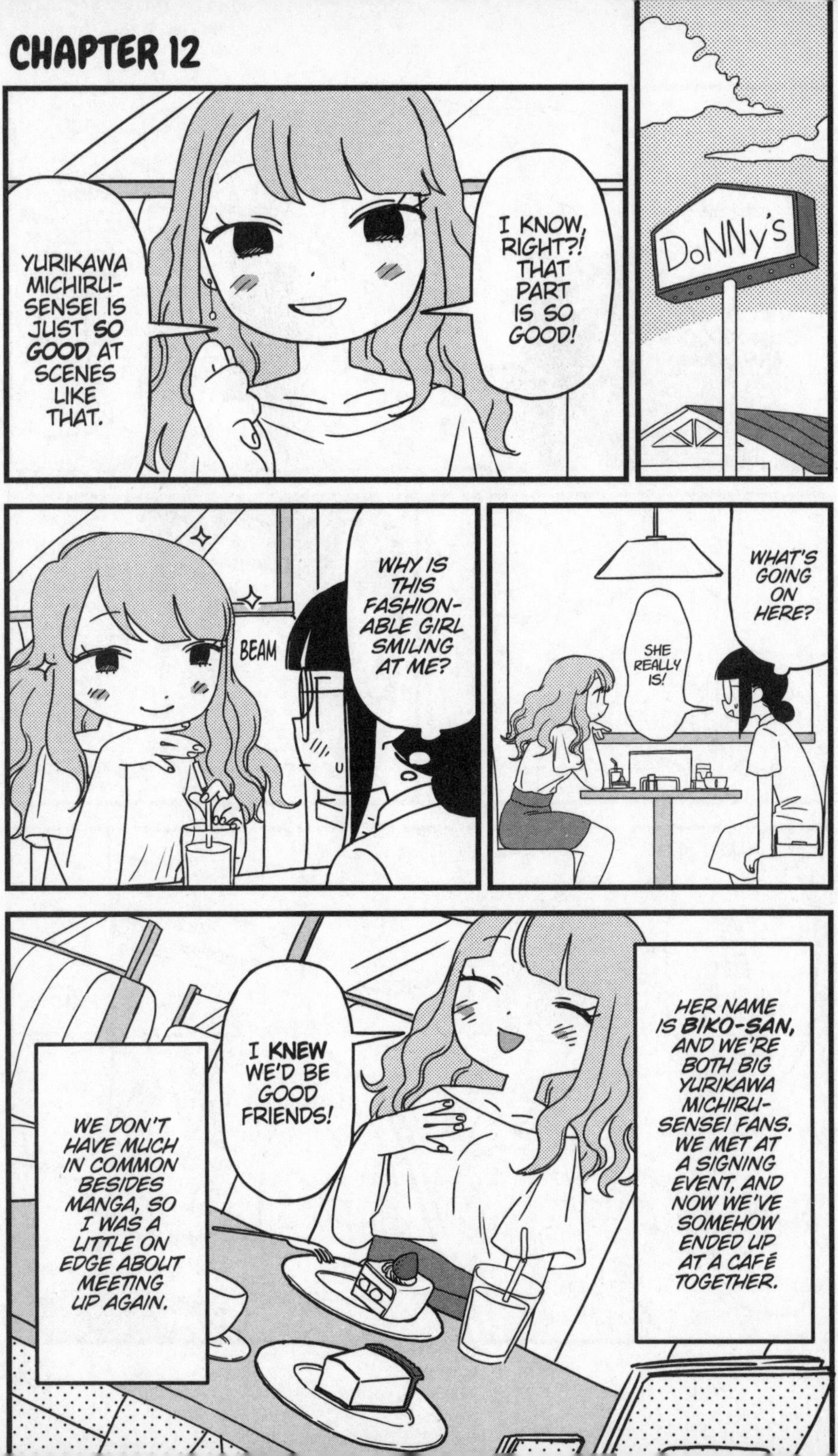
DoNNy's
I KNOW, RIGHT?! THAT PART IS SO GOOD!
YURIKAWA MICHIRU-SENSEI IS JUST SO GOOD AT SCENES LIKE THAT.
WHAT'S GOING ON HERE?
SHE REALLY IS!
WHY IS THIS FASHION-ABLE GIRL SMILING AT ME?
BEAM
HER NAME IS BIKO-SAN, AND WE'RE BOTH BIG YURIKAWA MICHIRU-SENSEI FANS. WE MET AT A SIGNING EVENT, AND NOW WE'VE SOMEHOW ENDED UP AT A CAFÉ TOGETHER.
I KNEW WE'D BE GOOD FRIENDS!
WE DON'T HAVE MUCH IN COMMON BESIDES MANGA, SO I WAS A LITTLE ON EDGE ABOUT MEETING UP AGAIN.

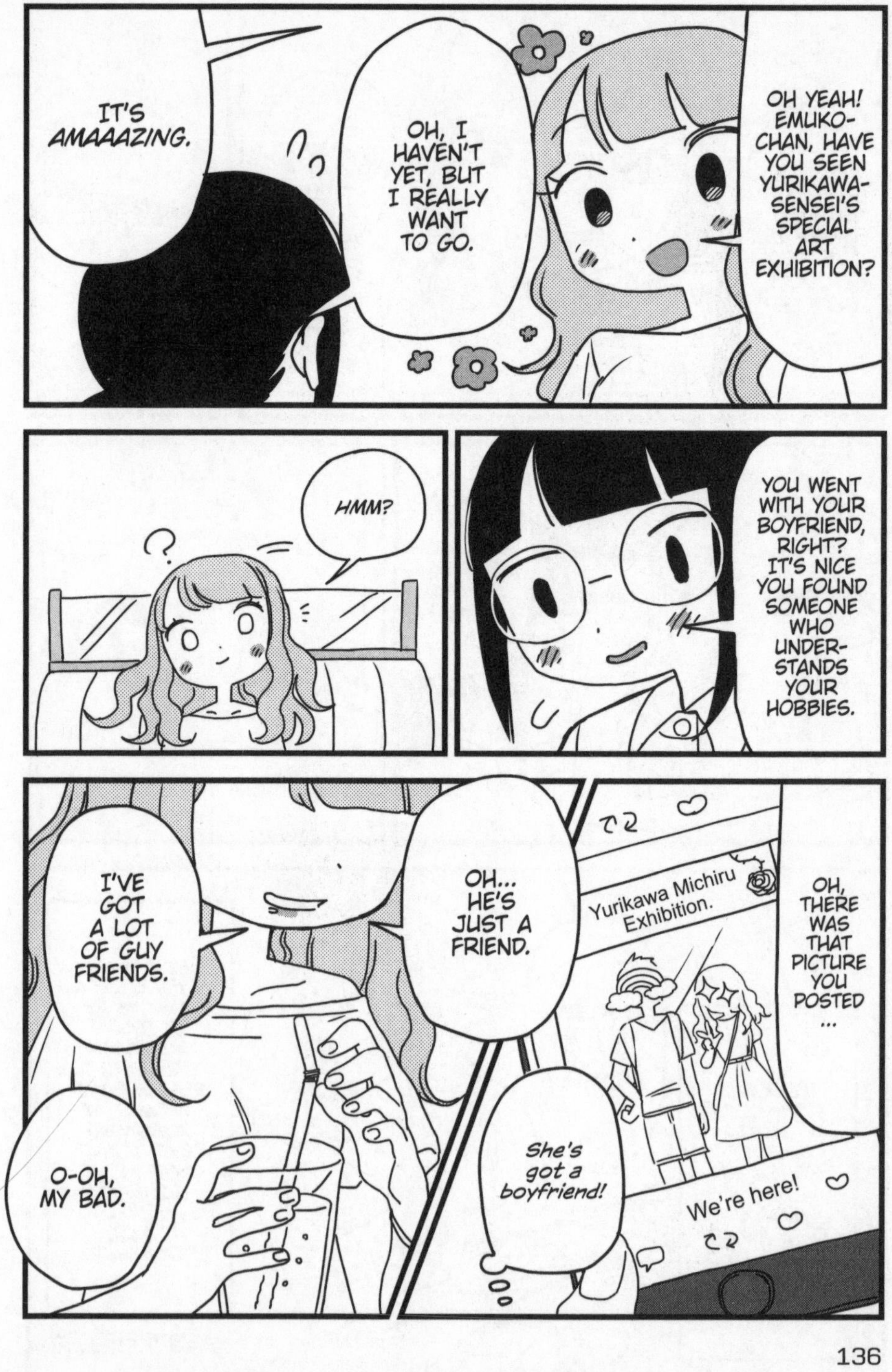
OH YEAH! EMUKO-CHAN, HAVE YOU SEEN YURIKAWA-SENSEI'S SPECIAL ART EXHIBITION?
OH, I HAVEN'T YET, BUT I REALLY WANT TO GO.
IT'S AMAAAZING.
YOU WENT WITH YOUR BOYFRIEND, RIGHT? IT'S NICE YOU FOUND SOMEONE WHO UNDERSTANDS YOUR HOBBIES.
HMM?
OH, THERE WAS THAT PICTURE YOU POSTED...
Yurikawa Michiru Exhibition.
We're here!
She's got a boyfriend!
OH... HE'S JUST A FRIEND.
I'VE GOT A LOT OF GUY FRIENDS.
O-OH, MY BAD.

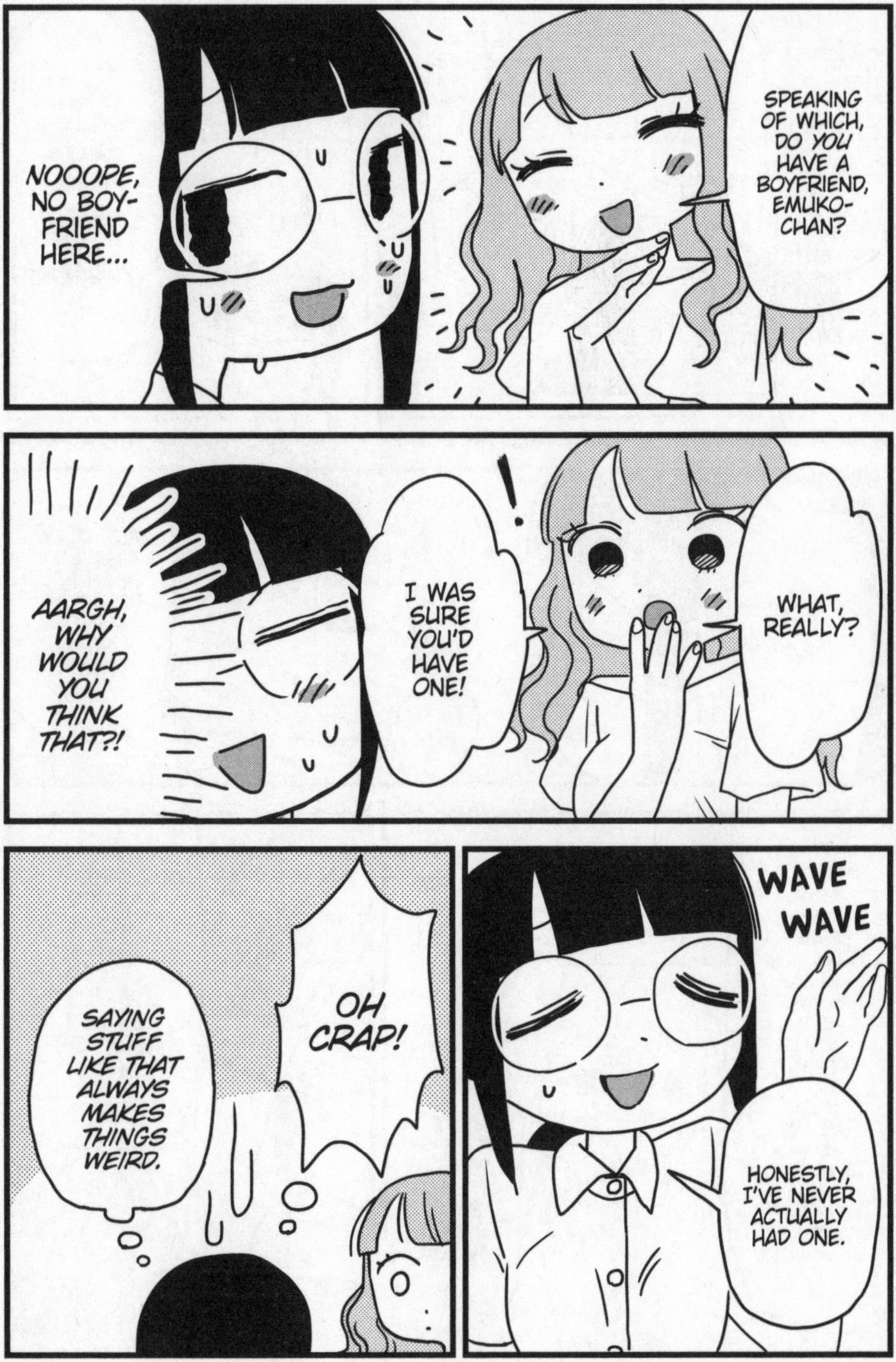
SPEAKING OF WHICH, DO YOU HAVE A BOYFRIEND, EMUKO-CHAN?
NOOOPE, NO BOY-FRIEND HERE...
WHAT, REALLY?
I WAS SURE YOU'D HAVE ONE!
AARGH, WHY WOULD YOU THINK THAT?!
WAVE WAVE
HONESTLY, I'VE NEVER ACTUALLY HAD ONE.
OH CRAP!
SAYING STUFF LIKE THAT ALWAYS MAKES THINGS WEIRD.

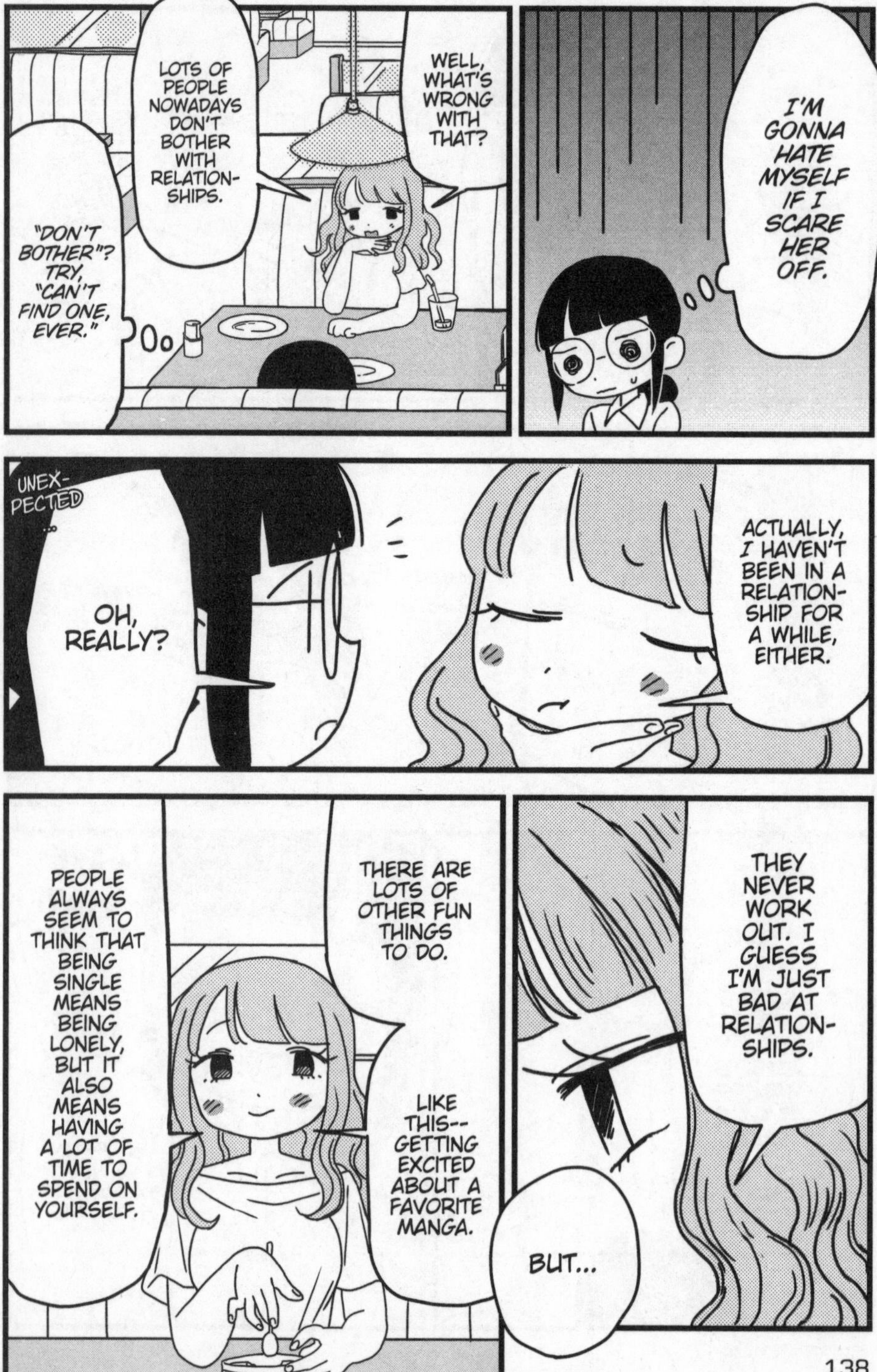
I'M GONNA HATE MYSELF IF I SCARE HER OFF.
WELL, WHAT'S WRONG WITH THAT?
LOTS OF PEOPLE NOWADAYS DON'T BOTHER WITH RELATION-SHIPS.
"DON'T BOTHER"? TRY, "CAN'T FIND ONE, EVER."
ACTUALLY, I HAVEN'T BEEN IN A RELATION-SHIP FOR A WHILE, EITHER.
OH, REALLY?
UNEX-PECTED
THEY NEVER WORK OUT. I GUESS I'M JUST BAD AT RELATION-SHIPS.
BUT...
THERE ARE LOTS OF OTHER FUN THINGS TO DO.
LIKE THIS-- GETTING EXCITED ABOUT A FAVORITE MANGA.
PEOPLE ALWAYS SEEM TO THINK THAT BEING SINGLE MEANS BEING LONELY, BUT IT ALSO MEANS HAVING A LOT OF TIME TO SPEND ON YOURSELF.

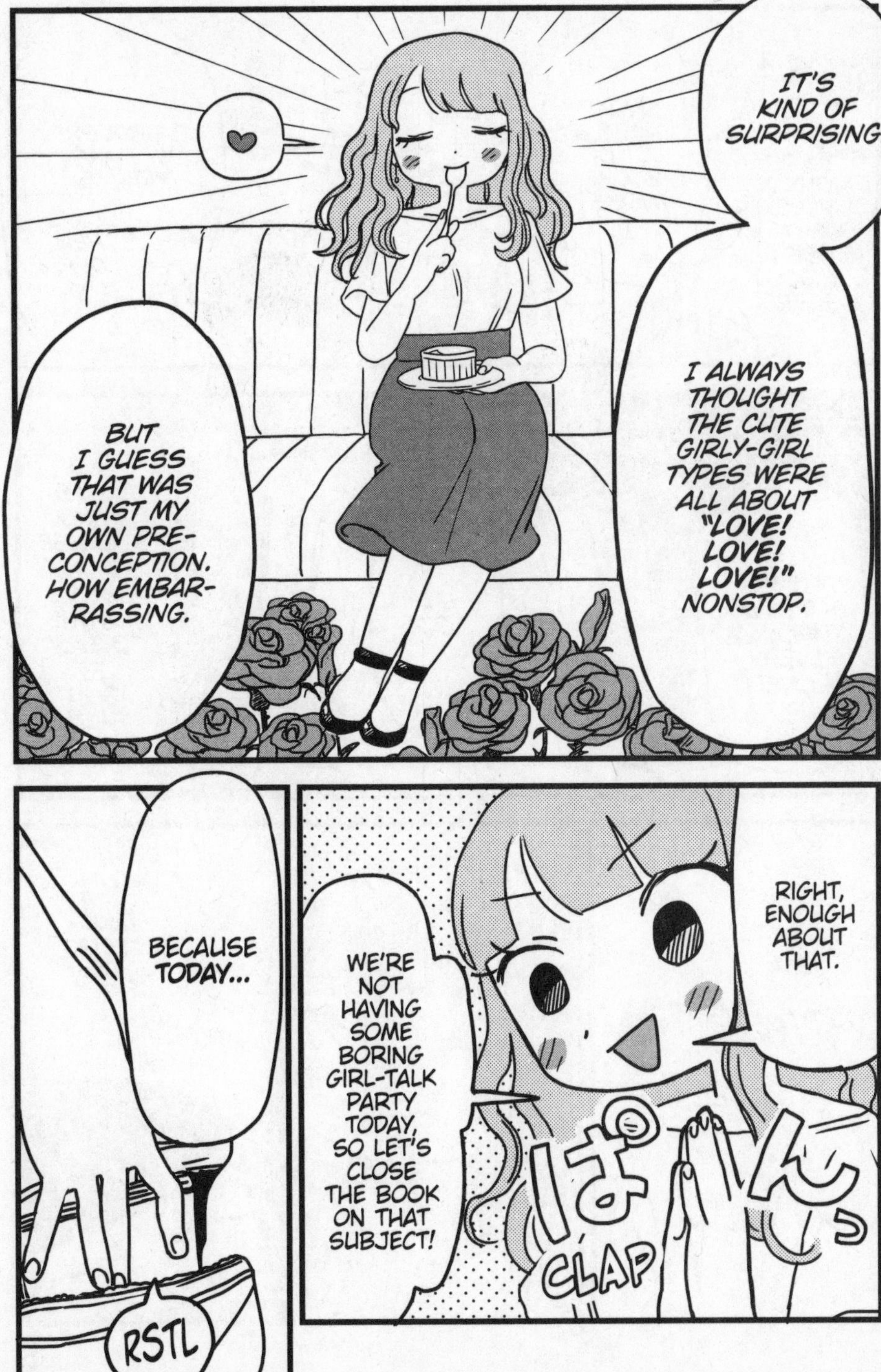
IT'S KIND OF SURPRISING.
I ALWAYS THOUGHT THE CUTE GIRLY-GIRL TYPES WERE ALL ABOUT "LOVE! LOVE! LOVE!" NONSTOP.
BUT I GUESS THAT WAS JUST MY OWN PRE-CONCEPTION. HOW EMBAR-RASSING.
RIGHT, ENOUGH ABOUT THAT.
WE'RE NOT HAVING SOME BORING GIRL-TALK PARTY TODAY, SO LET'S CLOSE THE BOOK ON THAT SUBJECT!
ぱんっ
CLAP
BECAUSE TODAY...
RSTL

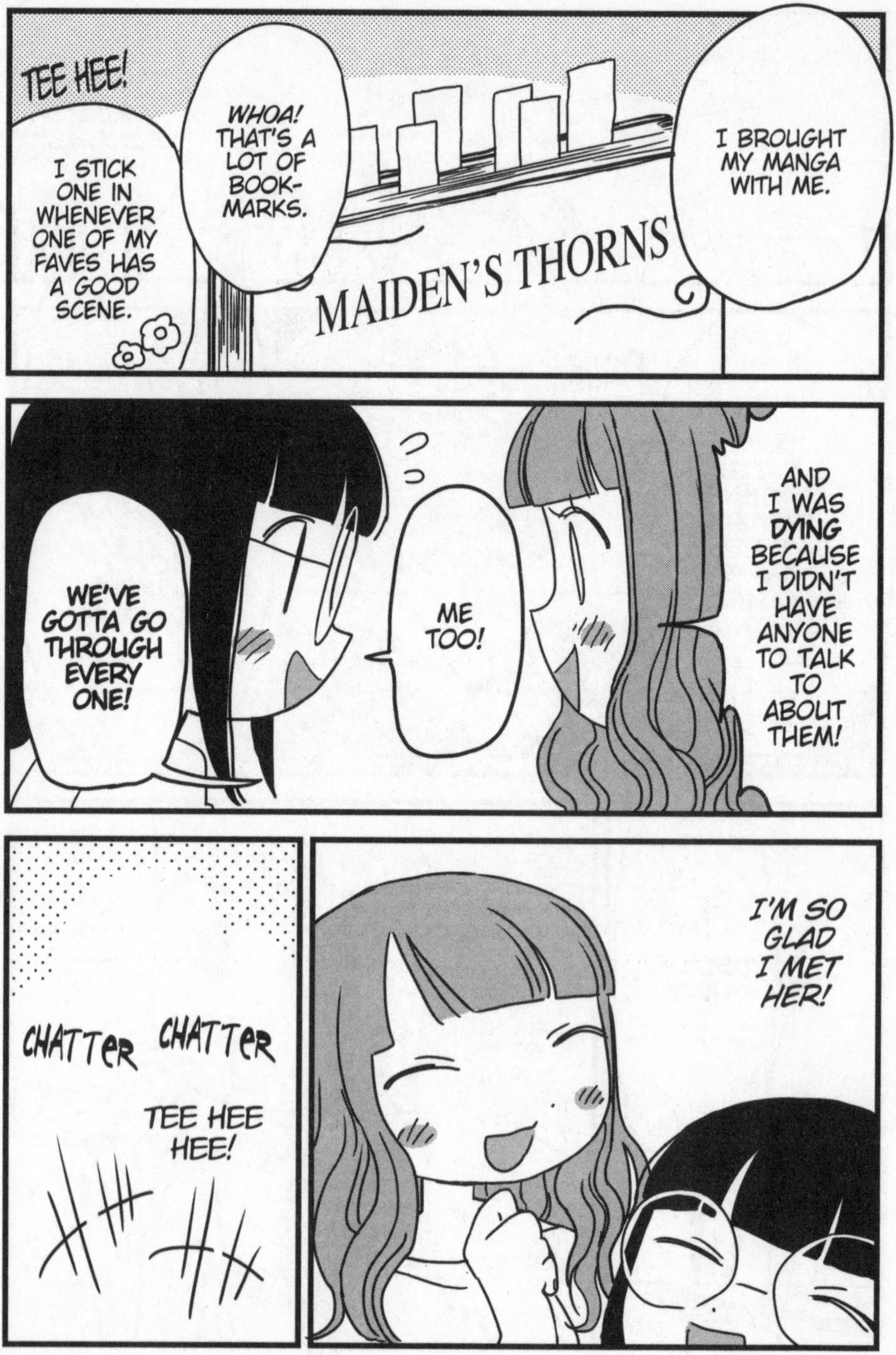
I BROUGHT MY MANGA WITH ME.
MAIDEN'S THORNS
WHOA! THAT'S A LOT OF BOOK-MARKS.
TEE HEE!
I STICK ONE IN WHENEVER ONE OF MY FAVES HAS A GOOD SCENE.
AND I WAS DYING BECAUSE I DIDN'T HAVE ANYONE TO TALK TO ABOUT THEM!
ME TOO!
WE'VE GOTTA GO THROUGH EVERY ONE!
I'M SO GLAD I MET HER!
CHATTER CHATTER
TEE HEE HEE!

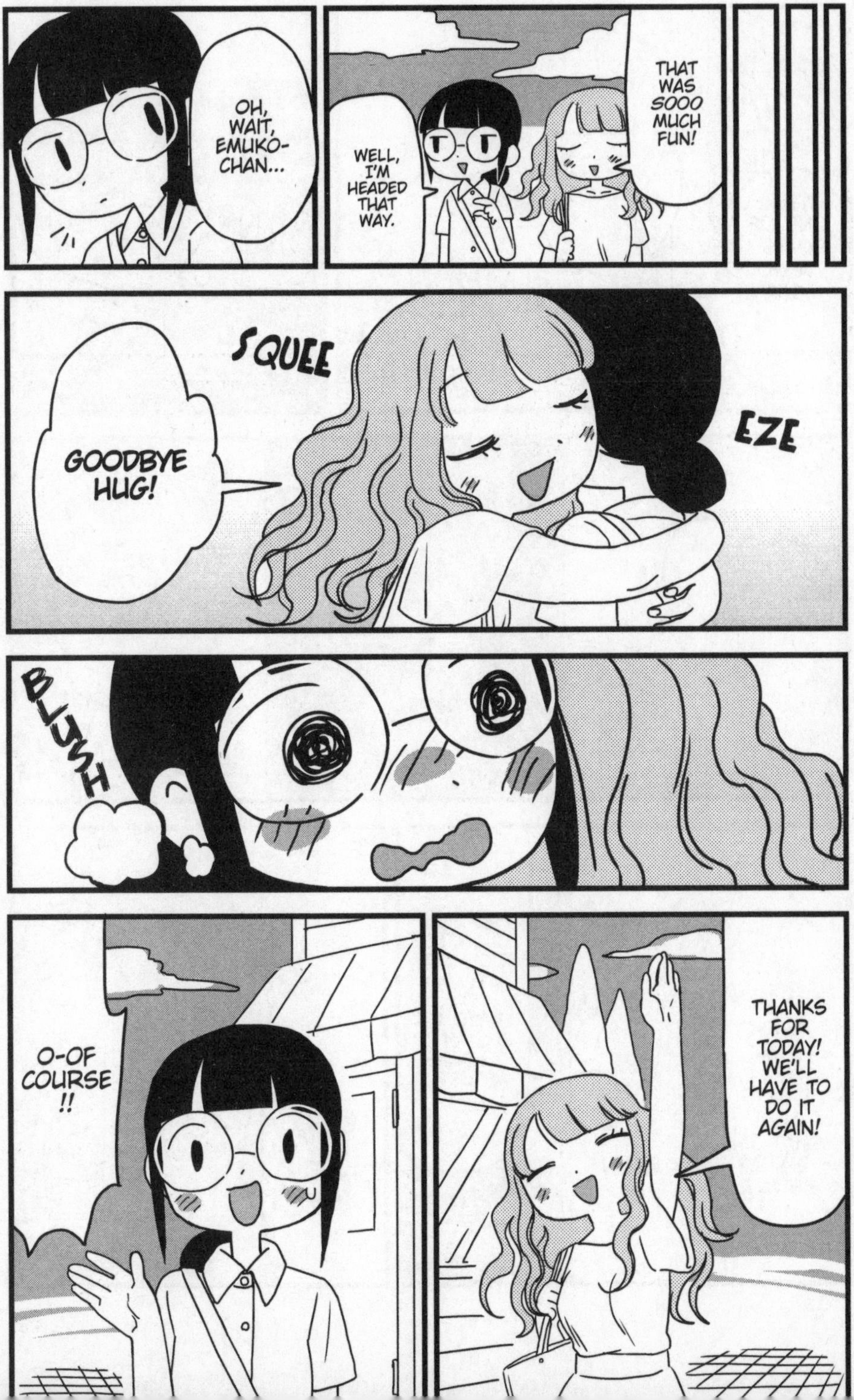
THAT WAS SOOO MUCH FUN!
WELL, I'M HEADED THAT WAY.
OH, WAIT, EMUKO-CHAN...
SQUEE
EZE
GOODBYE HUG!
BLUSH
THANKS FOR TODAY! WE'LL HAVE TO DO IT AGAIN!
O-OF COURSE !!

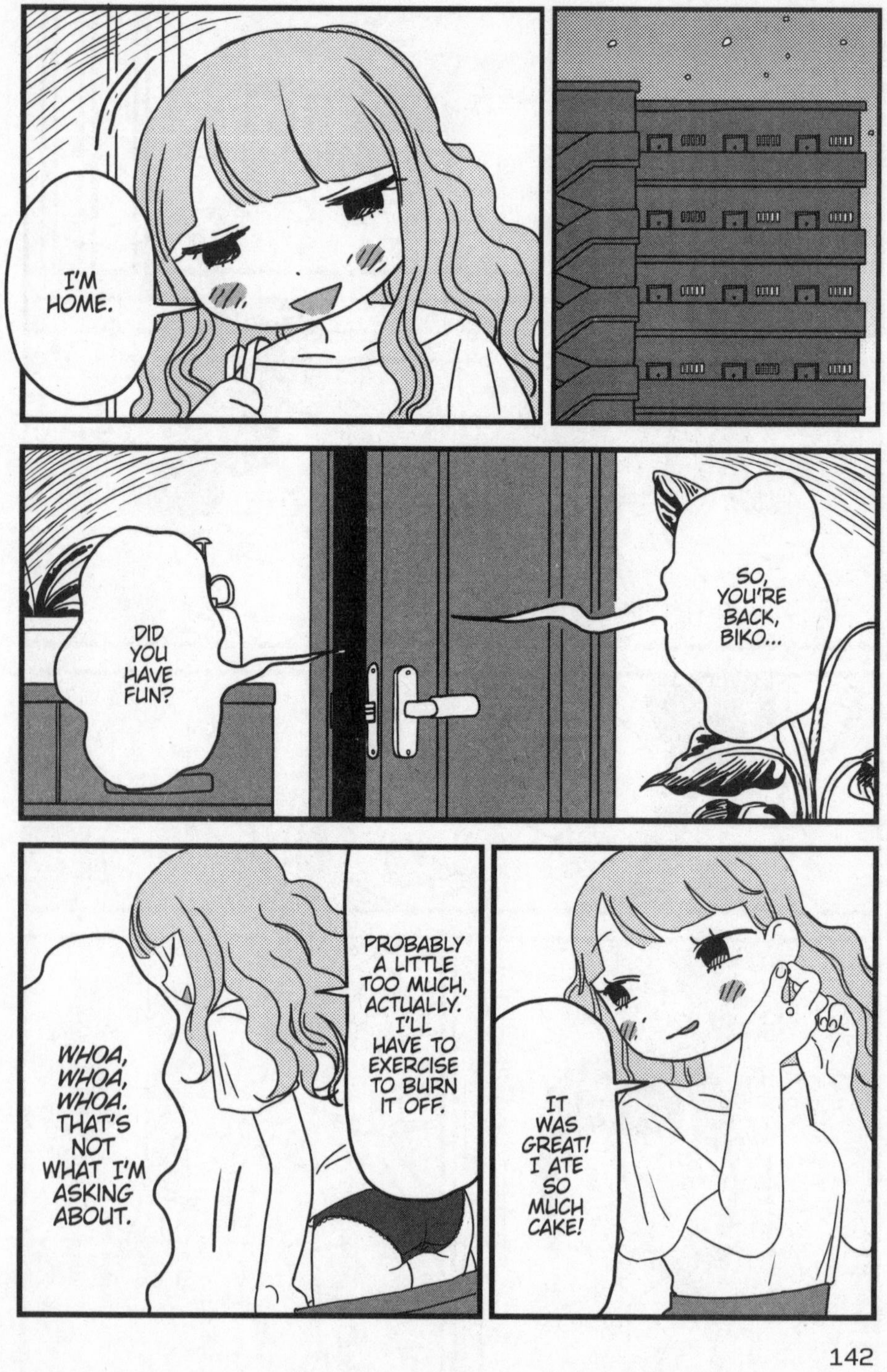
I'M HOME.
SO, YOU'RE BACK, BIKO...
DID YOU HAVE FUN?
IT WAS GREAT! I ATE SO MUCH CAKE!
PROBABLY A LITTLE TOO MUCH, ACTUALLY. I'LL HAVE TO EXERCISE TO BURN IT OFF.
WHOA, WHOA, WHOA. THAT'S NOT WHAT I'M ASKING ABOUT.

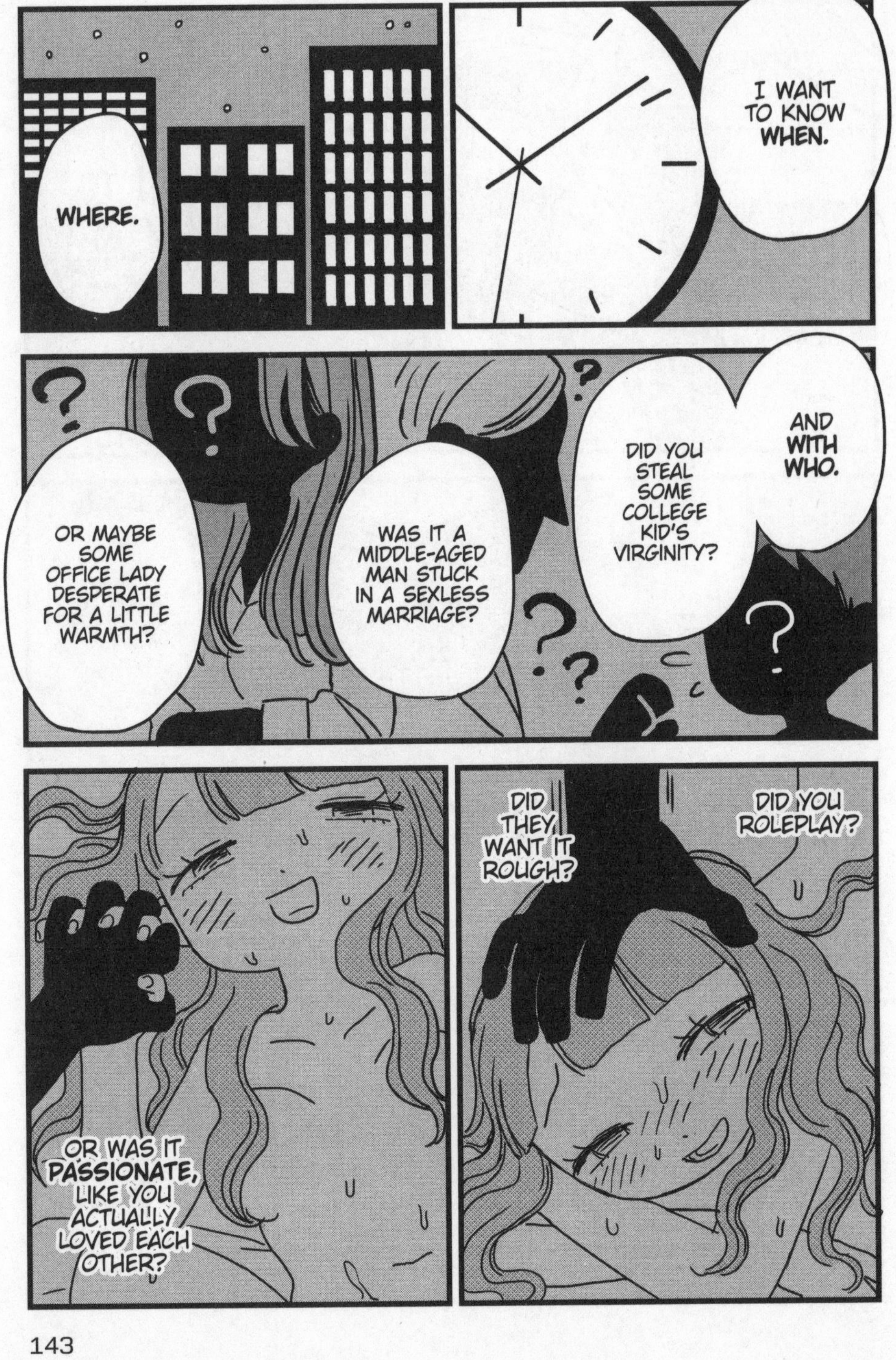
I WANT TO KNOW WHEN.
WHERE.
AND WITH WHO.
DID YOU STEAL SOME COLLEGE KID'S VIRGINITY?
WAS IT A MIDDLE-AGED MAN STUCK IN A SEXLESS MARRIAGE?
OR MAYBE SOME OFFICE LADY DESPERATE FOR A LITTLE WARMTH?
DID YOU ROLEPLAY?
DID THEY WANT IT ROUGH?
OR WAS IT PASSIONATE, LIKE YOU ACTUALLY LOVED EACH OTHER?

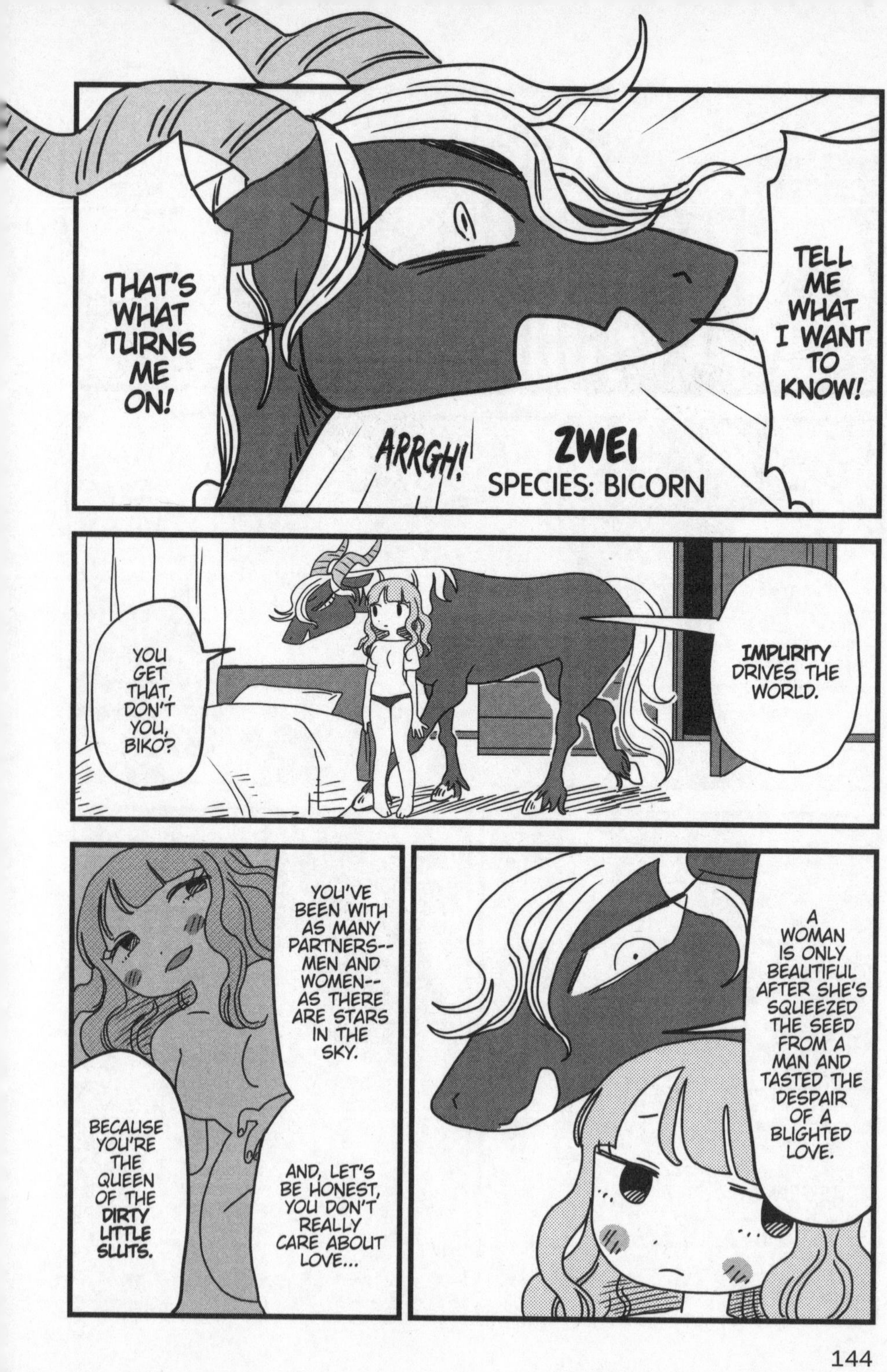
TELL ME WHAT I WANT TO KNOW!
THAT'S WHAT TURNS ME ON!
ARRGH!
ZWEI
SPECIES: BICORN
IMPURITY DRIVES THE WORLD.
YOU GET THAT, DON'T YOU, BIKO?
A WOMAN IS ONLY BEAUTIFUL AFTER SHE'S SQUEEZED THE SEED FROM A MAN AND TASTED THE DESPAIR OF A BLIGHTED LOVE.
YOU'VE BEEN WITH AS MANY PARTNERS--MEN AND WOMEN--AS THERE ARE STARS IN THE SKY.
AND, LET'S BE HONEST, YOU DON'T REALLY CARE ABOUT LOVE...
BECAUSE YOU'RE THE QUEEN OF THE DIRTY LITTLE SLUTS.

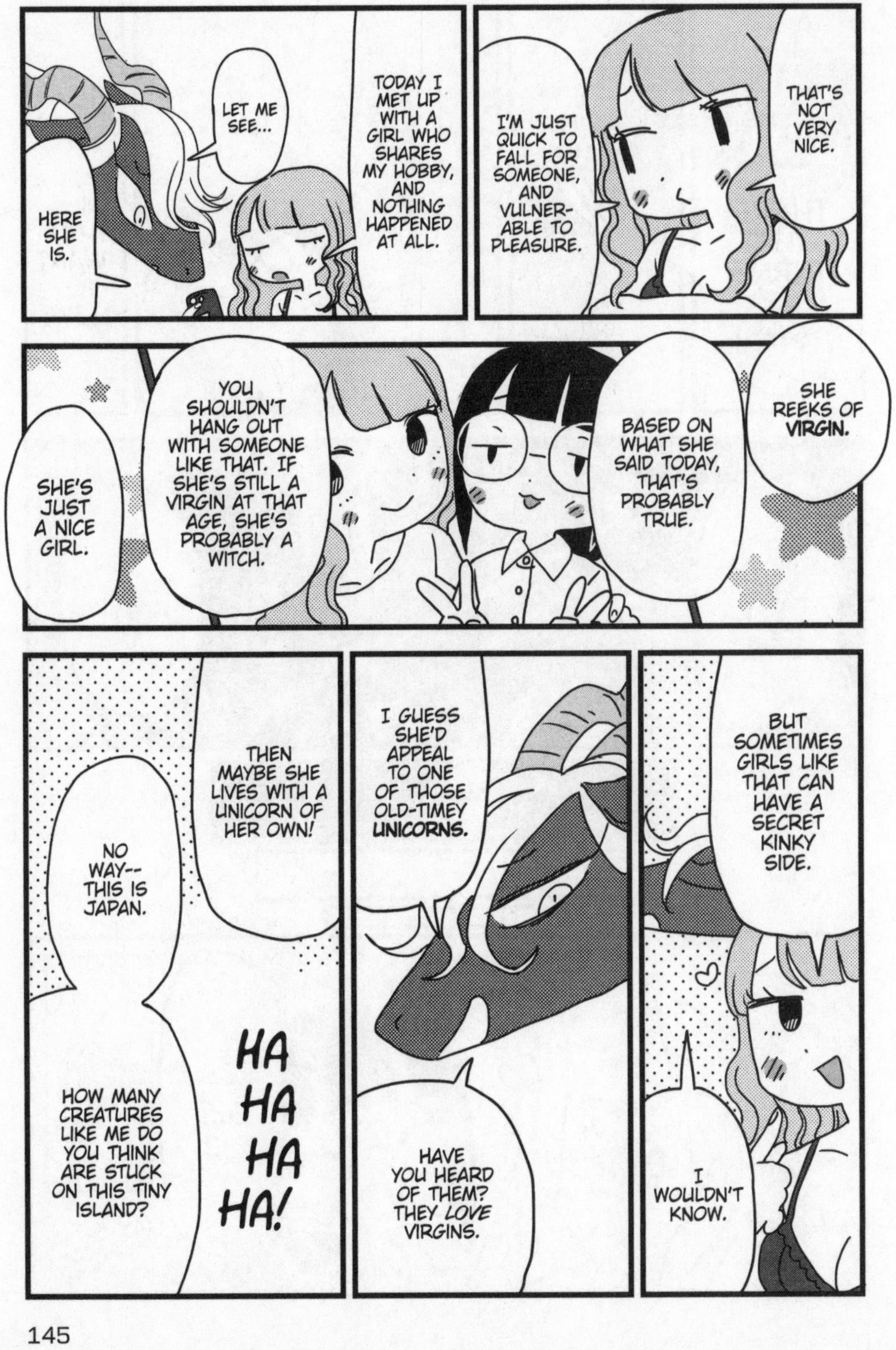
THAT'S NOT VERY NICE.
I'M JUST QUICK TO FALL FOR SOMEONE, AND VULNERABLE TO PLEASURE.
TODAY I MET UP WITH A GIRL WHO SHARES MY HOBBY, AND NOTHING HAPPENED AT ALL.
LET ME SEE...
HERE SHE IS.
SHE REEKS OF **VIRGIN.**
BASED ON WHAT SHE SAID TODAY, THAT'S PROBABLY TRUE.
YOU SHOULDN'T HANG OUT WITH SOMEONE LIKE THAT. IF SHE'S STILL A VIRGIN AT THAT AGE, SHE'S PROBABLY A WITCH.
SHE'S JUST A NICE GIRL.
BUT SOMETIMES GIRLS LIKE THAT CAN HAVE A SECRET KINKY SIDE.
I WOULDN'T KNOW.
I GUESS SHE'D APPEAL TO ONE OF THOSE OLD-TIMEY **UNICORNS.**
HAVE YOU HEARD OF THEM? THEY *LOVE* VIRGINS.
THEN MAYBE SHE LIVES WITH A UNICORN OF HER OWN!
NO WAY-- THIS IS JAPAN.
HA HA HA HA!
HOW MANY CREATURES LIKE ME DO YOU THINK ARE STUCK ON THIS TINY ISLAND?

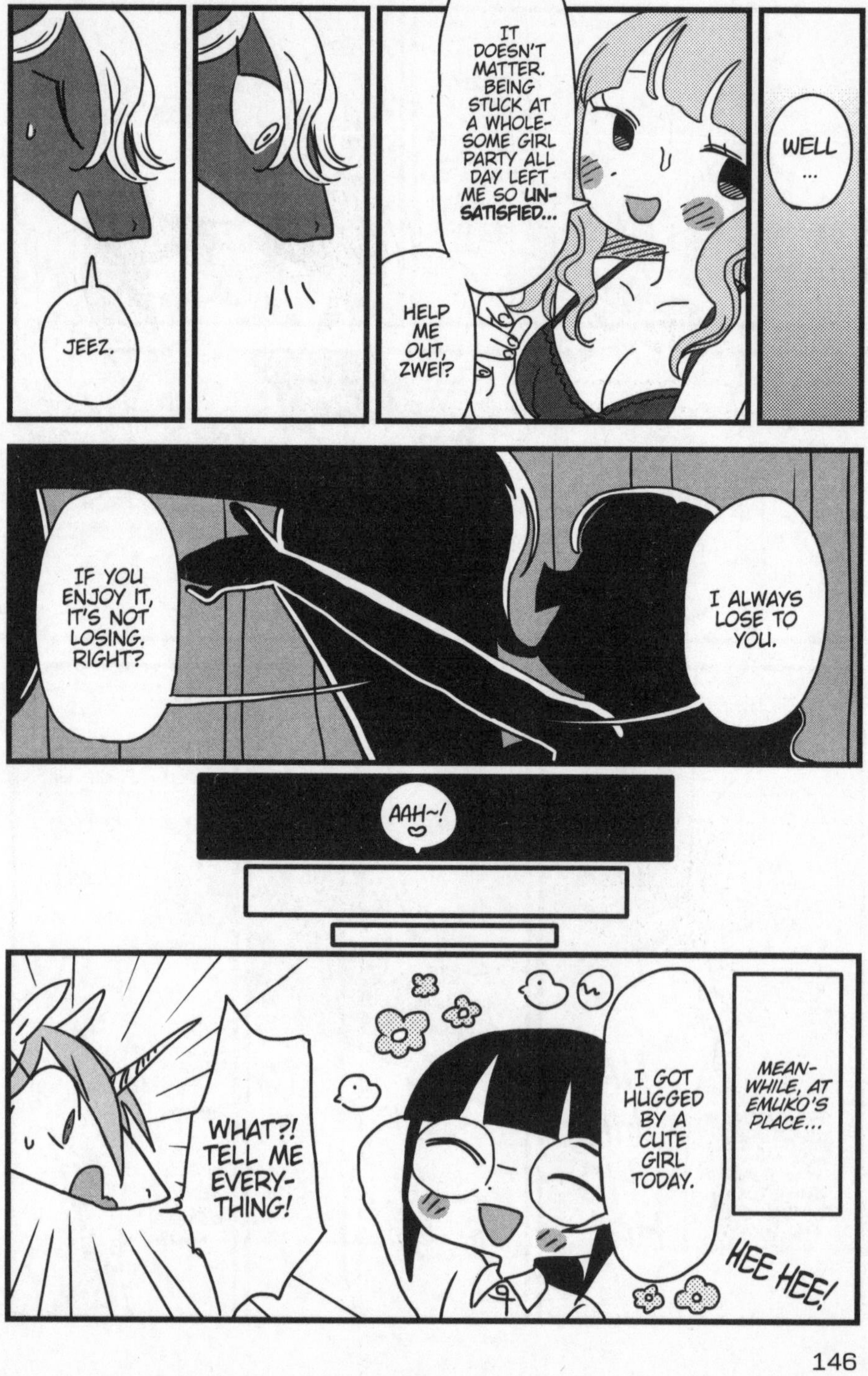
WELL ...
IT DOESN'T MATTER. BEING STUCK AT A WHOLE-SOME GIRL PARTY ALL DAY LEFT ME SO UN-SATISFIED...
HELP ME OUT, ZWEI?
JEEZ.
I ALWAYS LOSE TO YOU.
IF YOU ENJOY IT, IT'S NOT LOSING. RIGHT?
AAH~!
MEAN-WHILE, AT EMUKO'S PLACE...
HEE HEE!
I GOT HUGGED BY A CUTE GIRL TODAY.
WHAT?! TELL ME EVERY-THING!

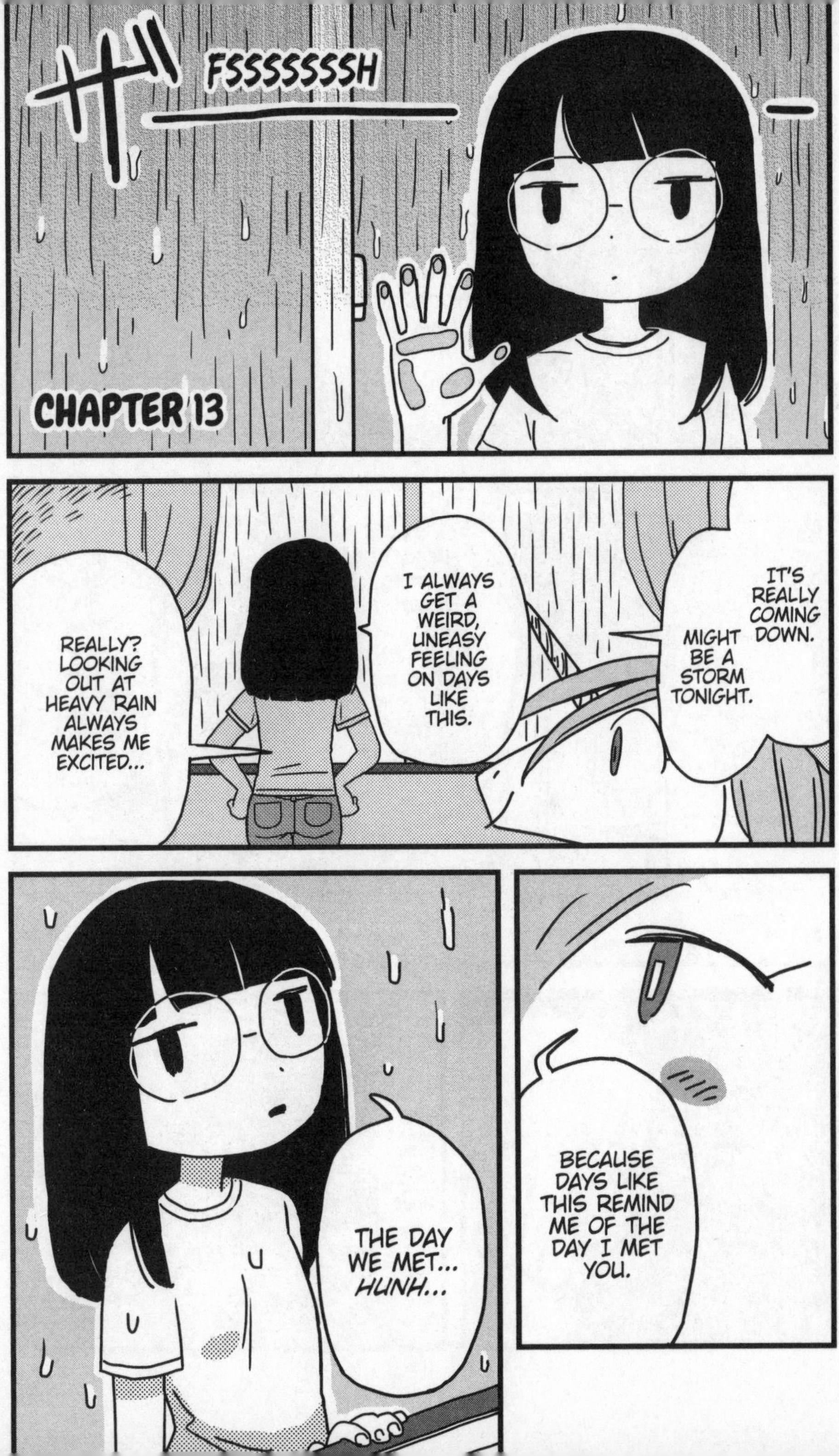
FSSSSSSSH
CHAPTER 13
IT'S REALLY COMING DOWN.
MIGHT BE A STORM TONIGHT.
I ALWAYS GET A WEIRD, UNEASY FEELING ON DAYS LIKE THIS.
REALLY? LOOKING OUT AT HEAVY RAIN ALWAYS MAKES ME EXCITED...
BECAUSE DAYS LIKE THIS REMIND ME OF THE DAY I MET YOU.
THE DAY WE MET... *HUNH...*

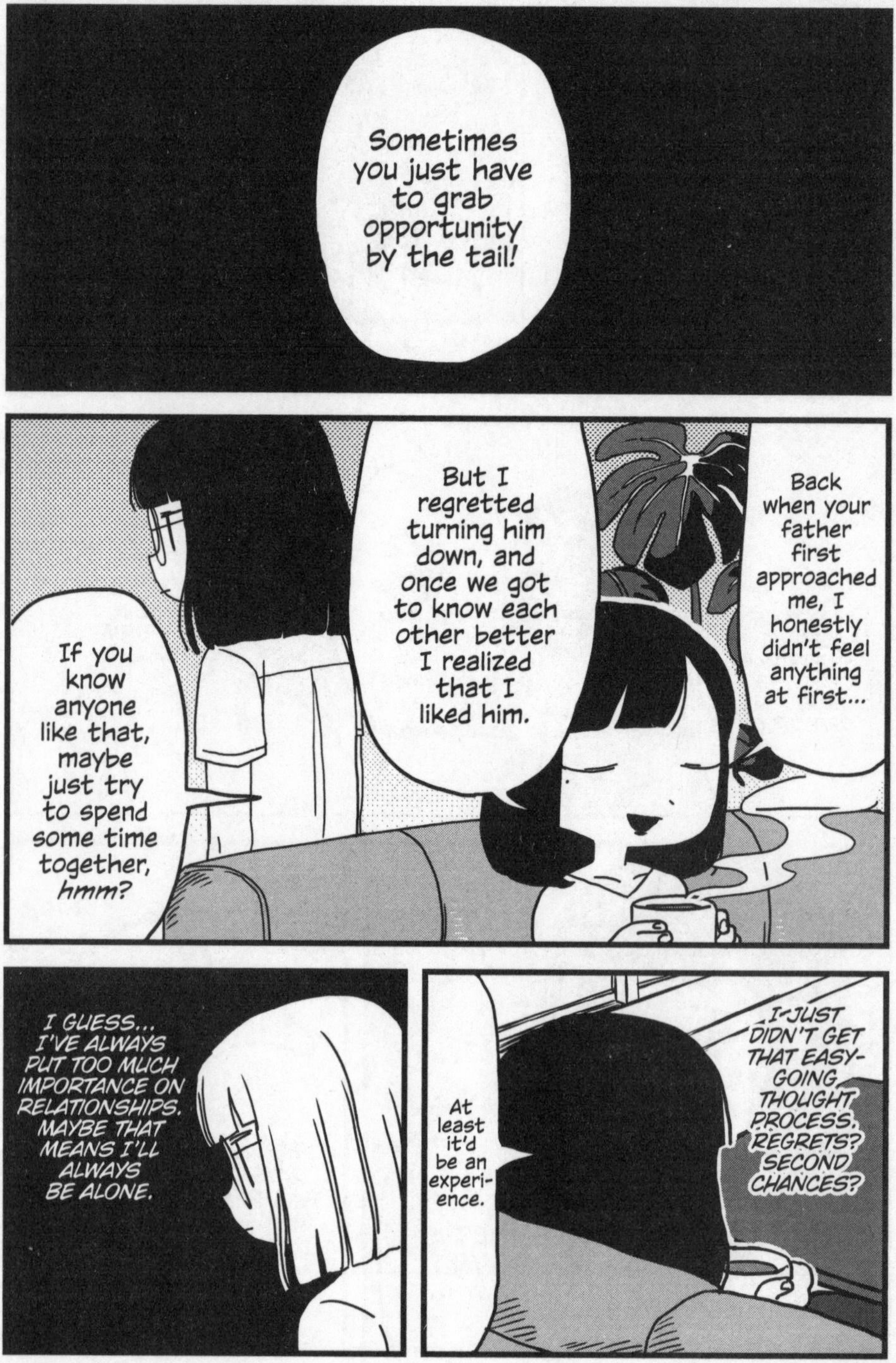
Sometimes you just have to grab opportunity by the tail!
Back when your father first approached me, I honestly didn't feel anything at first...
But I regretted turning him down, and once we got to know each other better I realized that I liked him.
If you know anyone like that, maybe just try to spend some time together, *hmm?*
I-JUST DIDN'T GET THAT EASY-GOING THOUGHT PROCESS. REGRETS? SECOND CHANCES?
At least it'd be an experi-ence.
I GUESS... I'VE ALWAYS PUT TOO MUCH IMPORTANCE ON RELATIONSHIPS. MAYBE THAT MEANS I'LL ALWAYS BE ALONE.

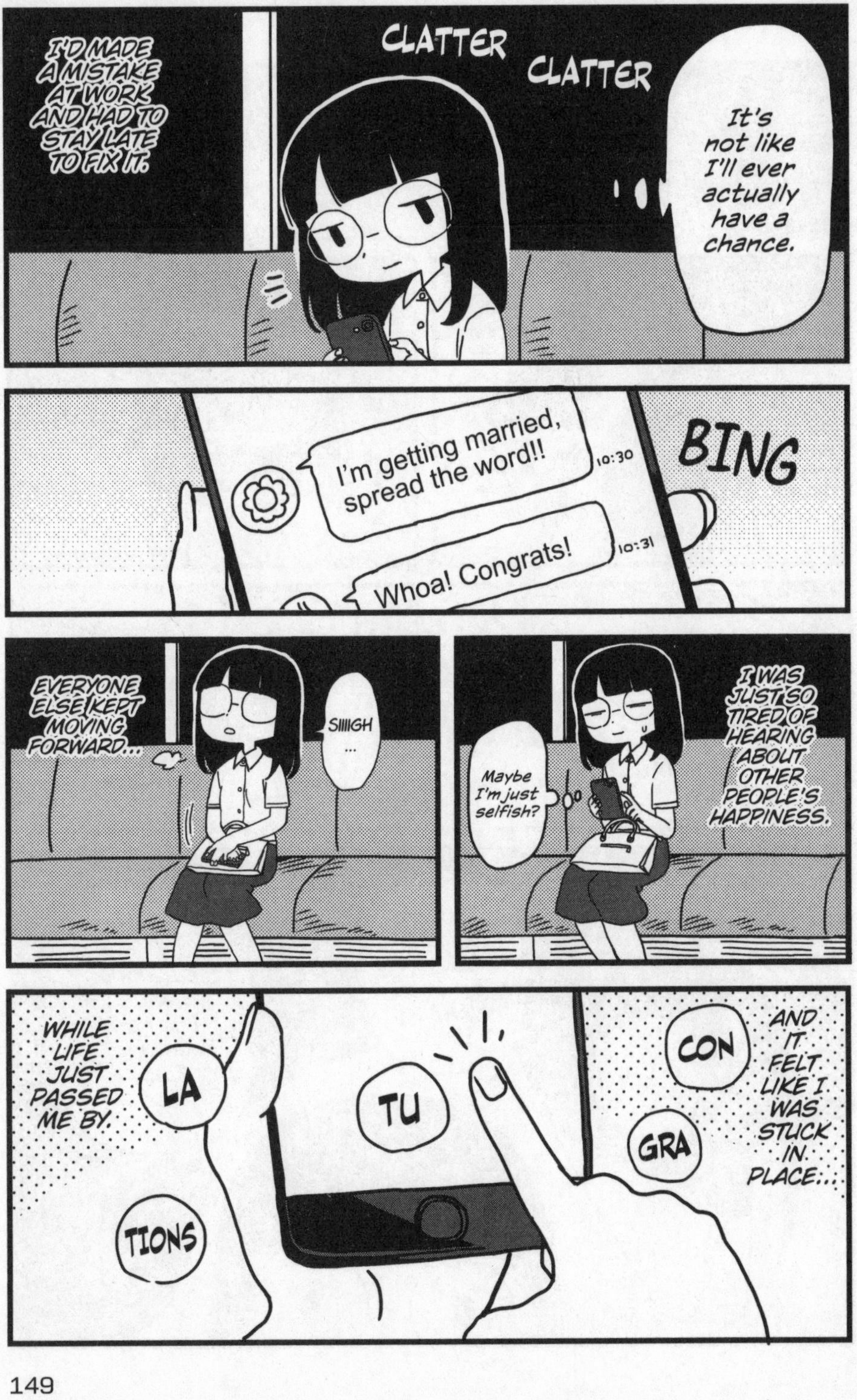
It's not like I'll ever actually have a chance.
CLATTER
CLATTER
I'D MADE A MISTAKE AT WORK AND HAD TO STAY LATE TO FIX IT.
BING
I'm getting married, spread the word!!
10:30
Whoa! Congrats!
10:31
I WAS JUST SO TIRED OF HEARING ABOUT OTHER PEOPLE'S HAPPINESS.
Maybe I'm just selfish?
SIIIGH ...
EVERYONE ELSE KEPT MOVING FORWARD...
AND IT FELT LIKE I WAS STUCK IN PLACE...
CON
GRA
TU
LA
TIONS
WHILE LIFE JUST PASSED ME BY.

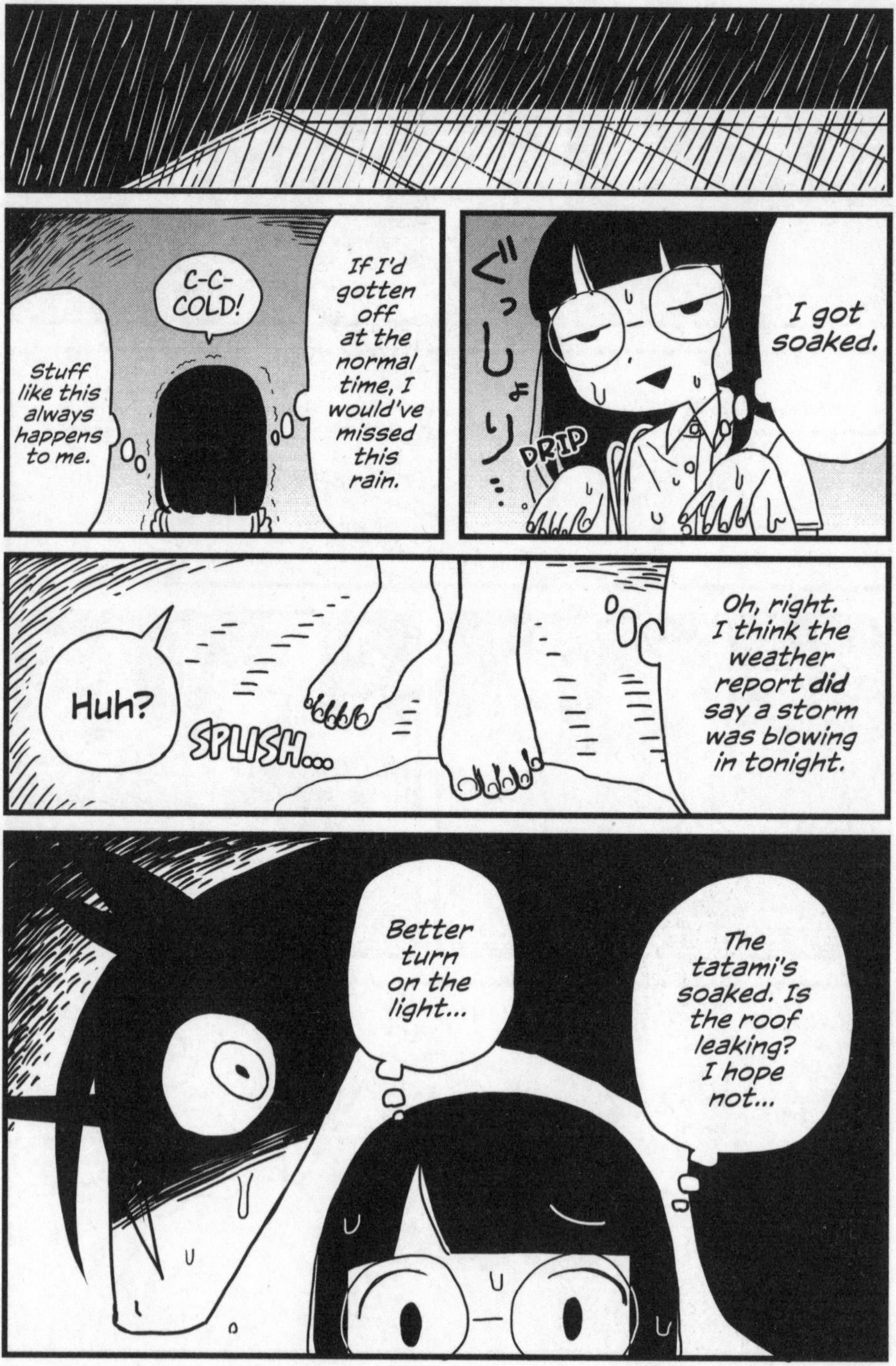
I got soaked.
ぐっしょり
DRIP
If I'd gotten off at the normal time, I would've missed this rain.
C-C-COLD!
Stuff like this always happens to me.
Oh, right. I think the weather report did say a storm was blowing in tonight.
SPLISH...
Huh?
The tatami's soaked. Is the roof leaking? I hope not...
Better turn on the light...

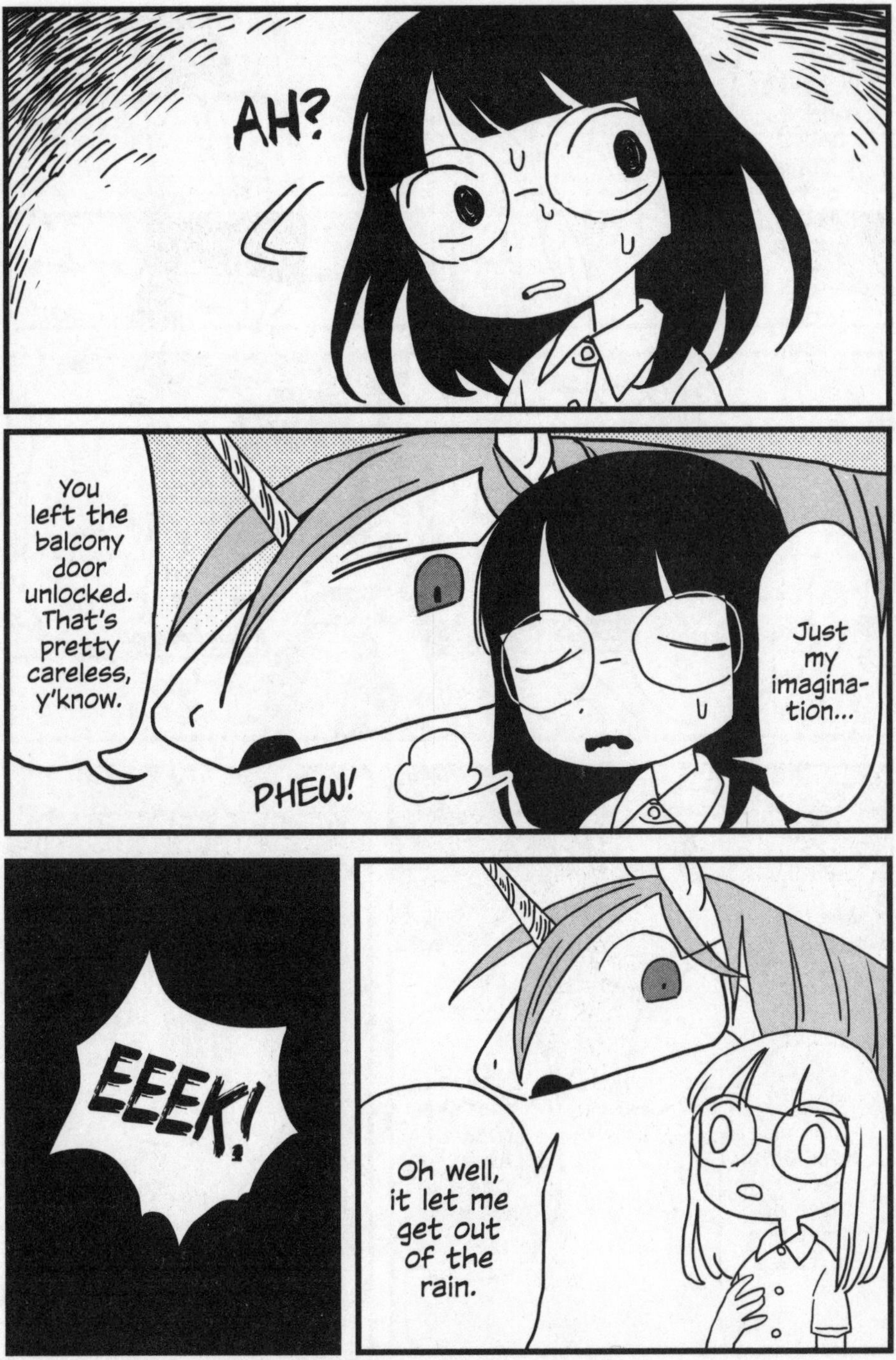
AH?
Just my imagination...
PHEW!
You left the balcony door unlocked. That's pretty careless, y'know.
Oh well, it let me get out of the rain.
EEEK!

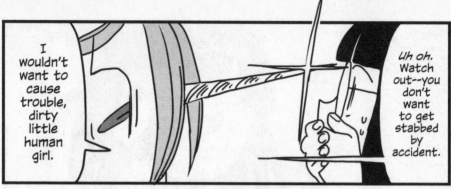

Uh oh. Watch out--you don't want to get stabbed by accident.
I wouldn't want to cause trouble, dirty little human girl.
WH... WHA... WHAT ARE YOU...?
FWUMP...
YOU CAN'T JUST COME INTO SOME-ONE'S HOUSE...
I am...
a wandering unicorn.
I made a mistake reading the skies as I roamed.
Normally I'd never do something like this...

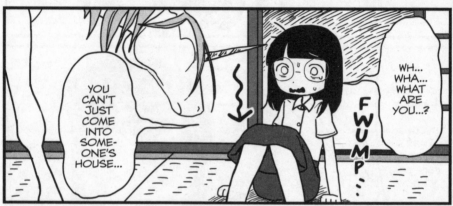

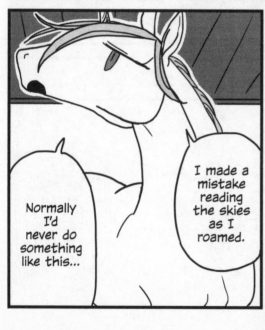

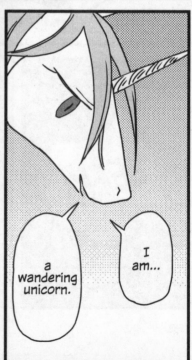

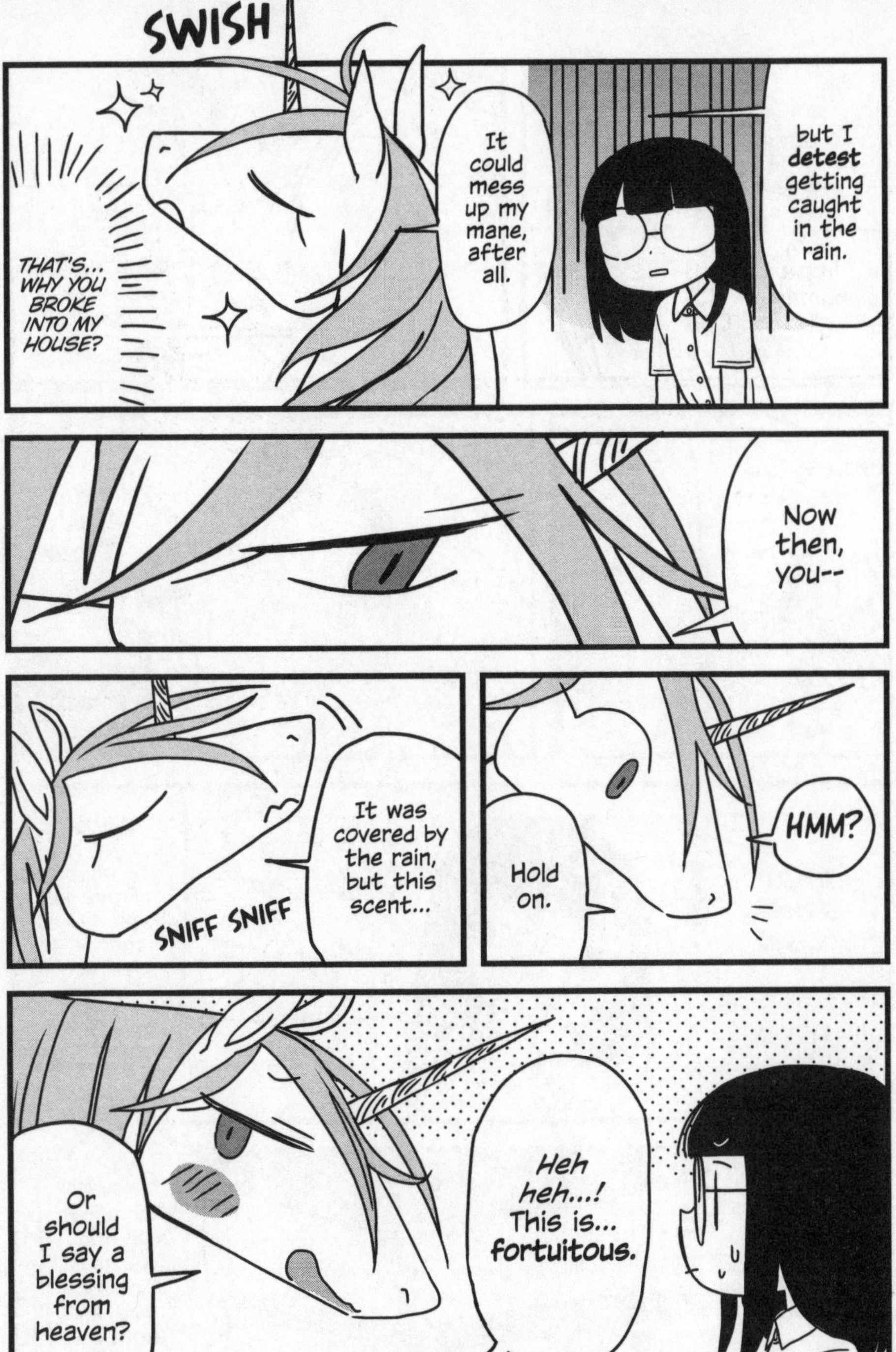
but I detest getting caught in the rain.
It could mess up my mane, after all.
SWISH
THAT'S... WHY YOU BROKE INTO MY HOUSE?
Now then, you--
HMM?
Hold on.
It was covered by the rain, but this scent...
SNIFF SNIFF
Heh heh...! This is... fortuitous.
Or should I say a blessing from heaven?

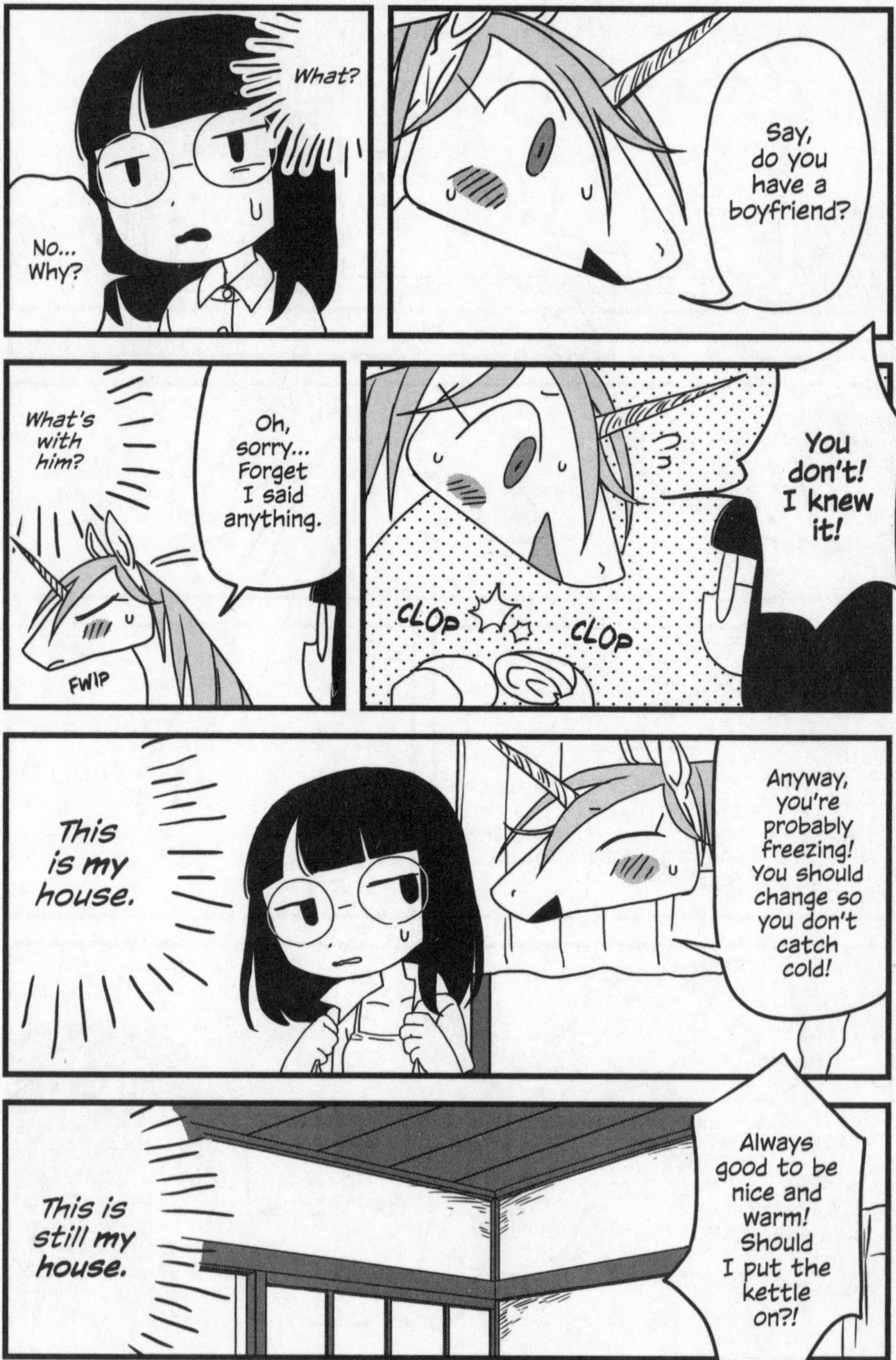
Say, do you have a boyfriend?
What?
No... Why?
You don't! I knew it!
CLOP
CLOP
Oh, sorry... Forget I said anything.
What's with him?
FWIP
Anyway, you're probably freezing! You should change so you don't catch cold!
This is my house.
Always good to be nice and warm! Should I put the kettle on?!
This is still my house.

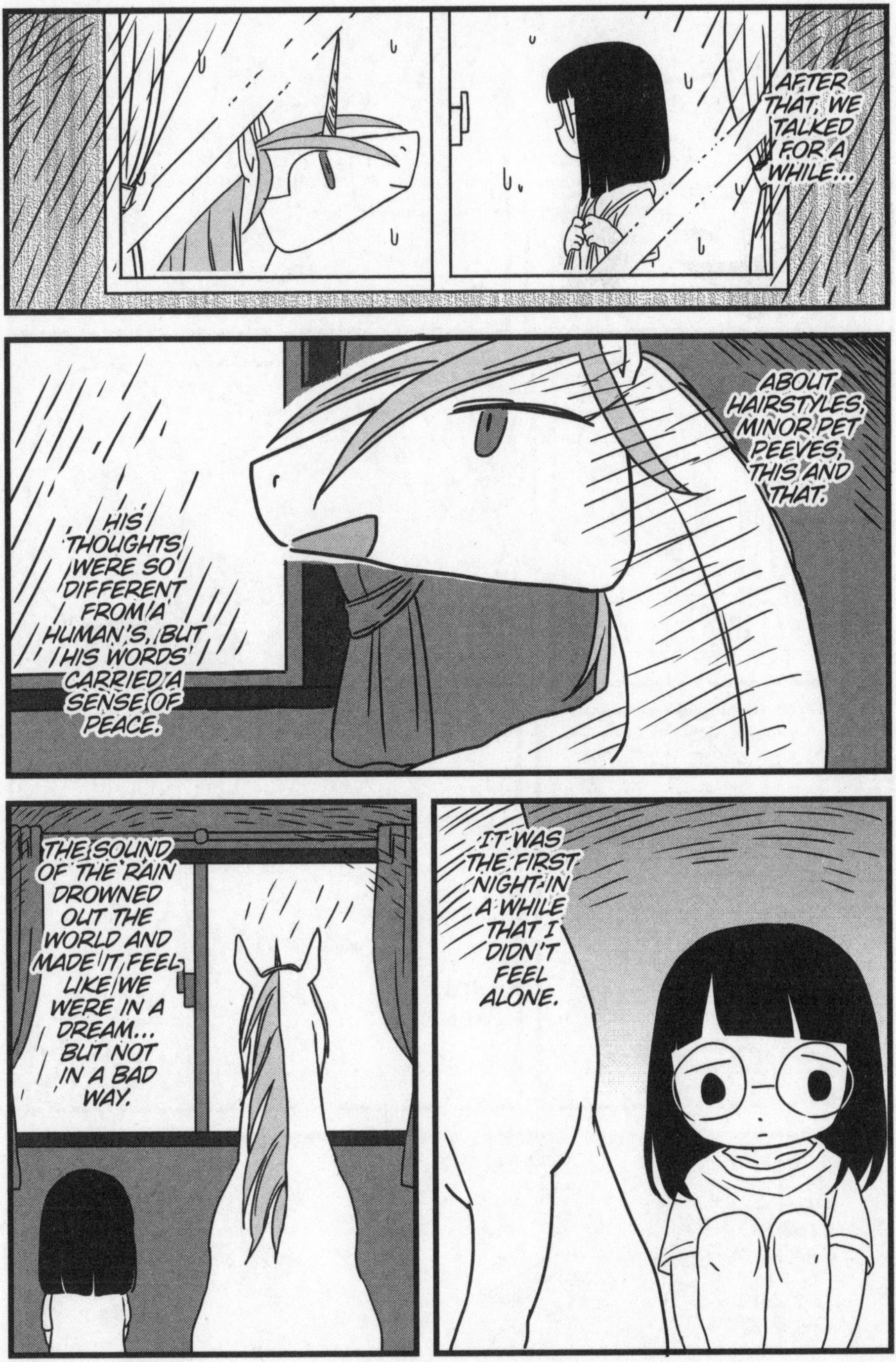
AFTER THAT, WE TALKED FOR A WHILE...
ABOUT HAIRSTYLES, MINOR PET PEEVES, THIS AND THAT.
HIS THOUGHTS WERE SO DIFFERENT FROM A HUMAN'S, BUT HIS WORDS CARRIED A SENSE OF PEACE.
IT WAS THE FIRST NIGHT IN A WHILE THAT I DIDN'T FEEL ALONE.
THE SOUND OF THE RAIN DROWNED OUT THE WORLD AND MADE IT FEEL LIKE WE WERE IN A DREAM... BUT NOT IN A BAD WAY.

Oh... looks like the rain's letting up.

I should take this chance to move along.

Well, I'm off.

I haven't talked to anyone in ages. This was fun.

HUP!

"SOMETIMES YOU JUST HAVE TO GRAB OPPORTUNITY BY THE TAIL!"

I'll miss you.

Fare-well.

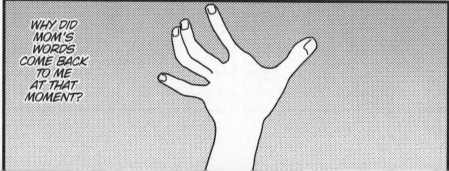

WHY DID MOM'S WORDS COME BACK TO ME AT THAT MOMENT?

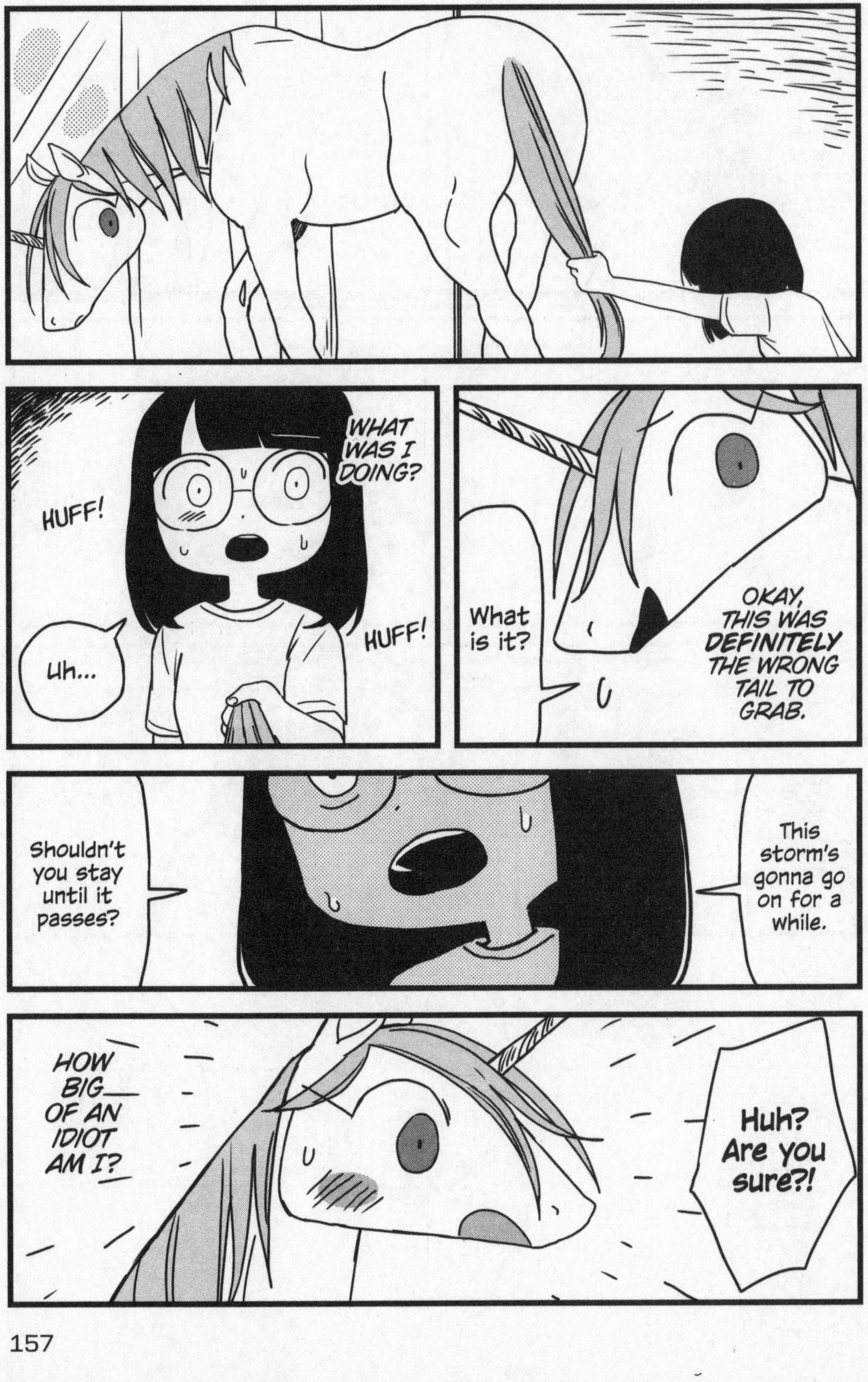
OKAY, THIS WAS DEFINITELY THE WRONG TAIL TO GRAB.
What is it?
WHAT WAS I DOING?
HUFF!
HUFF!
Uh...
This storm's gonna go on for a while.
Shouldn't you stay until it passes?
Huh? Are you sure?!
HOW BIG OF AN IDIOT AM I?

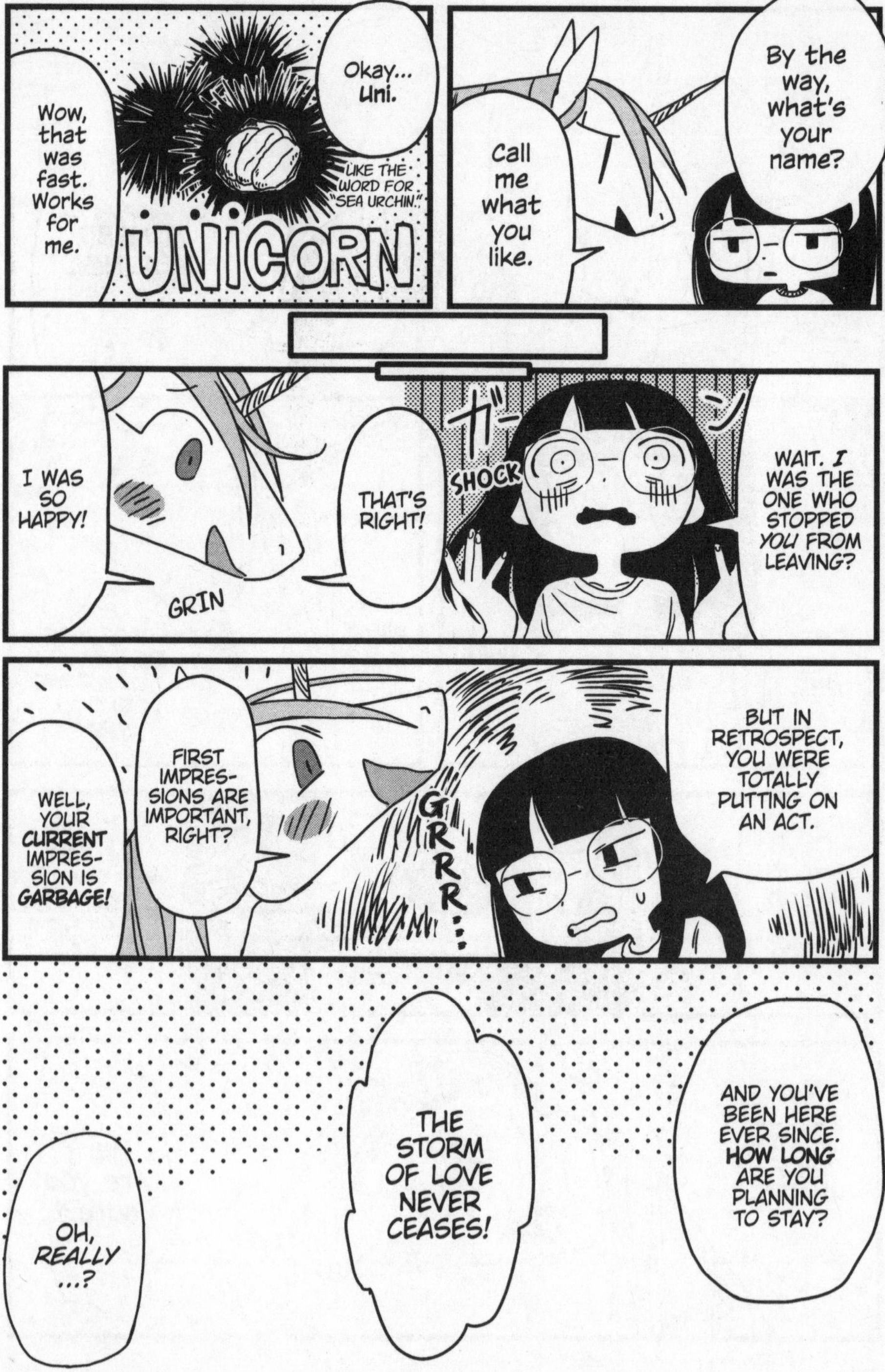
By the way, what's your name?
Call me what you like.
Okay... Uni.
UNICORN
LIKE THE WORD FOR "SEA URCHIN."
Wow, that was fast. Works for me.
WAIT. *I* WAS THE ONE WHO STOPPED *YOU* FROM LEAVING?
SHOCK
THAT'S RIGHT!
I WAS SO HAPPY!
GRIN
BUT IN RETROSPECT, YOU WERE TOTALLY PUTTING ON AN ACT.
GRRR...
FIRST IMPRESSIONS ARE IMPORTANT, RIGHT?
WELL, YOUR **CURRENT** IMPRESSION IS **GARBAGE!**
AND YOU'VE BEEN HERE EVER SINCE. **HOW LONG** ARE YOU PLANNING TO STAY?
THE STORM OF LOVE NEVER CEASES!
OH, *REALLY* ...?

BONUS

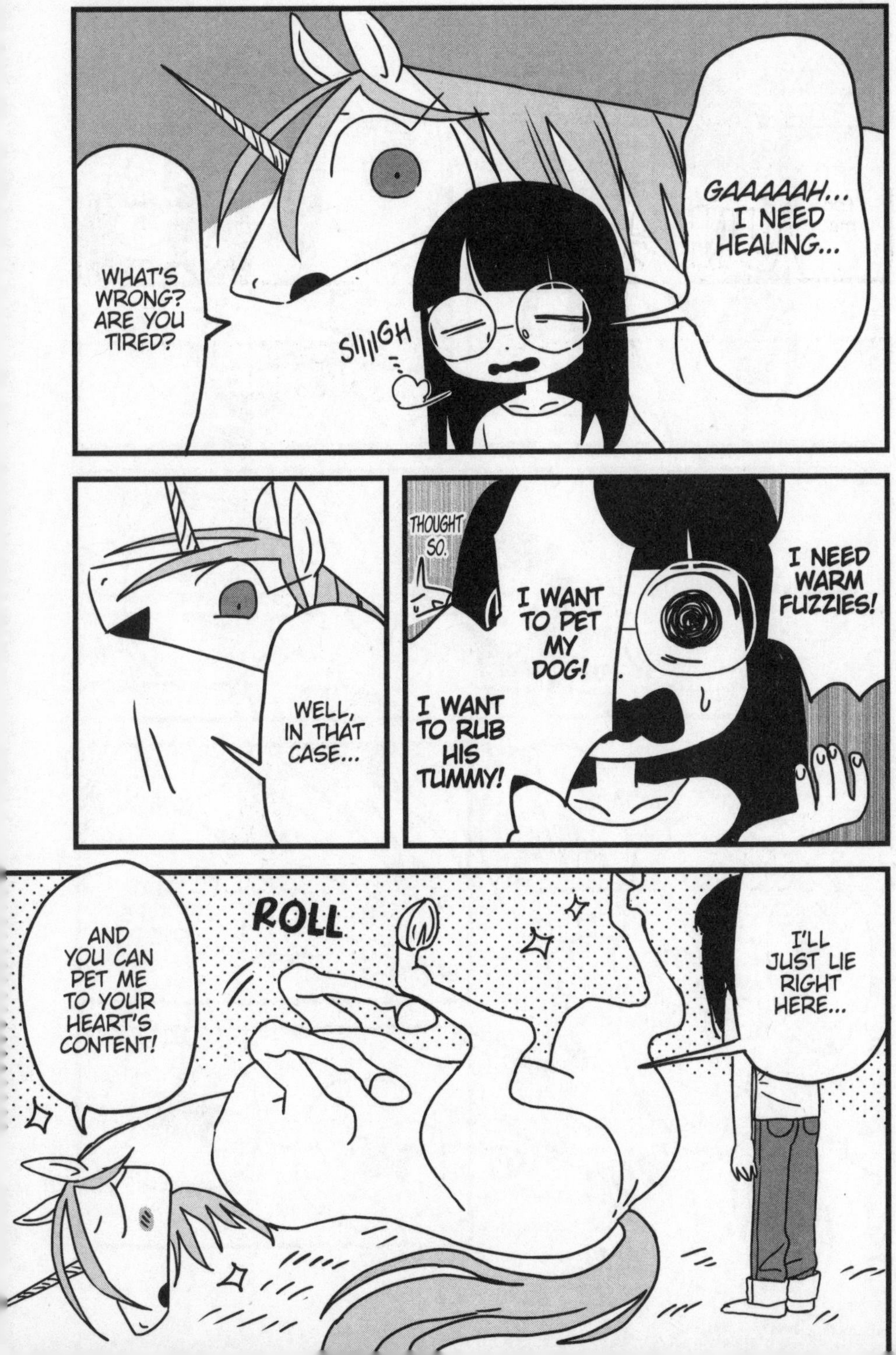
GAAAAAH... I NEED HEALING...
SIIIIGH
WHAT'S WRONG? ARE YOU TIRED?
I NEED WARM FUZZIES!
I WANT TO PET MY DOG!
THOUGHT SO.
I WANT TO RUB HIS TUMMY!
WELL, IN THAT CASE...
I'LL JUST LIE RIGHT HERE...
ROLL
AND YOU CAN PET ME TO YOUR HEART'S CONTENT!

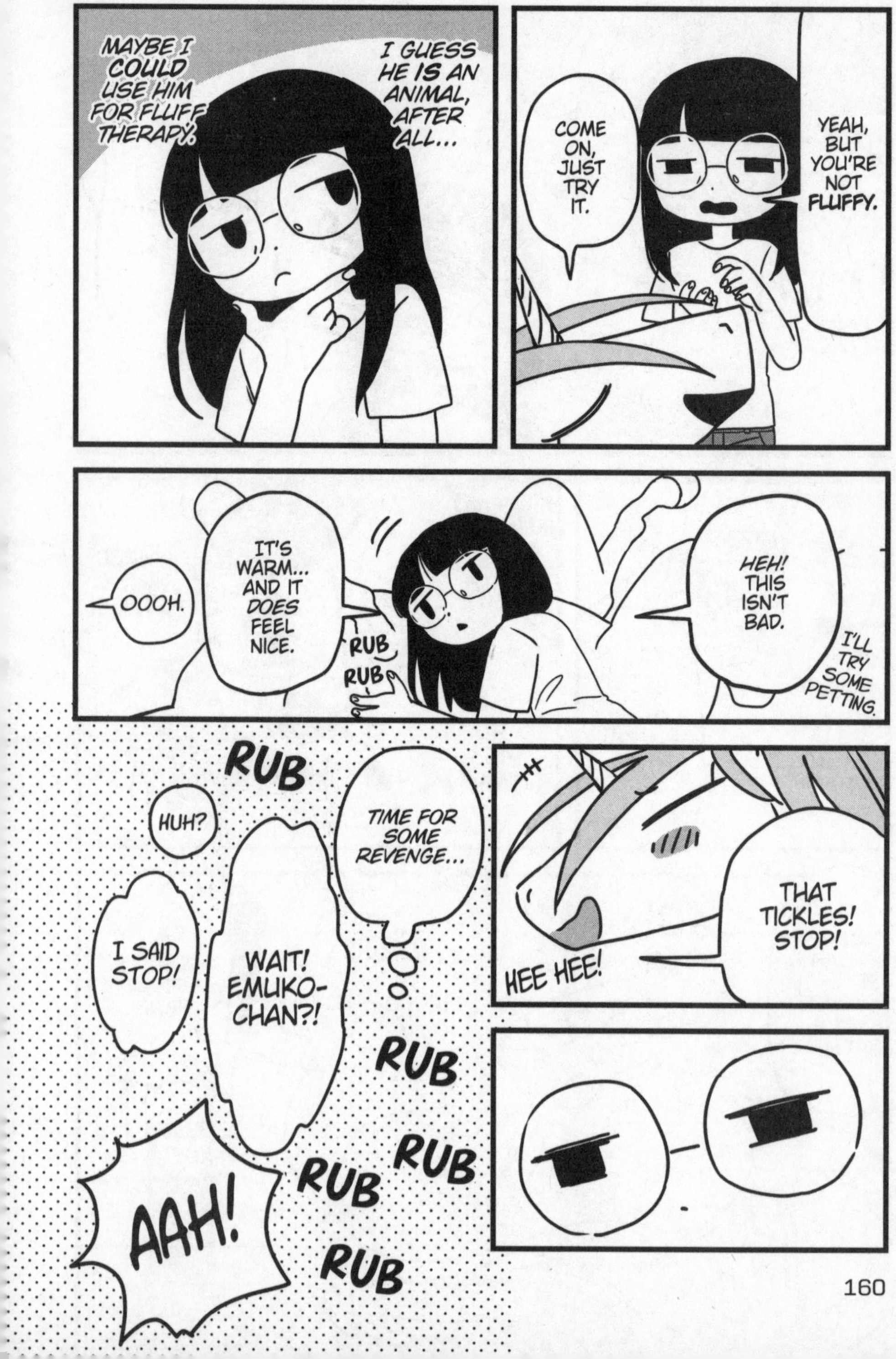
COME ON, JUST TRY IT.
YEAH, BUT YOU'RE NOT FLUFFY.
I GUESS HE IS AN ANIMAL, AFTER ALL...
MAYBE I COULD USE HIM FOR FLUFF THERAPY.
HEH! THIS ISN'T BAD.
I'LL TRY SOME PETTING.
IT'S WARM... AND IT DOES FEEL NICE.
RUB RUB
OOOH.
THAT TICKLES! STOP!
HEE HEE!
TIME FOR SOME REVENGE...
RUB
HUH?
WAIT! EMUKO-CHAN?!
I SAID STOP!
RUB
RUB
RUB
RUB
AAH!

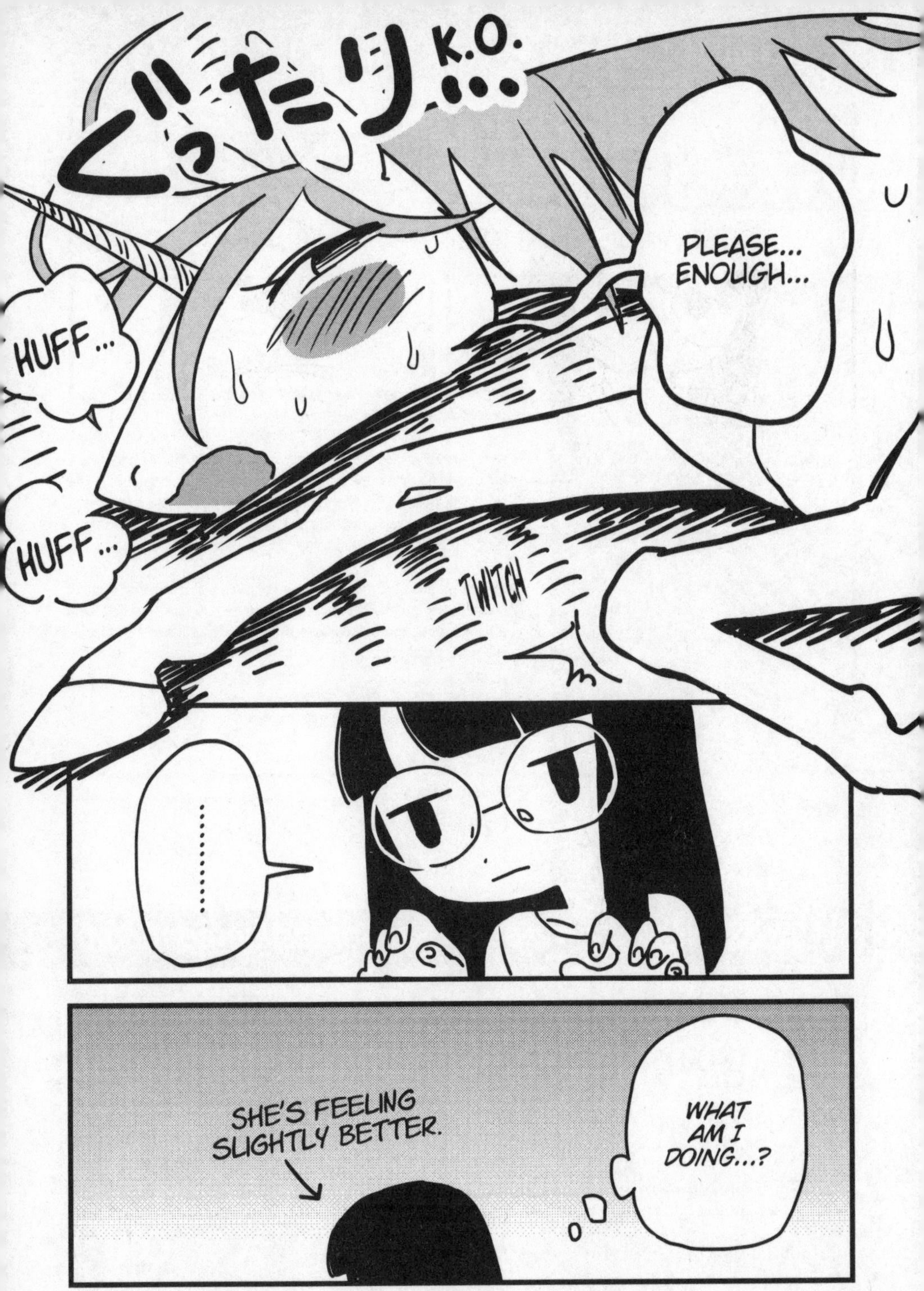
ぐったり K.O. ...
PLEASE... ENOUGH...
HUFF...
HUFF...
TWITCH
......
WHAT AM I DOING...?
SHE'S FEELING SLIGHTLY BETTER.

Unicorns Aren't Horny (1) - END

SEVEN SEAS ENTERTAINMENT PRESENTS

UNICORNS AREN'T HORNY

story and art by **SEMI IKUTA**

VOLUME 1

TRANSLATION
Wesley O'Donnell

ADAPTATION
Rebecca Scoble

LETTERING AND RETOUCH
Rina Mapa

COVER DESIGN
Nicky Lim
(LOGO) **George Panella**

PROOFREADER
Danielle King

EDITOR
Shanti Whitesides

PREPRESS TECHNICIAN
Rhiannon Rasmussen-Silverstein

PRODUCTION MANAGER
Lissa Pattillo

MANAGING EDITOR
Julie Davis

ASSOCIATE PUBLISHER
Adam Arnold

PUBLISHER
Jason DeAngelis

Seven Seas press and purchase enquiries can be sent to Marketing Manager Lianne Sentar at press@gomanga.com. Information regarding the distribution and purchase of digital editions is available from Digital Manager CK Russell at digital@gomanga.com.

ISBN: 978-1-64505-859-5

Printed in Canada

First Printing: November 2020

10 9 8 7 6 5 4 3 2 1

FOLLOW US ONLINE: ***www.sevenseasentertainment.com***

READING DIRECTIONS

This book reads from ***right to left***, Japanese style. If this is your first time reading manga, you start reading from the top right panel on each page and take it from there. If you get lost, just follow the numbered diagram here. It may seem backwards at first, but you'll get the hang of it! Have fun!!

1
2
3
4
5
6
7
8
9

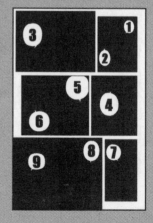